THE
YEARBOOK OF ENGLISH STUDIES
VOLUME 47

2017

VOL. 47
2017

THE YEARBOOK

OF

ENGLISH STUDIES

Series Editor

ANDREW HISCOCK

Walter Scott: New Interpretations

Guest Editor

SUSAN OLIVER

Modern Humanities Research Association

The Yearbook of English Studies

is published by the

MODERN HUMANITIES RESEARCH ASSOCIATION

and may be ordered from JSTOR
E-mail: participation@jstor.org

Further information about the activities of the Association and individual
membership can be obtained from the MHRA Membership Secretary, Peters, Elworthy & Moore,
Salisbury House, Station Road, Cambridge CB1 2LA, UK, email: membership@mhra.org.uk,
or from the website at: www.mhra.org.uk

The next volume of the *Yearbook* (2018) is entitled *Writing in the Age of William IV*.
Correspondence related to the *Yearbook of English Studies* should be addressed to:

Professor Andrew Hiscock
Series Editor, *Yearbook of English Studies*
School of English
Bangor University
Bangor
Gwynedd
Wales
LL57 2DG

Email: mhraassistant@bangor.ac.uk

ISSN 0306-2473 (print)
ISSN 2222-4289 (online)
ISBN 978-1-781882-93-1

TYPESET BY ALLSET JOURNALS & BOOKS, SCARBOROUGH, UK

FOREWORD

Welcome to the latest volume of the *Yearbook of English Studies* devoted to Walter Scott, published by the Modern Humanities Research Association. The first collection in this series rolled from the presses in 1971. The editor was Professor T. J. B. Spencer, who was at that time Director of the Shakespeare Institute and also Head of the Department of English Literature at the Institute. The 'Assistant Editor' was R. L. Smallwood. The introduction to the volume set out its purpose: it was to be a 'new annual publication [...] devoted to the language and literature of the English-speaking world'. As the editors underlined, the *Yearbook* had been 'established because of the continuing rise in the amount of good work in English studies offered for publication in the *Modern Language Review*, and the similar increase in the number of books on the language and literature of the English-speaking countries sent for review.' In 1976 the *Yearbook* moved a short distance to the University of Warwick with the editorial duties now taken on by G. K. Hunter and C. J. Rawson. R. L. Smallwood remained as the Assistant Editor, but was replaced in the following year by Jenny Mezciems. At this point a new policy for the *Yearbook* was implemented. While it might operate as 'an additional outlet' for *MLR* submissions, 'a substantial portion of each *Yearbook* will from now on consist of specially commissioned articles on a broad topic [...] in order to give each volume a greater centrality of interest and a wider readership.'

With this new policy in place, the 1978 *Yearbook* (vol. 8) became an 'American Literature Special Number'. By 1984, Claude Rawson was the sole editor of the *Yearbook* with Jenny Mezciems continuing as Assistant Editor. In addition, by this time, the *Yearbook* had acquired an 'advisory panel' which included John Beer, Malcolm Bradbury, Philip Edwards, G. K. Hunter, Derek Pearsall, Pat Rogers, R. L. Smallwood, J. B. Trapp, and Larzer Ziff. 1989 (vol. 19) saw the introduction of the first 'guest editor' for a *Yearbook*: J. R. (Dick) Watson of Durham University, who later became the Chairman of the MHRA. In 1990 Professor Andrew Gurr, Reading University, took up the editorship of the *Yearbook* with Phillipa Hardman as the Assistant Editor, and in 2000 (vol. 30) he re-introduced the practice of inviting guest editors to the series. In the years which followed, Nicola Bradbury, also of Reading University, edited and commissioned a number of volumes of the *Yearbook*. During these years, Professor John Batchelor, Newcastle University, became English Editor for *MLR*, and took on the role of Series Editor for the *Yearbook* in the period 2006–11. He experimented with new patterns of publication for the *Yearbook* (two annual volumes), introduced new cover designs, and edited two *Yearbook* volumes himself in this period: one devoted to Victorian literature, and another entitled

From Decadent to Modernist: and Other Essays. Indeed, during his period of office, John Batchelor commissioned me to edit the 2008 volume of the *Yearbook* devoted to Tudor Literature. I remain enormously indebted to John for sharing his extensive knowledge of the very distinguished scholarly history of the MHRA's *Yearbook of English Studies* for this introductory discussion. I would like to take this opportunity to extend my sincere thanks to him, to Richard Correll (the *Yearbook*'s editorial assistant), Gerard Lowe (the MHRA's Production Manager), and Samuel Rogers (my editorial assistant at Bangor University). In each case, their input and support has been invaluable.

I also wish to take this opportunity to thank the guest editor of the present collection devoted to Walter Scott, Susan Oliver. The subject of the 2017 *Yearbook* returns critical attention to one of the giants of British literature and this collection reviews his literary achievements and legacies with cutting-edge research by a premier team of Scott critics. Given the range of its ambition, I have no doubt that this *Yearbook* will make an invaluable and timely contribution to scholarship in reassessing the important figure of Walter Scott and excite further enquiries on the part of its readers.

With every good wish
ANDREW HISCOCK
Series Editor, *Yearbook of English Studies*

Contents

Contents

ABSTRACTS

Six Degrees from Walter Scott: Separation, Connection and the Abbotsford Visitor Books
CAROLINE McCRACKEN-FLESHER

Scott, we know, cast a long shadow for writers and readers alike. Yet the **author's house**, for all its blocky solidity, offers a challenge to any linear notion of literary and cultural inheritance. **Abbotsford** holds **visitor books** that date from the house's opening shortly after the author's death, and that have been consistently maintained through to today. These books provide unique data expressing how Abbotsford and author evolve in a tangle with quite other people and distant places. 'Six Degrees from Walter Scott' reads the walls of **signatures** in Abbotsford's guest books through theories of **actor networks** and the archive that raise important questions of signing, meaning and being for **author** and signatory alike.

The 'universal favourite': Daniel Terry's *Guy Mannering; or, The Gipsey's Prophecy* (1816)
ANNIKA BAUTZ

This essay explores the contemporary **reception** of the first **adaptation** of a Walter Scott **novel** for the **stage**, Daniel Terry's *Guy Mannering; or, The Gipsey's Prophecy* (1816). The essay shows that many more people, from a much wider socio-economic background, would have seen Terry's version between 1816 and 1824 than would have had access to the novel. **Reviews** of the play indicate that its popularity was enhanced by Scott's extraordinary fame and status, and, indeed, it was judged by its closeness to the novel. Terry's play paved the way for a rush of stage adaptations of Scott's novels, and presents one of the many spin-offs that Scott's works inspired and enabled. The play, in turn, contributed to shaping the reception of the most popular novelist of the **early nineteenth century**.

Handing Over Walter Scott? The Writer's Hand on the English and French Marketplace
CÉLINE SABIRON

This essay reassesses Scott's 'handing down' strategy in a Romantic context, from his 'multi-handed' **authorial technique** and his staging of the **transmission** process into **publication**, to the role of the often-intrusive hand of the **translator** and the question of the variability of the text. The essay begins by exploring the author's **fetishization** of the **hand motif** and the way it reflects on his own writing practices. Affected from an early age by chilblains, Scott literally had to rely on helping hands all through his career. As a writer, his relationship to the hand and the **act of writing** was therefore paradoxical. The hand as a motif in Scott's writing is shown to be displaced from its physical manifestation into the realm of **metaphor**, and from the literal to the **aesthetic** and poetic spheres.

Vanishing Mediators and Modes of Existence in Walter Scott's *The Monastery*
EVAN GOTTLIEB

In his **Magnum Opus** introduction to *The Monastery* (1820), Scott retrospectively clarifies that the White Lady of Avenel — who plays a more active role in the novel's plot than any other **supernatural** agent in the **Waverley Novels** — was not intended to be a truly otherworldly figure; she was meant, instead, to be 'connected with the family of Avenel by one of those **mystic** ties, which, in ancient times, were supposed to exist [...] between the creatures of the elements and the children of men.' She proved unpopular with readers and critics alike, and Scott dropped her from the book's sequel, *The Abbot* (1821). But what if the White Lady's true significance lies not in her specific **narrative interventions**, but rather in her role as an **ideological mediator** between the novel's Catholic and Protestant factions? In the first half of this article, I propose to account for Scott's remarkable creation with help from **Slavoj Žižek**, whose concept of the **'vanishing mediator'** helps clarify the White Lady's structural function as an agent of historical change. I then turn to **Bruno Latour**'s socio-anthropological theories to help reframe the novel's more wide-ranging representations of historical conflict. By re-describing *The Monastery* via Latour's recent rhetoric of **'modes of existence'**, each with its own set of truth-conditions, trajectories, and subject-effects, I aim to illuminate not only *The Monastery*'s historical stakes but also its ongoing relevance for us in the early twenty-first century, as we continue to negotiate a variety of seemingly mutually incomprehensible forces and belief systems.

'In Contrast to Those Whom We Have Called Materialists, Mr. [Scott] Is Spiritual': On Scott and Woolf, Romance and 'Fullness of Life'
MATTHEW WICKMAN

Virginia Woolf recognized Walter Scott's considerable influence on **literary history**, but she rejected Scott by appealing to a principle of 'life', a composite of delicate perception, vivid imagination, and what Woolf described as 'spiritual' rather than **'materialist' writing**. This essay extends Woolf's formulation to include 'fullness of life', a non-sectarian designation of **spirituality**, and renegotiates her relation to Scott on that basis. It argues that the spiritual for Scott and Woolf is found less in transcendence (a conventional feature of spirituality) than in the *failure* to reconcile 'life' to 'fullness', the 'energies' of individuals to the history that exceeds them. **Romance** becomes the record, indeed, the very form of this failure. It is this failure, precisely, that motivates belief — whether in history (Scott) or in what surpasses it (Woolf) — in the first place.

The Politics of Fear: Gothic Histories, the English Civil War and Walter Scott's *Woodstock*
FIONA PRICE

The post-**French Revolution** debate in Britain saw a battle over the meaning and political uses of the **gothic**, in which, this article argues, the **historical novel** of the **English Civil War** and the Commonwealth became an important site. Its pages restaged, in generic as well as political terms, the conflict between, on the one hand, radicalism and the dissent, and, on the other, Church and King. While radical writers deployed the gothic to evoke the horrors of oppression, both **Cassandra Cooke**'s *Battleridge* (1799) and **Jane West**'s *The Loyalists* (1812) positioned the radicals as themselves the terrorized source of terror. In the process they reclaimed medicinal and scientific authority for the royalists, a position that **William Godwin** problematizes in *Mandeville* (1817). Tracing the complexities of this debate, I argue that Walter Scott's *Woodstock* replies to both sides in a metafictional *tour de force*. Reading Scott's novel against these earlier historical fictions, it becomes evident that the novel is a bitter exposé of the battle over gothic as anything but rational.

Towards the Edinburgh Edition of Walter Scott's Poetry
ALISON LUMSDEN

In spite of a recent re-evaluation of Scott's work there is no scholarly edition of his poetry. This is a crucial lack that distorts our understanding of the nature of poetry in the Romantic period. However, such a **scholarly edition** in ten volumes is under preparation at the **University of Aberdeen** under the guidance of those who produced the Edinburgh Edition of the Waverley Novels. My article examines the questions that have been explored in order to develop a

methodology for **editing** Scott's poetry, the ways in which its creative evolution differs from that of his fiction, and outlines some of the discoveries that have been made along the way.

'Land Debateable': The Supernatural in Scott's Narrative Poetry
AINSLEY MCINTOSH

This essay investigates how Scott deploys the **supernatural** in his early **poetry**, asking what such imagery, motifs and storylines contribute to our understanding of his works. My argument is that they draw attention to broader thematic concerns about **politics** and **power**. Ultimately, Scott's engagement with the supernatural allows him to explore the possibilities of **language** and the limitations of poetic form. Interest in the supernatural also positions him in dialogue with Romantic contemporaries including **Samuel Taylor Coleridge** and **John Keats**, as well as situating his poetry within a **gothic Romantic aesthetic**.

The Lay of the Last Minstrel and Improvisatory Authorship
DANIEL COOK

This essay traces what superficially appear to be **contradictions** in the **improvisatory authorship** of *The Lay of the Last Minstrel*. Scott, it argues, seeks to dramatize in a modern printed poem anchored by historical notes the spontaneous and occasional remit of traditional **minstrelsy**. The story itself, moreover, turns on actions that are notionally unforeseen (*improvisus*) for an uninitiated reader of **romantic ballads**. Seemingly from memory, Scott, through his **surrogate compositional voices**, refashions a range of poetic and scholarly materials from a common stock and from the corpora of others, including, controversially, an as-then unpublished but widely recited fragment by Coleridge. By masterfully reining in his plot by the closing of the text, Scott asserts his **authorial control** over the poem as it exists on the page and yet still maintains in a kind of living archive the open-ended nature of improvised minstrelsy.

Sir Walter Scott's *The Antiquary* and the *Ossian* Controversy
NIGEL LEASK

This essay examines Scott's *The Antiquary* in relation to the controversy around **James Macpherson's** *Poems of Ossian*. Although explicit discussion of *Ossian* in *The Antiquary* is mainly confined to Jonathan Oldbuck's comic dialogue with his hot-headed Highland nephew Hector MacIntyre in volume I, chapter 3, the essay argues that the debate was actually central to the larger issue of the **ethnic origins** and **modern identity** of the **Scots**, dramatized in the arguments between the 'Gothic' Oldbuck and the 'Celtic' Sir Arthur Wardour throughout the novel. Oldbuck's planned **epic** *The Caledoniad* is discussed in relation to Macpherson's epic *Fingal*, and I conclude with a suggestion that the often-criticized 'invasion plot' of *The Antiquary* might have been inspired by that of *Fingal*, and also Macpherson's earlier poem *The Highlander*. Scott's irenic vision of Britain in *The Antiquary* thus resolves ethnic conflict between Goths and Celts in the interest of **national unity**.

'This right of mercy': The Royal Pardon in *The Heart of Midlothian*
TARA GHOSHAL WALLACE

The famous pardon scene in *The Heart of Midlothian* functions as a gratifying emotional resolution, so much so that readers have often deplored Scott's decision to continue the narrative beyond the climactic interview between Jeanie Deans and Queen Caroline. This essay considers the **royal pardon** itself, addressing how Scott distinguishes Effie Dean's trial for **infanticide** from practices governing both the crime and **judicial protocol**, and connecting criminal procedure with national politics and the royal prerogative itself. Scott emphasizes what is problematic about the mercy of the Hanoverians, but at the same time demonstrates, especially in the final chapters of the novel, the necessity and the propriety of what in *The Life of Napoleon* he calls 'this right of mercy' that was 'wrest[ed] from the crown' during the French Revolution.

Sir Walter Scott and the Caribbean: Unravelling the Silences
CARLA SASSI

My essay interrogates the striking **silences** in Scott's *oeuvre* in relation to Scotland's involvement as a partner of the **British Empire** in the **colonization of the Caribbean** and in the exploitation of **slavery** in this region. By drawing from **narratological theories** (especially those articulated by **Robyn R. Warhol** and **Ruth Rosaler**), I treat Scott's silences as examples of **'implicature'** — a 'conspicuous silence', which acquires and generates meaning through the interaction of **text** and **context**, and represents a form of **communication** in its own right. Through a discussion of samples from his *Letters*, *Tales of a Grandfather*, *Rokeby*, *Rob Roy*, *The Antiquary* and *Heart of Midlothian* I try to identify the invisible **maps** of meaning of the unsaid and 'unnarrated'. While suggesting that this approach allows us to articulate a more nuanced perspective on Scott and **Scottish-Caribbean relations**, I also claim that it allows us to critically rethink the problems and possibilities of engaging with Caribbean slavery in British and other European nineteenth-century fiction.

'All that is curious on continent and isle': Time, Place, and Modernity in Scott's 'Vacation 1814' and *The Pirate*
PENNY FIELDING

This article considers the interrelations of **temporality** and **spatiality** in the early nineteenth century. Comparing Scott's journal of his **tour of the lighthouses** of Great Britain and his fictional revisiting of the islands of **Orkney** and **Shetland** in *The Pirate*, I look at two different historical contexts: the (supposed) post-war summer of **1814** and the imperial expansion of the **1820s**. I explore the ways Scott uses the rarely visited **Northern Islands** to think about other spaces: war-torn Europe and the **archipelagic** empire. Setting the diary form against the novel, I then think about the form of the novel as genre in literary history, the progress of the **national tale**, and finally the uses of **georgic** as **metonymic** of literature as a whole.

Scott, India and Australia
GRAHAM TULLOCH

From early in his life Walter Scott had strong personal relations with **India** but his contacts with **Australia** came much later in his life and were fewer in number. However, even though India was not, like **New South Wales**, a **penal colony**, and the British had been in India for centuries whereas they had colonized Australia within Scott's own life time, Scott's personal relations with India and Australia are remarkably similar in kind, though not in quantity. They take place in a well-defined context of **imperial patronage** which Scott used with skill and success to support a number of young Scots including, in the case of Australia, convicts. On the other hand Scott's imaginative involvement with the two countries differs considerably: India figures quite prominently in his fiction, but in all his published writing there is only one passage on Australia and it deals with quite different issues from those concerning India. This article considers a number of individual cases of Scott's patronage in India and Australia and examines the similar ways in which he was able to further the careers of his protégés. It also compares his writing about India and Australia and suggests that, though the themes in his writing about each country are quite different, in each case the dominant theme is one that was taken up by Scott in his early years.

Trees, Rivers, and Stories: Walter Scott Writing the Land
Susan Oliver

This essay investigates Walter Scott's writing, across several genres, as a contribution to an **environmental historiography** of Scotland. One of the main research questions is whether that writing provides any evidence for an early **land ethic** that anticipates **Aldo Leopold**'s twentieth-century use of that term. Scott's response to **aesthetic discourses** of his time is another topic of discussion. The essay explores **ballads, poetry, fiction** and a range of **non-fiction** documents that includes **letters**, a **statement to parliament** and **minute books**. Scott's involvement in **oil gas production** is discussed, as is his concern about the depletion of river salmon stocks due to modern methods of **fishing** aimed at exploiting stocks to meet product demand from London. The essay is set in a framework of contextualized historical sources, as well as recent developments in **ecocriticism** and the **environmental humanities**.

NOTES ON CONTRIBUTORS

Annika Bautz is Associate Professor of English at Plymouth University and Head of the School of Humanities and Performing Arts. Her publications include *The Reception of Jane Austen and Walter Scott* (2007), as well as essays on Edward Bulwer-Lytton, Walter Scott, library history, and aspects of the history of the book in the Romantic and Victorian periods.

Address for correspondence: Dr Annika Bautz, School of Humanities and Performing Arts, Plymouth University, 6 Portland Villas, PL4 8AA, UK

Email: annika.bautz@plymouth.ac.uk

Daniel Cook is a Senior Lecturer in English and Associate Director of The Centre for Scottish Culture at the University of Dundee. He has published widely on eighteenth- and nineteenth-century literature in such journals as *Essays in Criticism*, *Review of English Studies*, and *Philological Quarterly*. He is the author of *Thomas Chatterton and Neglected Genius, 1760–1830* and the co-editor of *The Afterlives of Eighteenth-Century Fiction* and *Women's Life Writing, 1700–1850: Gender, Genre, and Authorship*.

Address for correspondence: School of Humanities, University of Dundee, Nethergate, Dundee, DD1 4HN, UK

Email: d.p.cook@dundee.ac.uk

Penny Fielding is Grierson Professor of English at the University of Edinburgh. Her books include *Scotland and the Fictions of Geography: North Britain, 1760–1830* and the *Edinburgh Companion to Robert Louis Stevenson*. She is a General Editor of the New Edinburgh Edition of Robert Louis Stevenson for which she is preparing an edition of Robert Louis and Fanny Stevenson's *The Dynamiter*. She was Principal Investigator for the AHRC-funded project 'Writing the North' <www.writingthenorth.com>.

Address for correspondence: Room 2.19, 50 George Square, Edinburgh, EH8 9LH, UK

Email: penny.fielding@ed.ac.uk

Evan Gottlieb is Professor of English at Oregon State University, where he teaches classes on eighteenth-century literature, British Romanticism, and literary theory. He is the author of four books, most recently *Romantic Globalism: British Literature and Modern World Order, 1750–1830* (Ohio State University Press, 2014) and *Romantic Realities: Speculative Realism and British Romanticism* (Edinburgh University Press, 2016). He has also edited or co-edited several volumes, including a new Norton Critical Edition of Tobias Smollett's *The Expedition of Humphry Clinker* (W. W. Norton, 2015). He is currently writing an introduction to contemporary theory for Routledge's Engagements with Literature series.

Address for correspondence: Moreland Hall 326, 2550 S W Jefferson Way, Corvallis, OR 97331, USA

Email: Evan.Gottlieb@oregonstate.edu

Nigel Leask has held the Regius Chair of English Language and Literature at the University of Glasgow since 2004. His book, *Robert Burns and Pastoral: Poetry and Improvement in Late-18th Century Scotland* (2010) won the Saltire Prize for the best Scottish Research Book of 2010. He has recently edited the *Collected Prose Writings of Robert Burns* for the AHRC-funded Oxford edition of the *Collected Works of Robert Burns*. He is currently co-investigator of the AHRC-funded

'Curious Travellers: Thomas Pennant and the Welsh and Scottish Tour, 1750–1820' (2014–18) <http://curioustravellers.ac.uk/en/> and is currently writing a book entitled *'Stepping Westward': The Scottish Tour, 1720–1820*. He is a Fellow of the British Academy and of the Royal Society of Edinburgh, and is a Vice President of the Association of Scottish Literary Studies.

Address for correspondence: School of Critical Studies, University of Glasgow, 5 University Gardens, Glasgow, G12 8QQ, UK
Email: nigel.leask@glasgow.ac.uk

Alison Lumsden is Chair in English Literature at the University of Aberdeen. She was a general editor for the Edinburgh Edition of the Waverley Novels and is lead editor for the Edinburgh Edition of Walter Scott's Poetry. She has published extensively on Scott and directs the Walter Scott Research Centre at Aberdeen. She is also Honorary Librarian for Scott's library at Abbotsford House.

Address for correspondence: The School of Language, Literature, Music and Visual Culture, King's College, Aberdeen, AB24 3UB, UK
Email: a.lumsden@abdn.ac.uk

Caroline McCracken-Flesher is Professor of English and George Duke Humphrey Distinguished Faculty (2016) at the University of Wyoming, and an Honorary Fellow of the Association for Scottish Literary Studies. Her publications include *Possible Scotlands: Walter Scott and the Story of Tomorrow* (Oxford, 2005) and *The Doctor Dissected: A Cultural Autopsy of the Burke and Hare Murders* (Oxford, 2012). She has edited volumes on Scottish Science Fiction, the Scottish Parliament, and Robert Louis Stevenson, and is currently co-editor of the Edinburgh Biographical Dictionary of Scottish Writing. She leads the 'UW at Abbotsford' project.

Address for correspondence: Department of English, 3353, University of Wyoming, 1000 East University Avenue, Laramie, WY 82071, USA
Email: cmf@uwyo.edu

Ainsley McIntosh is an independent scholar who lives and works in London. Her research interests lie in the literature, and particularly the poetry, of the Romantic period. Her critical edition of Walter Scott's *Marmion* (1808) will be published in 2017 as the first volume of the Edinburgh Edition of Walter Scott's Poetry.

Address for correspondence: 52 Rommany Road, West Norwood, London, SE27 9PX, UK
Email: ainsleymcintosh@gmail.com

Susan Oliver is Reader in Literature at the University of Essex. Her first book, *Scott, Byron and the Poetics of Cultural Encounter* (Palgrave, 2005), was awarded the British Academy Rose Mary Crawshay Prize, 2007. She is completing two further books: *Green Scott: Writing and National Ecology*, which is funded by the British Academy and Leverhulme Trust, and *Arbiters of Opinion: Transatlantic Periodical Culture, 1790–1860*. Her research interests are in Scottish literature, Romanticism, transatlantic studies, periodical studies and ecocriticism. She is an Advisory Board Member for the MLA International Bibliography and the North American Association for Studies in Romanticism. She also serves on the Executive Committee of the British Association for Romantic Studies. She is Honorary Fellow in Literary Studies at the University of Wyoming.

Address for correspondence: Department of Literature, Film, and Theatre Studies, University of Essex, Wivenhoe Park, Colchester, CO4 3SQ, UK
Email: soliver@essex.ac.uk

Fiona Price is Professor of English Literature at the University of Chichester. She is the author of *Revolutions in Taste, 1773–1818: Women Writers and the Aesthetics of Romanticism* (Ashgate, 2009) and of *Reinventing Liberty: Nation, Commerce and the Historical Novel from Walpole to Scott* (Edinburgh University Press, 2016). She is co-editor with Ben Dew of *Historical Writing in Britain, 1688–1830: Visions of History* (Palgrave, 2014) and editor of two historical novels, Jane Porter's *The Scottish Chiefs* (1810; Broadview, 2007) and Sarah Green's *Private History of the Court of England* (1808; Pickering and Chatto, 2011). She has published extensively on historical fiction, the Romantic period novel and women's writing.

Address for correspondence: Department of English and Creative Writing, University of Chichester, College Lane, Chichester, West Sussex, PO19 6PE, UK
Email: F.Price@chi.ac.uk

Céline Sabiron is Senior Lecturer in English literature at Lorraine University (Nancy) where she teaches literature and translation courses to undergraduate and graduate students. She is also a research fellow at Wolfson College, Oxford University. She is the author of various articles on Walter Scott and several books including a recent one on Scott's Scottish novels entitled *Écrire la frontière: Walter Scott, ou les chemins de l'errance* (Presses universitaires de Provence, 2016). Her research interests now lie in the relationships of eighteenth- and nineteenth-century literature with translation studies and cognitive science. She has been a member of the executive committee of the French Society for Romantic Studies since 2014 (as vice secretary and webmaster).

Address for correspondence: UFR Arts, Lettres et Langues, 42–44 Avenue de la Libération, BP 3397, 54015 Nancy cedex, France
Email: celine.sabiron@univ-lorraine.fr, celine.sabiron@wolfson.ox.ac.uk

Carla Sassi is Associate Professor of English literature at the University of Verona. She specializes in Scottish and postcolonial studies and is interested in the historical and the theoretical intersections between these fields, with special reference to the post-Union period. She is currently Affiliate Professor at the School of Critical Studies of the University of Glasgow. Among her books are *Why Scottish Literature Matters* (2005) and, as a co-author, *Caribbean-Scottish Relations* (2007). She has co-edited a special issue of the *International Journal of Scottish Literature* on 'Scottish-Caribbean Passages' (2008), the volume *Within and Without Empire: Scotland across the (Post)colonial Borderline* (2103) and edited the *International Companion to Scottish Poetry* (2016).

Address for correspondence: Departimento di Lingue e Letterature Straniere, Università di Verona, Lungadige Porta Vittoria 41–37129 Verona, Italy
Email: carla.sassi@univr.it

Graham Tulloch is Emeritus Professor of English at Flinders University and has written extensively on Scottish literature and language with a particular emphasis on Scott, Hogg and, more recently, Stevenson. He has edited Scottish and Australian literary texts, including Scott's *Ivanhoe* (1998), Clarke's *His Natural Life* (1997), Martin's *An Australian Girl* (1999) and, with Judy King, Hogg's *The Three Perils of Man* (2012) and Scott's *Shorter Fiction* (2009). He is the author of *The Language of Walter Scott* (1980) and *A History of the Scots Bible with Selected Texts* (1989) and has a long-standing interest in Scottish writers' involvement with Australia, having published a number of articles in this field.

Address for correspondence: College of Humanities, and Social Scienecs, Flinders University, GPO Box 2100, Adelaide SA 5001, Australia
Email: graham.tulloch@flinders.edu.au

Tara Ghoshal Wallace is Professor of English at George Washington University, specializing in eighteenth- and nineteenth-century British literature. Her books include *Jane Austen and Narrative Authority*, *Imperial Characters: Home and Periphery in Eighteenth-Century Literature*, *Women Critics, 1660–1820* (co-editor, with the Folger Collective), and Frances Burney's *A Busy Day* (editor). Recent articles include pieces on Burney, Alexander Pope, Walter Scott, and Mary Wollstonecraft. She was the keynote speaker for the annual Burney conference in 2016, and will be the keynote speaker for the Mid-Atlantic ASECS annual meeting in November 2017. Her current book project is on Walter Scott's representations of monarchy.

Address for correspondence: Department of English, George Washington University, 801 22nd St. NW, Washington DC 20052, USA
Email: tgw@gwu.edu

Matthew Wickman is Professor of English and Founding Director of the BYU Humanities Center at Brigham Young University, Utah. He is the author, most recently, of *Literature after Euclid: The Geometric Imagination in the Long Scottish Enlightenment*, as well as essays in journals including *PMLA*, *MLQ*, *Romantic Circles Praxis*, and *Scottish Literary Review*.

Address for correspondence: BYU Humanities Center, College of Humanities, Brigham Young University, 4103 JFSB, Provo, UT 84602, USA
Email: matthew_wickman@byu.edu

Introduction

SUSAN OLIVER
University of Essex

Just over half a century ago, Marxist critic Georg Lukács proposed that Walter Scott — writing more than a century earlier — was responsible for a new kind of historical narrative: readers, by identifying with everyday kinds of fictional characters, 'could re-experience the social and human motives which led men [and women] to think, feel and act just as they did in historical reality'.[1] That argument, according to which fiction does much more than remember cultural history through telling tales, because in addition it conveys a sense of thought and feeling, should at least have ensured Scott a renewed place in Romantic studies. If Wordsworth and Coleridge's *Lyrical Ballads* synthesized older (even ancient) poetry of feeling with narrative storytelling to make something bold and experimental, Scott did something similar with historical fiction in the form of the long narrative poem and in prose. All three of these first-generation Romantics believed in the power of remembering, during which the imagination could re-create feelings from the past, to improve their own and a future world.[2] Wordsworth added that such recreated feeling, based in intense personal experience, 'does itself actually exist in the mind'. Scott's achievement, according to Lukács, was to recover socially embedded feeling from beyond the boundaries of personal experience because located in the deeper past, but still in such a way that individuals could experience it in their minds. Through a figurative form of time travel, then, people could relate more sympathetically to one another and establish a better society, responding to understanding produced by feelings as well as by thought. Whether or not Scott is accepted as a mainstream Romantic, it would be difficult to imagine a writer more concerned about community. Furthermore, literature for him is the medium through which this process of remembering can go on in ways that look forward as well as to the past.

Scott's formal education included classics and law along with Scottish Enlightenment epistemologies of organization, systematic enquiry and empirical

---

[1] Georg Lukács, *The Historical Novel*, trans. by Hannah and Stanley Mitchell (Harmondsworth: Penguin, 1962), p. 42. The use of the masculine pronoun in the quoted passage from the Mitchells' translation will be objectionable to some readers, so the feminine is included.

[2] Wordsworth, 'Preface', in *Lyrical Ballads, With Other Poems* (London: Longman and Rees, 1800), pp. xxxiii–xxxiv. See also Samuel Taylor Coleridge, *Biographia Literaria*, ch. 13.

Yearbook of English Studies, 47 (2017), 1–15
© Modern Humanities Research Association 2017

deduction. That combination of knowledge evidently fits the model of an ordered imagination that Michel Foucault has defined as dominant in the late eighteenth and early nineteenth centuries.[3] A more personal world of reading in the allegories of medieval romance, interest in conjectural as well as stadial history (both developments of the Enlightenment), and a willingness to explore the vicissitudes of Romantic sensibility mark Scott out as someone who, more than is often acknowledged, preferred to live his imaginative life near to the edge of what he saw to be possible.[4] Almost everything he wrote confronts anxiety about worlds that are about to be lost or rendered obscure. His poems, novels, verse dramas, and collected ballads are in part an attempt to ward off cultural annihilation. At another level, sometimes crossing the threshold into mawkishness, they strive through nostalgia to compensate for guilt and grief over what has been lost. But at his best, while his political allegiances could not have been more different, Scott's authorial ambitions across several genres can be compared with Percy Shelley's argument that poetry 'arrests the vanishing apparitions that haunt the interlunations of life'.[5] Scott was a lawman by profession, serving as Sheriff-Deputy of Selkirk and Clerk to the Court of Session in Edinburgh; arrest and case studies were part of his day's work.[6] As a writer he was drawn to what remains mysterious and unsettling.

Yet despite a steady stream of attention from committed scholars, it was not until the late twentieth century that Scott returned to prominence in studies outside Scottish literature. In the 1980s, interest in his writing began to grow. An increase in criticism was accompanied by new approaches to editions of the original works. The Edinburgh Edition of the Waverley Novels, published between 1993 and 2009, made available for the first time since Scott's lifetime early versions of the prose fiction. I will say more in due course about that edition and about the major new edition of the poetry that is only now being produced. What is clear is that interpretation and attention to texts, along with scholarship extending beyond the page into architecture and land, to cultural influence globally and to conceptual issues such as homeliness and homecoming, have been moving with increasing momentum to push the boundaries of what we

---

[3] Michel Foucault, *The Order of Things: An Archaeology of the Human Sciences*, trans. by Alan Sheridan (London: Routledge, 2002).

[4] Compare Scott's account of his own education in his autobiographical fragment, in J. G. Lockhart, *Memoirs of the Life of Sir Walter Scott, Bart.*, 2nd edn, 10 vols (Edinburgh: R. Cadell; London: J. Murray and Whittaker & Sons, 1839), I, 56–62 with Marilyn Orr's account of his fictional treatment of education in 'Real and Narrative Time: *Waverley* and the Education of Memory', *Studies in English Literature*, 31.4 (Autumn 1991), 715–34.

[5] Percy Bysshe Shelley, 'A Defence of Poetry', in *The Major Works*, ed. by Zachary Leader and Michael O'Neill (Oxford: Oxford University Press, 2009), pp. 674–701 (p. 698).

[6] He was appointed Sheriff-Deputy of Selkirk in 1799 and served as Clerk to the Court of Session in Edinburgh from 1806 to 1811.

know about Scott. It is fair to say that not all of this criticism has been positive towards Scott, for a variety of reasons.[7] The purpose of the present volume is to represent some of the best examples of where Scott studies are positioned at the moment, and to account for some of the breadth as well as depth of that position. Caroline McCracken-Flesher has shown how Scott continues to make thinkable a future of multiple possibilities, in which his 'texts and his nation are alive in their constant retelling' and where meaning is emphasized by a wider 'differential play across place, plot, time, teller, and reluctant reader'.[8] The vital plurality of the texts and compulsion to keep retelling the stories — which, after all, is the original mode of the Scottish Border ballad that inspired Scott — is all-important here. That his writing has 'gusto', a favourite word of the younger Romantics, meaning art that has life, energy, spirit, and passion, would hardly now be denied.[9] For the reasons so far given, the essays that follow aim to identify and address reasons why Scott is relevant to the twenty-first-century world in which we live, as well as to the literary and cultural legacy of Scotland.

The five sections of this number of the *Yearbook* are designed to highlight areas in which studies of Walter Scott and his works are developing in new directions. While not everything can be included, the aim has been to represent as wide a range of approaches as is practical. In some cases, the essays build on previous areas of research. Others introduce new angles generated by contemporary world concerns, such as environmental studies. Scott has always been recognized for his interest in place and early nineteenth-century landscape aesthetics, but it is only with the development of ecocriticism as a critical and theoretical field that attention has being paid to evidence for the agency of the land in his work, or to his concern with ecology.[10] Anyone working on Scott will know, as Caroline McCracken-Flesher reminds us in her essay for this volume, that the twenty-first century has seen a surge of interest in Scott's onward literary and cultural influence. McCracken-Flesher's own *Possible Scotlands: Walter Scott and the Story of Tomorrow* (Oxford, 2005), Ian Duncan's *Scott's Shadow: The Novel in Romantic Edinburgh* (Princeton, 2007) and Ann Rigney's *The Afterlives of Walter Scott: Memory on the Move* (Oxford, 2012) are among several

[7] For example, John Sutherland's controversial *The Life of Walter Scott: A Critical Biography* (Oxford: Blackwell, 1995) was described by Marilyn Scott as 'pithy, cynical [and] irreverent' in her review 'Burying Scott', in the *London Review of Books*, 17.7 (7 September 1995), 10–11 (p. 10).

[8] *Possible Scotlands: Walter Scott and the Story of Tomorrow* (Oxford: Oxford University Press, 2005), p. 9 and Oxford University Press <https://global.oup.com/academic/product/possible-scotlands-9780195169676?cc=US&lang=en8#>.

[9] See William Hazlitt, 'On Gusto', first published in *The Examiner*, 26 May 1816, and included in *The Round Table* (1817). John Keats argued that poetry which could 'enjoy light and shade' lived 'in gusto'. See his letter to Richard Woodhouse, dd. 27 October 1818, in *The Letters of John Keats*, ed. by H. E. Rollins, 2 vols (Cambridge: Cambridge University Press, 1958), I, 193–94.

[10] For Scott, place and landscape, see James Reed, *Sir Walter Scott: Landscape and Locality* (London: Athlone, 1980).

monographs that have contributed to that area of scholarship, while *The Reception of Sir Walter Scott in Europe* (2006), edited by Murray Pittock, gives a much-needed and wide-ranging account of Scott's place in European literature. Meanwhile, Alison Lumsden's *Walter Scott and the Limits of Language* (Edinburgh University Press, 2010) has shown how Scott's incorporation of multiple languages and dialects, in his poetry and prose fiction, responded to theories of the Scottish Enlightenment by emphasizing the significance of Scotland's contemporary cultural diversity.

The archive as both material and conceptual record continues to be central to Scott studies, with what constitutes any such archive being taken into new areas. Caroline McCracken-Flesher develops her previous work on the author's home itself as an archive by investigating what can be learned from signatures in the visitor books that record tourism to Abbotsford during the years 1833 to 1935. Bringing Ann Rigney's and Ian Duncan's work into dialogue with Iain Gordon Brown's edited collection of essays on Abbotsford and Alastair Durie's socio-historical analysis of visitor numbers and trends, her opening essay for this volume uses theories of authorship and inscription along with archival scholarship to assess what tourism to Scott's home reveals, or fails to disclose, about the development of onward literary networks.[11] McCracken-Flesher points out that Thomas Carlyle likened visitors to Abbotsford to vermin feeding off the remains of the author's reputation, and regarded excessive tourism as no more than cultural vandalism. She goes on to explore what it means to sign — and thereby to leave a name — in a book that is designed to record the presence of people in a space associated with a writer.

McCracken-Flesher's essay brings a virtual as well as material 'house' of Scott to the foreground of critical enquiry. The intentionality behind maintaining visitor books raises further considerations. She looks beyond the inscription of signatures by major literary figures to consider also the many more obscure visitors. One problem here is the difficulty of reconciling names with numbers. In an age when big data and a bewildering amount of available information threaten to make meaning obscure or at least difficult to retrieve, McCracken-Flesher looks deeply into the actual and symbolic 'wadge of paper' that comprises the many volumes of the visitor books. The manner in which tourism informed Scott studies in the early years of the twenty-first century, for example in books by Nicola Watson and Susan Oliver, feeds into this new study of an indoor

---

[11] *Abbotsford and Sir Walter Scott: The Image and the Influence*, ed. by Iain Gordon Brown (Edinburgh: Society of Antiquaries of Scotland, 2000); Alastair Durie, 'Tourism in Victorian Scotland: The Case of Abbotsford', *Scottish Economic & Social History*, 12.1 (2010), 42–54 (p. 43) <http://www.euppublishing.com/doi/abs/10.3366/sesh.1992.12.12.42> [accessed 21 Nov. 2016]. Cited by McCracken-Flesher in her essay in this volume.

archive that contributes to the cult of the author and literary travel.[12] Beyond problems of palaeography, there are questions to be asked about why literary tourists, some of whom were authors in their own right, signed or assigned themselves into a place associated with Walter Scott as man and writer? Another question concerns considerations given to gender. McCracken-Flesher explores Susan Ferrier's desire, through visiting Abbotsford, to avoid becoming ensnared as a writer in Scott's historical storytelling. Ferrier provides a case study of visiting that itself begins in a historical context of Scott's time. Other authors whose presence is inscribed into the visitor books include Mark Twain, signing as Samuel L. Clemens, and Harriet Beecher Stowe. The part played by John Gibson Lockhart as journalist, man of letters and Scott's biographer, as well as his son-in-law, has always been contentious, and issues of memorialization — not least in the persona he constructed for his father-in-law in *Memoirs of the Life of Sir Walter Scott*, published across the nineteenth century in a variety of multi-volume forms — gain a new resonance from this opening essay.

Annika Bautz continues the volume's enquiry into Scott's legacy by exploring the context, production and reception of Daniel Terry's dramatic interpretation of *Guy Mannering* (1815), titled *Guy Mannering; or, The Gipsey's Prophecy: a Musical Play in three acts*. Her essay looks at how Terry's popular play, premiered at Covent Garden Theatre in 1819, brought the storytelling of the 'Author of Waverley' to a wider audience than would have read the novel. Critical attention has been paid over the years to theatrical adaptations of Scott's poems and other novels, and to the many operatic versions of his works, but Bautz gives us a much-needed study of the staging and reception of the first adaptation of Scott's prose fiction. Scott collaborated with Terry, advising him on his characterization — which is where there are some major differences from the novel. Bautz argues that each man gained, as the combined commercial success of the novel and play led to a continuing upward spiral in the popularity of both. Terry's adaptation also drew new attention to issues of social class, gender, and the political implications of relationships between the characters, which Bautz argues are emphasized in his departures from Scott's original story. Different relationships between individuals in the novel and its staged version are shown to function as markers in the onward life of a story. Bautz assesses those markers and the formal tensions they generate between author, playwright and reviewers, and between readers of the novel and playgoers. Finally, the essay compares reviews in a range of periodicals to assess the role that journalism took in mediating Scott's journey from page to stage.

---

[12] Oliver, *Scott, Byron and the Poetics of Cultural Encounter* (Basingstoke: Palgrave Macmillan, 2005) and Watson, *The Literary Tourist: Readers and Places in Romantic and Victorian Britain* (Basingstoke: Palgrave Macmillan, 2006).

While Annika Bautz explores one form of handing the onward tradition of Scott and his novels, Céline Sabiron looks at another. Motifs of labouring hands in nineteenth-century fiction have received plenty of critical attention, not least where the Victorian condition-of-England novel is concerned. Charles Dickens's *Hard Times, David Copperfield* and *Great Expectations* and Elizabeth Gaskell's *Mary Barton* are perhaps obvious examples. In each of those novels, the use and misuse of 'hands' is a theme as well as a motif. Ian Duncan took modern British literature's fascination with hands back to the beginning of the gothic tradition in the late eighteenth century, interpreting Horace Walpole's vivid dream of 'a titanic mailed hand on a banister' in *The Castle of Otranto* (1764) as a symbol of anxiety about authority and authorship.[13] Céline Sabiron's contribution to the present volume begins with an account of the real bodily discomfort that Scott suffered with his own hands, and to that extent she takes Scott criticism into the new area of disability studies. Her essay moves on to an analysis of specific instances of hand imagery in Scott's fiction. Sabiron makes connections between the lived experience of the writer and the product of his authorship, before addressing the processes of transmission or 'handing over' of his writing to publishers in Scotland and in France. She uses the term 'multi-handedness' to describe processes of making connections between the various people involved in preparing and transmitting early manuscript versions as well as finished works into press. Ina Ferris, Jane Millgate and Fiona Roberston have all written about the relationship between Scott's dictation of his novels and the inevitable issue of multiple authorship that emerges in the production of published books.[14] Sabiron takes forward some of the issues that their work raises. One of the most exciting features of this essay is the way in which practical issues involving pain and the body of the author are brought into relation with the fetishized imagery of hands in several of Scott's works. Why was Scott so interested in hand imagery in storylines of deception and the macabre, we might ask? Whether in the form of a mutilated pocket curiosity in *The Fair Maid of Perth* (1828) or as the agent of 'palmistry and jugglery' in *Quentin Durward* (1823), Sabiron shows how hands in Scott's fiction are gothic presences that haunt the text. It is perhaps salient to remember here that one of Scott's earliest works, published in 1799, was a translation into English of Goethe's play *Götz von Berlichingen mit der eisernen*

---

[13] Ian Duncan, *Modern Romance and Transformations of the Novel: The Gothic, Scott, Dickens* (Cambridge: Cambridge University Press, 1992), p. 28. Walpole's exact words were that 'on the uppermost bannister of the great stair-case I saw a gigantic hand in armour'.

[14] Ferris, 'Scott's Authorship and Book Culture', in *The Edinburgh Companion to Sir Walter Scott*, ed. by Fiona Robertson (Edinburgh: Edinburgh University Press, 2012), pp. 9–21; Millgate, *Walter Scott: The Making of the Novelist* (Edinburgh: Edinburgh University Press, 1984); Robertson, *Legitimate Histories: Scott, Gothic and the Authorities of Fiction* (Oxford: Clarendon Press, 1994). All are cited by Sabiron in her essay in this volume.

Hand, under the title *Goetz of Berlichingen with the Iron Hand*.[15] In the second half of the essay Sabiron explores the way Scott hands his own novels across language thresholds to French translators, including Auguste-Jean-Baptiste Defauconpret, and the onward influence of his work on French late Romanticism in the works of Balzac, Dumas, Vigny and Hugo. Theories of authorship and editing along with critical studies in book history infuse this essay in striking and instructive ways.

Section II of the volume is concerned with new theoretical approaches and genre studies. Evan Gottlieb is already known for his groundbreaking work taking Scott studies into new areas of theoretical enquiry, while he never loses sight of the importance of the novels themselves.[16] If a commonplace criticism of theory is that it displaces textual studies into a location where the original works of literature risk becoming inaccessible to readers who are not theory-oriented, that is not the case in Gottlieb's work. In his essay for the *Yearbook* he continues his attention to some of Scott's less commented-upon fiction, in a reading that casts a fresh illumination on Scott's interest in supernaturalism. Focusing on *The Monastery*, he investigates Scott's use of the 'vanishing mediator', a term taken from the work of Slavoj Žižek.[17] The spectral character of the White Lady in *The Monastery*, a gothic novel set in the middle of the sixteenth century, is shown to be a figure essential to the mechanism by which Scott treats one of the hottest periods of change in history for which his fiction is known. Gottlieb argues that while the White Lady is insubstantial in a conventional way, because a spirit, she is very substantial in a more complex sense by virtue of her contribution to the 'modes of existence' (from Bruno Latour) that mediate one of Scotland's most problematic social and cultural transformations: that is, the transition from an older culture based in Roman Catholicism to a modern civil society based on Presbyterianism. A study of these historical issues could easily make its argument in the form of a sophisticated gothic reading, but that is not where Gottlieb's enquiry goes. Bringing theories by Žižek and Bruno Latour into dialogue, firstly with one another and then with recent work in environmental justice by eco-cultural critics including Rob Nixon, the essay investigates the structural properties of modes of existence that are sometimes best understood, as Latour would argue, from a non-anthropocentric angle.

---

[15] Scott published *Goetz of Berlichingen with the Iron Hand: A Tragedy Translated from the German of Goethe* in 1799.

[16] See Gottlieb, *Walter Scott and Contemporary Theory* (London: Bloomsbury Academic, 2013).

[17] Žižek, 'Eastern European Liberalism and its Discontents', in *The Universal Exception: Selected Writings, Volume Two*, ed. by Rex Butler and Scott Stephens (London: Continuum, 2006), pp. 15–36 (p. 29). Cited by Gottlieb in this volume.

Matthew Wickman also brings under new scrutiny Scott's treatment of borderlines between the material and spiritual, the historic and the present. The comparison he makes here of Scott's third novel *The Antiquary* with Virginia Woolf's *To the Lighthouse* revisits a relationship between Romantic historicism and modernism that has remained tense for the best part of a century. Ever since Woolf published her essay 'Modern Fiction' (1925), which dismissed the legacy of Scott's historical mode, the historical novel has been under scrutiny for reasons that Wickman identifies in order to challenge. Woolf notably wanted to draw a line between the spirituality she saw to be at the forefront of modernism, with its attention to felt experience, and the constraining mode of past-ism she believed to be inherent in the historical novel. She strove in her own fiction, as Wickman shows, to break free from the kind of historical narratives she understood to be derived from Scott. Yet we could argue that novels such as *To the Lighthouse*, *The Waves* and *Orlando* are haunted by historical narratives that continue to produce powerful feeling (and new forms of feeling, furthermore). Wickman deconstructs and examines Woolf's main argument that fiction deriving from Scott's historical model lacks 'life', because it is preoccupied with what is already dead. In doing so he draws attention to the difference between late Victorian imitations of Scott and the original novels. Woolf's ambition for modernism was that it should privilege its responsibility to attend to life as it happens. Wickman scrutinizes the prominence with which *The Antiquary* re-emerges after 'Modern Fiction' through that novel's importance to Mr Ramsay in *To the Lighthouse*. Mr Ramsay's interest in nineteenth-century literature is notoriously never far from his mind, and Woolf makes much of his fascination with Scott's description of the episode in which antiquary Jonathan Oldbuck visits the Mucklebackit family of fisherfolk after the death by drowning of their young son and grandson, Steenie. Oldbuck's careful recording of Elspeth Mucklebackit's chanting of the Ballad of Hadyknute (a favourite ballad of Scott's) is one of the most commented-upon passages in *The Antiquary*. Wickman looks closely at Woolf's argument about that passage, at her notion of 'spirit', and at what Scott actually achieves in *The Antiquary*. His essay argues that far from lacking in life, *The Antiquary* continues to exert a vital agency in the liminal literary space that Woolf identifies between Scott's mode of historical fiction and the modernist text. The result, he argues, is that Scott's attention to feeling operates vitally as 'a kind of dialectic of enchantment and demystification'.

Fiona Price explores how Scott used metafictional techniques to participate in debates about literary genre and the representation of history. Her essay positions Scott in a long-running Romantic-period argument about the political uses of gothic and historical fiction. Price shows through her focus on the late novel *Woodstock; or, The Cavalier. A Tale of the Year Sixteen Hundred and Fifty-one* (1826) how Scott responded to earlier and continuing disputes about historical representation made by Edmund Burke, Mary Wollstonecraft, William Godwin, William Hazlitt, Cassandra Cooke and Jane West. The fusion in *Woodstock* of strategies of storytelling with a continuous, intertextual reflection on the uses of sentiment and terror in other works draws attention to the ways in which rhetoric and political self-awareness function in gothic fiction. The dualism of 'spirit' and 'the spiritual' again comes under scrutiny, with Scott using spectral imagery to explore real-world concerns about the spirit of liberty and of enthusiasm, and indeed, of the age.

Continuing with the theme of enchantment, Alison Lumsden's essay at the beginning of Section III reminds us that Scott's poetry was such a 'dazzling success' that he could barely keep pace with demand. The main focus of her essay is editing; more specifically, the problems that surround the production of a new edition of the poetry for the twenty-first century. Editing Scott's works is an area of scholarship that has received much attention recently, not least because the last twenty-four years have seen new editions of all of his novels. The Edinburgh Edition of the Waverley Novels under the series editorship of David Hewitt, while not alone in producing editions of the novels, took a new approach by turning for its base texts to the first and early editions rather than to the magnum opus that had supplied almost every base text since Scott's death.[18] Each volume includes information relating to the editorial process, lists of emendations, notes on procedure, historical notes, and a detailed glossary. Lumsden was editor or co-editor of four of the EEWN volumes. She is now series editor for Edinburgh University Press's scholarly edition of the poetry. As she points out, despite its initial popularity, Scott's poetry now receives far less attention than his prose fiction, which is disappointing since his narrative poems were experiments in literary historicism that not only built his reputation as an author but also contributed to the diverse form and subject matter that shaped Romantic poetry.[19] Lumsden brings into focus 'the generic innovation' of Scott's poems, arguing that they were in their time understood by reviewers to be 'new and radical'. She acknowledges the indebtedness of the novels to the plots, characters, modes of storytelling, and sources in the accumulating bank of notes of the poems. But she is more interested here in processes of production of the poetry itself. Again, processes of multiple authorship along with responses in subsequent editions to criticism show Scott to be an author who developed a highly social process of composition. Choosing base texts for the poetry edition has for these

---

[18] The series is published by Edinburgh University Press and will be referred to hereafter as EEWN.

[19] For book-length critical studies see Nancy Moore Goslee, *Scott the Rhymer* (Lexington: University Press of Kentucky, 1988), Susan Oliver, *Scott, Byron and the Poetics of Cultural Encounter* (Basingstoke: Palgrave Macmillan, 2005) and Maureen McLane, *Balladeering, Minstrelsy, and the Making of British Romantic Poetry* (Cambridge: Cambridge University Press, 2008).

and other reasons been complicated, as case studies here of *Marmion* and *The Lady of the Lake* show. Theories of poetry have always been at the centre of Romantic studies, but Scott is almost never read in that context. Lumsden asks us to think again, making the case for the essays on poetry published in the *Poetical Works of 1830* and in the subsequent (posthumous) edition of 1833 as participants in that dialogue. Arguably, Scott's essays on chivalry and romance for the *Encyclopaedia Britannica* could be included as well, for their exploration of the history of medieval and renaissance romance forms, to which he and his contemporaries responded.

Ainsley McIntosh continues the volume's attention to Scott's narrative poetry by exploring how gothic supernatural imagery extends beyond content and the conventions of genre to practical processes of creativity and publication. Scott famously used a metaphor of demonic agency, describing 'a dæmon who seats himself on the feather of my pen when I begin to write'.[20] The idea of the author in action being driven by a demon not only connects the supernatural with processes of communication, but also says something about forces that operate inside the text. For example, the agency of the book of spells in *The Lay of the Last Minstrel* has often been interpreted as a warning about the need for morally responsible reading. The role of the occult book in the story says more about the power of language and of interpretation than about the nature of authorship, although Scott does imply that an author's control over what she or he has written is precarious at best. Michael Scott has the daunting task — from the other side of the grave — of recovering his book and limiting the damage it can cause. Celeste Langan has argued that the *Lay*'s book motif contributes to a multimedial poem in which reading, song, and instrumental music come together as art forms to assert the magical (transformative) properties of language.[21] McIntosh takes Scott's three most influential poems, *The Lay* (1805), *Marmion* (1807), and *The Lady of the Lake* (1810) as case studies through which to investigate how supernatural imagery inside the text transcends the boundaries of the tale. The questions asked reassess the nature of the magic, enchantment and charm with which Scott's writing is associated.

The Lay of the Last Minstrel is given another new reading by Daniel Cook, who explores the text's evidence of literary sociability. It is commonplace almost to the point of cliché that the *Lay* attracted charges of negative sociability almost as soon as it was published, with Samuel Taylor Coleridge accusing Scott of

---

[20] For 'printer's devils' see *Oxford English Dictionary*, Online <http://www.oed.com> [accessed 14 December 2016]. For Scott's words, see *The Fortunes of Nigel* (1822), ed. by Frank Jordan, EEWN (Edinburgh: Edinburgh University Press, 2004), p. 10. Both cited by McIntosh in this volume.

[21] Celeste Langan, 'Understanding Media in 1805: Audiovisual Hallucination in *Lay of the Last Minstrel*', *Studies in Romanticism*, 40.1 (2001), 49–70.

plagiarizing a short passage from his own *Christabel*. The grounds for that complaint and the rancour of Coleridge's accusation have received almost as much attention as the *Lay* itself. Cook revisits the plagiarism argument, but for new reasons, and drawing other conclusions about intertextuality in Scott's first long poem. Through a close reading, along with attention to the growing paratext of Scott's explanatory notes and introductory essays, he shows how the *Lay* was a hybrid composition always aware of its own conversational interaction with other poets and their works. Cook develops his position out of Maureen McLane's argument that the *Lay* asserts its place in poetry and poetics through what might be called a 'minstrelsy complex'.[22] The final canto, which Scott himself curiously said was 'altogether redundant', is shown by Cook to make a case for the poem as a manifesto for a minstrelsy in touch with the past but also, through its rejection of closure, looking forward to the future. That prophecy underpins Scott's own entire project as an author.

Nigel Leask opens Section IV on new approaches to Scott and history with an essay looking at the relationship between *The Antiquary* (1816) and James Macpherson's *Ossian* fragments. Even before he became well known as an author, Scott's education in historical theories of the Scottish Enlightenment and his growing reputation as an antiquarian led to his being involved in the debate over authenticity and the treatment of history in *Ossian*. The public face of that involvement included an essay published in the *Edinburgh Review* in 1805, in which Scott reviewed both the Highland Society of Edinburgh's commissioned report on *Ossian* and a new two-volume edition by Malcolm Laing. Scott was at that time still keen to write for the *Edinburgh*, and editor Francis Jeffrey was more than pleased to secure his expertise on a matter that continued to attract attention. Parts of Scott's review are notorious for their apparent attempt to put to rest Macpherson and his poems, but Leask's essay insists on a reappraisal. The need to look further into Scott's writing career to understand the extent to which *Ossian* haunted Scott's imagination, and (more specifically) the ways in which Macpherson may have continued to exert influence on his approach to fiction as social historiography, is based on evidence found in his third novel. In his literary-historical investigation, Leask considers versions of *Ossian* by other authors and Ossianic imitations within the storyline of the *Antiquary*. He also explores wit and issues of taste surrounding Scott's use of humour in weighing debates about ethnic prejudice towards Highlanders, and the more sinister concern of Jonathan Oldbuck to show that the Picts were of Gothic rather than Celtic ancestry, and therefore of Germanic rather than Irish origin. Questions to be asked include whether Oldbuck represents Scott's own position on Scottish identity politics, and whether he is an object of satire and/or self-parody. These

[22] McLane, *Balladeering, Minstrelsy, and the Making of British Romantic Poetry*, pp. 144, 151–52.

matters resonate beyond Scott studies, because they draw attention to a history of class, religious and racial prejudice that continued to affect Scotland's cultural development and political economy.

Law and its interpretation, historically and in his own time, is understandably a prominent feature in Scott's writing, given his training as an advocate and service as Sheriff-Deputy of Selkirk. Likewise, his support for monarchy as the head of a constitutional Union that recognizes Scotland's legal autonomy informs almost everything he published. A question arises, then, as to whether his poetry and prose fiction might be read as the voice of a constitutional lawyer as well as a commentary on jurisprudence by of one of the leading public intellectuals of his time. Tara Ghoshal Wallace addresses these questions, putting Scott's interest in the biopolitics of sovereign power in post-Union Scotland under fresh scrutiny in an exploration of the often-derided fourth volume of *The Heart of Midlothian*. As Wallace notes, criticism of Scott's seventh novel has been animated and diverse: James Kerr and Ian Duncan, among others, have described *The Heart of Midlothian* as a 'romance' or 'fable' of 'national regeneration', while biographer John Sutherland conversely dismissed it as a propagandist apology for the Hanoverian dynasty.[23] Theories of the body by Michel Foucault, Giorgio Agamben, and Roberto Esposito underpin this much-needed reassessment of Scott's treatment of Royal Prerogative and its effects on male and female subjects of the sovereign state. The relevance of social class is also taken into consideration. Wallace maintains a strong dialogue with a wide range of critical positions, taking forward her own study of statutory law relating to the concealment of pregnancy and infanticide dating from the late seventeenth century, as applied over one hundred and thirty years to the Regency period in which Scott was writing.

Carla Sassi takes this number of the *Yearbook* into the field of postcolonial studies and the history of slavery. Her essay investigates silences that attend Scott's mediation of Scotland's history in the colonization of the Caribbean and its part in the transatlantic slave trade. Sassi bases her analysis on a condition of 'conspicuous silence', which she also terms 'willed' or 'unwilled amnesia'. More widely, she argues, such silence constitutes a lapse of memory that can only be explained as 'a form of [cultural] forgetfulness that appears more radical in Scotland than in other European countries, also involved in the exploitation of slavery in the Caribbean'. A question asked from the outset in this essay is whether Scott's or his nation's willed or unwilled amnesia specifically emerges in connection with slavery, in which case it could be motivated by a particular instance of guilt; or whether, by contrast, it grows from more universal roots in

---

[23] James Kerr, *Fiction against History: Scott as Storyteller* (Cambridge: Cambridge University Press, 1989), p. 64; Duncan, *Modern Romance*, p. 154; Sutherland, *The Life of Walter Scott*, p. 209. All are cited by Wallace in this volume.

'the teleological philosophy of history conceived and diffused by the Scottish Enlightenment', which Murray Pittock has shown involves 'the analysis of the past [...] not on its own terms, but in the light of what it could contribute to an account of progress towards the present'.[24] Sassi evaluates Scott reticence over slavery in a range of examples, some of which contain other references to cultures of the Caribbean and the Americas. Her case studies are the long poem *Rokeby*, novels including *The Antiquary*, *Rob Roy* and *The Heart of Midlothian*, the historiographical *Tales of a Grandfather*, and Scott's correspondence. Narratological theory informs her argument and she furthermore asks why Robert Burns's silence over slavery has received so much more critical attention than Scott's reserve. Sassi proposes that such an uneven comparative treatment of two of Scotland's most influential writers emphasizes the need for further enquiry into Scott's position, because of his role 'as historiographer and myth-maker in nineteenth-century Scotland'.

The final section of the volume assesses where Scott studies stand at their intersection with some key twenty-first-century concerns: namely, literary geographies, the environment, and ecology.

Penny Fielding looks at Scott's writing about the sea and the northern islands of Orkney and Shetland, first in a travel journal and then in his novel *The Pirate* (1821). Her essay explores how time, space, and place tend to converge at imagined borders (which may be internal, cultural, between land and sea, and/or textual). Fielding's main argument concerns the anxieties that emerge when 'the formation of a national geography around a political centre [...] or by a dominant cultural figure [Scott] leaves fluid and unresolved spaces' that do not easily fit within 'the taxonomic geographic decisions that borders require'. As a historian educated in Scottish Enlightenment theories of social progression, and as an antiquarian with conservative political convictions, Scott looked for continuities and trajectories that would enable him to understand the past's relationship with the present in a teleological framework. Fielding asks what happens when extreme peripheral geographies intervene in that process. The result is that we see Scott reaching after disappearing rituals and stories in an attempt to retrieve and record them before they are gone. Among the examples that Fielding discusses is a sword-dance that Scott witnessed in Shetland, an experience recorded in the unpublished diary of his 1814 journey accompanying the Commissioners of the Northern Lights on their annual inspection of the lighthouses around the coast of Scotland. She also comments on the eagerness with which Scott yearned, like so many other antiquarians, to 'discover traces of

[24] Murray G. H. Pittock, 'Historiography', in *The Cambridge Companion to the Scottish Enlightenment*, ed. by Alexander Broadie (Cambridge: Cambridge University Press, 2003), pp. 258–79 (p. 258). Also cited in Sassi's essay for this volume.

the Picts, the supposed aboriginal people of Scotland and the subject of a continuing debate over their language and ethnicity'. Her essay asks questions about the term 'vacation', which Scott uses in the title he gave his diary. Most of all, Fielding confronts here a number of previously unasked questions about how Scott responded to the archipelago of the northern isles as places where 'fractal geometries' and an 'uncertain temporality' arise out of evidence of international migration and transcultural connections. What Scott experienced could not but destabilize his received ideas about history as a coherent national project. His novel *The Pirate* is proposed here as a response that first revisits, then reimagines, Orkney and Shetland as global rather than particularly Scottish locations.

While Scott's role in the literary culture and social history of his own nation continues to attract critical enquiry, almost no attention has been given to his engagement with Australia. Partly, that is because Scott did not write much about what was then regarded largely as a penal colony with only a recent history. Graham Tulloch confronts the omission, bringing to the foreground Scott's correspondence with several colonial representatives, free settlers, and transported convicts. The context for his enquiry is imperial and colonial patronage, with the prolific level of attention to India in the letters providing a means of assessing a relatively scant Australian presence. The importance of a comparison with India, together with a quantitative critical approach, cannot be overstated here, because what can be learned about Scott and Australia casts new light on the role of folklore and mythology in the building of a Scottish cultural identity at home and in diaspora. Letters exchanged with governors Lachlan Macquarie and Sir Thomas Brisbane, a chain of correspondence with free settler George Harper, flippant asides to Adam Ferguson about convicted Borderers sent to 'botanize' for a while, and a letter from a convicted forger provide a framework for Tulloch's enquiry. Of particular interest is Harper who, being neither a colonial office holder nor a prisoner, was the kind of everyday observer and messenger that Scott needed in a distant land where he could not conduct his own research. Harper not only returned the favour of a letter of introduction from Scott with gifts of seeds and wildlife (some of which were at best dubiously welcome) but, as Tulloch shows, acted as go-between with Macquarie in acquiring for Scott published stories about bushrangers that could be seen as counterparts to the Scots Border reivers of ballad tradition.

Susan Oliver concludes the volume with an investigation of Walter Scott's writing across several genres — anthologized ballads, original poetry, fiction, and a range of non-fiction documents that include letters, statements to parliament, and minute books — assessing his contribution to an environmental historiography of Scotland. Her approach is material and literary, being informed by period responses to the land and by ecocritical theories of agency in the nonhuman world. One of the questions she asks is whether Scott's writing provides any evidence for an early land ethic that might anticipate Aldo Leopold's first use of that term in *A Sand County Almanac and Sketches Here and There*, published in 1949. Scott's approach to the land may in many ways be considered ethical, but do those ethics extend beyond a human interest in conservation and land use to include the interests of the wider biotic community? Oliver explores Scott's involvement in an early debate about pollution and fossil fuels, when as Chairman of the Edinburgh Oil Gas Light Company he presented a statement to Parliament arguing that oil gas was a cleaner fuel than coal gas.[25] She explores his concern about the depletion of salmon and trout stocks, firstly with reference to the formation of the River Tweed Commissioners and then in his storytelling in *The Tale of Old Mortality*, *Redgauntlet* and *The Antiquary*. Scott's entire *oeuvre* is traced through its evolution from the *Minstrelsy* ballads back to the soil of Scotland itself, both materially and symbolically, through analysis that draws on Heather Sullivan's 'dirt theory' and Jane Bennett's *The Vitality of Things*. Oliver's essay provides a fitting end to this year's *Yearbook*, by positioning Scott studies in areas where they have not previously featured to any considerable extent; that is, in environmental humanities, ecological historiography, and ecocriticism.[26]

---

[25] *Edinburgh New Gas-Light Bill. Statement for Sir Walter Scott, Bart. Chairman, the other Directors, and the Proprietors of the Edinburgh Oil Gas Company, applying for a repeal of a Prohibition in their Act of Parliament to make Gas from Coal.* Sess. 1827. National Library of Scotland.

[26] 'Dirt Theory and Material Ecocriticism', *Interdisciplinary Studies in Literature and Environment (ISLE)*, 19.3 (Summer 2012), 515–31 (p. 515); Jane Bennett, *Vibrant Matter: A Political Ecology of Things* (Durham, NC: Duke University Press, 2010).

SECTION I

Walter Scott:
Transmission and Afterlives

Six Degrees from Walter Scott: Separation, Connection and the Abbotsford Visitor Books

CAROLINE McCRACKEN-FLESHER

University of Wyoming

Recent considerations of Scott's afterlives and shadow foreground the author and his works as a cultural inheritance.[1] The trajectory, however, trends linear — from author to monument or through the anxiety of literary influence. Another record suggests a less direct descent. In the visitor books at Scott's home in the Scottish Borders, which record name after name of those who wandered the house from 1833 to the present day, shadows and lights flicker from disparate signatures illuminating distant places and different times.[2] From them, Alastair Durie has tabulated the numbers of tourists to Scott's carefully constructed jewel-box of a home; he has traced waves of popularity by visitors' geographical origin.[3] We might pursue signatures into street registries and business records to establish who, exactly, visited. Still, does the concatenation of names across generations reveal any meaningful link between Walter Scott and the locals, aristocrats, works parties and international travellers who traipsed through Abbotsford after the author had gone and who left their mark to accumulate with the archives of the past? To whom did the writers seek to communicate, and why? What, thereby, do the visitor books tell us about the networks of literary meaning and being?

Thomas Carlyle would not expect these books to tell us anything good. Reviewing J. G. Lockhart's memoir of his father-in-law, Carlyle argued that, even

Acknowledgements: this chapter was developed with the help of the Abbotsford Trust, the University of Wyoming Institute for Humanities Research, UW International Programs, and the University of Edinburgh's Institute for Advanced Study in the Humanities. My thanks to the Abbotsford Trust for permission to reference the Visitor Books, and to the trustees of the National Library of Scotland for permission to quote Major Scott's letter.

[1] See Ann Rigney, *The Afterlives of Walter Scott: Memory on the Move* (Oxford: Oxford University Press, 2012); Ian Duncan, *Scott's Shadow: The Novel in Romantic Edinburgh* (Princeton, NJ: Princeton University Press, 2007).

[2] Alastair Durie studies registers from 1837 forward. See Alastair Durie, 'Tourism in Victorian Scotland: The Case of Abbotsford', *Scottish Economic & Social History*, 12.1 (2010), 42–54 (p. 43) <http://www.euppublishing.com/doi/abs/10.3366/sesh.1992.12.12.42> [accessed 21 Nov. 2016]. Under the Abbotsford Trust, visitor books have been recovered that start in 1833.

[3] Ibid., pp. 45, 46, 49, 50.

during Scott's life, traffic to Abbotsford exposed author–visitor relations in a negative dynamic. Suspicious of Scott's popularity as a person and as an author, he sneered:

> Abbotsford became infested to a great degree with tourists, wonder-hunters, and all that fatal species of people [...] all paths were beaten with the feet and hoofs of an endless miscellany of pilgrims. As many as 'sixteen parties' have arrived at Abbotsford in one day [...] 'the flesh-flies;' buzzing swarms of bluebottles, who never fail where any taint of human glory or other corruptibility is in the wind.[4]

Scott's visitors are animalistic, sustaining their atavistic tendencies by feeding off a too-productive author, too dependent on applause, and past his sell-by date. 'Mr Lockhart thinks', Carlyle mocks, that 'there was no literary shrine ever so bepilgrimed'. Visitors add no patina to Abbotsford; rather, Scott's undue popularity brings an accumulation of *grime*.

In this context, literary tourism enacts a vandalism that reveals the tawdriness of its object. Carlyle's opinion, that is, anticipates the 'broken window' theory of graffiti. Here, urban blight produces low-level criminality, including what we now (in telling contrast) often call 'street art'.[5] To Carlyle, Abbotsford was ruinous in the fullest sense of the term: Scott was ruined financially and morally in the struggle to keep his expensively tacky house by over-writing. It was this 'corruption' that produced the detritus of tourists, guest books, and the signatures of all and sundry.

Yet is the touristic urge to mark the space of remembrance akin to vandalism or to leaving stones on a grave? The tension between honour and damage is informatively expressed at Petrarch's home. Fiona McDonald notes that during the Grand Tour, it was typical for tourists

> to scrawl their initials, full names, and the dates of their visit onto the walls of Petrarch's house (but never on the tomb itself). To remedy this vandalism [...] it was decided in 1787 to provide a visitors book [...] The original book is now on display in the house [...].
>
> [...] some of the earlier [graffiti] is also now part of the visiting experience. There is a piece written by a group of Austrian students back in 1564.[6]

Such graffiti seeks a relationship to an author on a personal level — some people write on the house. But it also expresses a relationship of honour — these people did not write on the tomb. Further, the inscriptions themselves direct today's

---

[4] Thomas Carlyle, 'Review of *Memoirs of the Life of Sir Walter Scott, Baronet*. Vol. i–vi', *London and Westminster Review*, 6.12 (1838), 293–345 (pp. 328–29).

[5] See James Q. Wilson and George L. Kelling, 'Broken Windows: The Police and Neighborhood Safety', *Atlantic Monthly* (March 1982) <http://www.theatlantic.com/magazine/archive/1982/03/broken-windows/304465/> [accessed 21 Nov. 2016]. The theory has been challenged for its formulation, conclusions, and resulting policing practices.

[6] Fiona McDonald, *The Popular History of Graffiti: From the Ancient World to the Present* (New York: Skyhorse, 2013), p. 67.

reader toward their writers and different times and places.

What kind of relationships insist within the Abbotsford visitor books, where the names of the good, great and inconsequential are marshalled into well-behaved but impenetrable rows? Under Durie's analytic lens, visitors emerge in singularity. We can see who toured and from where. Durie's study of numbers, the rules of the house, available modes of transportation and accommodation hints at individuals as they are produced by contemporary circumstances. Specific hours of opening, that train, this hotel allow these lines in the guest book.

Yet the concreteness of many volumes, the solidity of wadges of paper, the walls of names point, too, to the impossibility of a name in isolation. Page after page of unknowns accumulate not just into an intensity of appreciation for Walter Scott or for Abbotsford, but into a multi-valenced challenge to the very notion of a chosen relationship. Here worlds and times stand cheek by jowl. Scott is only the occasion, Abbotsford only the place. Solid pages with their implied individuals betoken the unpredictable play of relationship and a resulting possibility.

Theories of tourism, then, prepare the ground for analysing the Abbotsford visitor books. But these accretions to Abbotsford beseech Derridean ideas of the archive. To Carolyn Steedman, researchers every day confront the '*ordinariness, the unremarkable nature of archives*'.[7] In actual archives, she explains,

> though the bundles may be mountainous, there isn't in fact, very much there [...] The Archive is made from selected and consciously chosen documentation from the past and also from the mad fragmentations that no one intended to preserve and that just ended up there [...] It is indexed, and catalogued, and some of it is not indexed and catalogued, and some of it is lost. But as stuff, it just sits there until it is read, and used, and narrativised.[8]

How much more deliberate, ordinary, accidental, unyielding and yet serendipitously productive is the signature in a visitor's book?

As much as the archive, the signature intrigues Derrida for its 'impossible idiom'.[9] He extrapolates from the claim of singularity in the grammatical person and the proper name that we love '*the proper*: what is proper to [ourselves], proper to the other, proper, that is, to the always singular thing'.[10] Yet the signature is also an effacing, redoubling, erasure of the self, 'so you must certainly sign, but it is as well also not to sign [...] The bar does not pass between the signature and the absence of signature, but *through the signature*. Which is

---

[7] Carolyn Steedman, *Dust: The Archive and Cultural History* (New Brunswick, NJ: Rutgers University Press, 2002), p. 9.

[8] Ibid., p. 68.

[9] Jacques Derrida, *Signéponge/Signsponge*, trans. by Richard Rand (New York: Columbia University Press, 1984), p. 28.

[10] Ibid., p. 30.

therefore always overflowing'.[11] To sign is to make a claim on presence but to leave a marker of deferral; the signature in a book registers the absence and implies the multiplicity of the one who signed. The Abbotsford guest books, then, are full of nobodies posing problems to themselves. What they can show to us is the making of meaning, and maybe of being, in temporary space and contingent time.

This is the more so because these particular books stand central in a network of ironies that constitute a case for theorizing the self as signed. Excessively full of nobodies, as Carlyle would have recognized, they nonetheless express a community he was never invited to join in Scott's lifetime and that, through his trenchant review of Lockhart's *Memoir*, he refused to join thereafter. Yet Scott, too, viewed such assemblages of admiring strangers and even friends with feelings publicly known to be mixed. Thus the Abbotsford visitor books, unlike those of other literary lions, both provide data for and are installed within a critique of the contemporary and later celebrity culture to which they bear witness.

Scott had a realist's attitude to the accumulations of people he occasioned. His friend John Morritt noted that early in his career, on an 1809 visit to London, 'the homage paid him would have turned the head of any less gifted man of eminence'. It 'neither altered his opinions, nor produced the affectation of despising it'.[12] Still, Scott's preference was to avoid it. Ten years later he claimed that although in Germany he could be

> free from the pursuit of those alarming hunters of wild animals so common at Harrowgate Cheltenham and our English spaws who cannot suffer a poor *lion* like myself to come quietly thither for the benefit of his health [...] On the whole I incline to sit quiet at home this vacation.[13]

At home, Scott displayed the same instinct for hospitality, but preference for its limits.

Even before Scott's new house at Abbotsford could supply adequate accommodation, we find him assembling sympathetic groups of family, friends and writers. 'Our house in Castle Street', he tells Matthew Weld Hartstonge in 1813, 'is so small [...] we have no spare bed. But we would reckon upon your being our dear and constant guest'.[14] Amid the mess of an Abbotsford under construction, he hails Daniel Terry to 'a *pew*' and encourages Miss Smith that though 'Our house is the least that ever harboured decent folks since the

[11] Ibid., p. 34.

[12] J. G. Lockhart, *Memoirs of the Life of Sir Walter Scott, Bart.*, 7 vols (Edinburgh: Robert Cadell, 1837–38), II, 244–45.

[13] Walter Scott, *Letters of Sir Walter Scott*, ed. by H. J. C. Grierson, 12 vols (London: Constable, 1932–37), V, 409 (8 July 1819). To John B. S. Morritt.

[14] *Letters*, III, 270 (10 May 1813). To Matthew Weld Hartstonge.

traditionary couple who lived in the Vinegar bottle [...] if you come [...] we will find a corner for you'.[15] In 1818, with Abbotsford in a better state of preparedness, over a few days he awaits Lord and Lady Melville and entourage, defers Terry because 'we shall be full with these great folks & the people I must ask to meet them', and makes plans with Lady Compton to add her family, including its children, along with a John Richardson who is a solicitor for his relatives.[16]

However, not every guest who was welcomed was either invited or enjoyed. 'Two sons of Sir James Hall came here yesterday', Scott lamented during the electioneering season in 1819, 'and with their fathers philosophical spirit of self-accomodation establishd themselves for the night [...] my head and stomach sufferd so much [...] that I had a return of the spasms'.[17] The problem was such that when Scott began to establish himself at Abbotsford, Joanna Baillie warned against 'idle Travellers' who might try to 'make an Inn of your house [...] that they may boast in their stupid Tours afterwards of the great attentions they received from their *Friend* Mr Scott'.[18] Baillie hints to keep his spare rooms few and small. And certainly, Scott suffered under the influx of strangers. J. G. Lockhart, on his first visit to Abbotsford, 'found Mrs Scott and her daughters doing penance under the merciless curiosity of a couple of tourists [...] tall, lanky young men, both of them rigged out in new jackets and trowsers of the Macgregor tartan'. Imagining they carried letters of introduction that would connect them, somehow, to Scott, Charlotte Scott duly passed the afternoon with them. Scott, on his return, presumed upon their ease and familiarity, and also welcomed them until realization dawned and he released them before they could wait out the dinner hour, saying he 'could not tresspass further on their time'.[19]

Abbotsford, that is to say, enjoyed a reputation among friends and strangers as a welcoming house. Scott operated on the principle of 'Wellcome the coming speed the parting guest'.[20] But under pressure, he thought that Abbotsford was 'haunted by too much company of every kind', and in his private journal quietly declared his dislike, especially, of foreigners with the 'impudence that pays a stranger compliments and harangues about his works in the Author's house [when] they know nothing about what they are talking of'.[21] To Lockhart, the press of company was certainly too much. His *Memoir* asserted: 'The hospitality

[15] *Letters*, III, 514 (10 November 1814), 411 (13 February 1814). To Daniel Terry and Miss Smith.

[16] *Letters*, V, 201–03 (5 October 1818). To John Ballantyne and Lady Compton.

[17] *Letters*, V, 377. To Lord Montagu, dd. 6 May 1819.

[18] Joanna Baillie, *Collected Letters of Joanna Baillie*, ed. by Judith Bailey Slagle, 2 vols (Madison, NJ: Fairleigh Dickinson University Press, 1999), I, 282–83.

[19] Lockhart, *Memoirs*, IV, 200–01.

[20] Walter Scott, *The Journal of Sir Walter Scott*, ed. by W. E. K. Anderson (Edinburgh: Canongate, 1998), p. 204 (30 July 1826).

[21] Ibid., p. 13 (23 November 1825).

of [Scott's] afternoons must alone have been enough to exhaust the energies of almost any man'.[22]

Importantly, Scott himself occasionally went absent from the mêlée, and was known so to do. In 1818, in one of many such instances, he fled the 'travelling esquires and bankers' for a few 'quiet days with Lord Melville'.[23] After 1837, Scott's admirers knew from the *Memoirs* that he had often decamped to the nearby home of his daughter and new son-in-law to avoid what Lockhart termed 'the solemn applauses of learned dulness, the vapid raptures of painted and periwigged dowagers, the horse-leech avidity with which underbred foreigners urged their questions, and the pompous simpers of condescending magnates'.[24] Those who went to Abbotsford itself once the house was accessible to paying visitors were personally disabused of Scott's open welcome. They saw the library and, as William Howitt reported, 'a gallery, by which [Scott] could get to and from his bedroom, and so be at work when his visitors thought him in bed. He had only to lock his door, and he was safe'.[25] Abbotsford stood as a welcoming house, but raised questions about the tolerable level of visitors' presence and participation in this author's home.

Scott also anticipated concerns about the signature itself. During his life, Abbotsford kept no record of guests — and Lockhart actually regretted that though 'It is the custom in some [...] country houses, to keep a register of the guests [...] nothing of the sort was ever attempted at Abbotsford'.[26] Lockhart knew that 'It would have been a curious record — especially if so contrived [...] that the names of each day should, by their arrangement on the page, indicate the exact order in which the company sat at dinner'. The memoirist wanted to see the 'many persons of distinction in rank, in politics, in art, in literature, and in science'. Here, Lockhart is thinking of a record like the Dinner Books for the Duke of Buccleuch's nearby hunting lodge at Bowhill and his other properties, where someone — perhaps the butler — entered attendants at dinner.[27] Chance visitors, however, were another matter.

Scott, in fact, exemplified across his life and in very public ways why no one should sign. Scott recognized the persistence of a name. To Joanna Baillie, when she styled herself 'Mrs', as older women of the time found necessary to do, he joked: 'Well you may call yourself what you please [...] but I will warrant you never get posterity to tack either *Miss* or *Mrs* to the quakerlike Joanna Baillie'.[28]

---

[22] Lockhart, *Memoirs*, v, 2.

[23] Scott, *Letters*, v, 188 (10 September 1818). To Lady Abercorn.

[24] Lockhart, *Memoirs*, v, 123.

[25] William Howitt, *Homes and Haunts of the Most Eminent British Poets*, 2 vols (New York: Harper Brothers, 1847), II, 218.

[26] Lockhart, *Memoirs*, v, 5.

[27] Dinner Books for Buccleuch properties are in the National Records of Scotland, Register House.

He acknowledged, too, the performative power of a name, refusing to set his own to a history for it would 'lead to great disappointment in the public [...] When a man puts his name to so grave a matter as a History, it should be something very different from the [...] sketch which I intend to furnish'.[29] Naming made a hostage of your being; it confined you within expectation and potentially shifted your reputation. Thus while others might sign, Scott often would not.

Scott, indeed, actively resisted the signature. In his journal entry for 28 December 1825, he remembered that 'When I first saw that a literary profession was to be my fate I endeavourd by all efforts of stoicism to divest myself of that irritable degree of sensibility [...] which makes the poetical race miserable and ridiculous'.[30] It was this Walter Scott who, when starting as a novel writer in 1814, refused to sign his name.

After his bankruptcy, Scott would recognize the monetary value of naming. Then, he worked to reassemble his copyrights by aligning his texts with his name. He actually cultivated literary value through that unique name, noting that 'If I have the command of a new Edition and put it into an attractive shape with notes, introductions and illustrations that no one save I myself can give I am confident it will bring home the whole purchase money with something over'.[31] But left to his own preference, Scott abjured the signature, publishing *Waverley* anonymously in 1814, and then appearing/disappearing behind the derivation 'the Author of Waverley'. It was a game he enjoyed, writing even to close friend Joseph Train to acknowledge that a story Train had shared had appeared in print, and to deny his own hand in the process: '"Why," Scott coyly observed, "the author should conceal himself, and in this case even change his publishers as if to insure his remaining concealed is a curious problem."'[32]

It was a problematizing of the self through the abrogation of the signature that Scott went on vigorously to pursue. By 1819, the elision of Scott as signature had actually become a crowd-sourced affair. Now he wrote to a friend who was in the know alongside Scott's publishers, editors and transcribers:

I own I did mystify Mrs. ***** a little [...] She came up to me with a great overflow of gratitude for the delight and pleasure, and so forth, which she owed to me on account of these books. Now, as she knew very well that I had never owned myself the author, this was not *polite* politeness, and she had no right to force me up into a corner and compel me to tell her a word more than I chose [...] I denied the charge [...] I suggested Adam Fergusson.[33]

[28] *Letters*, III, 536 (1814). To Joanna Baillie, n.d.
[29] *Letters*, IV, 280 (26 October 1816). To Archibald Constable.
[30] *Journal*, p. 60.
[31] Ibid., p. 429.
[32] *Letters*, IV, 323 (21 December 1816). To Joseph Train.
[33] *Letters*, V, 294-95 (18 January 1819). To J. Richardson.

And Scott blithely accepted and colluded in many a sobriquet such as 'the Great Unknown' and the 'Wizard of the North', while multiplying his texts' narrator/editors — and putting them in discourse with one another or the ever-retreating 'Eidolon, or Representation, of the Author of Waverley'.[34]

Scott, of course, recognized the importance of his written hand to others, thus he did not always withhold it. On his last voyage, when told he should not tip the seamen crewing the *Barham*, he asked whether instead he could give the captain an autographed copy of the Waverley Novels.[35] For Basil Hall, the facilitator of the voyage, he agreed to sign the manuscript of *The Antiquary*, now in Hall's possession. 'You would add great value to this writing, Sir Walter, if you would be so kind as to put your name to it', Hall encouraged.[36]

Yet Scott always pondered the dynamics of a signature to make or to undo. In 1826, in the throes of bankruptcy, he wondered if publishing *Chronicles of the Canongate*

> without my name (*nomme de guerre* I mean [The Author of Waverley]) the event would be a corollary to the fable of the peasant who made the real pig squeak against the imitator while the sapient audience hissd the poor grunter as if inferior to the biped in his own language [...] were I to fail [...] and then vindicate my claim to attention by putting 'by the Author of Waverley' in the title my good friend *Publicum* would defend itself by stating I had tilted so ill that my course had not the least resemblance to my former doings [...] Therefore I am firmly and resolutely determined that I will tilt under my own cognizance.[37]

The Chronicles of the Canongate was thus Scott's first substantial fiction to come out under the name, 'Walter Scott'. Nonetheless here, too, Scott elided that name. '[It] was my original intention never to have avowed these works during my lifetime', he declares in the introduction.[38] Time and presence should never meet. But naming himself, he immediately began to overwrite that name with others: Joseph Train gave him the history of Old Mortality; an unknown lady sent him the story that produced *The Heart of Midlothian*.[39] Worried that he had now become the 'Too well Known', and that his journal, with its persistent inscription of the self, made him 'intolerably selfish', in the chronicles he disappears in the network of others' signatures.[40] Signatures offer a site, but not the reality of

---

[34] Consider Cleishbotham and Pattieson of the *Tales of My Landlord*, or Clutterbuck and Dryasdust. Clutterbuck meets the Eidolon in *The Fortunes of Nigel*. See Walter Scott, *The Fortunes of Nigel*, ed. by Frank Jordan, EEWN (Edinburgh: Edinburgh University Press, 2004), pp. 4–5.

[35] Basil Hall, *Fragments of Voyages and Travels*, excerpted in Fiona Robertson, ed., *Lives of the Great Romantics II*, vol. 3, 'Scott' (London: Pickering and Chatto, 1997), pp. 82–122 (p. 86).

[36] Robertson, p. 118.

[37] *Journal*, p. 244 (17 October 1826).

[38] Walter Scott, *The Chronicles of the Canongate*, ed. by Claire Lamont, EEWN (Edinburgh: Edinburgh University Press, 2000), p. 3.

[39] Scott, *Chronicles*, pp. 4–5.

[40] *Journal*, p. 48; p. 179.

authenticity. Through Scott's career, and visibly to a public always on the verge of his secret, the author hinted toward the unmaking that came with a known and inscribed name.

Still, if Scott publicly manifested a critique of the written self, he was held to have given his signature in stone at Abbotsford. To Horace Smith, who visited in 1827, Abbotsford's every detail 'prate[d] of his whereabout'.[41] Harriet Beecher Stowe similarly saw Scott as represented in his house during her 1853 visit: 'it was throughout his own conception, thought, and choice; [...] he expressed himself in every stone that was laid'.[42] Harald Hendrix has observed that 'Besides being a product of a writer's imagination or ambition, his house may also be a source of inspiration in its own right, or a material frame necessary for the production of literature'.[43] Nicola Watson goes a step further. Abbotsford, she argues, triangulates the relation between author, works and visitor; it was 'designed as a literary puzzle, explicitly alluding to the settings of the poems that had made Scott's fortune [...] and covertly performing Scott's secret identity as "The Author of Waverley"'.[44] So if Scott typically refused his signature, at Abbotsford he seemed presented and perhaps caught in place, written within the very stones of his house.

How did visitors relate to this signature in stone? Promptly after Scott's death in 1832 there was a rush of memorialists all keen to inscribe themselves alongside Scott at Abbotsford. Great and little, with the embarrassment of Scott and his non-signing gone, they assembled themselves: in 1833, Basil Hall quickly expanded his *Fragments of Voyages and Travels* to narrate his long relationship with the author, and his role in Scott's last voyage;[45] the next year (1834) James Hogg published *Familiar Anecdotes of Sir Walter Scott* in America, and it promptly was pirated back to Glasgow as *The Domestic Manners and Private Life of Sir Walter Scott*;[46] in 1835, Washington Irving recounted his 1817 experience of visiting an Abbotsford under construction, based on the introduction provided by his books and a letter from Thomas Campbell.[47] And so it went through the century as notable authors penned their autobiographies.

---

[41] Horace Smith, 'A Graybeard's Gossip about his Literary Acquaintance', *New Monthly Magazine*, 82 (February 1848), p. 252; Robertson, pp. 292–99 (p. 294).

[42] Harriet Beecher Stowe, *Sunny Memories of Foreign Lands*, 2 vols (Boston, MA: Phillips, Sampson and Company, 1854), I, 132.

[43] Harald Hendrix, ed., *Writers' Houses and the Making of Memory* (New York: Routledge, 2008), p. 4.

[44] Nicola Watson, *The Literary Tourist: Readers and Places in Romantic and Victorian Britain* (Basingstoke: Palgrave Macmillan, 2006), p. 94.

[45] Hall's essay 'Sir Walter Scott's Embarkation at Portsmouth in the Autumn of 1831' ended volume 3 of *Fragments of Voyages and Travels*, third series (Edinburgh: Robert Cadell, 1833). Excerpted in Robertson, pp. 82–122.

[46] Robertson, pp. 44–78 reviews this history and prints excerpts from *Domestic Manners*.

[47] Washington Irving (as 'The Author of "The Sketch-Book"'), *Abbotsford, and Newstead Abbey* (London: John Murray, 1835), is excerpted in Robertson, pp. 126–62.

What was the purpose of signing oneself into the space that signified Walter Scott? This was more than a strategy to place each money-spinning memoir next to the Waverley Novels in sales catalogues and on bookshelves from Edinburgh to the antipodes. Paul Westover gives a suggestion. Focusing on Irving, he notes that

> the aspiring author associates himself with the canon, not only discursively [...] but also physically, placing himself bodily beside a great precursor [...] he both participates in the precursor's aura and adds a layer to it, invoking the power of association on his own behalf.[48]

Susan Ferrier's report in this context seems an exception, but it adds nuance to the rule. Fiona Robertson terms Ferrier's a 'strange and electrifying description'.[49] It was published in 1874, twenty years after Ferrier's death, and roused critical wrath for its wish that '[Scott's] noble faculties had been exercised on loftier themes than those which seemed to stir his very soul.'[50] Ferrier disliked Scott's efforts to entertain her with stories that tangled her among historic times and local antiquities. What was she seeking? Robertson notes that Ferrier writes of her encounters with Scott as if he were considerably older than she — they were separated by eleven years, only.[51] Moreover in the first visit, although she appreciates the hospitality, Ferrier feels no great proximity to Scott — who was still only a poet, and worked in the law with her father. Her later visits, in 1829 and 1831, came after the death of Scott's wife, his own bankruptcy, and the departure of all but one child. Abbotsford was replete with things and with memory, but Scott was in decline. Thus the Ferrier who, by virtue of long friendship, is admitted into the family circle, uses her eye as a now-successful novelist to triangulate between herself and Scott. She is inscribed in the same space as Sir Walter, but asserts a remove in time, knowledge and reputation.

Lockhart rushed to defend Scott from such hordes of auto/biographers poised over his remains. Working to produce his own authoritative biography, he worried that overly familiar friends like the Abbotsford steward, William Laidlaw, and that other farmer-poet, James Hogg, would devalue Scott's works and reputation.[52] He might not have worried so much, for as Ferrier demonstrates, Scott was not the issue, although he did provide the occasion. Scott was signed into the stones of Abbotsford, but he wasn't there. Authors from

[48] Paul Westover, *Necromanticism: Travelling to Meet the Dead, 1750–1860* (New York: Palgrave, 2012), p. 122.

[49] Robertson, p. 346. Ferrier's comments were published as 'Recollections of Visits to Ashistiel and Abbotsford' in *Temple Bar*, 40 (1874). See Robertson, pp. 348–54.

[50] Robertson, p. 351; Susan Ferrier, *Memoir and Correspondence of Susan Ferrier, 1782–1854*, ed. by John A. Doyle (London: John Murray, 1898), p. 240.

[51] Robertson, p. 346.

[52] Walter Scott [Major] to Robert Cadell, 29 July 1833. National Library of Scotland MS 21003, fols 164–65. In the end, Laidlaw did not publish his memoir.

Hogg to Stowe, whatever their contact with Scott, now could only assemble belatedly, if publicly, round an absence. Writing oneself into Abbotsford said more about the person who wrote than it did about Walter Scott.

But what can we make of the walls of ordinary names — of names made ordinary by their massing in year after year of visitor books? Shakespeare's visitors at Stratford became notorious for taking pieces of the place. Joseph Sabin reported in 1869 that a chunk had been cut from the beam over the chimney, and was told that 'some Americans had sawn it out' after tricking the attendant out of the room.[53] Visitors routinely wrote on the walls.[54] And Scott himself joined the many to inscribe his name on the window glass.[55] In Alloway, Burns's birth cottage suffered less writing on the wall but, Howitt saw in 1847, visitors were 'cutting [their] names into the furniture'.[56] Two tables showed space 'neither on the top, the sides, nor the legs, even for another initial'. New furniture became similarly inscribed. By contrast, at Abbotsford, which perhaps was not so symbolically 'ruinous' as Carlyle imagined, and was, of course, still occupied, signatures went into the book.[57] That is, people who had no personal connection to Scott and, relatively speaking, no desire for a piece of him, left an inscription of themselves in volumes designed for such inscription. Today, at Jane Austen's Chawton cottage and at the newly reopened Abbotsford, signatures and dates share space with invited comments, and those comments can be assembled to leverage donations and grants. The first century of visitor books at Abbotsford, however, self-replicating in the individual and in the mass, have a blocky solidity and ordered impenetrability that point to something else.

If authors sought to locate themselves according to Walter Scott, can these visitor book names, reduced into nobodies by their accumulated numbers, nonetheless triangulate toward meaning? Or do these pages simply inscribe generations of grime, as Carlyle might have thought? In this context, it is worth considering what such visitors sought at Abbotsford. Going by the testimony of travel guides, baronial Abbotsford stood in part as a guide to architectural style, interior decorating, and landscaping. The 1831 *Scenes in Scotland* noted its 'strange fantastic structure, setting utterly at defiance those principles of uniformity, to which modern architects attach so much importance'; it admired the inside 'as singular in its appearance, as [Abbotsford] is externally', and the

[53] See Washington Irving and F. W. Fairholt, *Shakespeare's Home* (New York: J. Sabin and Sons, 1877), pp. 55–80 (p. 57) for Joseph F. Sabin's 'A Letter-Stratford-on-Avon', dated May 1869.

[54] Julia Thomas, *Shakespeare's Shrine*, pp. 141–46, analyses the shift from graffiti to visitor book in the 1860s.

[55] Sabin, in Irving and Fairholt, p. 57.

[56] Howitt, I, 400.

[57] Durie notes that as the Victorian period progressed, guest books became commonplace. See Durie, p. 43.

way 'Sir Walter has clothed the banks of the Tweed [...] with young woods'.[58] *Black's Picturesque Tourist* (1842) commended the house's 'extraordinary proportions' and found the hall 'most interesting of all the apartments' with its stag horns and oak panelling.[59] The guidebooks' litany of train timetables, tours, entrance times and fees points to the service this vision of Abbotsford performs. By its ninth edition (1852), *Black's* was even adding in rates for meals on the road, and appropriate tipping practices.[60] That is, a substantial written apparatus works to place a traveller in precisely the right place at the right time, to see and appreciate the right, domesticated landscape. A wander into the wilderness represented by Scott's novels and their environment, but carefully managed in a network of official inscription, allowed what Katherine Grenier calls the subsequent return to domesticity, to 'real life'.[61]

This brings the inscriptions within the Abbotsford guest books into a new perspective. Here people did their own writing. For a hundred unbroken years they wrote within official visitor books, line after regimented line. Of course, the house's popularity waxed and waned, as did Scott's. In 1907, W. S. Crockett mapped the changes in Abbotsford's reputation from 'a perfect picture of the wonderful owner's mind' to 'ugly Abbotsford'.[62] Yet still people came and wrote their names in the visitor books. The tour itself shifted according to who was living in the house. Crockett is alert to the changes, regretting that 'for the present-day visitor, the exterior of the edifice is little in evidence'.[63] Still, people kept on coming, and kept on signing.

If authors sought to align their reputations according to a Scott written in stone, perhaps signatories to the visitor books hoped to validate or fix themselves at home according to the relations they seemed to establish with Scott's house and other culturally loaded sites. But wave after wave of signatures point to the problem behind such assertions of self, depending, as they do, on places and people triangulated across the shifts of time.

To Susan Stewart, we inscribe the world to mediate our 'terror of the insignificance of a world without writing'.[64] Abbotsford, if it recuperated anxiety against the natural or burgeoning industrial world, also exposed what was at stake. Though Scott may have been present first in reality and then in memory

---

[58] John Leighton, *Scenes in Scotland* (Glasgow: Richard Griffin, 1831), pp. 35–36.

[59] See *Black's Picturesque Tourist of Scotland*, 2nd edn (Edinburgh: Adam and Charles Black, 1842), p. 121.

[60] *Black's Picturesque Tourist of Scotland*, 9th edn (Edinburgh: Adam and Charles Black, 1852), pp. vii, viii.

[61] Katherine Haldane Grenier, *Tourism and Identity in Scotland, 1770–1914* (Aldershot: Ashgate, 2005), p. 55.

[62] W. S. Crockett, *Footsteps of Scott* (Philadelphia, PA: George W. Jacobs, 1907), p. 86.

[63] Ibid., pp. 87–88.

[64] Susan Stewart, *On Longing: Narratives of the Miniature, the Gigantic, the Souvenir, the Collection* (Durham, NC: Duke University Press, 2007), p. 31.

for his auto/biographically minded friends, he was not here any more. In fact Scott continued to recede according to the excessive presence of his guests — even from his remaining inscription at Abbotsford. Those seeking Scott often noted the pathos of the last clothes he wore in health, on display in the library. Charles Dickens was touched and revolted to see these 'in a vile glass case [...] it associated itself in my mind with broken powers and mental weakness from that hour'.[65] A story from Willis's 1830s visit that mentioned the housemaid taking out the coat and giving it a shake and a wipe was immediately footnoted in *Black's* and was repeated down the years.[66] It, too, was a story of increasing lack: 'It is well that the coat is under a glass case', wrote 'Cuthbert Bede' in 1863, 'for if it was to be taken down, and shaken and wiped for the inspection of every visitor, the stoutest cloth would ere this have given way'.[67] Scott's chair was failing, also. Early on, it had been common to sit where he had penned his novels. William Wells Brown, who escaped slavery in 1834 Kentucky, sat in it at Abbotsford in 1851; Charles Dickens junior, denied the privilege by the attendant, solicited the 'present representative of Sir Walter' and got to sit in it anyway.[68] Small wonder 'Cuthbert Bede' was soon told that though '99 out of very 100 visitors wished to sit', they were 'very properly forbidden'. 'Fancy', he exclaims, 'three or four excursion trains in a day, and every excursionist wishing to ensconce himself in the chair, and assist in rubbing it to destruction!'[69] That is, however strong an imprint may be, it fades into time. It disappears even as we attempt to fix it for ourselves. With what, then, and how, do we triangulate?

Perhaps this concern explains the assertive signing that continued down the years of visitor books. During the author's lifetime, some of his guests participated in a kind of competitive hostility as they tried to fix their position in relation to Scott. If old friend Joanna Baillie thought Scott should keep visitors to a minimum, Maria Edgeworth, a new guest in 1823, immediately pronounced on who should share proximity with Sir Walter. At Scott's Edinburgh house 'our whole last evening was spoiled by that odious Caledonian bore [Mr Hall] and his wife [...] Heaven forbid they shd come to Abbotsford while we are there — for which they made great pushes'.[70] When John Henry Newman stayed at Abbotsford in 1872, the dynamic still maintained: he bemoaned intrusive

---

[65] Charles Dickens, *The Letters of Charles Dickens*, 3 vols (Leipzig: Bernhard Tauchnitz, 1880), I, 272–73.

[66] Willis's 1832–36 letters for the *New York Mirror* were collected in N. P. Willis, *Pencillings by the Way*, new edn (London: George Virtue, 1842). See p. 440; *Black's*, 2nd edn, p. 123.

[67] Cuthbert Bede [Edward Bradley], *A Tour in Tartan-Land* (London: Richard Bentley, 1863), p. 368.

[68] William Wells Brown, *Three Years in Europe* (London: Charles Gilpin, 1852), p. 191; Charles Dickens, Jun., 'Raids over the Border', *All the Year Round*, 10 December 1870, pp. 37–42 (p. 41).

[69] Bede, p. 368.

[70] R. F. Butler, 'Maria Edgeworth and Sir Walter Scott: Unpublished Letters, 1823', *The Review of English Studies*, 9.33 (February 1958), 23–40 (p. 35). Maria Edgeworth letter, dd. 24 June 1823.

'excursionists [...] — Cooke's — walking past the windows [...] before the windows at 6 o'clock in the morning [...] Some poke their heads into the windows'.[71] Just as earlier guests might jostle to sit in Scott's chair, and somehow hold closer to the vanishing author, all might aspire to overwrite the last person in the visitor book with their own mark of presence. But if the chair that once held Walter Scott still can seat only one bottom at a time, similarly, there is always a signature on the next line.

The visitor books, then, in some respects manifest a lost cause. The signature, indeed, is the crux of the problem it is intended to address. This is a problem that Scott himself pointed out and that Derrida has theorized. To sign is to claim space, to attempt to fix oneself in time. But the signature is alien from the 'self'; it displaces the self and points to its multiplicity, subjects it to mutability. As Nicholas Royle has it, 'The name is double, the double is already in the name'.[72] Placed in the context of tourism, the signature is a 'marker' for the self in space and time, but the marker puts that self under question according to signatures that succeed it.[73] Worse, the signature in the visitor book, with all those lines before it and after, connects the 'self' to quite different places and other times.

This is where those walls of ink become interesting. To the scanning eye, important names come into focus. Charlotte Brontë, Charles Dickens, Oscar Wilde — all are easy to pick out, and feature in the Visitor Centre displays at today's Abbotsford. Names fall into patterns: 'Wm. Wells Brown' marks the fleeting presence of the escaped slave on 21 February 1851. A year later, Brown published his travels; a year after that, in April 1853, 'H. B. Stowe' arrives — and records her travels in 1854. More notably — because at odds with his public pronouncements on Scott, but in line with Scott's ideas on the signature — Mark Twain has lurked unrecognized as 'Samuel L. Clemens' of Hartford, Conn. until the most recent investigations of the visitor books. That is, the luminaries of America's antislavery discourse passed through Abbotsford. Still, that in itself is not surprising. It is interesting, though, to see that Clemens came with his wife (who did record a plan to visit Scott's house in her letters) and the editor of the Scotsman, Mr Russell, with his wife.[74] In the visitor books, they have kindly bracketed their names together.

More interesting again, significant people fall into relation with the names of nobodies. As, today, Queen Elizabeth's signature on the reopening of Abbotsford

---

[71] In Ian Ker, *John Henry Newman* (Oxford: Oxford University Press, 2010), p. 672.

[72] See Nicholas Royle, *The Uncanny* (Manchester: Manchester University Press, 2003), p. 191.

[73] See Jonathan Culler, *Framing the Sign: Criticism and its Institutions* (Norman: University of Oklahoma Press, 1988), p. 159, for Dean MacCannell's idea of the site marker.

[74] From Olivia L. and Samuel L. Clemens to Olivia Lewis Langdon, 2 and 6 August 1873, online at the *Mark Twain Project*, <http://www.marktwainproject.org/xtf/view?docId=letters/UCCL 00959.xml;style=letter;brand=mtp> [accessed 21 Nov. 2016].

is rumoured to share space with that of a tourist, Brown, Stowe and Clemens appear alongside quite other people. Clemens came on a day with a host of Americans and a handful from Halifax and Falkirk; Stowe forgot to date her entry (she came on Tuesday 26th, but the last date is 23rd), and so her party shares the page with a Mr and Mrs Charleton from Sunderland.

Any name in the Abbotsford visitor books is thus a node that shifts in a network of absences and spectral presences. We are left wondering, for instance, whether 'Mr. Stevenson & party' of 17 Heriot Row Edinburgh — Robert Louis Stevenson's parents — on 10 September 1867 brought with them their sixteen-year-old son, or whether he was petulantly or enthusiastically getting ready to head to the University of Edinburgh, where he would begin studies in November of that year. Did they come with the Baillies, Frasers and Thorburns, also of Edinburgh, who succeed them in the book? And if so, why? Did they engage at all with those who follow them in the book — 'Mr. & Mrs. W. Lockhart' of Ashestiel, Scott's home before Abbotsford, and likely the author's indirect relatives?

The lines of connection can sweep less determinately than this, and at the same time, more productively, too. In the twentieth- and twenty-first-century viewer's eye, 'D. G. Farragut' (30 June 1868), may not be known as a Union naval officer during the American Civil War. But through *Star Trek* and Federation ships that follow United States traditions of naming, he comes back into focus in the past, and projects into a future that now features 'Starship Farragut' as an online webseries producing classic *Star Trek* video.[75] Three years after the battle of Mobile Bay, where Rear Admiral Farragut was popularly held to have declared 'Damn the torpedoes, full speed ahead', here he was at Abbotsford. And here he is, connected through the US Navy to distant futures and popular audiences in ways he could not possibly have imagined.

As Durie has pointed out, over the years changing transportation brought all classes to Abbotsford and produced the era of mass tourism.[76] Famous names disappear among Lodge outings and mechanics' unions; workers on day trips occupy the same space and take on the same importance as transatlantic voyagers.[77] And if each unknown links across time to unexpected people, they themselves weigh unpredictably on the web of relationship. Consider, for instance, Professor Libby, of Spartanburg South Carolina. Libby draws attention to himself in the visitor book; around him cluster groups labelled for the

[75] See online at <http://www.starshipfarragut.com> [accessed 21 Nov. 2016].

[76] Durie, 'Tourism in Victorian Scotland', pp. 45–47.

[77] See, for example, 13 June 1891, which features an unnamed group of twenty-eight from Edinburgh. The Stirling Master Builders helpfully bracket their twenty-six or so members — some from Bridge of Allan or Bannockburn — on 18 June.

American South, and on 3 September 1911 he sketched in his diamond travel logo for 'The Libby Travel Club'. On 31 August 1912 here he is again, this time sticking a red diamond luggage label in the middle of the page to tout 'Professor and Mrs. Libby, Spartanburg S.C., Tours of Europe, the Orient, and Around the World'. Libby claimed a distinctly commercial presence and spoke across the visitor books to a potential clientele. The random checking allowed by the burgeoning resource that is Google, however, gives Libby a life beyond his luggage label. The *Spartanburg Herald* of 27 July 1915 shouts 'Prof Libby Saw Great Disaster'.[78] Apparently, when the SS *Eastland* capsized as it prepared to depart the Chicago waterside, loaded with Western Electric workers on a company outing, 'Professor Arthur S. Libby, European tourist and college professor', was on the quay. Libby helped by operating the pulmotor, which he opined could have snatched some of the 220 fatalities from death, except that it really needed to operate for an hour on each victim to reactivate the lungs. The unknown Libby, in other words, was Spartanburg's man in the world. Present in the visitor books he connects Abbotsford and America, international tourism, Chicago workers, and modern medicine.

Nicola Watson suggests that since the 1840s, 'Visiting Abbotsford has been a melancholy experience'.[79] The house has an 'embarrassing Victorian fossilized quality'. Certainly, as Susan Stewart says, one of the roles of such places is to serve as 'still life [...] concealing history and temporality [and producing] an illusion of timelessness'.[80] That role seems met for Durie, who despite changes to Abbotsford's extent, façade, access and tour routes, argues that 'What is not a factor of significance is any change in what Abbotsford had to offer. What the visitor saw remained unchanged'.[81] And yet, the visitors change.

As Carolyn Steedman observes, 'stuff' in the archive 'just sits there until it is read, and used, and narrativised'.[82] Basic research in the Abbotsford visitor books reveals individuals in networks. Signatures on lines are produced by fashions in tourism, modes of transportation, needs for self-confirmation — and the randomness of particular lives. In Bruno Latour's terms, there is no 'Abbotsford' as a society; rather societies are constantly being remade by the shifting presence of Abbotsford's visitors.[83] More, those visitors' signatures, constellated in books

---

[78] 'Prof. Libby Saw Great Disaster', *Spartanburg Herald*, 27 July 1915, p. 3. <https://news.google.com/newspapers?nid=1876&dat=19150727&id=5k4sAAAAIBAJ&sjid=48kEAAAAIBAJ&pg=6771,1117995&hl=en> [accessed 21 Nov. 2016].

[79] Watson, *The Literary Tourist*, p. 105.

[80] Stewart, *On Longing*, p. 29.

[81] Durie, 'Tourism in Victorian Scotland', p. 45.

[82] Steedman, *Dust*, p. 68.

[83] Bruno Latour, *Reassembling the Social: An Introduction to Actor-Network Theory* (Oxford: Oxford University Press, 2007).

and within the eye of the reader — informed by the networking made possible online — transgress time and establish connection in every direction.

Abbotsford, arguably, may be an inert monument. But through the visitor books it is inscribed with signatures that make it a waypoint linking lives and times.

The 'universal favourite':[1] Daniel Terry's *Guy Mannering; or, The Gipsey's Prophecy* (1816)

ANNIKA BAUTZ

Plymouth University

The first adaptation of a Walter Scott novel for the stage was *Guy Mannering; or, The Gipsey's Prophecy*, by Scott's friend Daniel Terry, premiered at Covent Garden Theatre in March 1816 and published in the same month. Following the success of Terry's play, each of Scott's succeeding novels was adapted within months, or sometimes within weeks, of the novel's respective publication, for both major and minor playhouses.[2] Theatrical productions based on Scott's works were so numerous in the nineteenth century that their number was exceeded only by productions of Shakespeare.[3] However, critical studies of adaptations of these novels are rare. There are surveys of dramatizations of Scott's works, such as H. Philip Bolton's masterly overview, or Richard Ford's catalogue, as well as accounts of some adaptations of Scott's novels, including Ann Rigney's compelling discussion of play versions of *Rob Roy* and *Ivanhoe*, and David Buchanan's comparative analysis of two adaptations of *The Heart of Mid-Lothian*. Jerome Mitchell's two books about operatic adaptations of Scott remain the seminal studies of that area of adaptation.[4] But to date, no extended study exists of Terry's *Guy Mannering*, or of its reception.[5]

I am grateful to Susan Oliver and James Gregory for their comments on this article.

[1] William Oxberry, 'Memoir of Mr D. Terry', in *Oxberry's Dramatic Biography* (London: G. Virtue, 1827), p. 7.

[2] Scott novels were turned into 'whatever type of play, musical play, drama, operatic drama, opera, burletta, melodrama, burlesque, or pantomime might be required for [theatre managements'] particular situation'. Barbara Bell, 'The Performance of Victorian Medievalism', in *Beyond Arthurian Romances*, ed. by Jennifer Palmgren and Lorretta Holloway (Basingstoke: Palgrave Macmillan, 2005), pp. 191–216 (p. 213).

[3] Ann Rigney, *The Afterlives of Walter Scott: Memory on the Move* (Oxford: Oxford University Press, 2012), p. 60. Also see William Knight's account of the Surrey Theatre: here, and elsewhere, Scott adaptations were 'all the rage'. *A Major London 'Minor': The Surrey Theatre, 1805–1865* (London: The Society for Theatre Research, 1997), p. 34. Some overviews of theatre in the nineteenth century do not mention Scott adaptations at all; for example, *The Performing Century: Nineteenth-Century Theatre's History*, ed. by Tracy Davis and Peter Holland (Basingstoke: Palgrave, 2007).

[4] Jerome Mitchell, *The Walter Scott Operas: An Analysis of Operas Based on the Works of Sir Walter Scott* (Tuscaloosa: University of Alabama Press, 1977) and *More Scott Operas: Further Analyses of Operas Based on the Works of Sir Walter Scott* (Lanham, MD: University of America Press, 1996).

[5] H. Philip Bolton, *Scott Dramatized* (London: Mansell, 1992); Richard Ford, *Dramatisations*

Yearbook of English Studies, 47 (2017), 36–57
© Modern Humanities Research Association 2017

This study is concerned with the reception of Terry's play during the first decade after its initial performance. In addition to being itself an adaptation, the play was mediated in different on-stage versions as well as in luxury and cheap print editions. In London, it was performed at both of the Theatres Royal, Covent Garden and Drury Lane. Terry's *Guy Mannering* was also performed all over the United Kingdom, and widely reviewed beyond London, but that and other productions are beyond the scope of this study.[6] Gauging reception by quantifying the number of performances and discussing the editions of the play text, I also explore reviews of the play as indicators of what aspects of the drama appealed to critics and how their reactions to the play compared to responses to Scott's novel.

The purpose here, then, is to establish a critical analysis of the reception of the play and to relate reviews of performance to those of the novel, in order to determine how the play contributed to shaping the reception of the most popular novelist of the early nineteenth century.

The Novel

Walter Scott was the most popularly admired novelist of his time. As John O. Hayden has said, it is difficult to emphasize quite how superlative his reputation was.[7] His works sold in unprecedented numbers and to extraordinary critical and popular acclaim, both in Britain and abroad. Scott's first novel, *Waverley*, was published in July 1814 during what the publishing world called the 'dead season', yet was immediately and extraordinarily successful. The first edition of one thousand copies (already more than the 500–750 copies printed on average for novels) sold out in less than a month, and a second edition of two thousand copies had sold within weeks. Before the end of the year, the novel had gone through seven editions.[8] *Waverley* produced unparalleled profits for its author and publisher: Archibald Constable had not been confident enough to buy the copyright outright for the thousand pounds that Scott had demanded, so *Waverley* was published on the basis of half profits. As John Gibson Lockhart, Scott's son-in-law, commented: 'Well might Constable regret that he had not ventured to offer £1000 for the whole copyright of *Waverley*!'[9]

of *Scott's Novels: A Catalogue* (Oxford: Bibliographical Society, 1979); Ann Rigney, *The Afterlives of Walter Scott*; David Buchanan, 'Popular Reception by Dramatic Adaptation: The Case of Walter Scott's *The Heart of Mid-Lothian*', *European Romantic Review*, 22.6 (2011), 747–65.

[6] For the popularity of Scott adaptations particularly in Scotland, as 'National Dramas', see for example Barbara Bell, 'The National Drama', *Theatre Research International*, 17.2 (1992), 96–108.

[7] *Scott: The Critical Heritage*, ed. by John O. Hayden (London: Routledge, 1970), p. 1.

[8] Editions numbered according to title page; four of these were not new editions in a bibliographical sense but reissues. Annika Bautz, *The Reception of Jane Austen and Walter Scott* (London: Continuum 2007), p. 23; William Todd and Ann Bowden, *Sir Walter Scott: A Bibliographical History, 1796–1832* (New Castle, DE: Oak Knoll, 1998), pp. 309–16.

[9] J. G. Lockhart, *Memoirs of the Life of Sir Walter Scott, Bart.*, 7 vols (Edinburgh: Robert Cadell; London: John Murray, 1837), III, 296.

Scott's ensuing novels were even more successful. *Guy Mannering; or, The Astrologer*, his second novel, appeared in February 1815 in a first edition of two thousand copies priced at a guinea each. Stocks sold out on the day of publication.[10] This was the first novel of the many that followed, with 'by the author of Waverley' given as the authorial identification on the title page. Two further editions of *Guy Mannering* were printed in 1815, a fourth edition in 1817, a fifth and sixth edition in 1820.[11] *The Antiquary*'s first edition, in May 1816, comprised 5000 copies, while *The Heart of Mid-Lothian* (July 1818) and *Rob Roy* (December 1817) were published in runs of ten thousand each, with the latter selling out within a fortnight of its release. The popularity of Scott's novels was superlative and led to innumerable spin-offs that included theatre versions, songs, operas, pantomimes, the circus, high and popular art, and book illustrations.

Enormous though these publication figures were, access to the novels was restricted by their price. Further to the guinea (21 shillings) required for *Guy Mannering*, *Rob Roy* sold at twenty-four shillings and *Kenilworth* retailed at an almost unheard-of one guinea and a half (thirty-one shillings and sixpence) in 1821.[12] Working-class men were earning between nine shillings and, very exceptionally, forty shillings a week throughout the period,[13] so even where literacy was not an obstacle, members of those classes were unlikely to spend a week's wages, or more, on the latest novel. High prices meant, as Jane Austen lamented, that 'people are more ready to borrow & praise, than to buy'.[14] Yet even through libraries, novels were unlikely to have reached very far below the middle classes: subscription or proprietary libraries charged annual fees ranging between ten shillings and two or even three guineas (and did not necessarily hold novels).[15] Circulating libraries varied more in price, depending on, for example, the size and location of the establishment, and while they often held primarily novels David Allan has shown that was not always the case.[16] However, arguably

---

[10] Bautz, *Reception*, p. 31.

[11] Todd and Bowden, pp. 361–68.

[12] Todd and Bowden, p. 537. *HOM* retailed at 32 shillings because it contained four volumes rather than the usual three.

[13] Kathryn Sutherland, '"Events … have made us a world of readers": Reader Relations, 1780–1830', in *The Romantic Period*, ed. by David B. Pirie, Penguin History of Literature, vol. v (London: Penguin, 1994), pp. 1–48 (p. 9).

[14] Jane Austen, letter to Fanny Knight, November 1814; in *Jane Austen's Letters*, ed. and coll. by Deirdre Le Faye (Oxford: Oxford University Press, 1995), p. 287.

[15] Thomas Kelly, *Early Public Libraries* (London: The Library Association, 1966), p. 128; William St Clair, *The Reading Nation in the Romantic Period* (Cambridge: Cambridge University Press, 2004), pp. 667–68; Annika Bautz, 'The Foundation of Plymouth Public Library', in *Before the Public Library*, ed. by Mark Towsey and Kyle Roberts (Leiden: Brill, 2017).

[16] David Allan, *A Nation of Readers: The Lending Library in Georgian England* (London: British Library, 2008), pp. 134–39.

the most successful circulating library in the early nineteenth century, William Lane's Minerva library, had a subscription fee of between two and five guineas in 1814, well above a working man's means.[17] Most of the libraries open to working-class readers were those funded by benevolent donors, and generally did not include fiction. For large sections of the population then, reading the novel on, or soon after, its publication would not have been possible.

Theatres and Audiences

Attending a performance at the theatre was much more affordable, and, importantly, did not require literacy. As David Worrall points out, 'the role in communication of audible rather than literate communication should not be underestimated'.[18] Ticket prices differed widely, but admittance to the theatre could be obtained for a fraction of the cost of access to the book. Prices for Drury Lane and Covent Garden, the only two theatres that could legitimately show drama, ranged between one shilling for the upper gallery and seven shillings for regular boxes (with the private boxes usually being taken by wealthy patrons for a whole season).[19] So-called minor, or illegitimate, houses offered admission from sixpence.[20] The Adelphi, an illegitimate but fashionable theatre, charged one shilling for the gallery, two shillings for the pit, and four shillings for a box. Until the Theatres Regulation Act was eventually passed in 1843, which finally abolished the monopoly of the patent theatres (after more than a decade of campaigning by Edward Bulwer Lytton and others), illegitimate theatres could not officially offer the spoken word. Theatre managers and playwrights found ways around that law, however, through using song and recitative to express words, but also, by the early nineteenth century, through introducing spoken word interlaced with music.[21] In consequence, the forms shown at the minor theatres were mainly burletta, melodrama and pantomime. Burletta in particular was drawn on as a form whose 'great usefulness consisted in the impossibility of defining it', and, as Joseph Donohue suggests, 'what cannot be defined cannot be prohibited'.[22]

The law however reserved the 'national drama', or the unaccompanied spoken word, for the patent theatres. Plays written for performance at the patent theatres

---

[17] Sutherland, p. 12.

[18] David Worrall, *Theatric Revolution: Drama, Censorship and Romantic Period Subcultures, 1773–1832* (Oxford: Oxford University Press, 2008), p. 274.

[19] Marc Baer, *Theatre and Disorder in Late Georgian London* (Oxford: Oxford University Press, 1992), p. 22.

[20] Joseph Donohue, 'Theatres, their Architecture and their Audiences', in *The Cambridge History of British Theatre*, vol. II: 1660–1895, ed. by Joseph Donohue (Cambridge University Press, 2004), pp. 292–308 (p. 295).

[21] Joseph Donohue, 'Burletta and the Early Nineteenth-Century English Theatre', in *Nineteenth-Century Theatre Research*, 1 (1973), 29–51 (p. 43).

[22] Donohue, 'Burletta', p. 30.

had to be submitted for approval to the Examiner at the Lord Chamberlain's office. Few plays were rejected at that point, largely because playwrights and theatre managers would self-censor prior to submission. The Examiner from 1778 to 1824 was John Larpent, who was known to be sensitive to any references to politics, religion and aristocratic scandals.[23] As Elizabeth Inchbald noted: 'The Novelist is a free agent. He lives in a land of liberty, whilst the Dramatic Writer exists but under a despotic government.'[24] As we shall see below, Terry's *Guy Mannering* certainly contained nothing to which Larpent could have taken exception.

Performances at major and minor theatres lasted an entire evening, starting around 6pm and often not ending until 11pm or later. Both legitimate and illegitimate theatres offered half-price admission to the gallery and pit, usually following the first play, and sometimes before the third act (of, usually, a five-act play), so that even the lower classes would have access to the theatre, though the view from the gallery was restricted.[25] *Guy Mannering* the play was therefore accessed by far more people in a few weeks than could have obtained access to the novel in a year.

At the Royal, or patent houses — Drury Lane and Covent Garden, and in the summer, when the other two were closed, the Haymarket — the gallery and pit admission prices were upheld for decades. That was famously so following the Old Price Riots of 1809, which showed how essential audiences deemed affordable admission to the national theatres, the only ones that were permitted to show drama, as a right. When the rebuilt Covent Garden opened in 1809 after the old theatre had burnt down a year earlier, John Kemble and the managers charged new, higher prices: four shillings instead of three shillings and sixpence for the pit, seven instead of six shillings for the regular boxes.[26] Furthermore, the restructure in favour of more private boxes meant the upper gallery, though no more expensive, was less desirable than it had previously been because of its more restricted lines of sight. As Marc Baer has shown, Kemble and the management argued within a new political economy, 'which suggested that rising costs should be met by the consumers of theatre', whereas 'many among the audience were operating within the framework of a competing "moral economy"'.[27] But the audience's cry for 'old prices' was so loud and consistent that after sixty-seven

---

[23] Jeffrey Cox, 'Re-viewing Romantic Drama', *Literature Compass*, 1 (2004), 1–27 (p. 9); Worrall, *Theatric Revolution*, esp. pp. 104–32.

[24] Elizabeth Inchbald, 'To The Artist' [*The Artist*, No. xiv, 13 June 1807], cited from Appendix to Inchbald, *Nature and Art*, ed. by S. Maurer (London: Pickering and Chatto, 1997), p. 143.

[25] Frederick Burwick, *British Drama of the Industrial Revolution* (Cambridge: Cambridge University Press, 2015), p. 6; Baer, p. 30.

[26] Baer, p. 22.

[27] Baer, p. 22.

nights of rioting, Kemble and the management capitulated. The old prices for the pit were restored, although the new prices for the boxes were retained.[28]

The differing prices served to uphold at least the illusion of a strict class division in the theatre auditoriums. Both legitimate and illegitimate theatres were built with separate entrances, while seating, too, was separate and consolidated as one of the ways in which 'antagonistic relations among various segments of theatre-goers had become unmistakably clear'.[29] In the new 1809 Covent Garden building, only about a third of the audience would have been accommodated in the gallery, with the much more expensive open and private boxes as well as the pit holding the majority.

Yet as Worrall argues, 'social exclusivity or segregation of the classes was an impossibility within these spaces'.[30] Most of the audience in the East End playhouses came from the immediate neighbourhood: journeymen, mechanics, shopkeepers, clerks, sailors, and women and children. But new bridges and improved transport made the East End houses more easily accessible for more affluent audiences from elsewhere in London. Famously, in the early 1820s, Queen Caroline visited Astley's, the Surrey and the Coburg theatres.[31] At the legitimates, too, there was a high proportion of labourers in the audiences. Worrall has shown that among audience members arrested at the old price riots there were 'Cheapside shopmen, Hackney coal merchants, footmen in livery, Shadwell brewer's clerks, a Soho "respectable tradesman" and a journeyman courier', as well as 'a Smithfield oil and colourman, a hairdresser, two silver-spoon makers, a major in the army'.[32] Worrall points out that these theatres, 'like their mirror images the churches, reached audiences drawn from all the social classes',[33] and enabled the mixing of social classes in the same space.

The differences between the social classes of theatre goers also manifested themselves in the kinds of productions that were favoured. Theatre managers had on the one hand to please the 'wealthy patrons who might reserve a box for the season', but at the same time, and for the same performances, they also had to attract spectators from much lower down the social scale.[34] Entertainments were varied, and the legitimate houses put on an increasing number of the more vocal productions that were shown at the illegitimates: burletta and melodrama.[35] In Jeffrey Cox's words, in terms of productions, 'there was more traffic between

---

[28] Baer, p. 36.

[29] Donohue, p. 225.

[30] Worrall, p. 229.

[31] Jane Moody, *Illegitimate Theatre in London, 1770–1840* (Cambridge: Cambridge University Press, 2000), pp. 165 ff; Worrall, pp. 196 ff.

[32] Worrall, pp. 228–29.

[33] Worrall, p. 274.

[34] Burwick, p. 6.

[35] Donohue, pp. 224.

"legitimate" and "illegitimate" theaters than the law imagined'.[36] The competition between major and minor houses intensified as they increasingly vied for the same audiences. Furthermore, the new Covent Garden and Drury Lane buildings were so vast that straight plays were difficult to stage, as large sections of the audience would not be able to hear the spoken word. Consequently, plays written for performance at the patent theatres increasingly contained a high proportion of sung words, and one of the most popular examples of a musical play was *Guy Mannering*.

Daniel Terry's Guy Mannering; or, The Gipsey's Prophecy: *Performances and Audiences*

Guy Mannering; or, The Gipsey's Prophecy: a Musical Play in three acts, by Daniel Terry, Esq., of the Theatre-Royal, Covent-Garden, was first performed on 12 March 1816, just over a year after the publication of Scott's novel in February 1815. The play established a precedent for stage adaptations of Scott's prose fiction, largely because, from the first night onwards, it was immensely popular. Many other Scott adaptations followed, including other versions of *Guy Mannering*, but none of the rival versions came close to Terry's in popularity, and most were derived from his.[37] Terry was said to have 'absolutely netted the immense sum of thirteen-hundred pounds by his operatic version of Sir Walter Scott's "Guy Mannering"'.[38] Scott had advised Terry on the script, and in the following years sent him proofs of his novels to give him a head start over other playwrights who would rush to produce an adaptation of the latest Scott novel.[39] Reviewers attribute the play's popularity partly to it being an adaptation of one of the most popular novels of the age, expecting the 'celebrated title, bestowed for the first time upon a musical drama, [to] draw after it a crowded house'.[40] It was then shown in every season from 1815–16 to 1823–24, and in these nine years was performed at least ninety-three times at Covent Garden,[41] besides being shown at Drury Lane and other London venues. Within weeks it was performed elsewhere in the United Kingdom, as well as abroad, repeatedly drawing 'one of the most crowded audiences of the season'.[42] While the novel's fame fed into the play's popularity, the play also enhanced the novel's popularity and the life of its characters.

[36] Jeffrey Cox, p. 9.
[37] Bolton, p. 57. Notably among early versions are J. R. Planche's 'The Witch of Derncleugh' (1821), and Douglas Jerrold's 'The Gipsy of Derncleugh' (1821).
[38] Oxberry, p. 7.
[39] Philip Cox, *Reading Adaptations: Novels and Verse Narratives on Stage, 1790–1840* (Manchester: Manchester University Press, 2000), p. 80.
[40] *The Times*, 13 March 1816, p. 3.
[41] Bolton, p. 56.
[42] *The Times*, 3 December 1817, p. 2.

Not only did contemporary reviewers comment on its extraordinary popularity at the time, but decades later critics still discussed the longevity and enduring popularity of this play. For example, a memoir of Terry published in 1827 states:

> If, too, popularity is a test of excellence, *Guy Mannering* stands in the first rank; for no drama has been a more universal favourite; it has been adapted by both our regular stages, and played in almost every theatre throughout the country; indeed we much doubt if a single exception can be found. This is no light praise, and to this, in its utmost extent, the author of *Guy Mannering* is truly and honourably entitled.[43]

At the time Terry's *Guy Mannering* was first performed, the capacities of Drury Lane and Covent Garden were 3100 and 3000 respectively.[44] In the ninety-three Covent Garden performances over the nine years following the first production of Terry's *Guy Mannering* on stage alone, even if we assume the house was not full to capacity — and it must have been fairly full for the play to be put on this frequently — the audience figures will have been at least 250,000, and are likely to have been higher. This dwarfs the readership of Scott's novel based on publication figures;[45] even if we assume many readers for each copy of the book, just the Covent Garden audience of *Guy Mannering* the play in these nine years is likely to have been at least five times higher than the readership of the novel in the whole kingdom for the same period. And Terry's play was put on in theatres throughout the country, so that, overall, many more people would have encountered the staged versions of Terry's Meg Merrilies, Guy Mannering, Lucy Bertram and Dominie Sampson, than would have read Scott's characterizations.

The Play's Text

The text of the play was printed in 1816 and would likely have been available to buy in the theatre (and elsewhere) from the first performance onwards. It was published by Miller, retailing at two shillings and sixpence, a fraction of the price of the novel; by 1817 the text stated on its title page that it was in its third edition, by 1818 in its fourth. Terry's *Guy Mannering* was the version that featured in the numerous collections of the *Waverley Dramas*, because, unlike some other Scott plays where there were competing adaptations, Terry's, as the first adaptation of any Scott novel, continued by far the most dominant, with 'virtually no other English versions [...] ever published'.[46] The play quickly

---

[43] *Oxberry*, pp. 7–8.
[44] Jeffrey Cox, 'Romantic Drama', pp. 9–10; Joseph Donohue, 'The Theatre from 1800–1895', in *The Cambridge History of British Theatre*, vol. II: 1660–1895, pp. 219–271 (p. 224).
[45] Todd and Bowden, pp. 361–68.
[46] Bolton, pp. 56–57.

FIGURE 1. John Dicks' illustrated one-penny edition of Terry's *Guy Mannering* (part of Dicks' *The British Drama* series, 1864). The illustration depicts Meg Merrilies' heroic death in Act III, Scene 3, in which she saves Harry Bertram's life and reinstates him as the heir, but knows this is at the cost of her own life.

© The British Library Board (Shelfmark: 11770.bbb.4).

became part of standard collections of British plays, such as William Oxberry's *New English Drama* (1818), and held its place in the canon, being included in collections such as Cumberland's *British Theatre* of 1843, or John Dicks' innovative — because extraordinarily cheap — illustrated one-penny series of *The British Drama* (1864).

Not surprisingly, Terry introduced some changes to plot and characters in his rendering of the novel for the stage, such as reducing the number of characters and collapsing periods of time. Julia Mannering becomes Guy Mannering's sister, not daughter, and Lucy Bertram ends up marrying Guy himself. Charles and his father Sir Robert Hazlewood can therefore be written out of the drama. One of the effects of the Lucy and Guy love plot is to render Lucy more conservative even than she is in the novel. She is represented as a passive model of propriety who needs Guy Mannering's protection from the start and later marries the man in whose house she lives, who was her father's friend and who acts as her guardian. While his gallant behaviour to Lucy Bertram is noticeable from the start, as well as her proper response, from the beginning of Act II Julia Mannering makes clear that his gallantry is more than disinterested: 'A lion in the toils! Oh, Lucy, dear Lucy! If you knew what meshes have been spread for that proud Colonel, in vain.'[47] Lucy gives voice to her feelings in a song to Julia that proves her modesty and decorum:

> *Air.* [Miss Bertram.]
>
> Oh! Blame me not, that such high worth
> Hath rais'd of love the gentle flame;
> Yet, as I own it — quicker throbs
> The timid, trembling pulse of shame.
> When pity dries the falling tear,
> Love, unperceiv'd, will venture in;
> And kindness to a wounded heart,
> Is sure that wounded heart to win.
>
> My faultering tongue, my downcast eyes,
> Reveal my bosom's thoughts too plain;
> But where love wore a form so good,
> Ah! Tell me, could it plead in vain?
> This heart, without a resting place,
> Was like the wandr'ing weary dove,
> Return'd from sorrow's storms, to seek
> A shelter in the ark of love.[48]

Many of the songs from the play became popular as stand-alone pieces. The sheet music could be bought immediately, and songs were included in collections, offering additional channels through which Scott's characters would have been

---

[47] Daniel Terry, *Guy Mannering* (London: John Miller, 1818), Act II, Scene 1, p. 25.
[48] Terry, *GM* (Miller, 1818), Act III, Scene 1, p. 49.

known and taken shape.[49] In this case, the song emphasizes Lucy's falling in love with the hero in a way stereotypical to heroines of the period's conservative novels, in line with conduct manuals: unintended, unperceived, ashamed of the — gentle — emotion once realized, as a response to being loved by an older kind man, and in need of protection and guidance. The double wedding at the end of the play, just after Meg's dramatic death, is a more easily pleasing scene than the eponymous hero's single status at the end of the novel.

To make Julia Guy's sister rather than daughter on the one hand collapses time, and on the other makes it possible for her to banter with Mannering throughout in a way a sister might. It also perhaps renders her disobedience to Mannering in her relationship with Captain Brown (alias Henry Bertram) a little less exceptional. The play allows her to give in to a reluctant meeting with Brown as her lover, although this soon turns into a comic hide-and-seek scene where first Sampson and then Mannering himself enter the room and Brown has to hide in various places before he can escape, while Flora and Julia have to make excuses for noises and other evidence. After Brown's escape, she reflects:

> I declare I am frightened at my own imprudence! Should my brother discover this business, what will be the consequence? Oh, dear! I wish he would but sympathise a little more with love, and a little less with honour — but alas![50]

While Julia is imprudent here by talking to her lover in her boudoir at midnight, her servant Flora is always present. Moreover, she has neither arranged nor sanctioned the interview, although she does then conceal Brown's presence from her brother. Julia does not venture beyond reluctant verbal replies, so that honour and gender boundaries can be upheld, and in the end love and honour can be combined because Brown turns out to be Bertram, the heir to the estate of Ellangowan.

While out of necessity there are fewer characters in the play than in the novel, there are still characters from various social classes. The main focus is on the four lovers, and on Meg Merrilies, Dandie Dinmont and Dominie Sampson, but other gipsies and minor characters such as Mrs MacCandlish, the innkeeper, are of significant interest and importance, which, given the mixed-class audiences at the theatres, may have contributed to the broad appeal the play enjoyed for many years. Meg in particular is given significance, partly by being in the subtitle — 'The Gipsey's Prophecy', as compared to the novel's subtitle of 'The Astrologer' — but also by the climax centring on the heroic death that she goes to knowingly

---

[49] For example, *'Oh! Rest thee babe', sung in Guy Mannering, written by D. Terry, Esq., Music by John Whitaker* (London: C. Sheard, *c.* 1820), or, for a collection: *The Universal Songsters; or, Museum of Mirth: forming the most complete, extensive, and valuable collection of ancient and modern songs* (London: Jones, 1829).

[50] Terry, *GM* (Miller, 1818), Act II, Scene 1, p. 32.

in order to save Harry Bertram's life and reinstate him as heir. Perhaps to keep her as a character apart from the others, she and Guy Mannering, the hero and older lover, are the only main characters who are not given a song (where she has verse in the play the directions specify 'Meg speaks', not sings).

The prophecy itself has also been changed. While in Scott's novel both Guy Mannering and Meg predict little Harry's future, in the play neither does. Guy Mannering is told the story of Harry's loss at the beginning of Act I, when he arrives in a Scottish inn after many years' absence in India. He 'heard [old Bertram] had a son',[51] but he has not seen him, let alone predicted the boy's future. His connection to the Bertram household is older; he describes old Bertram as 'my earliest, and best friend'.[52] The backstory is therefore altered, with Guy listening to the narration of the innkeeper, and Meg barely featuring in it. Meg's prophecy is in fact about herself, as the saviour of Harry Bertram and the House of Ellangowan, as she makes clear in Act III:

> Now then, to complete the work of Fate, tho' every step I take be on a corpse. I was born to raise the old House of Ellangowan from its ruins — and the moment is at hand when all shall behold —
> Bertram's right, and Bertram's might,
> Meet on Ellangowan's height.[53]

In the play then, the only person who has powers to see the future is a Scottish gipsy, not a rational English gentleman.

Overall, and whether for dramatic effect or driven by ideology or politics, the changes made to the novel in Terry's adaptation have the effect of making the plot and the characters more conservative, particularly in terms of gender expectation. Terry's *Guy Mannering* as staged and printed therefore contains nothing that any member of the audience or the Examiner at the Lord Chamberlain's office could take exception to. None of the middle-class characters oversteps boundaries. At the same time, however, Meg is not held to rules of either propriety or realism so that the outlandishness, power and pathos of the novel's Scottish gipsy is preserved in the play.

Upmarket and Abridged Versions

The various early editions of the play text of *Guy Mannering* are a good indication of its popularity. Some editions of the play text were more upmarket and included prefatory remarks and images, such as Oxberry's *New English Drama* Series, in which *Guy Mannering* was included in volume XII (1818, then reprinted several times) as the first of five plays in that volume, followed by *Cymbeline*,

---

[51] Ibid., Act I, Scene 1, p. 7.
[52] Ibid., Act I, Scene 1, p. 10.
[53] Ibid., Act III, Scene 1, p. 52.

MR LISTON,

AS DOMINIE SAMPSON.

Engraved by Woolnoth, from an original drawing by Wageman

Published 1820 by Simpkin & Marshall, Stationers C.º & Chapple Pall Mall.

FIGURE 2.   Oxberry's 1820 Edition of *Guy Mannering*, showing Mr Liston as Dominie Sampson. © The British Library Board (Shelfmark: 11770.f.12).

Twelfth Night, The Confederacy (by Sir John Vanbrugh, first performed in 1705) and *Douglas* (the 1755 tragedy by John Home that had also been popular for many years). To be included alongside four plays that had all acquired the status of classics — two Shakespeare plays, and two other well-known plays that had both been performed for decades — emphasizes the high esteem Terry's *Guy Mannering* is held in. Each play in Oxberry's edition was headed by a frontispiece of a famous actor playing one of the characters. In the case of *Guy Mannering*, the frontispiece shows Mr Liston as Dominie Sampson, the faithful but comic schoolmaster companion to Lucy Bertram, a choice that emphasizes the importance of characters that may seem marginal to the plot but are central to how the play (and the novel) is received.

The introductory remarks give biographical information about Terry as a 'master' dramatist, which again emphasizes the play's status, as its author is someone the reader should be interested in. The introduction discusses *Guy Mannering*'s genre as 'a very near kinsman of the melodrama' and recognizes that this kind of play is now 'infinitely more popular than any classical composition'.[54] However, the author cannot be blamed for this shift in audience taste, and instead needs to be praised for the skilful way in which he has adapted the novel into a play. While there is a recognition that the drama performed at the patent theatres is increasingly similar to that performed at the minors, the emphasis is still on the quality of this particular play, even as a melodrama. Oxberry's edition must also have been intended to be used for amateur performance as it gives exact stage directions, costume instructions, timings, and positioning of characters. This again testifies to the popularity of the play.

Alongside these editions of Terry's play retailing at two shillings and sixpence or more were cheaper, abridged versions, down to the production of a penny dreadful.[55] William Hodgson, for example, brought out an abridged version of Terry's *Guy Mannering* in 1822 in his company's Juvenile Drama series. This edition was edited to fit twenty-four pages, so consisted of two sheets, and was priced at sixpence, which was much more affordable than Miller's edition of Terry's text and cost a fraction of the price of the novel. Hodgson even entered his edition at the Stationers' Hall and the Stamp Office to give the text more authority. Probably to protect himself from piracy charges, Hodgson changed the words of Terry's text, though not in ways that materially altered the meaning of the sentences, or affected the characters. For example, the question of Mrs MacCandlish, the innkeeper, to Colonel Mannering, 'I beg your Honour's

---

[54] 'Remarks', in *GM* by D. Terry, ed. by W. Oxberry (London: Simpkin and Marshall, 1820), p. i.

[55] Bolton, p. 56.

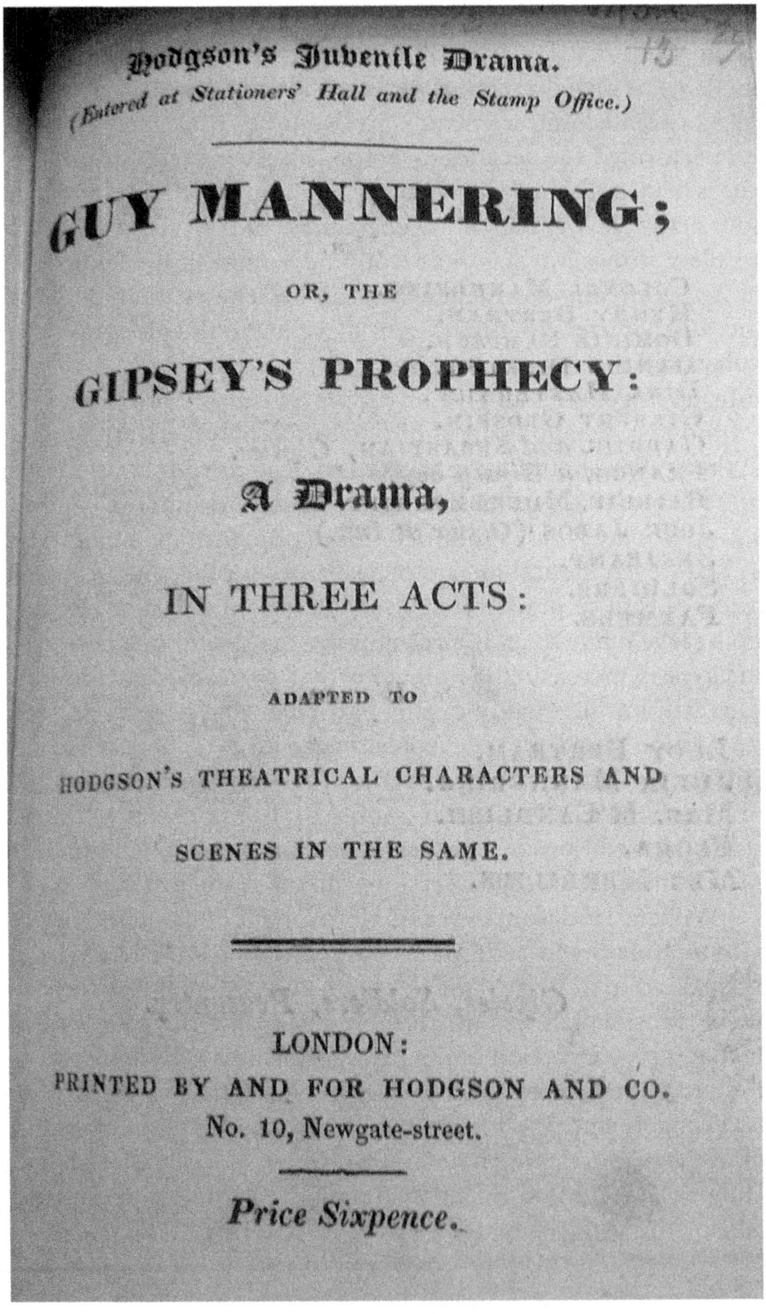

Hodgson's Juvenile Drama.
(Entered at Stationers' Hall and the Stamp Office.)

GUY MANNERING;

OR, THE

GIPSEY'S PROPHECY:

A Drama,

IN THREE ACTS:

ADAPTED TO

HODGSON'S THEATRICAL CHARACTERS AND

SCENES IN THE SAME.

LONDON:
PRINTED BY AND FOR HODGSON AND CO.
No. 10, Newgate-street.

Price Sixpence.

FIGURE 3. Example of an abridged version of Terry's play: Hodgson's Juvenile Drama Series, *Guy Mannering* (1822), Price Sixpence.
© The British Library Board (Shelfmark: 840.b.34.(13.)).

pardon. Would your Honour choose any refreshment after your ride?' in the original becomes 'Will your Honour take anything?'[56]

The play of *Guy Mannering* entered the market at various levels, as a performance, as an official play text, as a text that could be used for private theatricals, and in cheaper versions that could be had for sixpence.

Reviews of the Novel and the Play

While print runs, runs of performances, numbers and kinds of editions, prices of texts and theatre tickets give indications about popularity, they do not tell us what it was about the novel and the play that appealed (or otherwise) to readers and audiences. The present study focuses on reviews in contemporary periodicals, so does not attend to other kinds of reception such as more popular opinions that may have been recorded in diaries and letters. While reviews are not necessarily representative of a more popular reception, they give an indication of how some contemporaries reacted, and crucially, they show how critical opinions of novel and play compare.

The first decades of the nineteenth century were a heyday of periodical criticism. As William Hazlitt wrote in *The Edinburgh Review* in 1823, '"We are nothing, if not critical" Be it so: but then let us be critical, or we shall be nothing.'[57] Over sixty periodicals in the period carried reviews of literary texts and theatrical performances, most being published anonymously. Theatrical reviewing changed significantly during the period: the 'puffs' typical of the late eighteenth and very early nineteenth centuries, written by contributors who received payment or free seats in exchange for positive reviews, were being replaced by what Jeffrey Cox and Michael Gamer describe as 'some of the most perceptive criticism the theatre has ever received'.[58]

Reviews of novels, too, were not always highly regarded, largely because of fiction's low status. As Ina Ferris points out, reviews and novels alike represented 'a borderline discourse, neither fully literary nor fully commercial'.[59] For a novel to be reviewed at all was already a significant achievement. However, Scott's novels were all reviewed, in several periodicals, and often in long articles. Relating reviews of the play to those of the novel makes it possible to identify which aspects of the story appealed more broadly, and which were specific to the play.

---

[56] Terry, *GM* (Miller, 1818), p. 5; Terry, *Guy Mannering* (London: Hodgson, 1822), p. 4.

[57] William Hazlitt, '*The St James's Chronicle* — *The Morning Chronicle* — *The Times* — *The New Times* — *The Courier, &c.* — *Cobbett's Weekly Journal* — *The Examiner* — *The Observer* — *The Gentleman's Magazine* — *The New Monthly Magazine* — *The London, &c. &c.*' ('The Periodical Press'), in *The Edinburgh Review*, 38, May 1823, pp. 349–78 (p. 351).

[58] Jeffrey Cox and Michael Gamer, 'Introduction', in *The Broadview Anthology of Romantic Drama*, ed. by Cox and Gamer (Orchard Park, NY: Broadview, 2003), p. xvii.

[59] Ina Ferris, *The Achievement of Literary Authority; Gender, History and the Waverley Novels* (Ithaca, NY: Cornell University Press, 1991), p. 30.

Guy Mannering appeared in February 1815 and, like *Waverley*, was noticed by many more reviewing periodicals than the average novel would have been. Though the overall verdicts were generally positive, the majority of reviews also included criticism that centred particularly on the way romance and realism are combined in the novel's use of astrology. Both Meg Merrilies and Guy Mannering predict Harry Bertram's fate, but it is only to Mannering's involvement that the reviewers took exception. Mannering as an Oxford scholar from the late eighteenth century is a figure of realism that they expect to act in a recognized and approved way. That he should make use of astrology is a 'monstrous absurdity':[60] he can have contact with the world of romance by travelling to Scotland, a land of romance, but he has to behave there in accordance with codes of conduct of his origin and time.

Meg also predicts the future. Reviewers sanction that behaviour as acceptable because she is a figure of romance. As a Scottish gipsy matriarch she is exotic, and her actions and manners represent 'a class of people formerly so common in [Scotland]'.[61] Like ordinary characters of romance she is fictitious, but she also represents a class of people that existed. The novel is set in the past, albeit a very recent past, and Meg is a gipsy as well as Scottish, so that she is removed on several counts from an English readership. Her exoticism and her romantic qualities render the image the novel draws of her a realistic one: her dealings 'may be true to nature, as the Scotch have not yet thrown off their belief in witchcraft, and continue bigots to the influence of second sight'.[62] Meg's believing in the power of astrology is acceptable because it does not deprive her of realism: what is a 'monstrous absurdity' in an Englishman forty years ago is 'true to nature' in a female Scottish gipsy of the same period.

In spite of the criticism of Mannering's involvement in astrology, reviewers' overall verdicts show an extraordinary level of admiration which also becomes evident in reviews of Terry's adaptation of the novel into a musical play.

Reviews of the Play

Reviews of the play were overwhelmingly positive, emphasizing the favourable reception by the audience: 'the general effect of the Opera was so superior, that its announcement for repetition this evening was received with tumultuous probation by the audience'.[63] In addition to considering the play, they also

---

[60] *The Quarterly Review*, 12.24, January 1815, pp. 501–09 (p. 507). Attrib. J. W. Croker.

[61] *The Scots Magazine*, August 1815, pp. 608–14 (p. 609). The Scottish reviewer emphasizes the historical nature of the plot, emphasizing the distance that English reviewers stress in their focus on geography.

[62] *The Critical Review*, 600.3, June 1815, p. 601.

[63] *The Morning Post*, 14 July 1821, p. 1. All newspapers and periodicals cited below accessed through *Nineteenth-century UK periodicals*; *Nineteenth-century British Library Newspapers*; *British Periodicals*; *The Times Digital Archive* [all accessed May–July and December 2016].

discuss individual performers. The focus is overwhelmingly on Meg, the Scottish gipsy, and the performance of the actor playing her. The *Morning Post* applauded the successful blend of 'the terrific and the affecting', with the display of 'extreme emotion [making] the character appropriately dominant'.[64]

Particularly in the very early reviews, however, while also praising the play there are warnings that the adaptation can never reach the quality of the novel. A review in *The Times*, published the day after the opening of the play at Covent Garden, on 12 March 1816, still struggles to come to terms with the idea of adapting a novel by the Wizard of the North for the stage at all:

> scarcely any degree of skill in the adaptation of it to the stage, or of genius in the principal actors, could transfer to the play even a faint resemblance to that fervid and ungovernable interest which agitates us through so many pages of history itself.[65]

As is typical of reviews of Scott, his novels are seen as being in a league of their own, and are therefore also deemed to be above adaptation. This is perhaps particularly evident in the discussion of Meg Merrilies: while Sarah Egerton played her 'with considerable ability and feeling', it was impossible, even for her, 'to embody in ordinary mortal form, and to give expression through human organs to the spirit of that indefinable being, tinged with melancholy, clothed with fierce grandeur, and breathing prophecy'.[66] Other early reviewers' comments are similar in not blaming Mrs Egerton for what they perceive as a relative failure, but rather the sheer impossibility of rendering Scott's character accurately on stage:

> Mrs Egerton's Meg Merilies [*sic*] possesses great vigour without surpassing nature; and this is all we have a right to expect from the actress. Still, in the prophetess, we look for the wildly rolling eye of superhuman agency, [a voice] which approaches sublimity, and invests the character with awful grandeur.[67]

The play is as good an adaptation as possible, and the acting, too, could not humanly be better, and yet for Meg this is insufficient because she needs to be more than human to reach Scott's Meg.

For theatre reviewers, following the novel closely improves the play because the novel's status as superlative is never questioned; in fact, 'in the novel from whence the plot is taken, [Terry] found the characters already dramatised', but the adapting he had to do he executed 'with a considerable degree of acuteness and discrimination'.[68] Reviewers found 'the dialogue extremely well written'.[69] Fidelity to the novel also means reviews do not need to take up 'our readers' time

[64] *The Morning Post*, 10 September 1818, p. 1.
[65] *The Times*, 13 March 1816, p. 3.
[66] Ibid.
[67] *The European Magazine and London Review*, 69, April 1816, pp. 334–40.
[68] *Theatrical Inquisitor and Monthly Mirror*, 8, June 1816, pp. 440–42.
[69] *Theatrical Inquisitor and Monthly Mirror*, 8, March 1816, pp. 228–32.

FIGURE 4.   Mrs Egerton as Meg Merrilies. 'If ever the dead come back among the living | I'll be seen in that glen many a night.' *Guy Mannering*, Act III, Scene 1. Print engraved by J. Thomson from a drawing by S. De Wilde, *c.* 1820. © Victoria and Albert Museum, London.

in detailing [the plot]'[70] as 'the novel from which the story is taken is […] generally known',[71] expecting the audience, or at least those among the audience who are likely to read a review, to be familiar with the novel.

Over the ensuing years, all of Scott's novels were adapted for the stage. Reviewers, more used to the idea of Scott adaptations, therefore make explicit references to the novel less frequently. Even these later reviews, however, which discuss the play less and focus on the acting as the element that is new, bestow the highest praise when acting comes as close as possible to depictions of the characters in the novel. For example, Miss Byrne's performance as Julia Mannering is described as having 'raised the character to a rank it had not before attained in the opera. Her style of acting, and even of dressing the part, reminded us more strongly of the novel than any previous representation of the play',[72] and so, by implication, it was superior to any previous rendition. Similarly, because 'Miss Povey's Julia Mannering was not that of the novelist', she was not among the best actors that night.[73]

Generally, the actors employed were the period's first-rate, well-known actors. They were usually cast as a character in the play for a season and beyond, and made the character their own, for example through the inclusion of songs that were not in Terry's play text. The songs chosen often have only a loose connection to the plot of the play, and sometimes none at all. For example, John Braham, who played Henry Bertram at both Covent Garden and Drury Lane for several seasons, added ballads such as, 'Scots wha hae wi' Wallace bled', 'Bruce's Address to his Army', and 'The last words of Marmion'.[74] This choice of songs emphasizes the drama's cultural 'Scottishness' and historicity as well as the Scott connection, all of which reviewers remark upon.[75] The interspersed songs further stressed the difference between the lives of the audience and that of the characters on stage, as well as the celebrity status that the author of Waverley's name brought, but they also became a means for the actor to render his or her version of the character distinct.

Connected to the focus on Meg as the most exciting and distinctive character are comments on the qualities of the other female characters. Just as reviews of the novel accept Meg as outlandish and able to make prophesies, but not Guy

---

[70] *The New Monthly Magazine and Universal Register*, 5.27, April 1816, pp. 250–52.

[71] *Theatrical Inquisitor and Monthly Mirror*, March 1816, pp. 228–32.

[72] *The Literary Chronicle and Weekly Review*, 1.31, 18 December 1819, pp. 494–95.

[73] *The Literary Chronicle and Weekly Review*, 1.22, 16 October 1819, p. 351.

[74] Commented on for example in *The Times*, 3 December 1817, p. 2; *The Times*, 18 September 1819, p. 2; *The Morning Post*, 19 September 1820 ('Braham was as rapturously applauded as ever in all his songs. That of "Scots wha hae wi' Wallace bled" he was obliged to sing three times …'); *The Literary Chronicle and Weekly Review*, 22 May 1822, p. 351.

[75] See, for example, *The Observer*, 6 May 1822, p. 4.

Mannering, because he falls into their experience as an English gentleman, reviewers of the play accept Meg as different because she is Scottish and a gipsy while expecting the other women to be acted in 'chaste' and 'sweet' ways.[76] In particular, Lucy Bertram is perceived as a stereotypically helpless and conservative model of a heroine in the play, and reviewers wanted her to be acted as such. Maria Tree's rendering of Lucy Bertram is commended because of her 'modest propriety, a natural and touching simplicity of manners, which powerfully interested the audience'.[77] Similarly, 'the sweetness and simplicity of Miss Carew' as Lucy Bertram is admired, whereas Mrs Gibbs as Flora 'requires the severest reprobation [...] by a disgusting indecency of dress'.[78]

Importantly then, acting at the Theatres Royal, especially female acting, was expected to be respectable, on and off stage. Catherine Stephens, playing Lucy in the first performance, is highly celebrated in all reviews, again for the 'sweetness and simplicity' of her acting and singing.[79] Judith Pascoe's words on the influence of Sarah Siddons, who, 'in character roles and in the role of respectable matron, served as an enabling model for other women looking for ways to enter the public sphere without damaging their personal reputations in the process',[80] might perhaps be applied to Stephens, who became Countess Dowager of Essex.[81] Similar to reviewers' comments on Miss Stephen's performances, Miss Carew's 'chaste acting', too, is commended,[82] and an unnamed young lady who 'made her first appearance in the arduous character of Lucy Bertram [evidently] has the manners of a gentlewoman'.[83] For reviewers, it is only Meg who is allowed to be unconventional and unbound by the rules of female propriety because she is a Scottish gipsy, so twice removed from reviewers' own lives, whereas the daughter of the English gentleman has to display chastity, sweetness and simplicity, perhaps especially on stage.[84] Overall, both the play and the 'actors of first-rate talent' contribute 'to preserve unsullied the high character of British drama'.[85]

---

[76] *The Ladies' Monthly Museum*, November 1818, p. 285 and *Theatrical Inquisitor and Monthly Mirror*, 11, September 1817, pp. 227–30 (p. 229) respectively.

[77] *The Ladies' Monthly Museum*, October 1819, p. 227.

[78] *Theatrical Inquisitor and Monthly Mirror*, 11, September 1817, p. 229.

[79] *The Observer*, 11 October 1819, p. 3.

[80] Judith Pascoe, *Romantic Theatricality: Gender, Poetry, and Spectatorship* (Ithaca, NY: Cornell University Press, 1997), p. 15.

[81] 'Bishop's National Operas', *The Athenaeum*, 2425, 18 April 1874, p. 536.

[82] *La Belle Assemblee*, 1 March 1817.

[83] *Ladies' Monthly Museum*, 1 November 1818, p. 285.

[84] Interestingly, Terry as an actor is also described as 'chaste', so both as an actor and as a dramatist he is deemed unexceptionable. See 'Memoir of the late Mr. Terry', *Dramatic Magazine*, August 1829, p. 189.

[85] *The Times*, 3 December 1817.

Conclusion

This exploration of the first stage adaptation of a Scott novel and its reception has shown four things: firstly, at Covent Garden alone, many more people saw Terry's version of *Guy Mannering* between 1816 and 1824 than would have read the novel across the United Kingdom during the same period. Many contemporaries would therefore have become familiar with the play's characters as given by actors and as presented in both Terry's version and abridgements of it. Secondly, Terry's adaptation renders the novel more conservative, for example in its representation of issues relating to gender. Lucy Bertram is passive in Scott's novel, too, but this is intensified in the play and reviewers expected actresses to present the character in 'chaste' ways. Thirdly, reviewers' — and the audiences' — reactions to the first stage adaptation of a Scott novel were largely positive. They interpreted the play as 'complimentary to the taste and study of Mr Terry',[86] partly because they believed him to have kept closely to the novel. Fourthly, reviews of the play discuss similar points to those raised in reviews of the novel, particularly in their focus on Meg and Scottishness. A crucial difference is that Guy Mannering does not predict the future in the play, so that the main point of criticism in reviews of the novels does not apply to reviews of the play.

While the novel informed the reception of the play, the play also contributed to enhancing the novel's popularity. Anastasia Nikolopoulou argues that 'Scott's popularity was increased by staging of his works rather than the other way around'.[87] However, regarding Terry's *Guy Mannering*, this essay concludes that popularity of play and novel fed each other: on the one hand, the play made plot and characters (albeit its version of them) accessible to a much wider socio-economic group and much sooner than editions of the novel did, but on the other, reviews show that the play's popularity was enhanced by Scott's extra-ordinary fame and status, and indeed, was judged by its closeness to the novel. Terry's play paved the way for a rush of stage adaptations of Scott's novels, and presents one of the many spin-offs that Scott's works inspired and enabled. The play, in turn, contributed to shaping the reception of the most popular novelist of the early nineteenth century.

---

[86] *The European Magazine and London Review*, April 1816, pp. 334–40.

[87] Anastasia Nikolopoulou, 'Historical Disruptions: The Walter Scott Melodramas', in *Melodrama: The Cultural Emergence of a Genre*, ed. by Michael Hays and Anastasia Nikolopoulou (New York: St Martin's Press, 1999), pp. 121–46.

Handing Over Walter Scott?
The Writer's Hand on the English and
French Marketplace

CÉLINE SABIRON

Université de Lorraine and University of Oxford

Suffering from delicate health throughout his life, and in particular from chilblains causing his fingers to swell and crack,[1] Walter Scott had to resort to helping hands very early on in his career as a writer. Both editor and publisher James Ballantyne and poet William Laidlaw — who even became Scott's official steward and amanuensis from 1817 — would regularly write to his dictation. In periods of acute pain, which worsened following his paralytic strokes from 1830, Scott literally handed down his authority to a scribe who wrote on his behalf.

The usual synecdochic relationship between the hand and the act of writing takes on a paradoxical dimension with Scott and is conceptualized throughout his work, playing on the motif of the hand. Regarded as a symbol of power and domination in politics or in law, the hand is often represented as mutilated in Scott's novels, as if to reflect on his own disabled limb.[2] In such cases the writing hand is disembodied; it is cut off from the body and no longer linked to the spirit that conjured the story. This objectification is illustrated through Sir John Ramorny's amputated hand in *The Fair Maid of Perth* (1828). Held up to the public gaze, the latter is described as a 'bloody token', a 'trophy' which Oliver

---

[1] Scott regularly alluded to his disability in his *Journal*. See entries dd. 22 January 1829, 'I am disabled from writing by chilblains on my fingers, a most babyish complaint. They say that the character is indicated by the handwriting. If so, mine is crabbed enough' (p. 571) and 15 March 1831, 'After breakfast Mr Laidlaw comes at ten, and we write together till one. I am greatly helped by this excellen[t] man, who takes pains to write a good hand, and supplies the want of my own fingers as far as another person's can' (p. 717) in *The Journal of Sir Walter Scott*, ed. by W. E. K. Anderson (Edinburgh: Canongate Classics, 1998).

[2] For the hand as a sign of power, see 'The Highland Widow', in *Chronicles of the Canongate*, ed. by Claire Lamont, EEWN (Edinburgh: Edinburgh University Press, 2001), pp. 82, 88: 'by the hand of my Chief' swears clan-member MacPhadraick to Elspat, the widow of the Chieftain Hamish MacTavish, known as 'the Man with the strong right hand'. All quotations from Scott's fiction are from the Edinburgh Edition of the Waverley Novels. For concision hereafter, I have used the following abbreviations: *Waverley* (*W*), *Guy Mannering* (*GM*), *The Black Dwarf* (*BD*), *The Fortunes of Nigel* (*FN*), *Quentin Durward* (*QD*), *The Highland Widow* (*HW*), *The Fair Maid of Perth* (*FMP*), *Chronicles of the Canongate* (*CC*).

Yearbook of English Studies, 47 (2017), 58–74
© Modern Humanities Research Association 2017

Proudfute has 'picked up from the ground'.[3] Desecrated, it is treated like mere refuse found littering the ground. It is a nameless object, referred to by the determiner 'that' ('this placard, and that which accompanies it'), whose only material value is the ring worn on one of its fingers.[4] The stiffened hand is further defiled by being carried around in a pocket like an ordinary item: 'Douglas took from a pocket in the bosom of his buff coat a human hand and a piece of parchment'.[5] This human organ — stylistically tied together with the old hallowed text, and yet separated from it through a zeugmatic effect in coordination — is both exhibited (the grammatical object being shifted towards the back of the sentence, taken out of its canonical post-verbal position for enhancement purposes) and embedded, being deeply enclosed between the two yellowish-brown skins that comprise the outer layer of the coat leather[6] and the piece of parchment. The circulation of the dead hand can be read as an allegory of Scott's text-wrapping through a multiple use of helping hands, from the scribe and editor to the translator when his writing travels beyond the English-speaking world, and in particular across the Channel.

Scott's fetishization of the hand motif, which is used in a metafictional way to reflect on his own writing practices, is demonstrated in *Quentin Durward* (1823) where Scott's sceptical interest in 'palmistry and jugglery', labelled as 'other fantastic arts of prediction' in his *Letters on Demonology and Witchcraft* (1830), is embodied by the sage Martivalle, 'inspect[ing] [Quentin's] palm, according to the form of the mystic arts which he practised'.[7] The writing, printing and translating acts are embedded in the hand metaphor — through words such as 'line', 'marked', 'impress' — with lines to be read, deciphered, and rephrased into prophetic tales. Building on Ina Ferris's work on the question of authorship, and on Roland Barthes's and Michel Foucault's definitions of the author, the present essay aims at reassessing Scott's 'handing down' strategy in a Romantic context,[8] from his own staging of the transmission process to the

---

[3] *FMP*, ed. by A. D. Hook and Donald Mackenzie, EEWN (Edinburgh: Edinburgh University Press, 1999), p. 43.

[4] *FMP*, p. 131. 'There should have been — there was — a ring, my lord, which was on the knave's finger. I fear I have been forgetful, and left it at home, for I took it off to show to my wife, as she cared not to look upon the dead hand, as women love not such sights. But yet I thought I had put it on the finger again.' In *FMP*, p. 86.

[5] Ibid., p. 131.

[6] In the novel the hand is never left unwrapped. It is first carried in a pouch and then in the pocket of a buff-coat.

[7] *QD*, ed. by J. H. Alexander and G. A. M. Wood, EEWN (Edinburgh: Edinburgh University Press, 2001), p. 155. *Letters on Demonology and Witchcraft Addressed to J. G. Lockhart* (London: John Murray, 1885), pp. 134, 276.

[8] For a general reassessment of Scott's relationship to Romantic aesthetics, see Fiona Robertson, 'Romancing and Romanticism', in the *Edinburgh Companion to Sir Walter Scott*, ed. by Fiona Robertson (Edinburgh: Edinburgh University Press, 2012), pp. 93–105.

role of the often-intrusive hand of the translator, and the question of the variability of the text.

* * *

Resorting to amanuenses was relatively common during the period in which Scott was writing. Many other writers of the late eighteenth and early nineteenth centuries, including William Wordsworth, Samuel Taylor Coleridge, James Hogg, Percy Shelley, Frances Burney and Jane Austen, chose to protect their anonymity for various, and sometimes multiple, reasons,[9] and not only to comply with 'the traditional image of self-sufficient, inward-looking Romantics'.[10] What is interesting in Scott's case is that he does not use anonymity to escape from any excessive media exposure, but paradoxically to seek for it through '*anonymous celebrity*'.[11] The modern concept of celebrity emerging in the early part of the nineteenth century is complicated in late Romantic literature by some anti-celebrity impulses after the strong media presence of writers such as Lord Byron and Mme Germaine de Staël. Scott plays with the hand motif and voluntarily treats his body as a commodity: as Eric Eisner has argued, 'the writer's personality and the writer's body take on a public significance and a market value of their own',[12] not in a Byronic fashion through the writer's appearance but in a more textual and scriptural way (as shown later). Enquiring into the question of authorship, both Ina Ferris and Fiona Robertson have demonstrated that from the outset of his career, 'Scott's novelistic authorship operate[s] under signs of multiplicity and proliferation', with the auctorial King, the bodiless and faceless 'Author of Waverley' being characterized by an 'inbuilt plurality'.[13] Scott's numerous pseudonyms range from the vague generic Author of Waverley, for his series of novels that became known as the Waverley novels, to the invented, pun-filled, fictitious storyteller Jedidiah Cleishbotham, for his work gathered in the *Tales of My Landlord*.[14] He sometimes even published simultaneously under

[9] There is an 'overriding use of the practice of anonymity in relation to new fiction (over 80 per cent of titles in the 1780s and 1790s, and nearly 70 per cent in the 1820s)', in Introduction to *Authorship, Commerce and the Public: Scenes of Writing (1750–1850)*, ed. by E. J. Clery, Caroline Franklin and P. D. Garside (Basingstoke: Palgrave Macmillan, 2002), p. 5.

[10] Angela Esterhammer, 'Identity Crises: Celebrity, Anonymity, Doubles, and Frauds in European Romanticism', in *The Oxford Handbook of European Romanticism*, ed. by Paul Hamilton (Oxford: Oxford University Press, 2016), pp. 771–87 (p. 772).

[11] Ibid., p. 782.

[12] Eric Eisner, *Nineteenth-Century Poetry and Literary Celebrity* (Basingstoke: Palgrave Macmillan, 2009), p. 3.

[13] Ina Ferris, 'Scott's Authorship and Book Culture', in *The Edinburgh Companion to Sir Walter Scott*, ed. by Fiona Robertson (Edinburgh: Edinburgh University Press, 2012), pp. 9–21 (p. 18); Fiona Robertson, *Legitimate Histories: Scott, Gothic and the Authorities of Fiction* (Oxford: Clarendon Press, 1994), p. 117.

[14] 'I am NOT the writer, redacter, or compiler of the Tales of my Landlord.' In *BD*, ed. by P. D. Garside, EEWN (Edinburgh: Edinburgh University Press, 1993), p. 6.

both names, as with *The Antiquary* (1816) written by 'The Author of Waverley', and *The Black Dwarf* and *Old Mortality*, which came out in the same year under the 'authorship' of Jedidiah Cleishbotham.

Yet, this staging of fake competing auctorial identities is more than just an anonymity game in Scott's case. It is also an act that reveals the 'multi-handed' writing technique through which he collaborated with scribes, editors and translators to compose his texts. Collective authorship, then, was normal despite the romantic myth of the 'man of letters' as a solitary genius conveyed by Thomas Carlyle, among others, in his essay 'Hero as Man of Letters' (1840). As such, Scott resorts to a conventional and pervasive trope of Romantic writing, which involves blurring the borders between the professions of writer, editor and translator, with the last often straddling the uncertain boundary line between that of faithful conveyor and rewriter of the author's text. Jane Millgate has pointed out that, '[d]etermined to finish the volumes of *Tales* in spite of his indisposition [in 1819], Scott began dictating — sometimes to John Ballantyne, sometimes to William Laidlaw',[15] while John Gibson Lockhart, his son-in-law and official biographer, suggests that '[i]t was in this fashion that Scott produced the far greater portion of *The Bride of Lammermoor* — the whole of the *Legend of Montrose* — and almost the whole of *Ivanhoe*'.[16] Lockhart, who wrote vividly detailed descriptions of Scott's dictation exercises in his *Memoirs*, records a conversation with John Ballantyne:

[Ballantyne] informed me that his 'illustrious friend' [...] was so much recovered as to have resumed his usual literary tasks, though with this difference, that he now, for the first time in his life, found it necessary to employ the hand of another [...] The *copy* (as M.S. for the press is technically called) which Scott was thus dictating, was that of the *Bride of Lammermoor*, and his amanuenses were William Laidlaw and John Ballantyne; — of whom he preferred the latter, when he could be at Abbotsford, on account of the superior rapidity of his pen; and also because John kept his pen to the paper without interruption, and, though with many an arch twinkle in his eyes, and now and then an audible smack of his lips, had resolution to work on like a well-trained clerk; whereas good Laidlaw entered with such keen zest into the interest of the story as it flowed from the author's lips, that he could not suppress exclamations of surprise and delight.[17]

The '*copy*' is potentially plural since the word etymologically refers to both the manuscript for a printer and a reproduction or imitation. Lockhart offers the contrasting image of two copyists: one professionally detached from the story that he merely writes down, and the other who emotionally responds to what is

[15] Jane Millgate, *Walter Scott: The Making of the Novelist* (Edinburgh: Edinburgh University Press, 1984), p. 170.

[16] John Gibson Lockhart, *Memoirs of the Life of Sir Walter Scott* [first edn 1837–38] (Edinburgh: Robert Cadell, 1845), p. 397 [complete in one volume]. Also quoted in Millgate, p. 170.

[17] Lockhart, *Life*, p. 397.

dictated to him and indirectly participates in the story. Whatever their degree of invisibility, Scott's helping hands influence his stories. Ina Ferris uses a metaphor of organic cultivation to argue that the process 'take[s] the form of re-composition, re-cycling and collaboration, and the author himself emerges as a distinctly 'rough-mixed' construct'.[18]

Scott's collaborative production is metafictionally illustrated, at the outset of *The Bride of Lammermoor*, through the metaphor of a womb-like writing laboratory in the frame narrative. The latter is suitably located at an atopic and atemporal fictitious village, ironically called Gandercleugh — from lowland Scots and meaning a goose basin (*gander* being goose, and *cleugh* a gorge or ravine). Typically a writer's den, as pens used to be made of hand-cut *goose* quills, the Wallace Arms can be interpreted not just as a public house, but also as an operating theatre.[19] Stories from the past are fabricated and stitched together there, thanks to the singular and improbable samples of human life taken in the inn, whose initials 'WA' remarkably mirror those of the Author of Waverley, AW. The public place becomes the narcissistic 'navel'[20] where 'novels' are conceived, delivered and 'birthed'. The cosy, warm, small and familiar apartment in which Jedidiah Cleishbotham lives is a procreative womb. It is the *sanctum* from where he allegedly only collects and arranges the tales written by his assistant in the local schoolhouse, Peter Pattieson, from stories recounted by the nameless Landlord of the village hostelry. This vignette, ironically taking the reader 'in*n*' — with the extra letter [n] highlighting the *mise en abyme* — i.e. inside the making of the text, reveals the literary operations at hand, as far as Scott's manuscripts are concerned.

Through a process of fictional self-construction, Scott plays with the Romantic artist's embodied poetics of suffering[21] by means of clichéd images of a convulsed, wounded, afflicted body. Jane Millgate points out that most of the manuscript of *The Bride of Lammermoor* survives in Scott's hand, as do his corrected proofs. Only the final chapters were clearly dictated.[22] And yet, as recorded by Lockhart in his *Memoirs*, Scott claimed that when correcting the proofs of *The Bride of Lammermoor* 'he did not recollect one single incident, character, or conversation

[18] Ina Ferris, 'Scott's Authorship and Book Culture', p. 18.

[19] *BL*, ed. by J. H. Alexander, EEWN (Edinburgh: Edinburgh University Press, 1996), p. 9.

[20] 'Gandercleugh is, as it were, the central part, — the navel (*si fas sit dicere*) of this our native realm of Scotland.' In *BD*, p. 5.

[21] For a study of the relationship between the diseased body and the Romantic writer, see Clark Lawlor, *Consumption and Literature: The Making of the Romantic Disease* (Basingstoke: Palgrave Macmillan, 2006).

[22] 'The manuscript [...] offers little support for Lockhart's account of a text whose major portion was dictated, and since it does not differ notably from that of Scott's earlier works — it is written in his usual small, neat hand and shows no obvious signs of distress.' In Millgate, *Walter Scott*, p. 170.

it contained!' Rather, 'he literally recollected nothing else — not a single character woven by the romancer, not one of the many scenes and points of humour, nor anything with which he was connected as the writer of the work'.[23] The author uses representations of the body to his own advantage, and the 'hand' motif becomes what James Allard has called 'a "product" of discursive mastery', which feeds his Romantic self-mythologizing.[24] Lockhart relays and reinforces Scott's 'branding' of this identity through lengthy paragraphs and detailed anecdotes on the author's body pain while in the act of dictating his stories:

> The affectionate Laidlaw beseeching him to stop dictating, when his audible suffering filled every pause. 'Nay, Willie,' he answered, 'only see that the doors are fast. I would fain keep all the cry as well as all the wool to ourselves; but as to giving over work, that can only be when I am in woollen.' John Ballantyne told me, that after the first day, he always took care to have a dozen of pens made before he seated himself opposite the sofa on which Scott lay, and that though he often turned himself on his pillow with a groan of torment, he usually continued the sentence in the same breath. But when the dialogue of peculiar animation was in progress, spirit seemed to triumph altogether over matter — he arose from his couch and walked up and down the room, raising and lowering his voice, and as it were acting the parts.[25]

The biographer dramatically stages the behind-closed-doors fighting between spirit and matter, body and soul, through stereotypical characters and hyperbolic expressions — with Laidlaw, assuming the role of 'the affectionate' friend, and Scott that of the suffering but resilient writer. This Romantic stance is aestheticized to the point of being illustrated by painters, such as Scottish history painter William Allan, the first author-approved illustrator of the Waverley novels, who paid Scott a posthumous tribute by portraying him dictating to his daughter Anne in the armoury at Abbotsford (1844).[26] Scottish portrait painter Sir Francis Grant even literally 'placed [his] easel between Sir Walter and his amanuensis, William Laidlaw'[27] in order to paint a cabinet picture of the author for Lady Ruthven, as he recalled in an 1872 letter addressed to Sir William Stirling Maxwell. This highly symbolic layout, welcomed by Scott himself, points at the aestheticization of his own act of writing.

---

[23] Lockhart, p. 402.

[24] James Allard, *Romanticism, Medicine, and the Poet's Body* (New York: Routledge, 2013), p. 128.

[25] Lockhart, p. 397.

[26] See <http://artuk.org/discover/artworks/sir-walter-scott-dictating-to-his-daughter-anne-in-the-armoury-at-abbotsford-196676> [accessed 6 January 2017].

[27] Walter Scott, Sir William Stirling Maxwell, David Laing and James Drummond, *A Descriptive Account of the Portraits, Busts, Published Writings and Manuscripts of Sir Walter Scott, Bart. collected and exhibited at Edinburgh on Occasion of the Scott Centenary in 1871* (Edinburgh: William Paterson, 1874), p. 79.

Scott's auctorial sleight of hand went beyond the limited confines of his home and the actual act of writing. It spread to the printing house and gained the literary market place for a particular case of '*anonymous celebrity*'.[28] The connection was made through a pivotal and multifaceted man, James Ballantyne, acting as Scott's friend and copyist, indeed, but also as his editor and printer, reading all the manuscripts very carefully, pointing out inconsistencies in the tales, clarifying the characters' names in the dialogues, and correcting punctuation and grammatical mistakes.[29]

* * *

If Scott's writing is characterized by its embodied Romantic poetics of suffering and self-mythologizing, the author acted more according to the principles of Scottish enlightenment economics when it came to the relationship he had forged with his publisher. He was fully involved in the commercial aspects of book production, as an unnamed partner (from 1805) and then as senior partner in the new publishing firm of John Ballantyne & Co. from 1809. Scott's viewpoint on the commercial aspect of his trade is dramatized through the dialogue between the Author of Waverley and Captain Clutterbuck in the introductory epistle to *The Fortunes of Nigel* (1822):

> I do say it, in spite of Adam Smith and his followers, that a successful author is a productive labourer, and that his works constitute as effectual a part of the public wealth, as that which is created by any other manufacture. If a new commodity, having an actually intrinsic and commercial value, be the result of the operation, why are the author's bales of books to be esteemed a less profitable part of the public stock than goods of any other manufacturer?[30]

Being an author is described as a hand-operated commercial activity ('labourer'; 'manufacturer', from Middle French *manufacture* meaning 'something made by hand') and the books he writes and produces are equated with other commodities. Scott 'redefine[d] the business of fiction according to a tradesman's code', as Kathryn Sutherland has shown.[31] Both 'master-manufacturer' and

---

[28] Esterhammer, p. 782.

[29] See David Hewitt's article on textual theories applied to Scott's Waverley novels: 'Scott was sent the proofs containing Ballantyne's corrections and notes, and went through them thoroughly. He did more than correct: he revised passages, and improved the style and the sense; he added words, phrases, even passages, to enhance his narrative.' In David S. Hewitt, 'Scott and Textual Multiplepoinding', *Text*, 4 (1988), 361–73 (p. 363).

[30] *FN*, ed. by Frank Jordan, EEWN (Edinburgh: Edinburgh University Press, 2014), p. 14.

[31] 'He inserts the successful author into the production process under two heads: in general terms, as the employer or master-manufacturer who has put into circulation for profit a certain capital sum; and more specifically, as the workman whose creative effort is one stage in the book's manufacture, the value of which will be added to the end-product in the same way as the labour of the printer or the binder.' In Kathryn Sutherland, 'Fictional Economies: Adam Smith, Walter Scott and the Nineteenth-Century Novel', *ELH*, 54.1 (Spring 1987), 97–127 (pp. 100–01).

'workman', he was so much involved in the book industry (even though clandestinely) that he elaborated a whole strategy of secrecy, his original manuscripts being copied, when they were from his own hand, so that his handwriting should not be seen in the printing house.

This unusually complex editing process is illustrated in *Guy Mannering* (1815) through another vignette and in particular the metaphor of the charm — containing Guy Mannering's astrological predictions — hanging around the neck of new-born Henry Bertram, a figure of the reader in the novel:

> [Mrs Bertram's] first employment, when she became capable of a little work [after her delivery], was to make a small velvet bag for the scheme of nativity which she had obtained from her husband. Her fingers itched to break the seal, but credulity proved stronger than curiosity, and she had the firmness to *inclose it*, in all its integrity, within two slips of parchment, which she sowed round it, to prevent its being chafed. The whole was then enclosed in the velvet bag aforesaid.[32]

In this *mise en abyme*, Mrs Bertram plays the part of James Ballantyne. She encloses the secret of Scott's paternity of the Waverley novels — here symbolized by the astrologer's piece of paper representing 'the scheme of nativity' — within two envelopes. The first is made of parchment, similar to Scott's palimpsest-like manuscript, written over by the copyist who blurs any handwritten traces that may betray the author's true identity, which is then stitched all around. The second envelope, the small velvet bag, functions as a book cover since it wraps and protects Guy Mannering's composition. The latter, like Scott's text, is the object of a transaction through the Bertram family: it is handed down from the astrologer to Mr and then Mrs Bertram. The Bertrams thereby feature as fictitious doubles of the Ballantyne brothers, with whom they share the same initials. In the passage just mentioned, the seal hermetically closing the composition is meant to be broken after five years.[33] Likewise, Walter Scott's signature, and consequently his authorship, was meant to be revealed, but not before his death and long years of identity play. His introduction to the *Chronicles of the Canongate* refers to that intention:

> it was my original intention never to have avowed these works during my lifetime, and the original manuscripts were carefully preserved (though by the care of others rather than mine), with the purpose of supplying the necessary evidence of the truth when the period of announcing it should arrive.[34]

Scott's insolvency, linked to that of the Ballantynes, forced him publicly to acknowledge his authorship. It is highly ironic that the 'detected masquerader'[35]

---

[32] *GM*, ed. by P. D. Garside, EEWN (Edinburgh: Edinburgh University Press, 1999), pp. 30–31.

[33] He therefore delivered the paper into Mr Bertram's hand, and requested him to keep it for five years with the seal unbroken.' Ibid., p. 30.

[34] *CC*, ed. by Claire Lamont, EEWN (Edinburgh: Edinburgh University Press, 2001), pp. 3–4.

[35] Ibid., p 4.

should have chosen the stage of a public meeting, called for establishing a professional Theatrical Fund in Edinburgh in 1827, to make this 'trompe l'oeil' revelation, and lay down his disguise.[36] The passage quoted above, then, metafictionally highlights Scott's anxiety about letting go of his work, as he keeps his hands on the manuscripts throughout the whole 'handing down' process to the publisher. This level of intimacy between writer and publisher, and more generally between artistic endeavour and manual, commercial enterprise is not commonplace in the Romantic era. The machinery points at his wish to protect his version of the text, and control the literary market, a desire which was even more challenged when his manuscripts were handed over to translators and read by a foreign readership. In France the 'handing over' process followed the same strategy of secrecy as Scott's within the Edinburgh printing house. 'Inviolable secrecy': such was the phrase employed by Scott's semi-official translator-in-chief in France, Auguste-Jean-Baptiste Defauconpret (1767–1843), in a letter written on 4 October 1822 to his editor after the Mephistophelian pact that the Faust-like publishers of Scott in London signed with the French publisher Charles Gosselin. Indeed, it was agreed that Scott's London agents Black, Young and Young would give Defauconpret the proof sheets of Scott's novels straight from the press in exchange for the translator's inviolable secrecy concerning this transaction. The benefit of this secret transaction was that from 1822 every work from Scott's pen came out on the same day both in English in Edinburgh and London and in French in Paris. Defauconpret had thus been given priority over his other French[37] and European counterparts, so that he could get his translations on the market long before his rivals. Defauconpret thus came to embody Scott in France, simultaneously conveying and refashioning the writer's hand for a French readership.

* * *

To analyse the intrusive hand of Scott's translator, who turned the Scottish writer into a 'French author',[38] as Michel Crouzet stated in the preface to his 1981 critical edition, it is necessary to understand Defauconpret's aesthetics in the general context of translation studies in the early nineteenth century. In an 1819 letter addressed to the *Journal des débats* [*Journal of Debates*], Defauconpret revealed his aesthetics of translation, which followed the manner of eighteenth-century translators absorbing the general sense of the original text but rendering it into the target language in their own terms to adapt to the new readership:

[36] Robertson, *Legitimate Histories*, p. 118.

[37] Other translators of Scott in France included Joseph Martin, Henri Villemain, and Amédée Pichot.

[38] Michel Crouzet, 'Walter Scott et la réinvention du roman', in *Waverley, Rob Roy, La Fiancée de Lammermoor*, coll. 'Bouquins' (Paris: Laffont, 1981), pp. 7–44.

I believe that in importing a *novel* from one language to another, a translator's first duty is to make it capable of pleasing the new readers that he wishes to acquire for it. The taste of the English does not always conform to our own [...] I have thus suppressed some details which might have appeared otiose to the French reader, and I have abbreviated the portraits of several characters that are quite unconnected to the action. I have taken the same liberty with respect to an author whose reputation, *pace* Lady Morgan, stands infinitely above hers in England, Mr Walter Scott; and the welcome accorded in France to *Old Mortality*, *Rob Roy* and only recently, *The Heart of Mid-Lothian*, has proved that I was not wrong.[39]

Defauconpret adopted the classical French model of translation as a *belle infidèle* which was derived from Horace's *Ars Poetica* in which the Roman poet clearly dismissed literal, word-for-word translations, and later from the seventeenth-century tradition which equated translation with exercise in creativity and novelty to counter what was considered as the inevitable loss of beauty in translation.[40] Criticisms first emerged in the late seventeenth century through English translator and poet John Dryden's (1631–1700) advising paraphrase rather than metaphrase — defined as literal translation — and imitation, i.e. free translation.[41] They were followed by a debate over French and German attitudes to translation in the Age of Enlightenment, a debate illustrated by Johann Gottfried Herder's complaint in 1776 that 'the French, who are much too proud of their own taste, adapt all things to it, rather than try to adapt themselves to the taste of another time'.[42] The strategy of foreignizing was eventually theorized in 1813 by Friedrich Schleiermacher,[43] who is often considered to have laid the foundations for the concepts of domestication and foreignization then developed by Johann Wolfgang von Goethe and conveyed by Mme de Staël in her article *De l'esprit des traductions* [The Spirit of Translation] (1816).[44] She was critical of the sense of cultural superiority of the French and saw translation as a way to renew the classical culture in France and Italy by introducing elements of foreign cultures.

[39] Quoted in Paul Barnaby, 'Another Tale of Old Mortality: The Translations of A.-J.-B. Defauconpret in the French Reception of Scott', in *The Reception of Walter Scott in Europe*, ed. by Murray Pittock (London: Continuum, 2007), pp. 31–44 (p. 37).

[40] Jeremy Munday, *Introducing Translation Studies: Theories and Applications* (New York: Routledge, 2001), p. 42.

[41] John Dryden, 'From the Preface to *Ovid's Epistles*', in *The Translation Studies Reader*, ed. by Lawrence Venuti, 3rd edn (New York: Routledge, 2012), pp. 38–42.

[42] J. G. Herder, 'From *Fragmente* (1766–1767)', in *Translation, History, Culture: A Sourcebook*, ed. by André Lefevere (New York: Routledge, 1992), p. 74.

[43] Friedrich Schleiermacher, 'On the Different Methods of Translating', trans. by Susan Bernofsky, in *The Translation Studies Reader*, ed. by Venuti, pp. 43–63.

[44] Germaine de Staël, 'De l'esprit des traductions', in *Œuvres Complètes* (Paris: Treuttel et Würtz, 1821), pp. 387–92.

If Defauconpret revised and retranslated Scott's texts in the late 1820s and early 1830s to adapt to this aesthetic change, most of his translations of Scott's fictions followed a domesticating translation strategy. The latter entailed an appropriation, or reduction, of the foreign text into target-language conventions and it made use of stylistic devices, which provided for a transparent and fluent reading.[45] Defauconpret's approach was oriented towards the target audience since his main objective, as clearly stated in the above-cited letter, was to conform to the French taste in order to provide his readership with pleasure, a feeling in full agreement with Romantic ideology. As underlined by Barnaby, 'Scott often undergoes a startling transformation at Defauconpret's hands',[46] since the translator proceeded to contextual and stylistic rewritings in order to refashion Scott's texts for a Catholic, conservative, legitimist, post-Napoleonic French readership. Defauconpret's aim was not only political, with his translations reflecting his 'pious and loyalist public stance',[47] but also commercial. Indebted by his bad speculations or his subordinates' appalling management of his solicitor's office, he had found refuge in London from 1816, probably to escape from his creditors. He thus urgently needed to earn a living, which is why after an early but failed attempt at original writing, he turned to translation. Defauconpret thus practised what Juliana House calls 'covert translation' — as opposed to 'overt translation' — i.e. 'a translation which enjoys the status of an original source text in the target culture'.[48] Indeed, his translations into French were read in Russia, Poland, Spain and Italy long before English versions, which often came out later on the literary market. As Barnaby adds, '[e]ven when European readers did not read Scott in French, they used translations derived from Defauconpret rather than from Scott's original'.[49] Whatever their quality,[50] there is no denying that they became the

---

[45] 'Translation, then, always involves a process of domestication, an exchange of foreign-language intelligibilities for those of the translating language. But domestication need not mean assimilation, that is, a conservative reduction of the foreign text to dominant value.' In Venuti, *The Translator's Invisibility: A History of Translation* (New York: Routledge, 1995), p. 20.

[46] Barnaby, 'Another Tale of Old Mortality', p. 32.

[47] Barnaby, 'Restoration Politics and Sentimental Poetics in Defauconpret's Translations of Sir Walter Scott', *Translation and Literature*, 20 (2011), 6–28 (p. 9). For an extended summary of Defauconpret's involvement in French politics, see pp. 9–10.

[48] Juliana House, *Translation Quality Assessment: A Model Revisited* (New York: Routledge, 2015), p. 56.

[49] Barnaby, 'Another Tale of Old Mortality', p. 32.

[50] Jacques Bereaud avoids discussing the polemical quality of Defauconpret's translations into French, and prefers stressing their importance with regards to the impact they had on the development of the novel in Europe: 'Beaucoup de critiques de l'époque se sont élevés contre ses premières traductions; mais d'autres, plus avertis, ont compris très vite leur importance'. In Jacques Bereaud, 'La Traduction en France à l'époque romantique', *Comparative Literature Studies*, 8.3 (Sept. 1971), 224–44 (pp. 230–31).

originals for a large portions of readers and played a major part in circulating Scott's fictions in Europe and abroad. Defauconpret's hand was a sorting hand which literally manipulated the source texts to curry favour with the restored Bourbon monarchy and the French readership. He thus practised a high level of textual manipulation on poetical and ideological grounds. His tendency towards simplification, clarification and thus Manichaeism was diametrically opposite to Scott's, constantly promoting a middle way through the blurring of antagonistic values or characters. A few examples of the level of intrusion of the translator's hand in Scott's texts in French can be assessed through a close reading of a couple of excerpts from *Waverley* (1814), using Juliana House's scheme for analysing and comparing original and translated texts which mostly focuses on the concept of register and includes lexical, syntactic and textual points of comparison.

He **might** be delivered up to the military law, which, **in the midst of the civil war**, was **not likely to** be scrupulous in the choice of its victims, or the quality of the evidence. Nor did he feel much more comfortable at the thoughts of a trial before a Scottish court of justice, where he knew the laws and forms differed in many respects from those of England, and **had been taught to believe, however erroneously,** that the liberty and rights of the subject were less carefully protected. **A sentiment of bitterness** rose in his mind against the government.[51] (my emphasis)

Si l'on me traduit devant un **conseil**

de guerre, se disoit-il, je ne dois m'attendre à **aucune indulgence**, pas même à l'examen réfléchi de l'accusation dirigée contre moi. Les circonstances où nous nous trouvons lui feront une loi de frapper **impitoyablement** tous ceux qui paroîtront avoir allumé la **guerre civile**. Je ne serai pas mieux traité si je parois devant la cour royale d'Ecosse; je sais qu'elle n'est pas très scrupuleuse sur le choix de ses victimes, et que la moindre apparence lui tient de preuve. Un nouveau sentiment d'aigreur l'irrita de plus en plus contre le gouvernement.[52] (my emphasis)

Overall, the translated extract strikes one as much more clear-cut and binary than Scott's original source text. The translator suppressed qualifiers, which gives the translated text a much more assertive tone. Whereas modals like 'might', modal periphrases such as 'not likely to', and circumlocutory expressions such as '[a] sentiment of bitterness rose in his mind' are used in English, the French version is deprived of any such lexical subtleties ('aucune indulgence', i.e. no

[51] *W*, ed. by P. D. Garside (Edinburgh: Edinburgh University Press, 2007), p. 176.
[52] Walter Scott, *Waverley, ou Il y a soixante ans*, trans. by A.-J.-B. Defauconpret, 6 vols (Paris: Charles Gosselin, 1828), II, 218–19. Defauconpret's first translation of *Waverley* was actually based on Joseph Martin's first translation of Scott's novel. The Bouquins collection edited by Robert Laffont in 1981 is not used here because the texts are based on Defauconpret's retranslations, made when he revised his original translations from the late 1820s in order to follow the new foreignizing trend in translation theories.

leniency; 'impitoyablement' or ruthless), while a feeling of bitterness ('un nouveau sentiment d'aigreur'; 'de plus en plus') towards the government has already settled in Waverley's mind. The accusation is fleshed out in the translated text. Defauconpret also changed the perspective of the narrative by suppressing references to the character's inner feeling ('did he feel'; 'he knew'; 'had been taught to believe'). The facts are thus presented as statements rather than subjective impressions. He eventually silenced the narrator's voice which had been subtlety inserted ('however erroneously') to counterbalance the eponymous character's viewpoint. These lexical and narratorial omissions contribute to conveying the image of a sombre time when injustice prevailed and human rights were scorned.

Translating Scott with the French audience in mind, Defauconpret toned down the historical and cultural background. The 'Reformed Kirk of Scotland' is for example simply translated as 'l'Église d'Écosse' without any reference to the Protestant Reformation. As a fervent Catholic, he sometimes inserted his own comments, like in the following extract with the additional 'Dieu me préserve d'avoir jamais la folle prétention d'oser marcher sur les traces de l'inimitable Cervantès' [May the Lord preserve me from ever claiming to have dared to follow in the footsteps of inimitable Cervantes]:

From the minuteness with which I have traced Waverley's pursuits, and the bias which these unavoidably communicated to his imagination, the reader may perhaps anticipate, in the following tale, an imitation of the romance of Cervantes. But he will do my prudence injustice in the supposition. My intention is not to follow the steps of that inimitable author, in describing such total perversion of intellect as misconstrues the objects actually presented to the senses, but that more common aberration from sound judgment, which apprehends occurrences indeed in their reality, but communicates to them a tincture of its own romantic tone and colouring. So far was Edward Waverley from expecting general sympathy with his own feelings, or concluding that the present state of things was calculated to exhibit the reality of those visions	D'après tout ce que nous avons dit sur les habitudes, le caractère et la tournure d'esprit du jeune Edouard, le lecteur s'imagine peut-être qu'on va lui offrir une suite des aventures de Don Quichotte. **Dieu me préserve d'avoir jamais la folle prétention** d'oser marcher sur les traces de l'inimitable Cervantès! Son héros avait un genre de folie qui ne lui permettait pas de voir les objets sous leur forme naturelle, mais qui les métamorphosait au gré de son imagination. **Entièrement occupé d'une seule idée, Don Quichotte aurait voulu la faire partager à l'univers entier;** Edouard, au contraire, cherchait si peu à communiquer ses sentiments, à les faire adopter, qu'il n'osait pas même espérer de réaliser un jour les illusions flatteuses auxquelles il s'abandonnait avec tant de plaisir, et il n'avait pas de plus grande crainte que celle qu'on ne

in which he loved to indulge, that he dreaded nothing more than the detection of such sentiments as were dictated by his musings.[53]

parvint à connaître sa manière de voir et de sentir.[54] (my emphasis)

In terms of style, he tended to flatten Scott's text, stripping the language of local colour, figurative boldness, and digressions. In the above extract Scott used an intertextual reference to Cervantes's *Don Quixote* as an excuse for a convoluted poetical musing on the abstract concepts of vision, perception, and reality. He resorted to a long complex sentence running over a few lines and composed of both adverbial phrases and relative clauses, with words such as 'misconstrue', 'occurrences', 'tincture', 'colouring', and 'musings'. Defauconpret's text, in contrast, is much more straightforward. The content has been rearranged as to clearly oppose Cervantes and Waverley and their dealings with illusions.

It was this translated corpus, rather than the source texts, that became understood as the 'Scott model' for a whole generation of French writers in the 1820s. In his foreword to *La Comédie humaine* (1842) Balzac paid tribute to the 'modern trouvere'[55] who '*walter-scotted*'[56] French History to use his neologism from the preface for *La Peau de chagrin* (1831). Even though Balzac probably discovered *Waverley* in its first translation by Joseph Martin in 1818, he was more familiar with Defauconpret's 1822 translation. *Le Dernier Chouan ou la Bretagne en 1800* (1829), retitled *Les Chouans ou la Bretagne en 1799* (1834), was his first novel published under his name and it seems to have been directly drawn from *Waverley; Or, 'Tis Sixty Years Since* (1814). On top of their echoing titles, both plots evolve around political and sentimental topics, with the failure of insurrections through the death of their chieftains, and the love affair between the two opposite parties, Jacobites and Hanoverians, Chouans and Republicans. Yet, the two novels completely diverge in terms of style and tone. Contrary to Scott, Balzac shows no tinge of nostalgia towards a romanticized past. Describing the Chouans' marginal culture, the narrator says:

ils s'efforcent de conserver les traditions du langage et des mœurs gaëliques; aussi leur vie garde-t-elle de profonds vestiges des croyances et des pratiques superstitieuses des anciens temps. Là, les coutumes féodales sont encore respectées. Là, les antiquaires retrouvent debout les monuments des Druides. Là, le génie de

---

[53] *W*, p. 20.

[54] Walter Scott, *Waverley, ou Il y a soixante ans*, trans. by A.-J.-B. Defauconpret, vol. 1 (Paris: Charles Gosselin, 1828), pp. 54–55.

[55] 'Walter Scott, ce trouveur (trouvère) moderne', in Honoré de Balzac, Avant-propos of *La Comédie humaine*, in *La Comédie humaine*, 12 vols (Paris: Gallimard, 1976–81), I, 11.

[56] 'comme il est aujourd'hui rassasié de l'Espagne, de l'Orient, des supplices, des pirates et de l'histoire de France walter-scottée', in Honoré de Balzac, *La Peau de chagrin*, ed. by Pierre Citron, in *La Comédie humaine*, ed. by Pierre-Georges Castex (Paris: Gallimard, 1979), X, 54.

la civilisation moderne s'effraie de pénétrer à travers d'immenses forêts primordiales.[57]

[They struggle to preserve the traditions of the language and manners of their Gaelic ancestors; their lives show to this day many remarkable and deeply embedded vestiges of the beliefs and superstitious practices of those ancient times. There, feudal customs are still maintained. There, antiquaries find Druidic monuments still standing. And there, the genius of modern civilization shrinks from forcing its way through those impenetrable primordial forests.]

The passage expresses a feeling of irritation towards these outdated mores and customs: the anaphoric repetition of the shifter 'là' [there] emphasizes the lack of structure and the absence of any connection between these scattered beliefs and practices, while the ternary rhythm conveys the image of a slow, mechanical, and repetitive feudal society. Hyperbolic expressions ('incroyable', 'brutal', 'complète') stress the negative aspects of this old-fashioned Breton society. Contrary to Scott, Balzac is no keeper of the past. In *Waverley*, the manor of the Bradwardine family was rebuilt to look like the original, but it is also modernized to take into account the new historical development, i.e. the union between England and Scotland symbolized by the painting representing the Englishman, Edward Waverley, and the chieftain Fergus Mac-Ivor in Highland dress. Conversely, Balzac does not bring the Chouannerie to life in his novel; it is a lost cause from the very beginning as epitomized by the aptly named Château de la Vivetière, the Chouans' den, looking like a corpse, a skeleton being eaten by birds of prey before its last burial through the extended lexical field of death. In *Les Chouans*, there is no romanticization of the past, no possible ideological union: 'On ne peut pas être longtemps à la fois l'homme des Chouans et l'homme des Bleus' [You can't keep up being a spy of the Blues and a spy of the Chouans very long],[58] says Corentin, one of the Republicans. Contrary to *Waverley*, no character actually changes sides to join the opposite camp.

Balzac's text shares these characteristics with other French historical novels by Dumas, Vigny or Hugo. Even fluent readers of English like Stendhal and Vigny probably read Scott in translation since the French versions came out ahead of the English-language ones published by the Galignani Brothers in Paris. In his *Journal d'un poète* Vigny even mentioned how easy he thought Walter Scott's historical novels were,[59] and my contention is that this appreciation can partly be attributed to the translator's hand. By bringing Scott's hero into line

[57] Honoré de Balzac, *Les Chouans*, in *La Comédie humaine*, ed. by Pierre Dufief and Anne-Simone Dufief (Paris: Omnibus, 2011), III, 830 (my translation).

[58] Balzac, *Les Chouans*, in *La Comédie humaine*, III, 1033 (my translation).

[59] 'Je pensais que les romans historiques de Walter Scott étaient trop faciles à faire'. In Alfred de Vigny, *Journal d'un poète* (Paris: Michel Lévy frères, 1867), pp. 249–50. <http://gallica.bnf.fr/ark:/12148/bpt6k10567388/> [accessed 6 January 2017].

with the conventions of French Classicism and by refashioning Scott's protagonists as sentimental heroes, I believe that Defauconpret's intrusive hand was inadvertently responsible for creating a highly influential hybrid form that not only caused the French historical novel to diverge radically from the model pioneered by Scott — helping give a new lease to the gothic, through the darker clear-cut tone adopted in his texts — but also played a significant role in the evolution of the French realist novel.

* * *

'[L']écriture est destruction de toute voix, de toute origine. L'écriture, c'est ce neutre, ce composite, cet oblique où fuit notre sujet, le noir-et-le blanc où vient se perdre toute identité, à commencer par celle-là même du corps qui écrit' [Literature is precisely the invention of this voice, to which we cannot assign a specific origin: literature is that neuter, that composite, that oblique into which every subject escapes, the trap where all identity is lost, beginning with the very identity of the body that writes],[60] Roland Barthes writes. If the author's voice, or rather his voices in Scott's case, are crucial and as such have been finely analysed by many critics,[61] it is his body and in particular his hand which has triggered the writing of this article.

An indispensable tool for any writer, the hand takes an even more central and paradoxical role for Scott who had to cope with a hand which recurring illnesses often made useless. Frequently unable to write down his own stories, he had to resort to helping hands, whether they were family members, friends or literary partners. It seems to me that his work revolves around a reflexion on the hand motif which is displaced from the physical to the metaphorical, from the literal to the aesthetic and poetic spheres. Caught between two images of the hand, Adam Smith's concept of the 'invisible hand' and the Romantic cliché of the pale and feverish sacred hand of the writer — with Roger Chartier talking about the fetishizing of the writer's hand in pre-Romantic and Romantic literary works[62] — Scott managed to combine his commercial venture and his literary enterprise. He aestheticized the dictating exercises through art and developed an embodied poetics of suffering in his writing, while at the same time acting as a businessman fully involved in the book industry. His investment in the printing company also reveals Scott's anxious wish to keep a grip on his productions at both ends of the manufacturing process. Yet, he did not succeed in keeping his hand in with the

---

[60] In Roland Barthes, 'La Mort de l'auteur', in *Le Bruissement de la langue* [1968] (Paris: Seuil, 1984), pp. 61–68 (p. 63).
[61] 'the multiplicity of voices [...] is a principal feature of Scott's text itself'. Robert P. Irvine, *Enlightenment and Romance: Gender and Agency in Smollett and Scott* (Oxford: Peter Lang, 2000), p. 117.

French translator. Ironically enough, it is Defauconpret's intrusive hand which left a lasting mark on his readership across the Channel and beyond.

The unique multi-handed nature of his work, which resulted in the coexistence of various versions of his texts is confirmed by the existence of The Edinburgh Edition of the Waverley Novels and its very rich critical appendix which looks at the genesis of the text, its composition, through a careful analysis of the original manuscripts and the subsequent editions, highlighting alterations by other hands. Yet, 'there is plenty of evidence for the process of creation continuing after [Scott] wrote the manuscript versions', and the sheets 'provide[d] space for rewriting'.[63] This quest for the author's original conception, for what David Hewitt calls the 'authentic Scott' is questioned by Kathryn Sutherland in her article 'Factory Settings'.[64] The manuscript constitutes 'a textual elsewhere, the elsewhere of writing that is the locus of all determining factors, the space of every traversal'.[65] In praise of the variant Bernard Cerquiglini's approach opens up the textual space where new versions, rewritings, pastiches like *Walladmor* (1823), and translations can cohabit through comparative, rather than archaeological, perspectives. There may be no need for systematically distinguishing the extrinsic from the intrinsic, the copy from the original, and the translated text from the source text. Each version comes with its own richness revealing of the socio-political, cultural and literary context of the time of its production, like Scott's *Magnum Opus* (1829–33) which became the version in which Scott's Victorian and Edwardian readership enjoyed him, and could be valued as such whatever its faults or lacks. There have already been several representations of Scott on the marketplace, in both the UK and France, and there are probably many more to come thanks to the multi-handed nature of his work and his atypical position between Romantic aestheticization and commercial commodification.

---

[62] Roger Chartier, *La Main de l'auteur et l'esprit de l'imprimeur. XVI–XVIIIe siècles* (Paris: Gallimard, 2015).

[63] Hewitt, 'Scott and Textual Multiplepoinding', p. 363.

[64] Kathryn Sutherland, 'Factory Settings', *The Times Literary Supplement*, 27 Sept. 2013, pp. 3–5.

[65] 'Ce qu'on appelle communément l'avant texte (ensemble des brouillons, manuscrits, etc.) constitue un ailleurs textuel du texte, ailleurs d'écriture qui est le lieu de toutes les déterminations, l'espace de toutes les traversées'. In Bernard Cerquiglini, *Éloge de la variante: histoire critique de la philologie* (Paris: Seuil, 1989), p. 10.

SECTION II

Theoretical Approaches and Genre

Vanishing Mediators and Modes of Existence in Walter Scott's *The Monastery*

EVAN GOTTLIEB

Oregon State University

In his late 'Magnum Opus' introduction to *The Monastery*, originally published in 1820, Walter Scott claims to have no idea why he chose to return to familiar fictional territory after the geographical and historical departures of his previous bestseller, *Ivanhoe* (1819):

> It would be difficult to assign any good reason why the author of [that novel], after using, in that work, all the art he possessed to remove the personages, action, and manners of the tale, to a distance from his own country, should choose for the scene of his next attempt the celebrated ruins of Melrose, in the immediate neighbourhood of his own residence.[1]

As always with Scott, we should not take him entirely at his modest word. Although *The Monastery* backtracks to the literal ground of Scott's earliest authorial endeavors — the Borders between Scotland and England — it shares *Ivanhoe*'s interest in the causes and outcomes of clashing traditions, identities, and belief systems, even as it changes historical setting from the aftermath of the Norman Conquest to the lead-up to the Scottish Reformation. Duplicating *Ivanhoe*'s critical success, however, proved difficult. Although *The Monastery* sold relatively well — at this point in Scott's career, anything featuring 'by the Author of Waverley' on its title page was effectively guaranteed to be profitable — and received positive notices in *Blackwood's* and *The Gentleman's Magazine*, it was generally considered a disappointment. Critics were especially hard on Scott's decision to give a prominent role to a supernatural figure, a spirit known as the White Lady of Avenel. The *Edinburgh Monthly Review* condemned her as 'absurd almost to childishness', while the *Edinburgh Magazine* found Scott's creation 'insufferable'.[2]

Of course, Scott had deployed supernatural 'machinery' in many of his previous texts, including the Bodach Glas or Gray Ghost that haunts Fergus MacIvor in *Waverley* (1814), the spirit-possessed Green Room of *The Antiquary*

---

[1] Walter Scott, 'Introduction', in *The Monastery* (London: Thomas Nelson and Sons, n.d.), p. v.
[2] See *The Walter Scott Digital Archive*, <http://www.walterscott.lib.ed.ac.uk/works/novels/monastery.html#reception> [accessed 30 March 2016].

Yearbook of English Studies, 47 (2017), 77–92
© Modern Humanities Research Association 2017

(1816), and the prophecies and curses surrounding the Ravenswood family in *The Bride of Lammermoor* (1819).[3] So why did critics reject the White Lady? Elsewhere in the 'Magnum Opus' introduction quoted above, Scott is casually dismissive of her, claiming that she was meant as nothing more than a representative of those 'spirits of the elements' common to popular superstition, and that her role in *The Monastery* consisted primarily in 'acting a varying, capricious, and inconsistent part in the pages assigned to her in the narrative'.[4] Scott here anticipates some of the modern objections to his novel, such as Donald Cameron's assertion that *The Monastery* fails primarily because the White Lady is 'too definite and too frequent [in her appearances]'.[5] This complaint is picked up by Daniel Cottom, who notes that the White Lady's substantial presence in a novel (as opposed to the earlier activities of supernatural creatures in Scott's poems) discomfits readers because it unsettles generic expectations of prose versus poetry and realism versus romance;[6] implicitly agreeing with this assessment, Ian Duncan has humorously called the White Lady a 'doggerel-chanting banshee' and a 'Border sprite'.[7]

More recently, however, critics have begun to take her seriously — a welcome move, albeit one that needs to be made carefully. Chad May has accounted for the White Lady's unusual centrality to Scott's novel, as well as the critical opprobrium she has consistently generated, by arguing that 'she stands as a marker for that which lies outside historical explanation, in this case faith'.[8] Certainly, the White Lady has important functions to play; calling her merely or purely a figure of 'faith', however, misrepresents both her role in *The Monastery* and the larger ramifications of Scott's depiction of faith in the novel. In what follows, I propose first that we can best understand the White Lady as a 'vanishing mediator' who simultaneously prefigures and complicates Scotland's historical transition from Catholicism to Protestantism. In this essay's second

---

[3] If this list were to include Scott's poetry as well as his fiction then it would grow much longer; see, e.g., the figures of Michael Scott and Gilpin Horner in *The Lay of the Last Minstrel* (1805).

[4] Scott, 'Introduction', in *The Monastery*, p. xiv.

[5] Donald Cameron, 'History, Religion, and the Supernatural: The Failure of *The Monastery*', *Studies in Scottish Literature*, 6.2 (1968), 76–90 (pp. 78, 88). See also Mody C. Boatright, 'Scott's Theory and Practice concerning the Use of the Supernatural in Prose Fiction in Relation to the Chronology of the Waverley Novels', *PMLA*, 50.1 (March 1935), 235–61 (pp. 250–51), which attempts to extrapolate Scott's 'rules' for the fictional use of the supernatural before demonstrating that *The Monastery* violates them.

[6] See Daniel Cottom, 'Walter Scott and the Spirit of the Novel', in *Spirits of Fire: English Romantic Writers and Contemporary Historical Methods*, ed. by G. A. Rosso and Daniel P. Watkins (Madison, NJ: Farleigh Dickinson University Press, 1990), pp. 131–52.

[7] Ian Duncan, *Scott's Shadow: The Novel in Romantic Edinburgh* (Princeton, NJ, and Oxford: Princeton University Press, 2007), p. 194. Duncan speculates that the White Lady may have been Scott's attempt to work some James Hogg-like supernaturalism into his historical fiction.

[8] Chad T. May, 'Sir Walter Scott's *The Monastery* and the Representation of Religious Belief', *Studies in Scottish Literature*, 41 (2015), 191–208 (p. 207).

half, I turn to Bruno Latour's sociological methods of non-anthropocentric description — in particular, his recent development of a system of 'modes of existence' — to outline an alternative way of understanding *The Monastery*'s vision of religious and social transformation as a whole. In these ways, I hope to demonstrate that Scott's most explicitly spiritual Waverley Novel, far from being 'absurd' and 'insufferable', offers a sophisticated account of the early stages of the Scottish Reformation, as well as a meta-commentary on the nature of what it means to be (in Latour's terminology) a being of religion.

As mentioned above, the novel's titular monastery of Kennaquhair is modeled closely on Melrose Abbey, the ruins of which lie very close to Scott's own Abbotsford.[9] Andrew Lynch notes that critics have been divided regarding their impressions of Scott's treatment of the Catholic/Protestant divide: some find him surprisingly fair-minded, whereas others are in no doubt that Scott favours the Protestant cause and denigrates Catholicism.[10] Indeed, although Scott frequently praises his Catholic characters for their devotion, he makes it clear that their ardour is misguided, since he describes Catholicism as a 'corrupted system of Christianity'.[11] By contrast, even though some of its proponents are markedly ignorant, Protestantism is represented as inherently superior because it is based on direct access 'to the volume on which Christianity itself is founded' (p. 84).[12] As in many of Scott's narratives, moreover, 'the volume' in question is literally materialized — not in the form of the stolen spell book of *The Lay of the Last Minstrel* (1805), but as a vernacular Bible kept by Lady Avenel in defiance of Church prohibitions.

To understand fully this Bible's significance, some scene-setting is required. When the novel begins, Lady Avenel and her young daughter, Mary, are in the process of abandoning their estate — which is being menaced by bands of English soldiers in the wake of their victory at the Battle of Pinkie Cleugh in 1547 — to share living quarters in a small tower on the monastery's lands owned by a commoner widow, Dame Glendinning, and her two sons. After Lady Avenel's untimely death, a local monk seizes the forbidden Bible, but before he can return

---

[9] Scott confirms that Kennaquhair is Melrose in his introduction to the Magnum Opus edition of *The Monastery*. Penny Fielding observes that the name creates a pun in Scots, 'kenna whair' roughly translating to 'know not where'. See Penny Fielding, 'Explanatory Notes', in Walter Scott, *The Monastery*, ed. by Penny Fielding, EEWN (Edinburgh: Edinburgh University Press, 2000), p. 443.

[10] Andrew Lynch, 'Simply to Amuse the Reader: The Humor of Walter Scott's Reformation', *Postmedieval: A Journal of Medieval Cultural Studies*, 5.2 (2014), 169–83 (p. 175).

[11] *The Monastery*, ed. by Penny Fielding, p. 84. Subsequent citations to this edition will appear parenthetically.

[12] This same passage asserts that the earliest reformers did not desire a full split from the Church, but in fact did what they could 'to avoid a schism, until the violence of the Pope rendered it unavoidable' (p. 84) — 'violence' here presumably referring to Pope Leo X's excommunication of Martin Luther in 1521.

to Kennaquhair he is tricked by the White Lady and the book disappears. Father Eustace, the Abbey's sharp-witted Sub-Prior, initially doubts Father Phillip's report that he lost Lady Avenel's 'Black Book' after being waylaid by a supernatural maiden. He sets off to the tower to discover what its inhabitants know. Surprisingly, the Bible turns out to have been returned to Glendearg already, courtesy of the White Lady. Father Eustace duly confiscates the forbidden text, only to be attacked in his turn by the determined spirit, who knocks him from his mule and reclaims the Bible once again (pp. 92–94). Chad May notes that Father Eustace represents the voice of reasonable scepticism in the novel;[13] nevertheless, after his own close encounter with the White Lady, even he must admit that 'This is more than simple fantasy' (p. 93). Subsequently the Bible in question reappears twice more, each time magically transported by the White Lady. First, after Halbert Glendinning becomes jealous of Mary's apparent preference for his brother, Edward, he summons the White Lady to help him, who leads him to a mystical underground chamber where the Good Book awaits him (pp. 113–20). Second, later in the novel, with Halbert erroneously presumed dead, she appears to Mary and shows her where to find the very same Bible under a loose floorboard of the Glendinning brothers' bedchamber (pp. 278–81).

Both Halbert's and Mary's encounters with Lady Avenel's Bible are conversion experiences, as noted by May in his astute article. Before investigating the nature of these conversions further, though, I want to stay with the surprising mobility of the book itself. The centrality of the printed text to the Reformation is very well established.[14] Even if, as some historians have concluded, Scottish literacy rates 'have been exaggerated as part of the national myth', the combination of high literacy and a small population 'provided a wider pool of educated people' than in many other European nations, and thus primed Scottish receptivity to a religious reformation spurred by the distribution and consumption of print, including not only the Bible itself but also the many pamphlets of John Knox, George Buchanan, Samuel Rutherford, and others.[15] Lady Avenel's Bible thus represents in miniature the power of printed texts to circulate and widely disseminate knowledge — especially religious knowledge, 'the mysteries of the Divine Word' as Scott terms it (p. 280) — outside the control of official Church doctrine and authority. Indeed, it is no stretch to say that Lady Avenel's Bible

---

[13] May, '*The Monastery* and the Representation of Religious Belief', pp. 198–99.

[14] See, for example, Elizabeth Eisenstein, *The Printing Press as an Agent of Change: Communications and Cultural Transformations in Early-Modern Europe*, 2 vols (New York: Cambridge University Press, 1979).

[15] Keith M. Brown, 'Reformation to Union, 1560–1707', in *The New Penguin History of Scotland: From the Earliest Times to the Present Day*, ed. by R. A. Houston and W. W. J. Knox (London: Allen Lane and Penguin Press, 2001), pp. 182–275 (p. 186).

enjoys a greater freedom of movement than any of the book's actual characters, who frequently find themselves apprehended (Henry Warden, an itinerant Protestant preacher), misled (Father Eustace), exiled (Sir Piercie Shafton), presumed dead (Halbert), and even locked into their own tower, which occurs when Shafton flees with Mysie Harper and they need to buy themselves time to avoid pursuit.

What should we make of a Bible that seems to possess more mobility than most of the novel's human actors? Notably, Lady Avenel's forbidden book acts differently when it comes into contact with different characters in *The Monastery*. The prohibited Bible does not 'stick' at all to either of the monks who attempt to confiscate it or take it out of circulation.[16] By contrast, it clearly wants to find its way into the hands of both Halbert and Mary. For the latter, it holds attractions both for its associations with her mother and for the spiritual wisdom it promises to deliver. As Scott relates when Mary discovers it beneath the floorboards in the tower, 'There were slips of paper inserted in the work, in which [...] the errors and human inventions with which the Church of Rome had defaced the simple edifice of Christianity [...] were pointed out' (p. 280). Moreover, it also contains Lady Avenel's compiled sheet of Bible quotations seemingly designed to provide comfort in times of trouble; and it is this list to which Mary is immediately drawn. Just as Augustine was converted to Christianity by opening a Bible and reading randomly, so Mary's conversion is immediate. And just as Andrew Piper notes that 'The conversion at the heart of *The Confessions* was an affirmation of the new technology of the book within the lives of individuals',[17] so Mary's conversion occurs as a direct result of her personal contact with 'the Black Book':

> She read the affecting promise 'I will never leave thee nor forsake thee,' and the consoling exhortation 'Call upon me in the day of trouble, and I will deliver thee' [...] and her heart acquiesced in the conclusion, Surely this is the word of God (281; Chap. 30).

Significantly, however, this is practically the only time anyone in the novel is depicted actually *reading* Lady Avenel's Bible. The aforementioned monks, of course, have no interest in performing such a blasphemous act. Furthermore, when Halbert recovers the same Bible earlier in the novel — reaching through mystical fire in a scene that May notes recalls any number of Biblical precedents[18]

[16] 'Stickiness' is a term used by the anthropologist Ian Hodder to describe the relative adhesion of objects to humans; see his *Entangled: An Archaeology of the Relationships between Humans and Things* (Malden, MA: Wiley-Blackwell, 2012), p. 17. My original analysis of *The Monastery* invoked an object-oriented reading that was ultimately counter-productive. I am grateful to Matthew Wickman for his feedback on an earlier draft and for helping to clarify this point.

[17] Andrew Piper, *Book Was There: Reading in Electronic Times* (Chicago, IL: University of Chicago Press, 2012), p. 2.

[18] See May, '*The Monastery* and the Representation of Religious Belief', pp. 203–04.

— his conversion occurs quite differently from Mary's. Previously, Halbert has led a carelessly rustic lifestyle, dismissing his brother's book learning as just 'muttering and scribbling' (p. 110). But he emerges a changed man from his supernatural experience in the underground grotto where the White Lady has temporarily stowed the Bible. Like Mary, Halbert is initially drawn to the Black Book more for its personal associations than for its spiritual value; by gaining possession of it, he hopes both to understand and to impress Mary, who has seemed to favour the more bookish Edward. Whereas Mary needs actually to read the Bible — or at least her mother's curated version of it — in order to have her conversion experience, Halbert is transformed merely by getting his hands on it; after the White Lady rejects his plea for assistance 'to read and understand this volume' (p. 118), Halbert returns to the tower apparently without ever opening the Bible. Yet both his bearing and his language are immediately elevated, as evidenced by his sudden ability to match wits with the loquacious Shafton: 'All eyes were turned on Halbert while he was thus speaking, and there was a general feeling that his countenance had an expression of intelligence, and his person an air of dignity, which they had never before observed' (p. 138). Later, it seems probable that Halbert reads enough of the Bible to make a credible conversion to Protestantism, a move that helps his career as well as his love life; but mere contact with the White Lady is apparently enough to transform him. Scott's description of Halbert's transformation, moreover, is both ambiguous and suggestive:

> Whether it was that the wonderful Being with whom he had so lately held communication, had bestowed on him a *grace* and dignity of look and bearing which he had not before, or whether the being conversant in high matters, and called to a destiny beyond that of other men, had a natural effect in giving becoming confidence to his language and manner, we pretend not to say. (p. 138; italics added)

Demurring to specify the precise cause of Halbert's emergence from the grotto as a changed man, Scott drops a significant hint with the highly resonant word 'grace'. Despite not being invoked in its strictly religious sense, grace would have been recognizable to Scott's readers, especially Scots, as a keyword of the Scottish Reformation. John Knox's *Letter Addressed to the Commonality of Scotland* (1558), for example, invokes it five times, including in its opening sentence: 'To his beloved brethren the commonalty of Scotland, John Knox wishes grace, mercy, and peace, with the spirit of righteous judgment.'[19] Indeed, the concept of grace appears regularly in Knox's writings, especially in connection with two adjunctive ideas: grace is egalitarian, meaning it is available to all regardless of rank or wealth (although perhaps not gender, thanks to Knox's infamous *First*

---

[19] John Knox, *Letter Addressed to the Commonality of Scotland* (1558), <http://www.swrb.com/newslett/actualNLs/ltrcommo.htm> [accessed 18 June 2016].

Blast of the Trumpet Against the Monstrous Regiment of Women [1558]); and it is 'unearned', or given to us by God regardless of our worthiness or lack thereof.[20] When Halbert in particular undergoes his conversion experience, he clearly fits both of these conditions, being previously neither well-born nor especially pious or even thoughtful.

From a Protestant perspective, then, nothing authentically spiritual can be achieved without the addition of that essential ingredient, grace. But of what, precisely, does grace consist? Even among Christians, it is a notoriously slippery term. According to *The Encyclopedia of Religion*, grace 'stands primarily not for human virtue but for God's presence. Grace is a divine activity in human history and human lives'.[21] At first glance, the most obvious candidate for this role in *The Monastery* would be the White Lady herself; not only is she literally inhuman, but also (as we've seen) she plays a key role in circulating Lady Avenel's Bible and facilitating the religious conversions of several main characters. Yet we've also seen that Scott's introductory materials make clear that the White Lady is *not* to be associated with Christian spirituality; she is a spirit of the elements, an avatar of folk superstition associated with the fate of the Avenel family and the natural fountain where she is most often found. The White Lady herself knows that she exists in a separate realm, spiritually, from the rest of the characters; when Halbert asks her to teach him to read the Bible, she demurs:

> Alas! Alas!
> Not ours the grace
> These holy characters to trace:
> Idle forms of painted air
> Not to us is given to share
> The boon bestow'd on Adam's race. (pp. 118–19)

And a similar chant accompanies her revelation to Mary of her mother's Bible's hidden location:

> Maiden, attend! Beneath my foot lies hid,
> The Word, the Law, the Path, which thou doest strive
> To find, and canst not find. — [...]
> [...]
> But do not thou at human ills repine,
> Secure there lies full guerdon in this spot
> For all the woes that wait frail Adam's line —
> Stoop then and make it your's [*sic*], — I may not make it mine! (pp. 278–79)

---

[20] See, for example, Knox, *Letter to the Commonality of Scotland*: 'as the whole multitude was delivered from the bondage of Egypt, by the mighty power of God alone; so was every member of the same, without respect of persons, sanctified by his grace: the rich, in that behalf, nothing preferred to the poor. For by no merit nor worthiness of man was he moved to choose and to establish his habitation and dwelling amongst them'.

[21] Mircae Eliade, *The Encyclopedia of Religion*, quoted in Adam S. Miller, *Speculative Grace: Bruno Latour and Object-Oriented Theology* (New York: Fordham University Press, 2013), p. 6.

These passages confirm that although the White Lady is a spirit, she is clearly not meant to be identified with the Holy Spirit.

If the White Lady is a vehicle for God's grace, yet is herself unable to participate in it, then how can we understand her function in Scott's narrative? I propose that we think of her as what Slavoj Žižek calls a vanishing mediator: 'what must disappear, must become invisible, for the new order to establish its identity-with-itself'.[22] One of Žižek's favourite instances of a vanishing mediator in the history of Western philosophy is Friedrich Schelling: although Schelling's theories and methodologies seem like dead ends, with little or no lasting direct influence — that is, he has more or less vanished from the contemporary philosophical scene — his paradoxical 'system of freedom' retrospectively appears entirely necessary for philosophy to make the leap from Kantian transcendentalism to post-Hegelian historicism. Furthermore, says Žižek, for at least a moment Schelling 'render[ed] visible something that was invisible beforehand and withdrew into invisibility thereafter' — namely, the necessity of a mythic narrative that accounts for the genesis of the absolute (which of course takes different forms in different philosophical systems).[23]

So how does this concept of the vanishing mediator apply to the White Lady? Certainly, she regularly, literally *vanishes*: every occasion of her appearance is marked by a slow disappearance that literalizes the idea of an intermediary whose presence gradually fades as it becomes unnecessary. I have already shown how she mediates Halbert's and Mary's conversions from Catholicism to Protestantism. We can add that she acts throughout the novel to facilitate their eventual marriage and social ascent, from guiding the Avenels to the tower of Glendearg in the novel's opening chapters, to healing Shafton after his duel with Halbert so that the latter is not responsible for his death and can eventually be raised to the rank of baron. Furthermore, she makes visible something important but subsequently obscured in the shift from Catholicism to Protestantism: despite the latter's claim to offer a purified form of Christianity free from what Warden calls 'the superstitious devices of Rome' (p. 294), both rely heavily on mediational 'devices' to complete the circuit between human and metaphysical worlds. For Protestants, and especially for Calvinists, only Jesus mediates between God and humanity; this is part of what Max Weber famously described as its 'ascetic rationalism', through which (in Vincent Pecora's words) Protestantism has tried 'since Luther [...] periodically [...] to purge true religion of all vestiges of archaic

[22] Slavoj Žižek, 'Eastern European Liberalism and its Discontents', in *The Universal Exception: Selected Writings, Volume Two*, ed. by Rex Butler and Scott Stephens (London: Continuum, 2006), p. 29.

[23] Slavoj Žižek, *The Indivisible Remainder: On Schelling and Related Matters* (London: Verso, 2007), pp. 8–9. See also Adrian Johnston, *Žižek's Ontology: A Transcendental Materialist Theory of Subjectivity* (Evanston, IL: Northwestern University Press, 2008), p. 70.

magic'.[24] Catholics, by contrast, can call on a host of saints to aid and transport their heavenly communications; one of the Virgin Mary's official titles given by the Catholic Church is 'the Mediatrix of all Graces'[25] — a title that could easily be applied to the White Lady. As a representative of precisely the kind 'superstitious device' that Protestantism explicitly disavows but quietly retains in the form of a heavenly Son whose radical hybridity makes him 'monstrous',[26] the White Lady both mediates the transition from Catholicism to Protestantism and makes visible the supernatural element they share, but which only the former acknowledges as a legitimate vehicle of grace.

To this point, I've argued for the White Lady as a Žižekian vanishing mediator who foreshadows and facilitates the shift from Catholicism to Protestantism in pre-Reformation Scotland, while simultaneously illuminating how both forms of Christianity rely on supernatural mediations to disseminate God's grace. Yet even as this critique has tried to explain the White Lady's function in *The Monastery*, it has also employed a hermeneutics of suspicion that feels somewhat untrue to both the novel and its author. Scott's treatment of the White Lady eschews the sceptical note he usually introduces, in his notes if not also in the texts themselves, when employing supernatural characters and devices.[27] Furthermore, his personal views on religion — while not an infallible guide to his fictional depictions — suggest a degree of tolerance toward a range of Christian practices and beliefs extending well beyond the Calvinism of his childhood and the Episcopalian adherence of his adult years.[28] In this vein, Scott's journal entry of 10 December 1825, written some five years after *The Monastery*'s publication, is worth recalling. Contemplating the moral necessity of the afterlife, Scott notes that 'There are few I trust who disbelieve the existence of God', before continuing:

[24] Vincent P. Pecora, *Secularization and Cultural Criticism: Religion, Nation, and Modernity* (Chicago, IL: University of Chicago Press, 2006), p. 101. The phrase 'ascetic rationalism' is quoted by Pecora from Max Weber's *The Protestant Ethic and the Spirit of Capitalism* (1905).

[25] Thanks to Robert Davis for pointing this out to me. See, for example, Father William G. Most, 'Mary, Mediatrix of all Graces', *EWTN: Global Catholic Network* (1996), <https://www.ewtn.com/faith/teachings/marya4.htm> [accessed 20 July 2016].

[26] See, e.g., Slavoj Žižek, 'The Fear of Four Words: A Modest Plea for the Hegelian Reading of Christianity', in Žižek and John Milbank, *The Monstrosity of Christ: Paradox or Dialectic?*, ed. by Creston Davis (Cambridge, MA: The MIT Press, 2009), p. 82: 'Christ is God's "partial object," an autonomized organ without a body, as if God picked his eye out of his head and turned it on himself from the outside. We can guess, now, why Hegel insisted on the *monstrosity* of Christ.'

[27] For a valuable general analysis of Scott's use of paratextual materials, see Robert Mayer, 'The Illogical Status of Novelistic Discourse: Scott's Footnotes for the Waverley Novels', *ELH*, 66.4 (1999), 911–37.

[28] A somewhat dated but still useful survey of Scott's religious attitudes is provided by Richard French, 'The Religion of Sir Walter Scott', *Studies in Scottish Literature*, 2.1 (1964), 32–44.

But they have a poor idea of the Deity and the rewards which are destined for the Just made perfect who can only adopt the literal sense of an eternal concert [as their vision of Heaven] [...] I rather suppose there should be understood some commission from the Highest, some duty to discharge with the applause of a satisfied conscience — that the Deity who himself must be supposed to feel love and affection for the beings whom he has calld [sic] into existence should delegate a portion of those powers I for one cannot conceive altogether so wrong a conjecture. We would then find reality in Milton's sublime machinery [...] Nay, we would approach to the Catholic idea of the employment of Saints, though without approaching the absurdity of Saint-worship which degrades their religion.[29]

Keeping in mind that Scott likely wrote his journal with the idea of its eventual publication (or at least with the knowledge that even his 'private' writings necessarily implicated the Author of Waverley[30]), we can see in these reflections his willingness to give credence to a variety of Christian beliefs; most importantly for our purposes, although he considers 'Saint-worship' absurd, he sympathizes with the idea of saints as a category of religious beings with extra-human powers. Accordingly, analysing the White Lady as a merely functional device, rather than as part of a relatively ecumenical vision of spirituality, feels at best incomplete and at worst unfaithful (pun intended).

* * *

In this second part of my essay I want to view *The Monastery* through a different analytical lens: the 'modes of existence' model that Bruno Latour has adopted and adapted over the last decade or so. Drawing on the innovative, neglected work of the twentieth-century sociologist Étienne Souriau, Latour has recently admitted that Actor-Network-Theory — the socio-philosophical method of tracing relations between many sorts of 'actants' with which he has been associated for several decades — is ill-equipped to deal in a nuanced way with the webs of relations that constitute what we commonly call 'the social'. Latour himself has acknowledged that Actor-Network-Theory not only tends to make every network sound the same, each being inevitably 'composed in heterogeneous fashion of unexpected elements',[31] but also routinely represents events in ways that are unrecognizable to the human actants in question. His *An Inquiry into Modes of Existence* (2012; English trans. 2013) represents an important

---

[29] *The Journal of Sir Walter Scott*, ed. by W. E. K. Anderson (Edinburgh: Canongate Books, 1998), p. 40.

[30] See, for example, James P. Carson, 'The Author of *Waverley* and the Problem of Romantic Authorship', in *Approaches to Teaching Scott's Waverley Novels*, ed. by Evan Gottlieb and Ian Duncan (New York: Modern Language Association of America, 2009), pp. 50–58.

[31] Bruno Latour, *An Inquiry into Modes of Existence: An Anthropology of the Moderns*, trans. by Catherine Porter (Cambridge, MA: Harvard University Press, 2013), p. 35. Subsequent citations will appear parenthetically.

methodological shift, in which Latour begins to consolidate his new attempts to map the variety of relations that characterize different modern modes of being.[32] Here, 'network' is only one of fifteen (or twelve, depending on how you count them) modes that Latour proposes constitute the panoply of modern practices of value-formation and subject-making; these include well-established and generally agreed upon modes such as politics and law, as well as more obscure (but potentially no less important) modes like habit, technology, and fiction.[33] As he and Isabelle Stengers note in their introduction to Souriau's *The Different Modes of Existence* (1943), 'it's not a matter of opposing pure existence to reality, but of enquiring of each mode what is its own way of "making reality"'.[34]

The overarching mode of existence in *The Monastery*, not surprisingly, is religion (which Latour shortens to [REL]). Living in mid-sixteenth-century Scotland, the book's characters, like Scott himself in the journal entry quoted above, never doubt that they exist in a universe overseen by a metaphysical deity. As Latour describes in *Rejoicing* (2002), his proto-modal book on [REL], this assurance typifies a pre-modern historical moment in which religiosity acted as a kind of universal backdrop for all communication and action: 'The presence of divinities was obvious in the air or the soil. They formed the common fabric of people's lives, the primary material of all rituals, the indisputable reference point of all existence, the ordinary fodder of all conversation.'[35] There is at least one atheist in the Waverley novels; famously, the gypsy Hayraddin Maugrabin in *Quentin Durward* (1823) proclaims his godlessness (and, perhaps not coincidentally, is killed before that novel concludes happily for its Christian protagonists). Nevertheless, [REL] is a useful starting point for thinking about the 'indisputable reference point' of British society during the hegemony of Roman Catholicism. From this perspective, *The Monastery* investigates what it looked and felt like when that hegemony began to fray under the mounting challenge of the Reformation. Belief in God still forms the 'common fabric' of all lives in the novel, but the question of how to articulate, perform, and live that belief is increasingly open to debate.

[32] I say 'has begun to consolidate' because the *Inquiry* was preceded by several shorter studies in which Latour began to turn away from Actor Network Theory and towards something else; the oft-delayed translation of these books, however, means that some of them were published in English close to or even after the *Inquiry*. See Bruno Latour, *Rejoicing, or The Torments of Religious Speech*, trans. by Julie Rose (Malden, MA: Polity, 2013); Latour, *The Making of Law: An Ethnography of the Conseil d'État* (Malden, MA: Polity, 2010).

[33] The two-page chart listing all of the modes and their various perturbations is printed without pagination at the back of the book. The *Inquiry* also exists as an interactive website. See <www.modesofexistence.org> [accessed 30 September 2014].

[34] Isabelle Stengers and Bruno Latour, 'The Sphinx of the Work', introduction to Étienne Souriau, *The Different Modes of Existence*, trans. by Erik Beranek and Tim Howles (Minneapolis, MN: Univocal, 2015), pp. 11–94 (p. 44).

[35] Latour, *Rejoicing*, p. 5.

When *The Monastery* opens in 1553, a combined army of Scottish and Catholic forces has been thoroughly defeated by Henry VIII's English, Protestant soldiers at the battle of Pinkie Cleugh.[36] Before Lady Avenel and her daughter come to the tower of Glendearg, Scott's narrative is focalized by the widow of the tower's owner, who fears for her family's safety despite their habitation on the Abbey's land. Approached by a band of roving English soldiers, Dame Glendinning decides to meet them with her two young boys at her side. Fortunately for her, the head of this English riding party is an honourable man who is also charmed by the fearlessness of the Glendinning brothers. When he stations a sergeant to protect them from further incursions and turns to leave, Dame Glendinning calls after him, 'God be with you, gallant southern', which evokes these responses from her sons:

> 'Mother,' said the elder boy [Halbert], 'I will not say amen to a prayer for a Southron.'
>
> 'Mother,' said the younger [Edward], more reverentially, 'is it right to pray for a heretic?' (p. 42)

In the first of these reactions, Scott deftly articulates a mode of existence that frequently appears alongside but must be distinguished from the religious mode: politics [POL]. Halbert's refusal to pray for an Englishman is classically political as it invokes group loyalties and identities that include some people (the Scots) and thereby exclude others (the English).[37] Along these lines, the most obvious representative of [POL] in the novel is Julian of Avenel. Halbert and Edward's uncle is a Border baron with no entrenched loyalties beyond his own self-enrichment, and little patience for religion in any of its forms. He supports the incipient Reformation, not out of any spiritual conviction but because he covets Kennaquhair's lands for himself; as he tells the Protestant preacher, Warden, when they argue about religion, 'thou mayst call it what thou lists, but to me it is recommended, because it flings off all those sottish dreams about saints and angels and devils, and unhorses the lazy monks that have ridden us so long, and spur-galled us so hard' (p. 224).[38] Julian represents a purely secular and political opportunism shorn of any spiritual dimensions.[39]

---

[36] As Penny Fielding points out, Scott compresses the novel's timescale, since the Battle of Pinkie actually took place in 1547, but is presented in the novel as having occurred quite recently. See Fielding, ed., *Monastery*, 'Historical Note', p. 434.

[37] For the friend–enemy distinction as the basis of politics, see Carl Schmitt, *The Concept of the Political*, expanded edn, ed. and trans. by George Schwab (Chicago, IL: University of Chicago Press, 2007).

[38] In the matter of Julian's character (albeit little else), I agree with Cameron in 'Failure of *The Monastery*', pp. 76–90.

[39] Not coincidentally, the White Lady never appears to Julian despite the fact that he is a full-blooded member of the Avenel family, and therefore presumably as liable as any of the others to be visited by her.

If we now return to the Glendinning brothers' complaints about their mother's blessing of an Englishman, the response of the younger boy, Edward, initially appears more simple insofar as it is based on purely religious grounds: the English captain, Stalwarth Bolton, should not be prayed for because he is a 'heretic'. But this is where Latour's understanding of the [REL] mode provides a series of potentially important insights. First, he distinguishes between religious *institutions* and religion as a *mode* of existence; while the former are various and even frequently at odds with one another, the latter — and here we should probably implicitly limit the reach of Latour's analysis to Christianity, as he explicitly does in his *Inquiry* (p. 305) — is unified inasmuch as it represents the lived experience of those who 'draw the certainty of [...] being unified and complete, [not] from our own resources but from elsewhere: we receive it as an always unmerited gift that circulates through the narrow channel of [a variety of] salutary words' (*Inquiry*, p. 303). The beings of religion, in short, perceive themselves as the 'recipients' of 'gifts' in the form of 'words *that bear beings* [whom Latour terms 'angels'] *capable of renewing those to whom they are addressed*' (p. 303; italics in original). While this language sounds odd, it helps to remember that Latour's new method tries to describe the various modes of existence in terms that the beings who exist in and through them, or to use the term Latour adopts from Souriau, who are 'instaured' by them, can recognize as true to their own experiences. Edward's reluctance to bless Stalwarth Bolton on the grounds that the latter is a heretic shows that the young boy is already operating fully within the [REL] mode. It thus makes perfect sense that it is Edward, not Halbert, who becomes the titular hero of *The Abbot* (1821), Scott's sequel to *The Monastery*. Furthermore, the beings of [REL] need not agree with the details of each other's systems in order to recognize and engage with each other within the same mode. As discussed in the previous section, the most sympathetic Roman Catholic figure in the book (other than Edward) is Father Eustace, Kennaquhair's Sub-Prior. Yet Scott's omniscient narration marks him from the start as misguided, as in the following passage: 'Thus spoke, at least thus thought, a man zealous according to his imperfect knowledge, confounding the vital interests of Christianity with the extravagant and usurped claimed of the Church of Rome, and defending his cause with an ardour worthy of a better' (p. 79). As a being of [REL], Father Eustace's mode of existence is comprehensible to other likeminded beings, but although Scott recognizes that the monk is simply thinking and acting along the lines of his training and upbringing, no amount of further instauration will bring the Sub-Prior closer to the true salvation, political as well as religious, offered by Protestantism.

This leads to the second insight provided by Latour's analysis that can shed light on Scott's text. For Latour, every mode of existence shares a key structural component: each is characterized by one or more breaks, or 'hiatuses', which appear to disrupt its chain of associations but in fact facilitate its eventual (re)production of the mode of existence it constitutes. These 'small interruptions' (p. 34) are frequently unperceived as such from within their particular mode; in one of Latour's examples, the laboratory director who has to '"go through" the patent application process in order to bring his project to fruition' soon accepts this 'pass' through what is actually a legal mode of existence ([LAW]) as a natural, or at least necessary, part of his work in the domain of Science.[40]

So what is the specific type of hiatus characteristic of the Religious mode? How do the beings of [REL] reproduce themselves via a 'pass' or 'discontinuity'? Put simply, they do more or less what the main characters in *The Monastery* do: they ceaselessly question their beliefs and values, and occasionally find that their faith is best renewed by abandoning their old doctrines and inventing, adapting, or adopting new ones. After all, the 'promise of religion', as Latour puts it, remains the same across all Judeo-Christian denominations: it is the paradox of 'some sense, some promise of plenitude [...] translated, very awkwardly to be sure, by "eternity" and "eternal life" — but in time, always taken up again in time' (p. 312). It is the timely promise of timelessness and, moreover, a pledge that must consistently be renewed or reprised via 'an uninterrupted chain — constantly broken — of renewals, conversions, reinterpretations, innovations, and fruitful or fatal betrayals' (p. 314). In this way, we see Halbert's faith, which is weak or at best default Catholic for most of the book, altered and strengthened by his encounters with the White Lady and the itinerant Protestant preacher Warden. The encounters are extended, slightly surreal episodes that each function as potential moments of blockage, or hiatuses, through which Halbert must move in order to find his faith ultimately transformed and intensified. By the same token, although Edward ultimately remains Catholic rather than converting, his faith too is strengthened after being 'tested' — another term Latour frequently uses to describe such hiatuses — by encounters with the White Lady. As important as these tests that occur more or less *within* the [REL] mode, however, are the *passes* through other modes that strengthen these men's faiths: in such respect, episodes that may seem digressive or mechanical can be re-viewed as essential processes of instauration, through which characters emerge even more fully as religious beings. Halbert's duel with Shafton and Edward's abortive courting of Mary are examples.

The fit between Latour's modes of existence and Scott's *Monastery* may go deeper yet. We have seen how the latter treats religion, especially Christianity, as what Latour calls the 'indisputable reference point' of human relations (and, by extension, relations between humans and other actants), and also how it

---

[40] There is no specific mode for science in Latour's schema, since the domain of science is produced by the crossing of several other modes.

shows [REL] sustaining itself over time via a series of irregular but necessary shocks: the discontinuities, hiatuses, and passes that allow the reproduction of modes and the instauration of modern (which is also to say, modal) subjects. Following this thread, we may even wonder whether the ultimate Western figure of [REL]'s continuity in discontinuity is the Christian Trinity itself: the God who becomes his own Son, who in turn is killed and reborn, thus facilitating the transmission of the Holy Spirit to the 'virtual spiritual community' of all Christians.[41] After all, the promise of rebirth is precisely what is held out to, and by, the beings of religion in a variety of guises that Latour lists as 'Presence, Creation, Salvation, [and] Grace' — the latter shown to be a central concept in *The Monastery* and the Scottish Reformation, as discussed in the first part of this essay — before settling on a final term: 'Incarnation' (p. 312).

But as fascinating as such doctrinal questions are, to pursue them — which is precisely what Scott's novel encourages us to do — is to prove the strength of Latour's primary thesis that modes of existence reproduce themselves via breaks, passes, and discontinuities, and that the religious mode in particular does this precisely via the kinds of debates, controversies, and conversions depicted in *The Monastery*. As Latour puts it, 'Groping, contradictory exegesis: this is religion itself' (p. 313). It remains to be added that this could also serve as a description of just about any act of interpretation, up to and perhaps especially including the literary critical type of which we are all practitioners, regardless of our other faiths. Influenced by Latour, Rita Felski has recently observed that literary critics have for too long privileged critique at the expense of understanding: we have become very good 'at documenting the insufficiencies of meanings, values, and norms [...] We are often stymied, however, when asked to account for the importance of meanings, values, and norms in all forms of life, including our own'.[42] Unlike the characters of *The Monastery*, we are not currently confronting a politico-religious crisis as momentous as the Scottish Reformation; nevertheless, declarations that we now live in a post-religious world have clearly proven premature. Moreover, we are still navigating a variety of modes of existence whose mutual incomprehension not infrequently results in violence, whether of the fast or slow varieties.[43] As Charles Taylor notes, we can no longer afford to invest unthinkingly in those 'stories of modernity in general, and secularity in particular, which explain themselves by humans having lost, or

---

[41] The phrase 'virtual spiritual community' is Žižek's Hegelian description of the Holy Spirit in 'The Fear of Four Words', p. 29.

[42] Rita Felski, *The Limits of Critique* (Chicago, IL: University of Chicago Press, 2015), p. 15.

[43] On 'slow', i.e. accretional violence, especially relating to the environment and environmental justice, see, e.g., Rob Nixon, *Slow Violence and the Environmentalism of the Poor* (Cambridge, MA, and London: Harvard University Press, 2013).

sloughed off, or liberated themselves from certain earlier, confining horizons, or illusions, or limitations of knowledge',[44] religion prominent among them.

To conclude, let's return to the scene of confrontation in *The Monastery* that was analysed earlier in this essay. After young Halbert says he won't bless the departing English captain because he's a 'Southron', and Edward asks whether it's right to bless a 'heretic', their mother replies: 'The God to whom I pray only knows [...] but these two words, Southron and heretic, have already cost Scotland ten thousand of her best and bravest, and me a husband, and you a father; and, whether blessing or banning, I never wish to hear them more' (p. 42). Dame Glendinning, in other words, already understands what Latour and others have later argued: that mutual understanding and recognition, if and when they can be forged, require putting aside the terms and domains to which we are accustomed, and necessitate attempts instead to describe as faithfully as possible the networks of relations through which our own and others' modes of existence are instaured. Only then might we make good on the promise of what Felski hopes lies beyond critique: 'a positive vision [...] that is willing to recognize the potential of literature and art to create new imaginaries rather than just to denounce mystifying illusions'.[45] Or as the White Lady puts it during her pivotal encounter with Halbert halfway through *The Monastery*,

> Happiest they of human race,
> To whom God has granted grace,
> To read, to fear, to hope, to pray,
> To lift the latch, and find the way;
> And better had they ne'er been born,
> Who read to doubt, or read to scorn. (p. 115)

[44] Charles Taylor, *A Secular Age* (Cambridge, MA: Belknap Press, 2007), p. 22.
[45] Felski, *Limits of Critique*, p. 187.

'In Contrast to Those Whom We Have Called Materialists, Mr. [Scott] Is Spiritual': On Scott and Woolf, Romance and 'Fullness of Life'

MATTHEW WICKMAN

Brigham Young University

In the final section of Part One in *To the Lighthouse*, Mrs. Ramsay sees her husband

> reading something that moved him very much. He was half smiling and then she knew he was controlling his emotion. He was tossing the pages over. He was acting it — perhaps he was thinking himself the person in the book. She wondered what book it was. Oh, it was one of Sir Walter's she saw.

At a dinner party earlier that night, discussion had turned to the influence of Walter Scott's fiction: '[H]ow long do you think it'll last?' said somebody. Mrs. Ramsay 'scented danger for her husband', a writer who, himself, courted influence. 'A question like that would lead, almost certainly, to something being said which reminded him of his own failure. How long would he be read — he would think at once.'[1] Later in the evening, Mrs. Ramsay finds her premonitions confirmed. 'Don't interrupt me, he seemed to be saying' to her as she gazes at him turning the pages;

> just sit there. And he went on reading. His lips twitched. It filled him. It fortified him. [...] This man's strength and sanity, his feeling for straightforward simple things, these fishermen, the poor old crazed creature in Mucklebackit's cottage made him feel so vigorous, so relieved of something that he felt roused and triumphant and could not choke back his tears.[2]

Given Mr. Ramsay's pathetic standing in the novel as an arch solipsist, a black hole consuming others' sympathy and good will, his love for Scott's novel *The Antiquary*, and specifically for the scene in which the family of Steenie Mucklebackit mourns the young fisherman's loss at sea, seems damning of Scott and his legacy. Accordingly, this episode in *To the Lighthouse* has attracted a fair degree of scholarly attention as a bellwether of literary history, a symbolic passing

---

[1] Virginia Woolf, *To the Lighthouse* (San Diego, CA: Harcourt Brace Jovanovich, 1927), p. 107.
[2] Woolf, *To the Lighthouse*, pp. 119–20.

Yearbook of English Studies, 47 (2017), 93–109
© Modern Humanities Research Association 2017

of the torch from Scott's historico-realism to modernist explorations of the psyche. Some critics observe that this episode in the novel accentuates a family drama of Woolf's own: Mr. Ramsay has long been seen as a type for Woolf's father, Leslie Stephen, whose love for the Waverley novels finds its mirror in the books that line the shelves of the Ramsays' Hebridean home.[3] Judith Wilt more expansively connects this Freudian primal scene to a Bloomian case of anxiety, with Mr. Ramsay's taste in fiction enabling Woolf to indicate, in negative, her own aesthetic departure from Scott. Against the vector of 'history' personified by the putative father of historical fiction, Woolf appeals to a literary principle of 'life', 'a personal allusive field of energies in which the data of the senses dance mote-like in the fitful rays of the imagination'.[4]

Wilt's reflections about this passage in *To the Lighthouse* echo Woolf's in her 1925 essay 'Modern Fiction'. The problem with 'materialists', as Woolf calls Scott's literary progeny (in this essay, realists like Arnold Bennett), is that they make fictions 'solid in [their] craftsmanship' but lacking in more essential qualities. What 'if life should refuse to live' in these edifices of material objects? Woolf wonders. For what 'life' demands of writers is that they 'record the atoms as they fall upon the mind in the order in which they fall'. Instead of expending 'immense skill and immense industry making the trivial and the transitory appear the true and the enduring' — instead of exhaustively delineating contexts, both tangible and historical, and thus moving, with Mr. Ramsay, from Q to R, or to realism and the history that subtends it — Woolf proposes that writers 'trace the pattern, however disconnected and incoherent in appearance, which each sight or incident scores upon the consciousness'.[5]

That said, Mr. Ramsay's choice of Scott's novels, *The Antiquary*, complicates any neat dialectic between 'life' and 'history' in *To the Lighthouse*. Wilt discerns as much; and so, she remarks, does Mr. Ramsay: '"Roused and triumphant," he recognizes "life" in Scott's "feeling for straight-forward simple things, these fishermen, the poor old crazed creature in Mucklebackit's cottage."'[6] And indeed, *The Antiquary* is hardly a conventionally 'historical' novel, for, set in the recent past, it deals less with historical events than with the relationship between *history* as a coherent, 'engineered' narrative of the past and *antiquarianism* as a random

---

[3] See, both substantively and indicatively, Alice van Buren Kelley, *To the Lighthouse: The Marriage of Life and Art* (Boston, MA: Twayne, 1987), pp. 31–38.

[4] Judith Wilt, 'Steamboat Surfacing: Scott and the English Novelists,' *Nineteenth-Century Fiction*, 35 (1981), 459–86 (p. 477).

[5] Virginia Woolf, 'Modern Fiction', in Woolf, *Collected Essays*, 2 vols (London: Hogarth Press, 1966), II, 104, 107. I refer to the scene in *To the Lighthouse* in which Mr. Ramsay muses that 'thought is like the keyboard of a piano, divided into so many notes, or like the alphabet is ranged in twenty-six letters all in order [...] He reached Q. Very few people in the whole of England ever reach Q [...] R is then — what is R?' (pp. 33–34).

[6] Wilt, 'Steamboat Surfacing,' pp. 479–80.

collection of the past's artefacts and anecdotes, a kind of *bricolage*.[7] Reflecting on this latter aspect of Scott's novel, and on his fiction generally, Ina Ferris remarks that '[n]ineteenth-century European novels [...] display a marked fascination with obsolescence', in an almost antiquarian-like manner, such that 'literature became the repository for what the culture at large had consigned to nonfunctional oblivion'.[8] The observation seems almost to unify Scott and Woolf, for 'life' in Woolf's terms does not *progress* per se; as such, it falls outside the ambit of 'history'. And if Woolf was drawn to *The Antiquary* in particular it may be because that novel demonstrates, more than a preoccupation with history's leading characters, what Jane Millgate calls 'a profound concern with the fullness of individual lives'.[9]

And yet, Woolf still found *The Antiquary* lacking in its essential commitment to an aesthetic of vitality, to the contingencies that 'history' overlooks. As she wrote in an essay on *The Antiquary*, 'There are some writers who have entirely ceased to influence others, whose fame is for that reason both serene and cloudless, who are enjoyed or neglected rather than criticized and read. Among them is Scott.' Who truly enjoys reading him? His 'style is execrable [...] Old metaphors out of the property box come flapping their dusty wings across the sky'.[10] He is 'slovenly' where Robert Louis Stevenson is 'precise'. What is worse, Scott has no capacity to capture the minutiae of consciousness, the atoms falling on the mind: 'we may as well talk of the hearts of seagulls and the passions and intricacies of walking sticks and umbrellas'. Are not Scott's characters, 'all of them, Ochiltrees, Antiquaries, Dandy Dinmonts, and the rest, merely bundles of humours, and innocent childish humours at that, who serve to beguile our dull hours and charm our sick ones, and are packed off to the nursery when the working day returns and our normal faculties crave something tough to set their teeth into?'[11] This is why, Wilt observes, Mr. Ramsay 'could not remember the whole shape of the thing' when he put down Scott's novel. For Woolf, *The Antiquary* 'is not a harmonious living thing but a flotsam of living water and dead fiddlesticks'.[12]

---

[7] Derrida expounds on engineering and bricolage as the difference between the manufacturing of a whole, seamless entity and the cobbling together of fragments. See 'Structure, Sign, and Play in the Discourse of the Human Sciences', in *Writing and Difference*, trans. by Alan Bass (Chicago, IL: University of Chicago Press, 1978), pp. 278–93 (p. 285).

[8] Ina Ferris, '"On the Borders of Oblivion": Scott's Historical Novel and the Modern Time of the Remnant', *Modern Language Quarterly*, 70 (2009), 473–94 (p. 483).

[9] Jane Millgate, *Walter Scott: The Making of the Novelist* (Toronto: University of Toronto Press, 1987), p. 92. See Natasha Tessone's fuller discussion of this principle by way of an analysis of Aristotle in 'Tending to the (National) Household: Walter Scott's *The Antiquary* and "that happy commerce" of the Enlightenment', *Eighteenth-Century Fiction*, 26 (2013/14), 261–80 (pp. 273–74).

[10] Woolf, '*The Antiquary*', in *Collected Essays*, I, 139.

[11] Ibid., I, 140, 142.

[12] Wilt, 'Steamboat Surfacing,' p. 483.

This forms the basis for a substantial drama unfolding in this episode of *To the Lighthouse*, for Woolf is the first novelist, Wilt argues, who escapes Scott's gravitational pull: 'The great modernists who are her contemporaries write distinctly within it [the Waverley tradition]. [...] Even those who hate "history" the most, Joyce and Lawrence, write novels of heroes whose unsuccessful attempts to "fly by the nets" of class, religion, race, nation, and sex seem a poignant recapitulation of the dilemmas of [such Scott protagonists as] Edward Waverley, Henry Morton, Quentin Durward, Wilfred of Ivanhoe, Edgar of Ravenswood, [and] Arthur Darsie Redgauntlet'.[13] Stephen Dedalus, Rupert Birkin (of Lawrence's *Women in Love*), and Edward Ashburnham (of Ford Madox Ford's *The Good Soldier*), for example, find themselves facing the dilemma whereby the world's inheritance passes irrevocably to those to whom it seemed not to belong; likewise, Edward Waverley, ultimately heir to a Scottish estate, was little more than an observer in the Jacobite Rebellion, but the vanquished Fergus Mac-Ivor personified it. 'One thinks above all of the perplexing ending of *Old Mortality*, the splendid demonic Burley suddenly dead in the river, the splendid angelic Lord Evandale suddenly shot on the estate, and the survivors, Edith and Morton, gazing shell-shocked, not at each other, but ahead, into a future which suddenly, finally, emptily, belongs only to them.'[14] Wilt's point here is not so much that Scott buries such characters *in* history as that he repeatedly deploys them to peek out *from* history in moments of 'life'. That archaeological sensibility, that unearthing of what history buries: that is the reliquary aura that Oldbuck, Ochiltree, and Mucklebackit exude in *The Antiquary*. Ultimately, however, Scott still *believes* in history, whereas the characters of Woolf's contemporaries — the Dedaluses and Ashburnhams — are merely trapped by it.

What thereby seems missing in these later novels, most notably, is the fusion of 'a providential as well as a self-created future'.[15] Stephen Dedalus feels little compulsion to reconcile himself to history, for there is little inherent meaning in it. 'Transcendentally homeless', as Georg Lukács put it, the modern subject is no longer at one with its environment, social or natural.[16] In a still more modern (and yet, in some ways deeply traditional) parlance, what this struggle underscores — what Woolf seems intent on refashioning — is a sense of *spiritual connectedness*.

It is Woolf who provides us with this term of analysis, the *spiritual*. It is an odd term, seeming at once so resonant with and yet contrary to present-day

[13] Ibid., p. 484.
[14] Ibid., p. 485.
[15] Ibid., p. 485.
[16] Georg Lukács, *Theory of the Novel*, trans. by Anna Bostock (Cambridge, MA: The MIT Press, 1971), p. 41.

sensibilities. The spiritual, both as Woolf intends it and as it exceeds her intentions (leading us back to Scott), is the subject of my essay. She employs it in 'Modern Fiction' to distinguish 'the work of several young writers from that of their predecessors'. These young modernists 'attempt to come closer to *life* [...] even if to do so they must discard most of the conventions which are commonly observed by the novelist.' Most noticeable here is Joyce: 'in contrast with those whom we have called materialists, Mr. Joyce is spiritual.'[17] This may appear to be an eccentric way to characterize the author of *A Portrait of the Artist as a Young Man*, given that novel's dramatic rejection of religion. But then again, spirituality is not necessarily a religious category.[18] One useful way to think about it as it figures in Woolf's essay — indeed, as it stretches from Woolf back to Scott — is as a set of 'intuitions that can lead to fullness of life'.[19] This broad definition, proffered by Elisabeth Hense (and echoing Jane Millgate's remark about Scott's concern with 'the 'fullness of individual lives'), provokes thought. While evoking fulfilment, it implies in the immediate sense a failure to secure it, a bifurcation of actual from ideal, or at least ameliorable, circumstances (in Joyce's case, the tendentious effort to evade history altogether) and thus suggests a kind of restlessness and an impulse toward revisionism. In *To the Lighthouse*, it characterizes, for example, the relationship between Lily Briscoe's various, occasionally humiliating encounters with the Ramsay clan and their guests (Tansley, Carmichael, and others) — the material facets of her existence in the novel — and her ultimate 'vision', the 'sudden intensity' that compels her to 'draw a line there, in the centre' of her painting, and on that basis to arrive at a sense of climactic meaning about her experience, if not her entire existence: 'It was done; it was finished.'[20]

While that last phrase from the conclusion of Woolf's novel is allusively religious (echoing Christ's last words on the cross[21]), the structure of 'spiritual' affect in that episode is nothing liturgical, but corresponds instead to the logic of romance in converting desire into closure and fragment into meaning. Romance is a key category for Scott, of course, representing not only a modality

---

[17] Woolf, 'Modern Fiction', in *The Collected Essays*, II, 106–07 (my emphasis).

[18] This is a trend that has garnered increasing attention. Paul Heelas and Linda Woodhead were bringing attention to it more than a decade ago: 'Survey after survey shows that increasing numbers of people now prefer to call themselves "spiritual" rather than "religious."' *The Spiritual Revolution: Why Religion is Giving Way to Spirituality* (Malden, MA: Blackwell, 2005), p. 1.

[19] Elisabeth Hense, 'Introduction: Present-Day Spiritualities in Confessional, Popular, Professional and Aesthetic Contexts: Contrasts or Overlap?', in *Present-Day Spiritualities: Contrasts and Overlaps* (Leiden: Brill, 2014), pp. 1–20 (p. 5).

[20] *To the Lighthouse*, p. 209. For a fuller, and different exposition of the meaning of spirituality in *To the Lighthouse*, see Sharon Kim, *Literary Epiphany in the Novel, 1850–1950: Constellations of the Soul* (New York: Palgrave Macmillan, 2012), pp. 109–26.

[21] King James Bible, John 19. 30.

of narrative but also the texture of history: the difference of fiction from fact and present from past.[22] But what, we might wonder, is to be gained by examining romance in concert with a broadly conceived spirituality and not as an agent of difference only? We may intuit one answer from conventional associations of spirituality with the immaterial, as Woolf did in differentiating Joyce from his realist peers and also from a tradition defined by history and its materialist premises. In that respect, Joyce is spiritual because he sublimates history into something at once more abstract and affective. Channelling 'life', Joyce is not (of) Scott (at least, if we agree with Woolf rather than Wilt). But is even Scott of Scott? Reflect for a moment on what we called, above, Scott's *belief* in history, a belief that is only necessary because history is not entirely *there* — that it, too, is at least partly immaterial, an abstraction. This is where the mediating presence of romance in evoking that history becomes most provocative, for romance lends that immateriality a gritty quality; it makes ethereality substantive by lending the past a sensible, narrative form. As Woolf decried, spirituality for Scott involves precisely these remainders — aspects of experience (or stylistic features of romance: the '[o]ld metaphors […] flapping their dusty wings') that, as Ferris observes, culture had consigned to obsolescence. In Hense's terms, romance for Scott thus yields intuitions of a fullness — composed not of narrative alone, but of a living past and vision of a future that takes narrative form — that would not be sought were it already found, and whose impetus is discovered less in historical traces per se than in their erasures, the evocative worlds that remain unrealized or unredeemed. Hence, 'fullness' as a romantic feature of non-closure (seeking to account for elements that fall outside its own narrative frame, or perhaps are displaced by it) exists in tension with 'life' as an aesthetic principle of modern fiction, an instant of almost transcendent self-sufficiency. And the 'spiritual', seeking a 'fullness of life' precisely because that union proves elusive, resides between them.

The present essay takes up these dynamics in *The Antiquary* and *To the Lighthouse*. Woolf's novel may conjure Scott for the apparent purpose of exorcizing him — what she deems spiritual may appear to be what is *not* Scott — but that introduces a contradiction. For, if Scott's version of romance retains traces of what otherwise would be forgotten, then his presence in a novel that seeks to surpass him converts him into an uncanny, not-to-be-forgotten totem, a haunting presence — indeed, a kind of *spirit*. Woolf thus returns to Scott in the very gesture of taking leave from him, a 'dispiriting' detail at the heart of her

---

[22] In his essay 'Of Romance', Scott observes that 'Romance and real history have the same common origin', but that romance retains the trace of past superstitions. Hence, romance is 'a fictitious narrative turning upon the marvellous or supernatural.' 'Of Romance', in *The Miscellaneous Prose Works of Sir Walter Scott*, 6 vols (Boston, MA: Wells and Lilly, 1829), VI, 103–04.

spiritual economy. To that extent, the spiritual for Scott and Woolf is found less in transcendence (a conventional feature of spirituality[23]) than in the *failure* to reconcile 'life' to 'fullness', the 'energies' of individuals to the history that exceeds them. Romance becomes the record, indeed, the very form of this failure. It is this failure, precisely, that motivates belief — whether in history (Scott) or in what surpasses it (Woolf) — in the first place.

* * *

While 'spirituality' is not a word one frequently encounters in studies of Scott, one occasionally breezes past *spirit*. Consistent with its usage elsewhere, spirit here is varied, more evocative than definitive, and usually a little obscure. For Wilt, the term bears at least three meanings: Scott's quasi-Hegelian ethos in the eyes of Thomas Carlyle ('What makes *Ivanhoe* the imaginative ground of *Past and Present*' is the way Scott depicts characters 'bound to each other subtly, beyond all genuine hostilities, by the prime Spirit at work in man, the Spirit that gets Work done'), a stylistic feature of Scott's fiction ('the spirit of th[e] reign' of 'carnal language'), and also an energy of mind or character (the 'carnal language' to which she refers features in a text like *Old Mortality*, 'stand[ing] beside the rival spirits, often "shining," "fiery," or highly colored, in each text of each novel').[24] Ian Duncan, to cite one other instance, invokes spirit to characterize something like an inner essence: the song with which Flora Mac-Ivor beguiles the young Edward Waverley as he is gradually inducted into the Jacobite cause 'is a translation, literally, the movement of the spirit', and Scott himself is plumbing 'the spirit of romance' as a 'poignancy of private feeling' 'outside historical meaning'.[25] In effect, the 'spirit of romance' is Woolf's 'life'.

These are only a few examples, picked largely at random from a vast corpus of iterations. But they effectively illustrate a range of meanings 'spirit' acquires in Scott criticism: rarely, if ever, sectarian (through reference, say, to the Holy Spirit), more frequently in association with history (by adopting the vocabulary of Hegel, Carlyle, or Hazlitt: the 'spirit of the age'), and perhaps most often bearing a colloquial but nonetheless conceptual charge (as with Duncan's analysis of the 'spirit of romance'). Usually the word itself goes undefined, evoking something redolent of mind or mood but left intentionally vague, such that *spirit*

[23] The Christian theological scholar Sandra M. Schneiders, for example, defines spirituality, generically, as 'the actualization of the basic human capacity for transcendence'. 'Approaches to the Study of Christian Spirituality', in *The Blackwell Companion to Christian Spirituality*, ed. by Arthur Holder (Malden, MA: Wiley-Blackwell, 2011), pp. 15–34 (p. 16).

[24] Judith Wilt, *Secret Leaves: The Novels of Walter Scott* (Chicago, IL: University of Chicago Press, 1985), pp. 10, 85.

[25] Ian Duncan, *Modern Romance and Transformations of the Novel: The Gothic, Scott, Dickens* (Cambridge: Cambridge University Press, 1992), p. 83.

is put to what we might call 'spiritual' use, pregnant with a meaning that never materializes into anything concrete. Scott himself was leery of such spirits, which is not to say he never trafficked in them. In a different essay from the ones I cite above, Woolf declared Wandering Willie's tale in Scott's *Redgauntlet* 'one of the finest ghost stories'.[26] '[T]he existence of spirits', Scott remarks in his 1830 *Letters on Demonology and Witchcraft*, is 'the universal belief of the inhabitants of the earth.' And he had 'travelled in the twilight regions of superstitious disquisitions. Many hours have I lost [...] in examining old, as well as more recent narratives of this character.'[27] Naturally, what follows this confession is more than 300 pages of such stories, such that, in their own way, the *Letters on Demonology* form something of a precursor to William James's early psycho-sociological study *The Varieties of Religious Experience*.

But this paints too narrow a picture of both Scott and things 'spiritual'. For Wesley J. Wildman, diverse branches of scholarly inquiry into the subject of spiritual experience yield a theory of *intensity*, a nexus of affective over-determination connecting 'phenomenological, neurological, evolutionary, [and] philosophical [as well as] theological claims'. For all the interdisciplinary range of these fields, it is of particular note that they bear on visceral states widely identified with literary history — the 'liminal, profound, numinous, extreme, transcendental, traumatic, sublime', and so on: William Wordsworth's para-digmatic 'state of excitement' and scores of subsequent avatars.[28] What is more, in naming existential qualities that negotiate the relationship between the mundane and the extraordinary (traditionally, in the religious correlation of seen and unseen worlds), spiritual experience also situates such experience in a space akin, if not homologous, to the one traditionally delimited by romance — the 'here' and 'there' of imagination expressed by way of the 'now' and 'then' of dialectical history (e.g., the religious sectarianism of ages past dissolving into folk history and literary culture: Scott's *Letters on Demonology*, for instance). In this respect, the unpacking of spiritual experience as an academic subject yields not only cultural evolution — the shift from religious to poetic faith evident in the secular appeal to something like what Duncan calls 'the spirit of romance' — but also a historical concept of fiction as a medium of transport between material and more ethereal (but evocative) states of being.

---

[26] Woolf, 'The Supernatural in Fiction', in *Collected Essays*, I, 294. See too Evan Gottlieb's essay in this volume.

[27] Walter Scott, *Letters on Demonology and Witchcraft: Addressed to J. G. Lockhart, esq.* (New York: A. L. Fowle, 1900), pp. 15, 14.

[28] Wesley J. Wildman, *Religious and Spiritual Experiences* (Cambridge: Cambridge University Press, 2011), pp. 104–05 and William Wordsworth, 'Preface' to *Lyrical Ballads*, ed. by W. J. B. Owen (Oxford: Oxford University Press, 1969), p. 158.

Note that I refrain from providing a theological definition of spirituality — the meaning of spirit in this or that religious tradition. Instead, my point is intentionally more general, more attuned to the status of spirit in Scott criticism. Simply put, spirituality in Scott invites reflection on the dialectical history of genre, one of the subjects in which Scott figures most centrally. The logic is circular: a reading *of* Scott yields an idea of reading *by way of* Scott. Better said, the logic is spiral-like, Hegelian, which is to say, spiritual (or *geistig*): the particular, present as 'spirit' in a text like Scott's *Letters*, resolves itself into the form of the general, or the 'spirit of romance' that Scott's work helps us conceptualize. The matter of spirit thus becomes integral to our understanding of Scott, just as Scott becomes central to our understanding of the spiritual as a modern category of literature.

What is more, the spiritual helps us conceptualize the difference between the incidents and economy of romance, between *what happens* (in a particular text) and *why it happens* (in *any* text), between the *contingencies* of individual narratives and the *desire* that fuels the appeal of the genre. Consider a distinction Wildman draws between 'anomalous' and 'ultimate' spiritual experiences. The former consist of singular events — 'hallucination[s], synesthesia [...] out-of-body experiences' and the types of supernatural or fantastic encounters of which Scott writes in his *Letters*.[29] 'Ultimate' spiritual experiences, meanwhile, 'bring orientation and coping power, inspire great acts of courage and devotion, underlie key life decisions, and heavily influence social affiliation.'[30] If incidents are the 'anomalous', contingent elements of narrative, 'ultimate' effects describe the impetus behind such narrative, a reason why we are drawn to stories in the first place. In essence, romance folds anomaly into ultimacy, incident into purpose. Hence, and to bring us full circle, if we fail to understand the meaning of the spiritual in Scott then we fail to understand both Scott and the concept of literature, the modern iteration of romance, that takes root in him.

In light of this disclosure, Woolf's implication that Scott is a 'material' rather than a 'spiritual' writer becomes more enigmatic. So does Scott's novel *The Antiquary*, which represents for Woolf a conflict between these literary principles. This was Scott's third novel, published in May 1816. It tells the story of two wayward lovers, Major Neville (known as Lovel throughout most of the novel) and Isabella Wardour, the daughter of a financially straitened Scottish baronet. Lovel and Isabella meet and fall in love in England, but because Lovel is believed to be the illegitimate son of Edward Neville, brother to the Earl of Glenallan, and because Isabella knows that her father would never approve of such a union, she breaks their courtship and returns to Scotland. Lovel follows

---

[29] Wildman, *Religious and Spiritual Experiences*, p. 82.
[30] Wildman, p. 84.

her, meeting en route Jonathan Oldbuck: the antiquary. Oldbuck is a friend and old foil to Isabella's father and takes compassion on Lovel as he comes to learn of his circumstances. Eventually, Oldbuck uncovers the truth of Lovel's birth, that he is actually the legitimate son and heir of the earl, enabling Lovel and Isabella to wed. So goes the main plot. In this novel, however, more even than in most Scott novels, the main story is less interesting than its subplots. For, along the way, we encounter a wide cast of colourful characters: Edie Ochiltree, a beggar who is also a storehouse of local knowledge; Herman Dousterswivel, a German charlatan who dupes the desperate Arthur Wardour out of his money in a treasure-hunting scheme; Steenie Mucklebackit, a young fisherman who assists Edie in subjecting Dousterswivel to his own chicanery; Captain Hector M'Intyre, Oldbuck's nephew, who becomes a temporary rival to Lovel and then is wounded by him in a duel; Elspeth Mucklebackit, Steenie's grandmother, an aged medium of folklore and dark secrets; and more. The novel, in fact, vacillates between unfolding its plot and indulging in set pieces designed around these characters — pieces that, in Woolf's mind, at once open and obscure windows onto 'spirit', onto 'life'.

Building on this impression, Scott presents *The Antiquary* as a kind of dialectic of enchantment and demystification (or, perhaps better said, enchantment and enchanted demystification). Similarly to *Guy Mannering*, the novel Scott had published the previous year, *The Antiquary* draws on elements of gothic fiction: characters with shrouded pasts, mysteries embedded in ancient locales, and so on. Oldbuck shares Scott's own bemused fascination with the supernatural, indulging repeatedly in what Ochiltree, the sage mendicant, calls 'auld-warld stories' that 'the mind o' man canna resist' pertaining to 'Strange and Wonderful News […] of certain Apparitions', tales of 'imagination […] akin to miracle-working faith', and 'theories out of premises which were often far from affording sufficient ground for them'.[31] At the same time, Oldbuck regards such stories with contempt when he is not their raconteur: although gullible when it comes to history (for instance, erroneously extrapolating from one of his books that a mound near his estate is the ruined site of a Roman settlement), he nevertheless, Ochiltree says, 'has unco little sympathy wi' ither folks' in their illusions. 'He'll listen the hale day, an' ye'll tell him about tales o' Wallace, and Blind Harry, and Davie Lindsay, but ye maunna speak to him about ghaists or fairies, or spirits walking the earth, or the like o' that.'[32] Belief for Oldbuck is thus conditional, ambivalent, causing him to quarantine the magical worldview he otherwise indulges.

---

[31] *The Antiquary*, ed. by Nicola J. Watson (Oxford: Oxford University Press, 2002), pp. 26, 37, 93, and 133.
[32] Ibid., p. 213.

But, of course, that is part of the more general enchantment of Scott's novel, such that the partial disbelief felt by Oldbuck (indeed, by several of Scott's characters) becomes a vehicle for the suspended disbelief of Scott's readers. These dynamics are on clear display in the subplot involving Dousterswivel, for example, whose attempt to defraud Sir Arthur takes the form of a treasure-hunting scheme in some rustic ruins on Wardour's own property. Dousterswivel leads Sir Arthur to the scene and pretends to discover buried riches through a theatrical 'suffumigation' that raises imaginary spirits from the dead to guide the search. But Ochiltree and Mucklebackit, who have learned of the scheme, hide in the ruins and stage supernatural effects that terrify Dousterswivel — causing the latter to believe that his game of make-believe is true despite its self-arranged artifice. '[T]hough far more an impostor than a dupe, he was not without a certain degree of personal faith even in the gross superstitions by means of which he imposed on others.'[33] But in one respect, Scott's readers are placed in a similar position to Dousterswivel: although they know all about the latter's plot, and are party to the counter-scheme prosecuted by Ochiltree and Mucklebackit, the dramatic ruins in which the scene is set — 'a cave [...] screened by the boughs of an aged oak [...] form[ing] an emblem of the cross, and indicat[ing] the abode of an anchoret of former times'[34] — is so evocatively portrayed that it gives natural expression to the enchantment of which the characters otherwise disabuse themselves. The raising of spirits in *The Antiquary* thus reflects Duncan's point concerning the status of astrology — and, more generally, romance — in *Guy Mannering*: 'No longer having faith in the truth of the imaginary science, [Mannering — here, Dousterswivel] engages it, in a complex way, as a fiction. Yet not despite but because of that mode of engagement, all is true.'[35]

By Scott's understanding of romance, the supernatural carries with it vestiges of the past. And, as part of a world of outlived forms, Dousterswivel's labile 'suffumigation' resonates (in an antique way) with what Ina Ferris calls 'a rich lexicon of words' that by 1800 'had achieved a high profile across a broad sector of European cultures: *traces, vestiges, relics, ruins, remains*, and so forth.'[36] Timothy Campbell shows how this 'lexicon' informed even the hyperpresentist logic of fashion, which 'reconstituted old models as new by infusing them with all the allure of novelty and presence', such that the past retained its power even through processes that purported to supersede it.[37] In *The Antiquary*, this logic

---

[33] Ibid., p. 241.

[34] Ibid., p. 202.

[35] Duncan, *Modern Romance*, pp. 129–30.

[36] Ferris, '"On the Borders of Oblivion"', p. 477, original emphases.

[37] Timothy Campbell, 'Pennant's Guillotine and Scott's Antiquary: The Romantic End of the Present', in *Romantic Circles* (2014), para. 22 <http://www.rc.umd.edu/praxis/antiquarianism/index.html> [accessed 19 July 2016].

inscribes competing versions of historiography. As Ferris argues in a different essay, antiquarianism, increasingly ridiculed by the early nineteenth century, nevertheless 'overlapped with the enlightenment historian in important ways', rooting historical labour in empirical fact and thus 'effecting a break with an older humanist mode of narrative political history.' Antiquarianism acquires force in Scott's novel precisely when, and because, it is no longer entirely present. The process is akin to what I am calling enchanted demystification: 'Even as he cannot quite let go of the antiquary, [Scott] finally aligns himself and his fictional project with historian's history.'[38]

These scholarly perspectives, drawing upon different nuances in *The Antiquary*, underscore not only the play of present and past, but also the *presence* of the past, the force it exerts on a modern era that has self-consciously, if not self-confidently, surpassed it. Duncan expounds on this point in language evocative of Woolf when he remarks that '*The Antiquary*, of all Scott's novels, is the one most devoted to a representation of common *life*', with the added wrinkle that '[n]ational character resides most distinctively among' this group of 'common' people 'because, in effect, they belong to a *still-living past*.'[39] The significance of this past even amidst its obsolescence, its retention of value on precisely this basis, is an expression of what I call, above, the spiritual quality of form in Scott's work — spiritual because the past's remainders, swept up into a system of romance, are given a charge of what Wildman calls 'intensity'. A better word, in fact, would be 'ultimacy', the term Wildman employs to denote experiences characterized by their meaning rather than their ('anomalous') strangeness. And this tells us something about the significance of romance for Scott. He may express ambivalence about ghosts, but the same is not the case with romance; the latter is not a *vehicle* of meaning in Scott's fiction, it is the overdetermined site and source of *meaning itself*. This is less a biographical observation about Scott than a formal one, as a novel like *The Antiquary* essentially takes romance itself (evident in the dance between antiquarian and enlightenment history — the sanctification-through-burial of older by more modern historical modes) as its subject matter. As such, *The Antiquary*, bringing romance under special scrutiny, goes a step further than conventional literary self-reflexivity. Where literary self-consciousness typically indicates awareness of the conditions whereby a work imagines itself into existence (think, for example, of *Hamlet*'s play within a play as a commentary on theatricality), *The Antiquary* dramatizes and almost exaggerates a feature of the Waverley novels generally: it expresses a desire not only to account for the conditions of the

---

[38] Ina Ferris, 'Pedantry and the Question of Enlightenment History: The Figure of the Antiquary in Scott', *European Romantic Review*, 13.3 (2002), 273–83 (pp. 274, 278).

[39] Ian Duncan, *Scott's Shadow: The Novel in Romantic Edinburgh* (Princeton, NJ: Princeton University Press, 2007), pp. 139, 140, my emphases.

present, but also to retain traces of what the present forgets, of what it renders *immaterial*. In thematizing the tension between the 'novel', the *new*, and the history it outmodes, *The Antiquary* accords *ultimacy* to what otherwise would seem to have disappeared. It makes the ethereal substantive. In Scott's hands, romance virtually sacralizes the past, rendering it essential in its apparent displacement.

This is what alternately draws and repels Woolf. Episodes in *The Antiquary* can seem so vital and yet so vacuous, so deft in capturing their moment even as they traffic in the kinds of gritty remainders, the leaden qualities, that taint the alchemy of pure inspiration. Hence, the 'fullness' of Scott's fiction is not quite the 'life' to which Woolf aspires in her own. As an illustration, we might think again of the episode to which Mr. Ramsay turns: the scene in Mucklebackit's cottage. The scene, Scott's narrator announces (with Oldbuck playing the voyeuristic stand-in for the reader), is one 'which our Wilkie alone could have painted',[40] invoking the intimate domestic genre portraits of the early nineteenth-century painter David Wilkie. Later, when Oldbuck returns to the cottage, the narrator invokes the play of light and shade characteristic of Rembrandt.[41] The narrative thus foregrounds its own artifice, and what proceeds is detailed attention to various corners of its canvas: the father ('whose rugged weather-beaten countenance, shaded by his grizzled hair [...] revolv[ed] his loss in his mind with that strong feeling of painful grief, peculiar to harsh and rough characters'[42]), the mother ('her face covered by her apron', but nevertheless visibly expressing sorrow by way of 'the convulsive agitation of the bosom which the covering could not conceal'[43]), two village 'gossips' ('officiously whispering into her ear the commonplace topic of resignation under irremediable misfortune'[44]), the grandmother, Elspeth (only half-conscious, reaching habitually, 'mechanically', for her 'spindle' and 'distaff' despite the fact that 'both had been laid aside', gazing 'upon the bed which contained the coffin of her grandson, as if she had once, and for the first time, acquired sense to comprehend her inexpressible calamity'[45]), and the clergyman, Blattergowl ('a dreadful poser', though 'a good man' who, nonetheless, fails to console or instruct anyone[46]). The contrast between Elspeth and Blattergowl is especially important, as the former forges 'a connecting link between the surviving mourners and the dead corpse which they bewailed',[47] whereas the latter incurs 'at least impatience, if not scorn

[40] *The Antiquary*, p. 298.
[41] Ibid., see p. 309.
[42] Ibid., p. 298.
[43] Ibid., p. 299.
[44] Ibid., p. 299.
[45] Ibid., p. 300.
[46] Ibid., p. 301.
[47] Ibid., p. 300.

of his counsel'.[48] Indeed, within the logical unfolding of the scene, the very point of the clergyman's appearance is to illustrate the transfer of spiritual authority — the gravitas of ultimacy — from the church to the folk, from traditional religious metaphysics to what Duncan, above, calls 'the still-living past'.

And yet, for readers like Woolf, this transfer remains incomplete to the extent that the narrative obtrudes on the folk through the ungainliness, the coarse materiality, of its own apparatus. 'Ultimacy' in the scene thus resides with the narrative rather than its subject. This is made evident through the imposition of awkward vernacular formalities (as when Mucklebackit's coffin draws the description of 'the last mansion of mortality'[49]) and broad socio-logical generalizations (as the narrative zooms out to pontificate about how 'the Scottish peasantry are still infected with that rage for funeral ceremonial'[50]), and also through the clear orchestration of the scene for a privileged viewer: Oldbuck and, by implication, the reader. Oldbuck even returns to the cottage for an encore performance: he 'had been so much struck with the deportment of the fisherman and his mother, that, moved by compassion, and perhaps also, in some degree, by that curiosity which induces us to seek out even what gives us pain to witness, he preferred a solitary walk up the coast, for the purpose of again visiting the cottage as he passed.'[51] None of this seems contrary to Scott's narrative purpose; rather, everything is brought to bravura effect. For Scott, the spiritual qualities of romance are thus found less in the *folk* than in the *form* that preserves them.

This conflict, in fact, seems to be what so moves Woolf's Mr. Ramsay:

> he went on reading. His lips twitched. It filled him. It fortified him. He clean forgot all the little rubs and digs of the evening [...] as [the dinner company] passed his books over as if they didn't exist at all. But now, he felt, it didn't matter a damn who reached Z (if thought ran like an alphabet from A to Z). Somebody would reach it — if not he, then another. [Scott's] strength and sanity, his feeling for straightforward simple things, these fishermen, the poor old crazed creature in Mucklebackit's cottage made him feel so vigorous, so relieved of something that he felt roused and triumphant and could not choke back his tears. Raising his book a little to hide his face, he let them fall and shook his head from side to side and forgot himself completely [...] forgot his own bothers and failures completely in poor Steenie's drowning and Mucklebackit's sorrow (that was Scott at his best).[52]

This is Woolf's 'spirituality' on display. It exhibits, seamlessly, the mind of a narcissist who loves not what Scott achieves that he, himself, has not, but rather

---

[48] Ibid., p. 302.
[49] Ibid., p. 303.
[50] Ibid., p. 304.
[51] Ibid., p. 305.
[52] *To the Lighthouse*, pp. 119–20.

that someone like himself would read Scott despite the latter's all-too-gross humanity (as others may — surely will — read his own work, too). This drama of reading reveals the inner turmoil of a conflicted character, the 'life' of a man at once tragic and absurd. But to the degree that it divulges Mr. Ramsay's projection of his own anxieties onto the scene of Scott's novel, it also mirrors Scott's narrative impositions on the lives of his portrait peasants.

Woolf's literary spirituality thus recapitulates, and accentuates, the apparent deficiencies of Scott's. For this scene too, in *To the Lighthouse*, is about remainders; indeed, it valorizes such remainders as what is most spiritually true about Mr. Ramsay, if not about fiction itself. The difference, of course, is that in this episode in *To the Lighthouse* the remainders are made to seem organic to Mr. Ramsay's psyche. Here, the dialectical conflict inherent to Scott's fiction, the tension between form and content (the 'life' in Mucklebackit's cottage and the 'dusty metaphors', the somewhat clunky, painterly self-consciousness, of its exposition), is resolved in a virtually Hegelian display of 'spirit'. And yet, what Woolf's novel 'spiritualizes' is, precisely, the venerable status of these remainders in both Scott and Mr. Ramsay. And, with that very gesture, by effectively superseding Scott's romantic aesthetic, *To the Lighthouse* reprises Scott's 'spiritual' economy, including its failings — the 'fullness' it never quite resolves into 'life'. Paradoxically, then, by purging Scott of his contingencies of style, Woolf does to literary history what Scott does, for example, to the Jacobite Rebellion in *Waverley*, lending Scott's legacy a 'finish' it otherwise lacks and thus ensuring that Scott himself 'remains'.

In *To the Lighthouse*, then, Scott outlives Scott. In this respect, he effectively becomes his own Elspeth Mucklebackit, chanting at his loom in a way that sings to the Mr. Ramsays of the world — dinosaurs who survive their own moment and are still very much with us, still very much the burden the Mrs. Ramsays and the Lily Briscoes (and, autobiographically, the Virginia Woolfs) are forced to carry. But if Scott is converted into a remainder in Woolf's novel, we must remember that he 'romanticizes' remainders very much like these. And, in punctuating this fact, Woolf amplifies Scott's legacy as assuredly, if ambivalently, as such victims of history as Joyce's Stephen Dedalus and Ford's Edward Ashburnham. Scott's 'material' presence in *To the Lighthouse* is minimal, then, but his 'spirit' is everywhere.

* * *

Does Scott exist? For a novel like *To the Lighthouse*, this is not a simple matter of historical fact. It is almost akin to questions concerning the existence of God. Unlike Nietzsche's God, Scott is not dead for Woolf, even if he was never fully 'alive' either. And unlike Freud's Moses, he was not murdered by his tormented literary progeny (by Joyce, say, in a fit of 'Bloomian' transumption) and then accorded supernatural power in memory.[53] In Woolf's novel, Scott *remains* — which is to say, he acquires substance in and from a literary project that seeks to purge him. This is the logic of romance we unpacked above: made part of the texture of the narrative past and brought into being as an emblem of fiction, of what is not 'real' (or 'material'), Scott is conjured and exorcised with the same gesture. More to the point, this is also what renders him a *spiritual* presence, of what is with us despite or because of its uncanny evanescence.

Dynamics pertaining to influence, memory, and the uncanny are familiar in literary studies; Ferris's list of terms is a useful refrain here: '*traces, vestiges, relics, ruins, remains*, and so forth.' Introducing spirituality into this matrix, in some ways, simply repackages this set of perennial subjects that negotiate the presence of the past. In part, the present essay does as much by addressing spirituality by way of literary form, specifically romance. In other ways, however, spirituality marks out a slightly different territory from traces, or relics, or ruins, 'and so forth'. Spirituality suggests other associations, other definitions: *intensity, ultimacy, fullness of life.* A literary history that organizes itself around these latter principles does not bind itself to conventional history; instead, it expresses affinities between texts (formal and otherwise) through a series of topological relationships, bending literary periods into shapes governed less by what Woolf calls 'materialism' than by principles of 'life'.[54] Wai Chee Dimock's delineations of literature across 'deep time' have made these new shapes, these uncanny correspondences between texts and traditions, more familiar (for all their unforeseeable variety); more recently, Rosi Braidotti's appeal to a spirituality rooted in Deleuzean vitalism and 'becoming' has projected an image of what Woolf's poetics might look like refracted onto the scene of twenty-first-century subcultures, causes, and political movements — a literature energizing a perpetually reconceived and reconfigured public domain.[55]

As Scott so brilliantly illustrates, these moments of vitality are matters *of* and *for* history, certainly; but as Scott and Woolf jointly attest, spirituality does not concern history *only*. What it does perhaps most insistently is impart a conviction that literature is an exploration of meaning. 'Meaning' here, however, is multi-faceted: it designates not signification alone, but involves a list that evokes and

[53] I refer to Freud, *Moses and Monotheism*, trans. by Katherine Jones (New York: Vintage, 1939) and, by way of a pun to Joyce's character Leopold Bloom, Harold Bloom's *The Anxiety of Influence: A Theory of Poetry* (New York: Oxford University Press, 1973).

[54] Eric Hayot's *On Literary Worlds* (New York: Oxford University Press, 2012) presents a theory of what a post-period-driven literary studies might look like.

[55] See Dimock, *Through Other Continents: American Literature across Deep Time* (Princeton, NJ: Princeton University Press, 2006) and Rosi Braidotti, 'The Residual Spirituality in Critical Theory: A Case for Affirmative Postsecular Politics', in *Transformations of Religion and the Public Sphere: Postsecular Publics*, ed. by Rosi Braidotti, Bolette Blaagaard, Tobijn de Graauw, and Eva Midden (New York: Palgrave Macmillan, 2014).

differs from Ferris's, and that certainly presents interpretive challenges — a list that includes such terms as value, purpose, *raison d'être*, 'fullness of life'. By this reckoning, as I have argued is the case between Scott and Woolf — and precisely because 'fullness' is a promise that remains unrealized — literature becomes an exercise defined by its capacity to entertain contraries: those subsisting between 'materialism' and 'life', or between what is tangibly *there* and what is more elusively associated with 'being-there' (or, perhaps, with what is missing).[56] But if Scott teaches us anything, it is that the logic of contrariety, or of tense (even uncanny) coexistence, is not the same as that of progress, or of passing from one state to another. Hence, if spirituality's viability as a category of analysis is one lesson drawn from *To the Lighthouse*, then perhaps what we learn from *The Antiquary* is that materialism and spirituality potentially call upon the same resources of narrative —even, perhaps, as Scott inspires us to imagine, from the same pool of experience. It is not that we know one because of its *difference from* the other (we do not know antiquarianism because of its difference from enlightenment history, for example), but rather that we know one *through* the other, as a *remainder of* the other. For this reason, and for all the materialist contributions of the present era of scholarship — its attentiveness to archives and ideologies and more — we can no more expunge spirituality from literary studies than Woolf could reflect on 'life' without seeing Scott.

[56] I refer to the English translation of Martin Heidegger's *Dasein*, his term for human 'being'. In *Being and Time*, Heidegger lists 'spirit' in a litany of words that describe what proves elusive about that 'being': 'the subject, the soul, the consciousness, the spirit, the person.' As Woolf would appreciate, Heidegger articulates this list in the context of a discussion of Wilhelm Dilthey's 'philosophy of life.' *Being and Time*, trans. by John Macquarrie and Edward Robinson (New York: Harper Perennial, 1962), p. 72.

The Politics of Fear: Gothic Histories, the English Civil War and Walter Scott's *Woodstock*

FIONA PRICE

University of Chichester

In his 1824 essay on 'Sir Walter Scott' in the *New Monthly Magazine* William Hazlitt apostrophizes 'Wickliff, Luther, Hampden, Somers', those who 'are the cause we no longer burn witches and heretics [...] who have abated the cruelty of priests, the pride of nobles, the divinity of kings in former times'.[1] Evoking four centuries of religious and political reform, Hazlitt enters into the post-French Revolution struggle about the meaning of history, a struggle that is also a contest for ownership of the gothic. Like Mary Wollstonecraft in her *An Historical and Moral View of the French Revolution* (1794), Charlotte Smith in *Desmond* (1792), or William Godwin in his historical novel *St Leon* (1799), Hazlitt seeks to demystify feudalism and to present reform as a rational removal of superstitious tyranny. Yet while Hazlitt asserts that Scott's historical fictions normalize gothic oppression, Jane West and other conservative writers claimed that it was the radicals and dissenters who gothicized history in order to drive irrational reform. In this battle to deploy gothic and to claim the rational political high ground, the historical novel of the Civil War and the Commonwealth became an important site. Its pages restaged, in generic as well as political terms, the conflict between, on the one hand, radicalism and the dissent, and, on the other, Church and King.[2] Reading Scott's *Woodstock* (1826) against these earlier historical fictions, it becomes evident that the novel is a bitter exposé of this battle as anything but rational.

Although parallels between 1789 and the Glorious Revolution were commonplace in the 1790s and early 1800s, associations between radicalism and dissent led the women historical novelists Cassandra Cooke and Jane West to compare the period of the French Revolution with the earlier, mid-seventeenth

---

[1] William Hazlitt, '35. Hazlitt and the Spirit of the Age', *New Monthly Magazine*, 4 (April 1824), repr. in *Walter Scott: The Critical Heritage*, ed. by John O. Hayden (Abingdon: Routledge, 1970), pp. 279–89 (pp. 288–89).

[2] For a nuanced account of public dissent and the political sphere, see Daniel E. White, *Early Romanticism and Religious Dissent* (Cambridge: Cambridge University Press, 2006), particularly pp. 87–118.

Yearbook of English Studies, 47 (2017), 110–124
© Modern Humanities Research Association 2017

century.[3] For West, radicals and dissenters had used historical gothic to generate a fictional past filled with sinister clergy and nobility. Instead of these ahistorical 'ogres of Mother Goose' (as West referred to them), Cooke's and West's tales of the mid-seventeenth century position radicals as themselves the terrorized source of terror, reclaiming medicinal and scientific authority for the royalists.[4] While Godwin's *Mandeville* (1817) problematizes such associations, Scott's *Woodstock* replies to both sides in a metafictional *tour de force*. This late novel has been read as Scott's response to the bankruptcy crisis of 1826.[5] Nonetheless, just as *The Antiquary* (1816) had, with a certain amount of cheerful misdirection, restaged the post-French Revolution quarrel over the nature of history, *Woodstock* encapsulates, in more rancorous terms, the Romantic period's generic contest for definition of the historical gothic.[6]

The difficulties that the low-status, feminized, sentimental and even 'sickly' gothic form represented for Scott have been explored, notably by Fiona Robertson and Michael Gamer.[7] In this context, *Woodstock*'s use of the explained supernatural is significant. In revealing how gothic is deployed politically, the novel also suggests what is at stake in the genre's denigration. Gothic terror emerges as a frequently deployed form of political violence — and one Scott himself is willing to invoke. Suggesting that the problem of violence is central to the Romantic period novel, Anthony Jarrells and Timothy Campbell oppose Godwin's open-ended depiction of violence to Scott's aestheticized alternative, which (particularly by concentrating on the 'Glorious' Revolution) 'opens up the space of representation just enough to close off the violence of the recent past'.[8] Yet *Woodstock*'s exposure of the political re-appropriation of gothic tropes, its cruel practical jokes and its barely veiled attack on Godwin all suggest that violence has not been foreclosed. On the contrary, for Scott, the vitriol and fear generated by an extended post-French Revolution debate has irrevocably harmed the British political future.

When Edmund Burke describes the 'spirit of liberty' in his *Reflections on the Revolution in France* (1790) his metaphor is scientific rather than supernatural.

[3] Anthony Jarrells, *Britain's Bloodless Revolutions: 1688 and the Romantic Reform of Literature* (Basingstoke: Palgrave Macmillan, 2005), *passim*.

[4] Jane West, *Letters Addressed to a Young Man*, 3 vols (London: Strahan, 1802), III, 126.

[5] See Kenneth M. Sroka, 'Fairy Castles and Character in *Woodstock*', *Essays in Literature*, 14 (1987), 189–201.

[6] See Fiona Price, *Reinventing Liberty: Nation, Commerce and the Historical Novel from Walpole to Scott* (Edinburgh: Edinburgh University Press, 2016), pp. 170–206.

[7] Fiona Robertson, *Legitimate Histories: Scott, Gothic and the Authorities of Fiction* (Oxford: Clarendon, 1994), p. 271; Michael Gamer, *Romanticism and the Gothic: Genre, Reception, and Canon Formation* (Cambridge: Cambridge University Press, 2000), pp. 163–200.

[8] Anthony Jarrells, 'Bloodless Revolution and the Form of the Novel', *Novel: A Forum on Fiction*, 37 (2004), 24–44 (p. 41); Timothy Campbell, '"The Business of War": William Godwin, Enmity, and Historical Representation', *ELH*, 76 (2009), 343–69.

Although he asserts the importance of 'illusion', or the 'drapery' of a 'moral imagination', to cover monarchical power, his scientific tropes allow him also to claim a kind of political empiricism. Alluding to experiments with air carried out by the dissenting preacher Joseph Priestley, Burke hints at the inferior rationality of those motivated by the 'wild *gas*' of freedom.[9] In this account, the Revolution is an experiment that requires historical perspective; that is, time for the gases to settle and be assessed. In reply, Wollstonecraft's *Historical and Moral View* claims 'science' (broadly conceived) for a progressive radical agenda; implicitly, the radical, scientific reading of history, directing attention to empirical experience, exposes the illusions of court life.[10] Issuing a counter-challenge, in *Letters Addressed to a Young Man*, West echoes Burke's use of Priestley: history is like 'experiments made by an air-pump' but it is also superior to its scientific counterpart, since, she implies, it reveals the falsity of radical dissent's terrifying reading of the past.[11] *Letters* condemns (radical) historical fiction, but the alternative was to reclaim the genre. In Clara Reeve's *Memoirs of Sir Roger de Clarendon* (1793), contrary to popular history, Richard II shows great mercy after the Peasant's Revolt of 1381, while heroines are warned to disregard gothic nightmares. Rationality belongs to the monarchy rather than to the Lollards; conservative historiography finds supporting evidence in the feudal past.

If feudal times were a popular subject for historical novelists claiming political rationality, the Civil War was more contentious. In *British Historical Fiction before Scott* Anne H. Stevens identifies seven pre-1814 historical novels with a seventeenth-century setting.[12] Of these, besides West's *The Loyalists* (1812), only one other, Cooke's *Battleridge* (1799), deals with the Commonwealth. Sharing West's anti-Jacobin credentials, Cassandra Cooke, cousin to Jane Austen's mother, had royalist connections on the Leigh side of the family. Moreover, the generic distinctions drawn by Cooke in the preface to *Battleridge* leave her politics in no doubt. She remarks that 'Mrs Radcliffe' is the only author of the 'tremendous' capable of managing the '*belle passion*', rejecting those 'late brilliant novelists' whose 'young female Novices are taught to abjure parental duty, eloping with their admirers upon *principle*'.[13] For Cooke, as later for West,

---

[9] Edmund Burke, *Reflections on the Revolution in France and on the Proceedings in Certain Societies in London Relative to that Event* (1790), ed. by Conor Cruise O'Brien (Harmondsworth: Penguin, 1968), p. 90, p. 169

[10] Mary Wollstonecraft, *The Works of Mary Wollstonecraft*, ed. by Janet Todd and Marilyn Butler, 7 vols (London: Pickering, 1989), VI, 18.

[11] West, *Letters*, III, 154.

[12] Anne H. Stevens, *British Historical Fiction before Scott* (Basingstoke: Palgrave, 2010), pp. 78–80.

[13] Cassandra Cooke, *Battleridge: An Historical Tale Founded on Facts*, 2 vols (London: Cawthorn, 1799), I, pp. vi–viii.

a radical new philosophy shapes dubious fictions which associate authority with (Catholic) past oppressions. As the word 'principle' hints, from Cooke's perspective such fictions have insufficient empirical grounding.

Set in the period of the Commonwealth, *Battleridge* attempts to police the gothic and its accompanying irrationalities. Sir Ralph Vesey is the legal heir to Battleridge Castle since his vicious Puritan elder brother, Lord Aumerl, has been disinherited. When Sir Ralph finds his deeds to the property missing, the pious and clear-headed Dr Scot locates them. In the work's final scenes, Dr Scot reveals that he was led to their location (in a secret chamber behind an ancestor's portrait) by a spectral messenger. Only he, the most well-balanced of the novel's characters, has been able to deal with this ghostly manifestation. Similarly to Clara Reeve's *Old English Baron* (1778), Providence supports the legitimate heir. Nonetheless, the narrative of correct succession has been moderated. As in the Act of Settlement that eventually followed the 'Glorious' Revolution, 'continuity' is observed but religious and political rectitude is more important than following the strict line of descent.[14]

Meanwhile, in contrast to the true Providential support granted the royalists, gothic irrationality is associated with Cromwell, who appears before Scot in an empty picture gallery like a guilt-stricken 'ghost, pale, emaciated and stiff'.[15] Cooke implies that there is no truth in the superstitions of radical dissent, and, extrapolating from an interpolated tale in the second volume, the radical rewritings of history are equally false. The at first sight irrelevant narrative ostensibly in praise of Dalzell's deeds for the Scottish King Kenneth dwells on the evil and lascivious behaviour of the Ethling, Agitha, supposed heir to Earl Renne. Yet Agitha, a lascivious experimenter, poisoner and false doctor, also proves to be an upstart imposter. Even in the feudal past, terror has been generated by presumptuous ambition rather than by the monarch or nobility. Only the ruler's true descendants and pious divines like Dr Scot possess the ability to heal.

In *The Loyalists*, West expands such medicinal claims by suggesting the scientific credentials of conservatism. In doing so, she makes the attack on late eighteenth-century radical dissent much more explicit. In particular, as I have discussed elsewhere, she rewrites the Birmingham Riots of July 1791 when the house of radical dissenter and scientist Joseph Priestley was attacked by a Church and King mob.[16] In West's novel, it is the study of the Anglican clergyman Dr Beaumont that is destroyed by rioting dissenters. Scientific and rational enquiry belongs to the Church of England. In contrast, nonconformity is

[14] Burke, p. 102.

[15] Cooke, *Battleridge*, II, 136.

[16] Fiona Price, '"Experiments Made by the Airpump": Jane West's *The Loyalists* (1812) and the Science of History', *Women's Writing*, 19 (August 2012), 315–32.

associated with irrationality and superstition. Both the dissenting Farmer Humphreys and the Cromwellian Lady Bellingham believe they have seen accusatory spirits. Reprising Hume's account in his *History of England* (1754–61) of the religious rather than medical advice received by Cromwell on his deathbed, West has both die terrified, surrounded by 'godly ministers', 'ghostly assistants' in 'fierce dispute'.[17] Yet, unlike in *Battleridge*, these supernatural torments are not real. No Providential ghost supports the King. Instead, the medically adroit royalists, Mrs Mellicent and Isabel, are able to use the rebels' gothic fears to hide an injured royalist. Loyalism is not dead but supported by the empirical knowledge of its adherents.

In *A Tale of the Times* (1799), West had denounced Godwin's ideas of 'visionary perfectability'.[18] There, Fitzosborne, amongst other things a philosopher, is suspected of a deism that will perhaps lead to atheism and revolution. Although Godwin (the atheist son of a Calvinist minister) insists that he is unwilling to 'dwell' 'on the rabble of scurrilities' that writers like West had published about him, his historical novel *Mandeville* replies to such fictions as much as to *Waverley* (1814).[19] Challenging the association of dissent with rebellion and superstition, in *Mandeville* a Protestant royalist is wracked by the gothic torture of religious hatred. West had imagined benign conversations between her Anglican clergyman and the misled dissenter; in contrast, having escaped the 1641 Irish Rebellion, Mandeville is exposed to the poisonous anti-Catholicism of his Presbyterian tutor, Hilkiah Bradford, until he 'wander[s] like a meagre, unlaid ghost'.[20] In addition, in *Mandeville* not only are political beliefs more shifting than West accepts but the narrator's royalism is consistently misunderstood. In an episode that recalls the Treason Trials of 1794 and the radical William Hone's trials of 1817, Mandeville is accused by his schoolmates of possessing satirical images of the monarch. Pleading guilty to protect a friend, Mandeville can never escape the suspicion of treachery. Conversely, his contemporary, Clifford, is praised, provoking Mandeville until he determines with a sensation of 'preternatural horror' that Clifford is his 'fate'.[21] Maddened, Mandeville, like the Irish before the Rebellion, finds even the principle of inheritance undermined: his lawyer tries to gain control of his estate. No healing results. For Godwin, the inescapable cause and effect of history generates terror.

---

[17] West, *Loyalists*, II, 243; III, 230.

[18] Jane West, *A Tale of the Times*, 3 vols (London: Longman and Rees, 1799), III, 374.

[19] William Godwin, *Thoughts Occasioned by the Perusal of Dr. Parr's Spital Sermon, Preached at Christ Church, April 15, 1800* (London: Taylor and Wilks, 1801), p. 11.

[20] William Godwin, *Mandeville: A Tale of the Seventeenth Century in England*, ed. by Pamela Clemit, in *Collected Novels and Memoirs of William Godwin*, 8 vols (London: Pickering and Chatto, 1992), VI (1992), 52.

[21] Godwin, *Mandeville*, VI, p. 254, p. 253.

Timothy Campbell suggests that Holloway, the corrupt lawyer who tries to gain control of Mandeville's inheritance, and whose descriptions of history prove so plausible, can be understood 'as a figure for Scott' and 'thus Mandeville, a frustrated practitioner of history, as a figure for Godwin himself'. In this account, Godwin/Mandeville struggles against *Waverley*'s portrayal of 'enmity' as 'pleasure' that can be 'controlled'.[22] Yet in *Woodstock* Scott replies in a way that suggests the literary-historic battle is not over and that enmity is far from enjoyable. In 1824 (the year of publication of the first volume of Godwin's *History of the Commonwealth of England* [1824–28]) Scott asked Robert Southey if he had 'ever observe[d] how easy it would be for a good historian to run a parallel betwixt the great Rebellion and the French Revolution, just substituting the spirit of fanaticism for that of soi-disant philosophy'.[23] Yet he had been aware of the possibility for some time. As Peter Garside and Angela Wright note, both *Waverley* and *The Antiquary* contain echoes of *The Loyalists*.[24] *Woodstock*, though, does more than construct a 'parallel' between the two periods. Rather, it interrogates the post-French Revolution strategies of earlier historical novelists, including West and Godwin.

In 'Scott, Story-Telling and Subversion', Christopher Worth traces *Woodstock*'s 'representation of intensely competitive mixing of disparate language paths' to the Bible and Shakespeare.[25] However, the novel's early pages connect this interest in a 'dialogization' that moves towards 'hybridization' with the political debates of the late eighteenth and early nineteenth centuries.[26] The first chapter contains references to two of the most recycled phrases in Edmund Burke's *Reflections*, itself one of the most regularly re-appropriated texts of the post-French Revolution debate. Although Lockhart associates the novel's heroine

[22] Timothy Campbell, '"The Business of War"', p. 358.

[23] Walter Scott to Robert Southey, 1824, in *The Letters of Sir Walter Scott*, ed. by Herbert John Clifford Grierson, Davidson Cook and W. M. Parker, 12 vols (London: Constable, 1932–37), VIII, 374–77 (p. 376). For other sources, see Walter Scott, *Woodstock*, ed. by Tony Inglis, with J. H. Alexander, David Hewitt and Alison Lumsden, EEWN (Edinburgh: Edinburgh University Press, 2009), pp. 419–26. Political differences stemming from the Civil War linger in Scott's *Peveril of the Peak* (1822), but since that novel is primarily set at the time of the Popish Plot of 1678 it falls outside the scope of this article.

[24] Peter Garside, 'Walter Scott and the "Common" Novel, 1808–1819', *Cardiff Corvey: Reading the Romantic Text*, 3 (September 1999), <http://www.cf.ac.uk/encap/corvey/articles/cc03_no2.html> [accessed 15 January 2015]; Angela Wright, 'Scottish Gothic', in *The Routledge Companion to Gothic Literature*, ed. by Catherine Spooner and Emma McEvoy (New York: Routledge, 2007), pp. 73–82 (p. 80).

[25] Christopher Worth, 'Scott, Story-Telling and Subversion', in *Scott in Carnival*, ed. by J. H. Alexander and David Hewitt (Aberdeen: Association for Scottish Literary Studies, 1993), pp. 380–93 (p. 384). For political Shakespeare see Lidia Garbin, '"Not fit to tie his brogues": Shakespeare and Scott', in *Shakespeare and Scotland*, ed. by Willy Maley and Andrew Murphy (Manchester: Manchester University Press, 2004), pp. 141–56.

[26] Worth, p. 387, p. 390.

with Scott's daughter, the apostrophe to 'Alice Lee' supposedly written by a 'contemporary annalist' also recalls Burke's description of Marie Antoinette. As the French queen symbolizes a system 'under which vice itself lost half its evil by losing all its grossness', the narrator suggests of the 'faults' of Alice Lee: 'so well did they show amid thy good qualities, that I think they made me love thee better'.[27] An improved domestic alternative to the French queen, aristocratic rather than monarchical, she will teach Prince Charles the difference between licentiousness and chivalry. Charles needs the lesson because for 'the lower orders' in the congregation in King John's chapel at Woodstock 'the church was [...] but a steeple-house, the clergyman, an ordinary person; her ordinances, dry bran and sapless pottage.'[28] The sectarians' refusal of illusion recalls Burke's sketch of the revolutionary logic that suggests 'a king is but a man, a queen is but a woman; a woman is but an animal, and an animal not of the highest order'.[29] Failure of belief in the spiritual power of monarchy spreads until morality is undermined. To prevent this, Scott hints that some imaginative 'drapery' is still necessary, protecting power. Scott's narrator may contend that Alice is 'no creature [...] of an idle romancer's imagination', but his gallantry fulfils the same visionary function.[30]

If the veil of romance is attractive, Scott knows that power requires other, less pleasing generic devices. *Woodstock*'s central incident, in which Cromwell's commissioners are disrupted in their acquisition of the estate by a supposed haunting, operates as a reminder of historical fiction's manipulation of 'ghostly machinery' to political ends.[31] Introducing the Magnum Opus edition of *Woodstock* Scott remarks:

> It was the object of neither of the great political parties of that day to discredit this narrative, which gave great satisfaction both to the Cavaliers and the Roundheads; the former conceiving that the license given to the demons was in consequence of that impious desecration of the king's furniture [...] while the friends of the Parliament, on the other hand, imputed to the malice of the fiend the obstruction of the pious work.[32]

Although Scott is aware of two versions of the story, George Sinclair's *Satan's Invisible World Discovered* (1685) and Henry More's continuation of Joseph Glanvill's *Saducismus Triumphatus* (1681), that give credence to the

---

[27] Burke, p. 170; Walter Scott, *Woodstock or the Cavalier. A Tale of the Year Sixteen Hundred and Fifty-One*, 3 vols (Edinburgh: Constable, 1826), II, 6–7; all subsequent references are to this edition unless otherwise stated.

[28] Scott, *Woodstock*, II, 9.

[29] Burke, p. 171.

[30] Scott, *Woodstock*, II, 7.

[31] Scott, *Woodstock*, II, 92.

[32] Scott, *Woodstock*, in *Waverley Novels*, ed. by Andrew Lang, 24 vols (London: Macmillan, 1912), XX, p. xxi; subsequently, Scott, *Woodstock*, ed. by Lang.

supernatural, he chooses to privilege the more sceptical version given in Dr Plot's *Natural History of Oxfordshire* (1677).[33] This sceptical approach means that the description of political cynicism also functions when applied to the use of gothic in the post-French Revolution debate — a genre exploited to evoke fears of feudalism by more radical writers and to generate fears of radical enthusiasm by their opponents. As such, the preface unveils the re-appropriations that take place in the search for power, while indulging in some political veiling of its own. Scott's reference in the 1832 introduction to *The Every-Day Book* (1825–26), 'published by Mr Hone', underlines that the process of re-appropriation and resignification is still at work.[34] After Hone's 1817 trial, Godwin had facilitated his access to the British Museum's Library, where Hone gathered materials for *The Every-Day Book*. Given this background, it is unsurprising Hone begins his article on *Woodstock* by referencing a correspondent's complaints about the novel's anachronisms. Scott passes over the accusation that the scene should have been set in 1649, instead re-appropriating at length the details of the haunting included by Hone. The gothic tale remains politically pliable long after its Civil War genesis.

With its recycled language and emphasis on political and literary plots, *Woodstock* signals its metafictional content. Like Dr Rochecliffe's 'plots' ('almost constantly detected'), Scott's deliberate metafictional exposure of loyalist tactics produces unsettling results.[35] In the battle to preserve what, according to Burke, was the 'hereditary principle' of the British constitution, the supernatural had steadily become a less effective weapon.[36] Cooke, like Reeve, imagined monarchical rule supported by Providence (if not by divine right) but West's spectres, like those of Scott's narrative poem of the English Civil War, *Rokeby* (1813), are psychological. The ghosts in *Woodstock*, however, draw attention to the decline in the monarchy's spiritual status. While psychological terrors persist, Scott is more explicit about the ways in which they can be deliberately manipulated than West had been. Mrs Mellicent only connived at the belief that Waverly Park was haunted. In *Woodstock*, in contrast, Joseph Tomkins, the Independent, accompanied by royalist conspirators, ensures that Cromwell's relative, Desborough, is 'set upon [his] head the whole night, and soused with ditch-water the next'.[37] Symbolizing the political world reversed and defiled, such unspiritual mischief reveals the ignoble way gothic terror protects the king's property.

[33] Robert Plot, *The Natural History of Oxfordshire* (London: n.pub., 1677), pp. 206–10; see p. 206 for Plot's scepticism. See Scott, *Woodstock*, Edinburgh edition, pp. 421–22.
[34] Scott, *Woodstock*, ed. by Lang, p. ixx.
[35] Scott, *Woodstock*, I, p. viii.
[36] Burke, *Reflections*, p. 105.
[37] Scott, *Woodstock*, II, 98.

Whereas in Scott's earlier fiction he had been willing to provide justification for such tactics, by 1826 the excuses appear thinner. Thus, in *The Antiquary* it is only when Dousterswivel (a supposed alchemist like the hero of Godwin's *St Leon*), attempts supernatural trickery that Edie Ochiltree and Mr Lovel stage a pseudo-supernatural counterplot against him. Gothic deceit on one side generates trickery on the other. In contrast, in *Woodstock*, although the royalists are provoked by the estate's attempted sequestration, it is only they (with Tomkins's help) who indulge in such ignoble jests. Between the paltry tricks played on Desborough and the supposedly spectral appearance of the slaughtered player Dick Robison to Harrison and of Joseph Albany (Rochecliffe) to Holdenough, such spectral antics mix bathos with cruelty. The 'drapery' covering royal authority is decidedly tatty.

As well as rewriting West, in *Woodstock* Scott also replies to Godwin, indulging in some political cruelty of his own. Defending himself against James Ballantyne's charge that he had imitated Mrs Radcliffe, Scott wrote in his journal:

> My object is not to excite the fear of supernatural things in my reader, but to show the effect of such fear upon the agents of the story — one a man in sense and firmness, one a man unhingd by remorse, one a stupid, unenquiring clown, one a learned and worthy but superstitious divine.[38]

With this emphasis on psychological enquiry, Scott claims the same territory as *Mandeville*. Yet in his list of haunted characters, Scott alludes to only one of the commissioners, Desborough (the 'stupid, unenquiring clown'); his portraits of the others, Harrison and Bletson, go unremarked. Scott's mild tone is deceptive. In fact, Scott's text justifies the ignobility of the loyalist tricks by displaying the unpleasantness of the commissioners. In *Regency Radical: The Selected Writings of William Hone*, Daniel Kent and D. R. Ewen comment on 'the heterogeneity of the term "radical"', embracing as it did aristocratic Whigs (Sir Francis Burdett), infidel intellectuals (William Godwin and Jeremy Bentham)' and 'religious zealots (Robert Wedderburn)'.[39] As well as suggesting the political differences between Cromwell's divided supporters, a subject Scott was familiar with from his editorship of the *Somers' Tracts*, Scott's portraits of the commissioners evoke, at times viciously, these distinct contemporary radical identities.[40] As 'a bloody-minded, ranting enthusiast, who read the Bible to such purpose, that he never lacked a text to justify a murder', Harrison shares William Hone's own ability to

---

[38] See Scott's journal entry for 3 February 1826: Walter Scott, *Extracts from the Journal, 1825–1826*, in *Scott on Himself: A Selection of the Autobiographical Writings of Sir Walter Scott*, ed. by David Hewitt (Edinburgh: Scottish Academic Press, 1981), pp. 137–243 (p. 181).

[39] Daniel Kent and D. R. Ewen, *Regency Radical: The Selected Writings of William Hone* (Detroit, MI: Wayne State University Press, 2003), p. 388. See also Marcus Wood, *Radical Satire and Print Culture, 1790–1822* (Oxford: Clarendon Press, 1994).

[40] See Scott, *Woodstock*, Edinburgh edition, p. 421.

appropriate scripture.[41] With Hone's suggestion at his 1817 trials that the cabinet minister, George Canning, had, amongst others, parodied the Bible, he had drawn attention to the kind of re-appropriation of the spiritually terrifying that *Woodstock*'s artificial ghosts also reference. Equally, alternating between a 'spirit of enthusiasm' and a ruthless 'indifference to pain or bloodshed', Harrison recalls Robert Wedderburn, who, according to Iain McCalman in *Radical Underworld*, was 'both a licensed dissenting minister of enthusiastic disposition and a ferocious infidel', a combination, McCalman suggests, that was not uncommon.[42]

If Harrison's qualities hover between the representative and the particular, with Bletson, Scott is at his most directly referential. Like Godwin in the second volume of *An Enquiry Concerning Political Justice* (1793), Bletson believes his own 'doctrines of the perfectibility of mankind'.[43] Arguing that cause and effect in the external world is analogous to what happens in the mind, Godwin had emphasized necessity: 'mind as well as matter, exhibits a constant conjunction of events'.[44] Occupying similar materialist ground, Bletson is similarly 'unwilling to refer any of the phenomena of nature to a final cause'.[45] As the only character to mention Chaucer, Bletson also shares Godwin's literary tastes. Trying to calm himself after the haunting, Bletson insists that Chaucer 'lays the whole blame of our nocturnal disturbance on superfluity of humours'.[46] The gap between Bletson's language and Chaucer's recalls Scott's accusation, in his anonymous review of Godwin's *Life of Geoffrey Chaucer* (1803), that the biographer had made his characters speak almost in the language of '*soi-disant* philosophy'.[47] Certainly, Desborough finds Bletson's 'description of the old poet' 'unintelligible'.[48] Although in 1822 Scott anonymously donated £10 to Godwin's relief fund, saying he disapproved of his politics but acknowledged his 'genius', in *Woodstock*, suffering his own financial difficulties, he is less kind.[49]

With these unsettling portraits, Scott rewrites both *Mandeville* and Godwin's *History of the Commonwealth* in a distinctly personal way. In his essay 'Of History and Romance' Godwin had suggested that histories of individuals not

---

[41] Scott, *Woodstock*, I, 50.

[42] Scott, *Woodstock*, I, 272; Iain McCalman, *Radical Underworld: Prophets, Revolutionaries, and Pornographers in London, 1795–1840* (Cambridge: Cambridge University Press, 1988), p. 50.

[43] Scott, *Woodstock*, I, 278.

[44] William Godwin, *An Enquiry Concerning Political Justice and its Influence on General Virtue and Happiness*, 2 vols (London: Robinson, 1793), I, 290.

[45] Scott, *Woodstock*, I, 278.

[46] Scott, *Woodstock*, II, 99.

[47] Walter Scott, 'Art. XVI. *Life of Geoffrey Chaucer, the Early English Poet*', *Edinburgh Review*, Jan. 1804, 437–52 (p. 448).

[48] Scott, *Woodstock*, II, 100.

[49] Scott, *Letters*, VII, 252.

only promote self-knowledge in the reader but also 'mark the operation of human passions' in a way that cannot be achieved through the study of mankind in the mass.[50] Rather than showing social forces shaping an individual's passions (as Mandeville's irrational hatred is caused by the interaction of religious intolerance, chivalry and the doctrine of spiritual equality), Scott supplies his commissioners with unworthy motivations based on political position and self-interest. The contrast between Bletson's supposed principles and his self-interested conduct is particularly marked. In suggesting the 'caution dictated by the timidity of the philosopher's disposition' ('conscious his doctrines were suspected, and his proceedings watched'), for example, Scott alludes both to Godwin's sense of paranoia and his supposed retreat from direct political engagement in the early decades of the nineteenth century.[51] Instead of Bletson facing the dangers he has generated, he, like Godwin, continues an educational project ('if he had an opportunity of talking in private with an ingenuous and intelligent youth') that Scott portrays as highly insidious.[52] Worse still, like the eponymous hero of *St Leon* (and Dousterswivel), Bletson is an experimenter. Unprepared to sacrifice himself, he is at the same time hypocritically indifferent to practical obstacles to change, 'for the miscarriage of his experiment no more converts the political speculator, than the explosion of a retort undeceives an alchemist'.[53] With this portrait, Scott's fiction reverses Godwin's psychologically complex historical fiction to produce, not a developmental portrait but a performance of enmity. The historian's desire to mete out 'impartial reward' that Godwin had expressed in his *History of the Commonwealth* is lacking.[54]

Yet having roundly abused the radicals in the first volume and given the royalists a rather mean-spirited victory, Scott comes to suggest that the state is, after all, terrifyingly haunted, distorted by the monarchy and tarnished by the circulation of political tropes. The one moment of psychological torture comparable to *Mandeville* occurs when Cromwell confronts Anthony van Dyck's portrait of Charles I on horseback, putting himself and implicitly the executed monarch to the trial of history. Oliver wishes to read Charles merely as a 'man'

---

[50] William Godwin, 'Of History and Romance', in William Godwin, *Things as They Are; Or, the Adventures of Caleb Williams*, ed. by Maurice Hindle (London: Penguin, 2005), pp. 359–74 (p. 363).

[51] Scott, *Woodstock*, I, 281–82.

[52] Scott, *Woodstock*, I, 281. Godwin warned Percy Bysshe Shelley against political activism but Brailsford doubts the effectiveness of this; H. N. Brailsford, *Shelley, Godwin, and their Circle* (New York: Henry Holt, 1913), p. 232.

[53] Scott, *Woodstock*, I, 277.

[54] William Godwin, *The History of the Commonwealth, from its Commencement to the Restoration of Charles III* (1824–28), intro. by John Morrow, 8 vols (Bristol: Thoemmes Press, 2003), I, p. vi. See Porscha Fermanis, 'Godwin's *History of the Commonwealth* and the Psychology of Individual History', *Review of English Studies*, 64 (2010), 773–800 (p. 781) for a discussion of Godwin's Commonwealth men.

with 'breath in his nostrils', rather than as a king, and the painting as a mere 'painted canvas' rather than a representation of divine truth.[55] Charles's eye, 'cold' but still 'complaining', suggests whichever of the king's two bodies Cromwell confronts, the republican will continue to be haunted.[56] Worse still, kingly iconography continues to shape Cromwell's rule.[57] In this scene, although Cromwell talks of his disinterested desire to protect 'injured liberties', he struggles to imagine government outside the familiar terms of direct personal rule. Fit only to dominate 'crouching Frenchmen, or supple Italians', Charles issues a challenge to Oliver to reign more completely.[58] Although Cromwell suggests that Tomkins's tricks only work on 'simple fools', the shows of monarchy terrorize and control this representative of the modernizing state.[59]

In *Battleridge* Charles I's absence from the empty gallery leads to a moment of sentimental reflection; in *Woodstock* the dead monarch remains all too present. Equally, in Cooke's novel the portrait of Sir Ralph Vesey's ancestor leads to the deeds that confirm legitimate ownership, whereas in Scott's work the portrait of Sir Victor Lee, Sir Henry's ancestor, suggests a more dubious narrative of acquisition. Confronted by the portrait in the style of Holbein of Victor Lee participating in the dissolution of the monasteries, Tomkins smiles, perhaps to see the 'grim old cavalier employed in desecrating a religious house', perhaps for 'some other ideas'.[60] The Reformation establishes a precedent for the Civil War. Further, in *An Historical and Moral View* Wollstonecraft had made the demystifying suggestion that rulers were 'individuals wishing to fence round their own wealth or power' and that their 'descendants' were at work to solder 'the chains they forged'.[61] Echoing this cynicism, Tomkins's smile hints the royalists were, like the commissioners, despoilers, and freebooters. In line with this idea of royalist ruthlessness, the labyrinth behind the picture facilitates Charles's escape, as in the Reformation it had aided the Catholic priests. Scott hints that images of terror (whatever their source) support the counter-revolutionary impulse. Even the labyrinth behind the portrait can be read as a nightmarish version of Burke's organic constitution. Behind the portrait of destructive royalism/banditry lies a confusion that defies healthy change.

---

[55] Scott, *Woodstock*, I, 219–20.

[56] Scott, *Woodstock*, I, 220.

[57] For Scott's Cromwell, see Regina Hewitt, *Symbolic Interactions: Social Problems and Literary Interventions in the Works of Baillie, Scott and Landor* (Lewisburg, PA: Bucknell University Press), p. 165; and D. J. Trela, 'Sir Walter Scott on Oliver Cromwell: An Evenhanded Royalist Evaluates a Usurper', *Clio*, 2 (1998), 195–220.

[58] Scott, *Woodstock*, I, 219.

[59] Scott, *Woodstock*, III, 287.

[60] Scott, *Woodstock*, I, 87.

[61] Wollstonecraft, *Works*, VI, 18.

Alongside such authoritarian hauntings, by royalists who may themselves be little better than reformist robbers, the re-circulation of tropes and behaviours is likely, Scott hints, to harm even the post-Restoration state. In the damaged polis the real cannot be separated from the illusory or opponents distinguished from friends. For Wildrake and Everard, sentimental ties overcome political differences, but Holdenough, on discovering that his companion Rochecliffe, 'one of the pillars of High Church', is still alive, quarrels with him. Unlike the dissenter Barton and the Anglican Dr Beaumont (whose discussions lead to common ground) in *The Loyalists*, and more viciously disputative than Oldbuck and Sir Arthur in *The Antiquary*, the combatants fight 'more like fierce polemics about to rend each other's eyes out, than Christian divines'.[62] Only their separation preserves harmony. The alternative to such division is even more darkly confusing. Unlike his significantly named ancestor 'Victor', Henry Lee cannot distinguish between victory and defeat — after the first fight between Tomkins and Sir Henry, Joseph lets the old royalist appear to win. Later the deceived knight almost kills his own son. Through a process of appropriation, re-appropriation and even collusion, the royalists are linked with their opponents as much as with their allies. And although the marriage of Everard and Alice indicates possible cross-party union, the shared licentiousness of Charles II and Tomkins suggests a more sinister space of agreement. Both meet their objects of sexual desire near Rosamond's well. Admittedly, Tomkins attempts to rape Phoebe, whereas, as Hewitt argues, Charles is re-educated by Alice.[63] Nonetheless, the sense of sexual threat still remains. When Alice is delayed in escorting the king out of the environs of Woodstock, her father feels 'deep anxiety'.[64] Even though the monarchy has been modernized, the post-Restoration state will be haunted by the threat of violent domination.

Scott reverses the medicinal symbolism of *The Loyalists* and *Battleridge*. In *St Ronan's Well* (1823), he associated the fountain, metaphor for the healthy polis, with Dr Quackleben's false healing and the fakery of a contemporary spa; in *Woodstock* the well's isolated environs are associated with violence along with fraud. Even Alice, the figure of reinvented political romance, cannot heal. Although Alice compares her instructional verbal sketch of the ideal king to 'the wholesomest medicines' which 'are often bitter', Charles answers with 'asperity': 'physicians are reasonable enough to expect their patients to swallow them, as if they were honeycomb'.[65] Whereas West's Mrs Mellicent offers healing 'sallads, oat-cake, and metheglin', Alice's medicine is not sweet enough and her ideal

---

[62] Scott, *Woodstock*, III, 331.
[63] Hewitt, *Symbolic Interactions*, p. 182.
[64] Scott, *Woodstock*, III, 345.
[65] Scott, *Woodstock*, III, 51–52.

portrait will, history instructs, never be painted in reality.[66] Even worse, claiming the language of 'wholesome medicaments', Cromwell rejects the 'honey-comb' Charles II craves. Using the 'canting drawl' of radical dissent, the politician suborns the words of spiritual purity needed by the country.[67]

Portraying sickness at the state's heart, Scott also complicates the ownership of scientific rationality that West claimed for Church and King. Dr Rochecliffe, a 'constituent member of the Royal Society' accepts the terms of Charles's question: 'Why, if a vessel is filled brimful of water, and a large live fish plunged into the water, nevertheless it shall not overflow the pitcher?'[68] The conservation of volume is overlooked in favour of royal assertion. West's conservative image of Anglican rationality is undermined. The admittedly humorous incident gains sinister resonance through Tomkins's use of a similar vessel. Before attempting to rape Phoebe, Tomkins gives her the time needed to fill a pitcher to agree to his advances. An Independent who possesses real scientific powers rather than the fraudulent magic of *The Antiquary*'s Dousterswivel, Tomkins might be read as a Godwinian whose actual political 'gunpowder' has ironically helped the monarch.[69] Alternately, with his many pseudonyms and 'wizard'-like moral qualities, Tomkins can be read as the author of *Waverley*.[70] Yet the Trusty Joe of the novel's prefatory material vanishes in the text. If Joe's (only ultimately) pro-royalist plots parallel Scott's own authorial activities, the character's viciousness signals self-doubt on the author's part. The struggle to claim political rationality is dangerous because its outcomes cannot be foreseen; the results of the plots of the *Waverley* novels remain uncertain.

Both West and Cooke claim a kind of medicinal empiricism for the followers of Church and King, while deploying gothic against their opponents. Eschewing the narrative of healing, Godwin reverses these associations. In his account, the terror caused by religious and political sectarianism has real mental force and to analyse such enmity is, implicitly, to possess (radical) rationality. In some sense, what West performs, Godwin analyses. However, these Civil War fictions do not just struggle over ownership of the gothic but over two ways of understanding historical process. Cooke's and West's approach allows for a first cause, for some divine influence on human affairs. Between *Battleridge* in 1799 and *The Loyalists* in 1812, this Protestant moderation of the divine right of kings becomes increasingly secularized, but Godwin's *Mandeville* even more firmly strips away

---

[66] West, *Loyalists*, III, 75.

[67] Scott, *Woodstock*, III, 165–66.

[68] Maria Edgeworth, *Belinda*, ed by. Siobhán Kilfeather, in *The Novels and Selected Works of Maria Edgeworth*, 12 vols (London: Pickering and Chatto, 1999–2003), III (2003), 78; Scott, *Woodstock*, I, pp. viii, ix.

[69] Scott, *Woodstock*, ed. by Lang, pp. xxvi.

[70] Scott, *Woodstock*, ed. by Lang, pp. xxvi, xxvii–xxviii.

the idea of supernatural intervention in the historical process. In its place, the sectarianism which relies on divine illusion, becomes part of the terrifyingly determined, inescapable process of history. Despite Scott's mockery of Godwin, *Woodstock* comes closer to this second position. However, it adds an unpleasant littleness to the picture of historical causality. As *Woodstock* considers the standpoints taken by earlier historical novelists, Scott suggests it is not so much sectarianism but the petty rhetoric of debate that drives historical process.

Scott's novel reveals the role of the gothic as a driver in such debate. Unlike Radcliffe, whose explained form of supernatural removes the cause of terror, Scott suggests gothic's continuing manipulation across the political spectrum to generate power. Scott wryly demonstrates that, by enabling particular accounts of historical causality, the gothic can be used to produce either a radical or a more conservative understanding of political change in the present. In *Woodstock*, however, while Church, King and radicals all use the gothic to generate fear, the radicals are most sincere, genuinely feeling the terrors of the past. At the same time, all sides denigrate its use by opponents. Nonetheless, genuine terror is not lacking amidst the metafictional humour of Scott's own account. While Godwin in his *History of the Commonwealth* had been concerned with tracing patterns of causation, Scott traces supernatural effects to the most banal of causes; play-acting and mimicry largely replace psychological solemnity. Yet in tracing historical causality in the operation of a series of practical jokes, Scott has exposed the weakness of the 'drapery of the moral imagination' and has shown authority's reliance on fear rather than romance. The gesture of litotes, the reduction of political and generic debate to farce, does not remove enmity or sooth political doubt. On the contrary, *Woodstock*'s meta-analysis reveals that the traces of former language and policies, of earlier processes of recuperation and compromise, linger to constrain the present. When past royalists can be mistaken for freebooters, a process of hybridization has taken place that renders both modernity and monarchy suspect. In the years before Catholic Emancipation (1829) and the Great Reform Act (1832), Scott finds it more difficult to distinguish between false devils and real phantasms than he had once supposed.

SECTION III

Scott's Poetry

Towards the Edinburgh Edition of Walter Scott's Poetry

ALISON LUMSDEN

University of Aberdeen

In 1807 Scott was given an advance of one thousand guineas for *Marmion*, an unprecedented sum of money for any poem; in 1810 the publication of *The Lady of the Lake* was the media event of the year and at least six editions (over 25,000 copies) were sold in the first year.[1] As Nicola Watson has demonstrated, the poem caused a wave of tourists to visit the region in which it is set.[2] In fact, readers could not get enough of Scott's poetry and his dazzling success in the field culminated in 1813 when he was offered, but declined, the poet laureateship. However, in spite of Scott's significance in the early nineteenth century his role in shaping our constructions of Romanticism has been occluded; Scott is only given passing reference in accounts of Romantic poetry, until recently there has been very little critical work on his poems, and Scott's work seldom appears in anthologies of Romantic verse.

But why has Scott's poetry been so eclipsed? This question can, of course, only be speculated upon. Scott's own, typically self-effacing position was that the emergence of Byron as a major (and arguably darker and sexier) poet caused him to abandon his poetic endeavours and turn to writing fiction instead. However, while this provides a neat narrative of Scott's writing career it does not really match with the actual circumstances of it. While what we now consider to be Scott's major poetic achievements *The Lay of the Last Minstrel, Marmion* and *The Lady of the Lake* were all published before the appearance of *Childe Harold's Pilgrimage Canto 1*, in 1812, Scott was to write several more significant narrative poems after this date, such as *Rokeby* (1813) and *The Lord of the Isles* (1815). Work on the volume of *Shorter Poems* for the Edinburgh Edition of Walter Scott's Poetry is demonstrating that Scott also wrote short and occasional verse

---

[1] For a full account of the publishing history of the poem see William B. Todd and Ann Bowden, *Sir Walter Scott: A Bibliographical History, 1796–1832* (New Castle, DE: Oak Knoll Press, 1998). Editions were being produced so rapidly between May and November 1810 that sheets were being recycled from one to the other but there are at least six genuine new editions.

[2] See Nicola J. Watson, 'Holiday Romances; or, "Loch Katrine and the Literary Tourist"', in *Literary Tourism, The Trossachs and Walter Scott*, ed. by Ian Brown (Glasgow: Scottish Literature International, 2012), pp. 56–69.

Yearbook of English Studies, 47 (2017), 127–142
© Modern Humanities Research Association 2017

throughout his life, and of course, as the Edinburgh Edition of the Waverley Novels has shown via its annotations, Scott wrote much original poetry within his fiction, both in the form of mottos and to represent the (sometimes not very laudable) poetic aspirations of his characters.[3] If, then, the idea that Scott simply gave up writing verse in the face of Byron's emergence as the great poet of the day does not hold water are there other reasons why Scott's poetry has been so woefully neglected?

In fact, many circumstances have probably contributed to this situation. One simple response is, of course, that there is now very little appetite for reading any narrative verse, the genre on which Scott's reputation was built. However, while this may account for a general lack of readership for Scott's poetry it does not wholly justify its critical neglect. A second reason may lie in Scott's astounding success as a novelist. The neat narrative which suggests that Scott abandoned verse in order to turn, albeit anonymously, to fiction leads to a belief that his poetry was eclipsed by his fiction or that it is only of interest as a prelude to it. While there is much interesting work to be done on the connections between Scott's poetry and his fiction, particularly in areas such as the ways in which he hones his narrative technique or in the methods by which he employs, exploits and presents his source material, it is a mistake to see the poetry only in this way and to do so overlooks both its enormous popularity and its critical success, both at the point of its publication and well into the nineteenth century. Herein, perhaps, lies a third reason for its demise: so popular was Scott's work that generations of readers were force-fed both his fiction and his poetry; while the claim that no one reads Scott is often repeated it is not unusual to encounter a generation who can still recite significant passages from his poems, even if they do not know that Scott is the author. Such encounters with poetry are not always the best way to endear readers to it, and the often easy recitation of Scott's verse (something which the rhythms and metre can lend itself to, the often recited 'Young Lochinvar' being an excellent example) does not encourage careful reading or, indeed, the kind of reading that notes the nuance and complexity which is at play within it.

The overarching reason for the neglect of his poetry, however, probably lies in the general demise of interest in Scott in the twentieth century. This has been well documented in recent criticism but it is certainly fair to say that if a modernist aesthetic that valued surface complexity, concision and the exact placing of every word above narrative coherence, story-telling and expansive prose did not lend itself to appreciation of Scott's fiction, then it was even more antithetical to his poetry. Within the aesthetics of modernist poetry Scott very

---

[3] The Edinburgh Edition of the Waverley Novels, ed. by David Hewitt and others, 30 vols (Edinburgh: Edinburgh University Press, 1993–2012).

rapidly came to look old-fashioned, and an 'easy' approach to reading it encouraged by generations of teaching it to school children did not lend itself to looking beyond its apparent surface simplicity to its greater complexities. If we want to look for a more practical reason why Scott's poetry has been neglected, however, we can find it in the fact that there is no good modern edition in which we might encounter it; Lockhart's 1834 'Magnum' edition is, as will be discussed later, inadequate for several reasons, and J. Logie Robertson's Oxford edition, published in 1904, is incomplete, at times flawed, and presents Scott's poetry to readers in a cramped and discouraging form, offering none of the support that a modern readership requires.[4]

A new critical edition of Scott's poetry therefore seems timely, but before discussing what this will involve and how it might change our perspective on Scott's poetry it is worth offering some brief thoughts on why we should be reading it at all. First and foremost, Scott clearly played a major role in how Romanticism developed and to overlook his poetry is to experience a version of it that is skewed in very particular and ahistorical ways. Such questions aside, however, a re-visiting of Scott's poetry also uncovers a far more intellectually challenging body of work than has hitherto been recognized by criticism. Such a re-evaluation of Scott more generally has, of course, been underway for the past thirty years, and our understanding of him as a novelist and of the nuances with which he approaches narrative has been transformed. Recent approaches recognize the subtlety with which he engages with questions of history, national identity, and larger questions of societal formation and individual and collective responsibility, as well as the ways in which he engages with and often enhances the literary trends of his day. As a consequence they have uncovered a far more relevant and interesting Scott than that bequeathed to us by earlier critical history.[5] However, with some notable exceptions, Scott's poetry has not been subject to a similar re-assessment.[6] Yet for contemporary critics of his work, it was precisely its complexity that was most stimulating. As has been discussed elsewhere, it was the generic innovation of Scott's poetry that most struck early readers; Scott himself claims that he 'scorns pedantic laws of verse' and while this was at times perplexing for critics, it also prompted a recognition that

---

[4] *The Poetical Works of Sir Walter Scott, Bart.*, ed. by J. G. Lockhart, 12 vols (Edinburgh: printed for Robert Cadell, 1833–34) and *The Poetical Works of Sir Walter Scott*, ed. by J. Logie Robertson (London: Henry Frowde, 1904).

[5] See, for example, work by Penny Fielding, Ian Duncan, Catherine Jones, Ina Ferris, Fiona Robertson and Caroline McCracken-Flesher.

[6] These exceptions include the volumes by J. H. Alexander cited later, Nancy Moore Goslee, *Scott the Rhymer* (Lexington: University Press of Kentucky, 1988), Andrew Lincoln, *Walter Scott and Modernity* (Edinburgh: Edinburgh University Press, 2007) and Susan Oliver, *Scott, Byron, and the Poetics of Cultural Encounter* (Basingstoke: Palgrave Macmillan, 2005).

something new and radical was at work within his poetry.[7] In fact, Scott was one of the most experimental poets of his day. As Ainsley McIntosh demonstrates, a poem such as *Marmion* was also politically controversial, and indeed, Scott uses his poems, just as he was later to employ his fiction, to engage with the social, political and societal problems of his time, to deal with questions such as the relationship between crown and state, the role of the nation state within larger political units, the nature of heroism within the contexts of modernity, and issues of gender inequality.[8] Such readings of his poetry, however, have been largely overlooked. One step towards redressing this situation, I suggest, lies with producing a good scholarly edition. While critical editions on their own cannot, of course, fully recover the critical reputation of literary figures they are an important step along the way. The critical reputation of Scott's fiction may have been recuperated by the criticism produced in the past thirty years but the Edinburgh Edition of the Waverley Novels has also been instrumental and at times has helped to facilitate such criticism. It is hoped that a companion edition of Scott's poetry will do much to prompt a similar re-evaluation of it and, more importantly, recapture something of the excitement that Scott's 'boundary breaking' poetry prompted when it was first published. Over the past six years a team led by the University of Aberdeen has been working to develop such an edition and the first volumes of the Edinburgh Edition of Walter Scott's Poetry (hereafter EEWSP) are about to be published by Edinburgh University Press. The remainder of this article will explore what this edition will involve and the methodological questions that have had to be addressed to 're-purpose' Scott's poetry for twenty-first-century readers.

One of the first questions that had to be addressed was the scope of the edition. While the body of Scott's fiction is fairly clearly defined the poetry is more problematic. Several models presented themselves, however. The first lies in following Lockhart's 1834 *Poetical Works* edition. However, this immediately raises questions; volumes 1–5 of that edition are comprised of edited works such as *Minstrelsy of the Scottish Border* and *Sir Tristrem* and very early in its discussions the EEWSP team decided that this material lay outwith the scope of the edition; editing ballad material involves its own particular skills and a project is currently underway under the directorship of Sigrid Rieuwerts at the

---

[7] Walter Scott, 'Introduction to Canto 5', *The Lay of the Last Minstrel* (Edinburgh: Archibald Constable, 1805). J. H. Alexander notes that 'We have still no agreed title to designate the genre to which Scott's longer poems belong'. See *Two Studies in Romantic Reviewing: Edinburgh Reviewers and the English Tradition: The Reviewing of Walter Scott's Poetry, 1805–1817*, 2 vols, Romantic Reassessment, 49 (Salzburg: Universität Salzburg, 1976), II, 245. Francis Jeffrey famously describes *The Lay of the Last Minstrel* as 'such a romance as we may suppose would have been written in modern times', in the *Edinburgh Review*, 6 (April 1805), pp. 1–2.

[8] See Ainsley McIntosh, *Marmion; A Tale of Flodden Field. A Critical Edition* (unpublished doctoral thesis, University of Aberdeen, 2009).

University of Mainz. Lockhart also includes Scott's early translations from the German and Scott's drama — *MacDuff's Cross* and *The House of Aspen*, for example — and whether to include these offered another point for discussion. A second model is offered by J. Logie Robertson's Oxford edition of 1904, which does not include *Minstrelsy* but does include Scott's original contributions to it. It also expands upon Lockhart's body of miscellaneous and shorter poems, although sources for some of these are not always given. More controversially, it also incorporates the poetry from the Waverley Novels. After much discussion it has been agreed that the EEWSP will include, as would be expected, the narrative poems and all the shorter and lyric poems that appear in Lockhart's edition. Several new shorter poems have come to light in the course of editing and these too will be included, thus significantly expanding Scott's body of work and our understanding of him. The edition will not include the work collected by Scott for *Minstrelsy* or in other of Scott's edited works, but Scott's original contributions will be represented. Scott's verse drama will appear on the basis that it has traditionally formed part of what has been regarded as the body of his poetic output; while there may be little appetite for verse drama at the moment, including it in the edition will hopefully facilitate scholarship on it, and more importantly, allows for a full representation of Scott's *oeuvre*. Whether to include the incidental original poetry in the Waverley Novels and other works was also debated among the team. Historically it formed part of Scott's poetic canon before Logie Robertson's edition and Scott himself sanctioned its separate collection and publication by Constable. On 9 March 1822 Constable wrote to Scott stating:

> I must now come to the concluding object of the present [letter] — which is to ask your approbation of a publication, of which I now take the liberty of sending you a specimen, The Poetry of the Novels, Tales, and Romances of the Author of Waverley — which abound with so many beautiful fragments and pieces of poetry, and of which I propose printing a small impression, something on the plan of the enclosed, which contains the poetry of the first volume of Waverley. Preparing the copy for the press would be a delightful amusement to me, and I shall take care that the whole be accurately printed. If there should be a demand for the work in this collected form, which I flatter myself there would be, the future editions would of course be printed in Edinburgh.[9]

Scott was happy with this arrangement and replies on 23 March:

> Though I have time but for a brief letter, I do not put off much time in assuring you that you have my entire approbation, were that of any consequence, in the publication you intend to form from the prose vols. It is odd to say, but nevertheless it is quite certain, that I do not know whether some of the things are original or not, and I wish you would devise some way of stating this in the title.

[9] Letter from Constable to Scott, 9 March 1822, printed in *Archibald Constable and his Literary Correspondents*, 3 vols (Edinburgh: Edmonston and Douglas, 1873), III, 205–06.

'The Author of Waverley, finding it inconvenient to look over books for a motto, generally made one without much scrupling whether it was positively and absolutely his own, or botched up out of pieces and fragments of poetry floating in his memory;' but that would have an awkward effect if he were supposed to found merit on them as original.[10]

In spite of Scott's endorsement, however, there are risks in reproducing this material in a modern edition. Leaving aside Scott's very valid observation that we cannot always be sure which of the poems he has actually written, some of Scott's characters who consider themselves to be poets are woefully bad (Waverley himself or Frank Osbaldistone, for example), and taken out of context such material may seem strange. More practically this material has, of course, already been edited by the EEWN team and the virtue of reproducing it had to be considered. On balance, however, it was agreed that such material should appear. Even since the publication of EEWN resources such as ECCO (which Scott himself would clearly have been grateful for) have allowed us to identify the sources for some of the poetry attributed to Scott in the novels and it was agreed that with careful contextualization no disservice would be done to Scott's poetic reputation by reproducing some of his characters' bad verse in the edition.[11]

A final area for discussion focused upon Scott's own essays on poetry, published as the 1830 Introductions to *Poetical Works* and in the 1833 edition.[12] While it is not true to say that Scott never provides us with a theory of fiction — for much of this can, in fact, be found embedded within the novels themselves, particularly in the introductory chapters, and, indeed, in his essays on and reviews of other authors — nowhere does he provide so comprehensive and extensive an account of it as he does in these essays on poetry. It was therefore decided that they should be made more readily available. The Edinburgh Edition of Walter Scott's Poetry will, therefore, consist of ten volumes: 1. *The Lay of the Last Minstrel*, 2. *Marmion*, 3. *The Lady of the Lake*, 4. *Rokeby*, 5. *The Vision of Don Roderick, The Bridal of Triermain, The Field of Waterloo* and *Harold the Dauntless*, 6. *The Lord of the Isles*, 7. *Shorter Poems*, 8. *Poetry from the Waverley Novels and Other Works*, 9. *Verse Dramas*, 10. *Scott's Reflections on Poetry*.

Having determined what was to appear in the edition, the next step for the team was to agree upon a methodology for editing it. Establishing a base text is arguably the most theorized aspect of textual editing and certainly an exploration

[10] Scott to Constable dd. 23 March 1822, in *Archibald Constable and his Literary Correspondents*, III, 206–07.

[11] A database of addenda and corrigenda is being compiled and will be located on the web site of the University of Aberdeen's Walter Scott Research Centre.

[12] *The Poetical Works of Sir Walter Scott, Bart.*, 11 vols (Edinburgh, 1830) and *The Poetical Works of Sir Walter Scott, Bart.*, ed. by J. G. Lockhart, 12 vols (Edinburgh, 1833–34).

of the options available is one of the crucial steps in the editing process. Ostensibly Scott presents fewer problems than other Romantic poets; because he predominantly writes long narrative poems rather than lyrics he does not constantly engage in acts of major recasting. While there are some exceptions in his shorter poems we generally do not have variations of Scott's poems as we do, for example, in the case of Coleridge; Scott's poems do not become alternative texts as he engages with them. However, less visible complexities arise in the transmission of his work, in part caused by its unprecedented popularity. As a consequence of this his work goes through many editions very rapidly; as noted above, for example, six editions of *The Lady of the Lake* were published between May and November of 1810, and over 25,000 copies sold. Moreover, there are numerous collected editions of the poems published in Scott's lifetime, culminating in J. G. Lockhart's Magnum edition of 1834 (published just after Scott's death). These texts do not remain stable, but evolve and change in subtle ways from one edition to the next. In such circumstances the choice of a base text is complex and the principles for intervening in it to produce a scholarly edition are more complex still.

The process of editing the Edinburgh Edition of the Waverly Novels has, of course, given us a very clear understanding of how Scott's fiction made its way from manuscript to print and how the texts evolved over the many editions published in Scott's lifetime. While much useful information was inherited by the poetry team we could not to assume that the conditions under which the poetry came into being were necessarily the same. Most crucially, while the novels were published anonymously, the poetry was published openly by Walter Scott. In addition, when Scott first started to write poetry he was a much younger and less influential figure, presumably with less control over his work than when the 'Waverley Machine' had reached top gear. Our first task, therefore, was to discover the processes by which a Scott poem as opposed to a Scott novel made its way from manuscript into print and what happened to it as it rapidly went through those many early editions. Only by this process could we fully understand the options available to us for the edition and the nature of the emendation that would have to be undertaken in order to produce robust and reliable texts.

The first investigations into this question were undertaken by Ainsley McIntosh who, for her Aberdeen doctoral thesis, explored a model for a scholarly edition of Scott's second narrative poem *Marmion*.[13] The primary aims of McIntosh's investigation were to determine what would constitute a suitable base text and to ascertain the ways in which it should be emended in order to produce a scholarly edition for the twenty-first century. Her methodology involved the

---

[13] McIntosh, 'Marmion; A Tale of Flodden Field. A Critical Edition'.

collation of all relevant textual witnesses and the examination of the poem's publishing history. Traditional editorial theory would suggest that there are normally several contenders for base text in any critical edition, namely the manuscript and the first and the last editions to appear in the author's lifetime. The manuscript, as with Scott's fiction, could easily be dismissed, since Scott wrote it in the knowledge that his holograph text was part of an evolving creative process; punctuation, for example, is often added in print.

In the case of Scott's poetry the 1833–34 *Poetical Works* edited by J. G. Lockhart and appearing just after Scott's death offered the model for *Marmion's* latest appearance in print. However, it quickly transpired that as a base text for a new edition it is problematic. There is no evidence to suggest that Scott was artistically engaged in the production of this edition and while Lockhart makes reference to the existence of an interleaved set of the poetry similar to that used in the preparation of the Magnum edition of the novels, he makes only one emendation to his edition of *Marmion* as a result of it.[14] Moreover, while he records 214 variant readings from the manuscript in footnotes to the text, he does not use any of these to emend the text. Their inclusion gives no indication of their textual relevance or relationship to the composition or transmission of the text, thus rendering his text highly problematic as the basis of a modern edition. Lockhart's approach to annotation also compounds the inadequacy of his edition as the basis for a scholarly edition. While Scott makes a clear distinction between end notes and what he calls 'glossarial' notes at the foot of the page Lockhart muddles this distinction and even adds his own observations about the poem and its reception amongst the annotation material.[15]

Lockhart's final edition was therefore inappropriate. Another option clearly lay with the first edition. While the Edinburgh Edition of the Waverley Novels never explicitly stated that the first editions of Scott's novels should form the base text for their new edition, arguing instead that this should be the first fully articulated version of the work, in nearly every case it was the first edition that was chosen, since there is very little evidence that Scott intervened in the texts of his novels between the first editions and the late Magnum project. McIntosh presumed that this model might be applicable to *Marmion*. However, a very different picture emerged from collation of the relevant textual witnesses and investigation of Scott's correspondence. Indeed, the lack of anonymity

---

[14] For a full discussion of this see McIntosh, p. 70.

[15] Scott makes this distinction in a letter to Robert Cadell of 8 October 1828 where he writes: '*No* notes except such as are merely *glossarial* or otherwise brief notices necessary to explain the text, are to be placed at the foot of the page [...] This practice must be observed in all cases'. See *The Letters of Sir Walter Scott*, ed. by H. J. C. Grierson et al., 12 vols (London: Constable and Co., 1832–37), XI, 5. While he is referring to the Magnum edition of his fiction here we can assume that he would have wished the same procedures to be followed in the *Poetical Works*.

surrounding the production of *Marmion* led to what McIntosh, taking the lead from Jerome McGann, identified as a highly 'socialized' form of development and production where dialogues and interactions between Scott and his audience had direct consequences for the development of the text in both its pre- and post-publication stages.[16] In the case of *Marmion* 8000 copies of three editions sold out within six months of its first publication, and during this rapid and, as it transpired, intense process the text continued to develop and evolve. Often this was in response to information that Scott received from his readers. For example, several new notes were added, others were expanded and revised, and the narrative itself was altered as correspondents suggested revisions to Scott. In short, Scott remained creatively engaged with the text at least up to and including the third edition where he was still responding to responses from readers and changing his text accordingly. As a consequence of McIntosh's discoveries it became clear that it would be wrong to follow EEWN practice and use the first edition as the base text for the new edition of *Marmion*. Instead, the third edition was chosen on the basis that it is the culmination of a single compositional process that began in the manuscript, continued almost certainly in the lost proofs, and on into the first three editions. In other words, if the early editions are taken as part of what may be defined as an initial creative process (and it must be remembered that early editions were appearing within weeks of each other), the third edition represents the earliest fully articulated form of the poem.

This work raised two crucial points both for an edition of *Marmion* and the EEWSP project as a whole. Firstly, it was clear that any critical edition of the poetry could share with the Edinburgh Edition of the Waverley Novels the realization that the standard 'Magnum' edition was an insufficient model for a modern scholarly edition of Scott's poetry. Not only did Lockhart fail to follow Scott's wishes about the notes, but it was clear that the text had deteriorated significantly in the process of transmission: compositors' errors, mis-readings, and variations in punctuation had all moved it very far away indeed from Scott's early texts. Secondly, and perhaps more interestingly, this work demonstrated that while the expertise of the EEWN can provide the backbone of an edition of the poems, its procedures cannot simply be transferred wholesale to this endeavour, since the circumstances of production surrounding the poems seems to raise new and complex issues concerning textual transmission. The next question for the edition, therefore, was to ask if the case of *Marmion* was typical, or exceptional? Do all of Scott's longer narrative poems emerge from a similar process of 'socialization' or is *Marmion* unique?

[16] Jerome McGann writes that 'Because literary works are fundamentally social rather than personal or psychological products, they do not even acquire an artistic form of being until their engagement with an audience has been determined'. See Jerome J. McGann, *A Critique of Modern Textual Editing* (Chicago, IL: Chicago University Press, 1983), pp. 43–44.

Establishing this was fundamental to the formulation of a broader editorial policy for the edition as a whole and it was at this point that a pilot project for the edition was established, with funding from both the British Academy and the Carnegie Trust for the Universities of Scotland. It was crucial to test McIntosh's discoveries against other of Scott's longer poems and to both collate the relevant editions of them and explore their publishing histories. Three further poems were chosen for this purpose: *The Lay of the Last Minstrel*, as Scott's first narrative poem, *The Lady of the Lake*, which is the next to be published after *Marmion*, and *The Lord of the Isles*, chosen deliberately for its later publication date and for the fact that it is produced after Scott had begun to publish fiction.

The results of this investigation were fascinating. To focus on one example, work on *The Lady of the Lake* suggests that, like *Marmion*, Scott's public nature as he was writing this poem results in a kind of pre-publication 'socialization'. Certainly, Scott is not slow to tell others that he is writing the poem, and that to claim that he will value their thoughts on it before it is published. The summer before its publication Scott went to the Trossachs with his family and J. G. Lockhart reports that 'He gave a week to his old friends at Cambusmore, and ascertained, in his own person, that a good horseman, well mounted, might gallop from the shore of Loch Vennachar to the rock of Stirling within the space allotted for that purpose to FitzJames. From Cambusmore the party proceeded to Ross Priory, and, under the guidance of Mr Macdonald Buchanan, explored the islands of Loch Lomond, Arrochar, Loch Sloy, and all the scenery of a hundred desperate conflicts between the Macfarlanes, the Colquhouns, and the Clan Alpine'.[17] Moreover, Lockhart suggests that 'At Buchanan House, which is very near Ross Priory, Scott's friends, Lady Douglas and Lady Louisa Stuart, were then visiting the Duke of Montrose; he joined them there, and read to them the Stag Chase, which he had just completed under the full influence of the *genius loci*'.[18] Lockhart also suggests that James Ballantyne, Scott's printer and publisher for this poem with his brother John, read selections of it to 'select coteries' as it advanced through the press. 'Common fame', we are told, 'was loud in [The Lady's] favour; a great poem was on all hands anticipated.[19] This could hardly be more different than the secretive processes that surrounded the production of a Waverley novel.

Scott himself also indicates that he is willing to show the poem to others before its publication. In March 1810 he sent a printed version of the first two cantos of

---

[17] J. G. Lockhart, *Memoirs of The Life of Sir Walter Scott, Bart.*, 7 vols (Edinburgh: Robert Cadell, 1837), II, 250.

[18] Ibid., p. 50.

[19] Ibid., p. 292.

the poem to Lady Abercorn, whose husband was the dedicatee, noting 'how desirous I am your Ladyship should think well of these Minstrel stanzas. The deuce take my lover I can make nothing of him; he is a perfect automaton. It is very odd that the Border blood seems to rise in my veins whenever I begin to try couplets however torpid on other occasions. I am in my own person as Hamlet says *indifferent honest* and a robber or Captain of Banditti never comes across me but he becomes my hero'.[20] Around the same time he also wrote to his friend Morritt 'My present attempt is a poem partly highland — the scene Loch Katrine [...] I hope to show this ditty to you soon in Portland Place for it seems determined I must go to London though the time is not fixed'.[21] Most tellingly of all, in his 1830 Introduction of the poem Scott recounts how he showed sections of the poem to a farmer friend prior to its publication and a result was prompted to make considerable changes. He reports:

> I determined rather to guide my opinion by what my friend might appear to feel, than by what he might think fit to say. His reception of my recitation, or prelection, was rather singular. He placed his hand across his brow, and listened with great attention through the whole account of the stag-hunt, till the dogs threw themselves into the lake to follow their master, who embarks with Ellen Douglas. He then started up with a sudden exclamation, struck his hand on the table, and declared, in a voice of censure calculated for the occasion, that the dogs must have been totally ruined by being permitted to take the water after such a severe chase. I own I was much encouraged by the species of reverie which had possessed so zealous a follower of the sports of the ancient Nimrod, who had been completely surprized out of all doubts of the reality of the tale.

However, much of the dramatic tension in the poem results from the fact that James IV traverses the Highlands in the guise of James Fitz James, the Knight of Snowdon, and Scott goes on to tell that in this respect his friend's comments were less favourable:

> Another of his remarks gave me less pleasure. He detected the identity of the King with the wandering knight, Fitz-James, when he winds his bugle to summon his attendants. [...] This discovery, as Mr Pepys says of the rent in his camlet cloak, was but a trifle, yet it troubled me; and I was at a good deal of pains to efface any marks by which I thought my secret could be traced before the conclusion, when I relied on it with the same hope of producing effect, with which the Irish post-boy is said to reserve a 'trot for the avenue'.[22]

While the manuscript of *The Lady of the Lake* includes many small revisions that might suggest an attempt to obfuscate the identity of the king there is no evidence for a more wholesale revision of the poem to this effect, reminding us that the stories of composition Romantic writers tell about their work may not always be

[20] Letter to Lady Abercorn, dd. 14 March 1810. *Letters*, II, 312.
[21] Letter to J. B. S. Morritt, dd. 2 March 1810. *Letters*, II, 306.
[22] 'Introduction' (April 1830) to *The Lady of the Lake*, in *Poetical Works* (1833–34), pp. 8–9.

true; however, the truth that is revealed here is that Scott is listening to the opinions of his friends as he writes this poem.[23]

What is equally clear is that, in spite of his assertion that he would be more private in his composition following *Marmion*, Scott is showing this new poem to friends and family before it is printed, and that he is taking their reactions to it on board. As with *Marmion*, but in a manner very different from the fiction, the production of this poem is, then, as McIntosh identifies, a social process, where Scott is seeking, and at times responding to, the reactions of others during composition.

But what happens to the poem after publication? As mentioned earlier *The Lady of the Lake* rapidly sold out and six editions were required within six months: a circumstance that allows for continued creative evolution in a period where Scott was still actively and artistically engaged with the poem. Critical response for *The Lady of the Lake* was almost without qualification positive; even Jeffrey (who had reviewed *Marmion* negatively) seems to have liked the poem and appears to have regretted his harsh treatment of its predecessor.[24] As J. H. Alexander notes 'For Lord Abercorn, the dedicatee, it was "the most delightful as well as interesting Poem I have read in any language"'.[25] Yet this does not mean that the poem was above criticism by reviewers, by Scott's friends, and even by very slight acquaintances. *The Scots Magazine* found James's wanderings improbable and imprudent,[26] and the *Christian Observer* thought that Roderick's death was 'a blot on James's character'.[27] Lady Hood, along with several others, objected to the soldier's song in the final canto, commenting 'I have only to quarrel with you for continuing the <u>Soldiers</u> song in the 2d edition it is really unworthy of your muse & the sentiments are such that I don't think it is your <u>own</u> composition, pray erase it, all your friends wish you wd'.[28] Alexander also reports that 'Lady Abercorn, encouraged by Scott himself, was openly contemptuous of Graeme's character'. She writes 'How much it is against

---

[23] The manuscript of *The Lady of the Lake* is owned by the Morgan Library and Museum, New York, MA443. J. H. Alexander provides a list of Scott's correspondents who expressed surprise at the revelation of the king's character. These include Lady Hood, Joanna Baillie, Richard Heber and Tom Scott, the poet's brother. See *The Reception of Scott's Poetry by his Correspondents, 1796–1817*, 2 vols, Romantic Reassessment, 84 (Salzburg: Universität Salzburg, 1979), II, 361.

[24] Jeffrey's extensive review of *The Lady of the Lake* appeared in the *Edinburgh Review*, 16 (August 1810), pp. 263–93. Alexander, *Two Studies*, provides a full list of all of the reviews of *The Lady of the Lake* and notes that 'Of the twenty reviews, thirteen were favourable (five of those enthusiastic), three were neutral, and four were critical (two of them very hostile)', II, 369.

[25] Alexander, *Two Studies*, II, 353. Alexander is quoting NLS Ms 3879, fol. 139ᵛ, a letter to Scott dated 2 July 1810.

[26] Ibid., p. 379. This review appeared in the *Scots Magazine*, 72 (May 1810), pp. 359–64.

[27] Ibid., p. 379. The review appeared in the *Christian Observer*, 9 (June 1810), pp. 366–89.

[28] Ibid., pp. 359–60. Alexander is quoting a letter of Lady Hood to Scott of 26 August 1810 to be found in NLS Ms 3879, fols 166ᵛ–67ʳ.

constancy that even you cou'd not make your Knight of love who never broke his vow a more interesting character, I am afraid I am more in love with any of them than I am with him'.[29] She was not alone in this respect and responses to Graeme differed widely. Morritt wanted Brian the hermit to reappear in the denouement,[30] and Southey thought the songs in the poem a mistake or at least misplaced.[31] Scott, however, does not seem to have been inclined to change his poem as a result of these criticisms, as Lady Hood's complaint that the soldier's song persists into the second edition implies. Her sense that he *might* have changed it is, nevertheless, interesting, for it implies an expectation that Scott would alter his work in response to public feeling, even after its publication. To other comments made about the poem he responds, but again does nothing to alter its composition. Both Southey and Ellis, for example, have reservations about the metre of the poem. Scott, of course, can do nothing to change this but instead offers a vigorous defence of his chosen style, outlining its benefits to Ellis.[32]

If Scott was reluctant to change the body of this poem in response to reader criticisms, however, he does seem to have been more willing to make changes to his notes. For example, Mrs Clephane, who had advised Scott in some of the Gaelic in the poem, writes to thank him for preserving a coronach which she had sent him but adds: 'you must correct one letter — "Thou hast forsaken us before S̱awaine" — in place of Lawaine'.[33] Scott duly makes this change in the second edition. Moreover, if Scott at times reserved judgment about altering *The Lady of the Lake* because of the suggestions of readers this does not mean that the poem was not evolving in its early editions, for collation shows that he is still artistically engaged with it and altering it in line with his artistic sensibilities. Again this is most pronounced in the notes. There are ten new notes in the second edition of *Lady of the Lake* and several existing notes are significantly expanded. Several errors in the notes are also corrected, such as in note 6 to canto 3 where it is pointed out that the Ben-Shie had been incorrectly equated with the Head of the Fairies, when in fact a female fairy should be implied. The note originally reads 'The Ben-Shie, or *Ben-Schichian*, implies the head, or chief of the Fairies' but is altered in the second edition to read 'The Ban-Shie implies the female Fairy' and a footnote added to state: 'In the first edition this was erroneously explained as equivalent to *Ben-Schichian*, or the Head of the

[29] Ibid., p. 367. Alexander is quoting a letter from Lady Abercorn to Scott of 18 July 1810 to be found in NLS Ms 3879, fol. 147ᵛ.

[30] Ibid., p. 370. See also NLS Ms 3879, fol. 108ᵛ, Morritt to Scott, 17 May 1810.

[31] Ibid., p. 371. See also NLS Ms 3879, fol. 8ʳ⁻ᵛ, Southey to Scott, 11 May 1810.

[32] See Lockhart, II, 296–304 and *Letters*, II, 340, 346–48. The letters from Southey and Ellis to Scott can be found in NLS Ms 3879 and are also reprinted in Alexander, *Two Studies*, I, 104–08.

[33] Ibid., p. 85 and NLS Ms 3879, fol. 110.

Fairies'.[34] Changes are also made to the body of the poem, with the majority of changes taking place between the first and second editions. Some of these are fairly routine but there are other changes that imply a more creative engagement. In Canto 1 stanza 12 a pine tree's 'scattered' trunk is altered to read 'shatter'd'. In canto 2 the rather awkward lines 'Not so had Malcolm strained his eye | The step of parting fair to spy' becomes 'Another step than thine to spy'.[35] In Canto 3 it is no longer simply the thunder that has split a pine, but a 'thunderbolt',[36] while in Canto 5 the king's description of Roderick Dhu as 'exiled' is changed to the more correct 'outlaw'd' (l. 197).[37] A more wholesale revision again occurs in the description of the prison room at Stirling Castle where several lines are added and others significantly re-written.

Without pre-empting the new edition these examples give just a flavour of the changes that occur to the poem between the first and second editions. Fewer, but at times significant changes have also been found in later editions. All this suggests that, as with *Marmion*, Scott continued to be artistically engaged with the poem beyond its first appearance in print, and that the first edition is not, perhaps, the end point of its creative evolution. A similar pattern emerged in our investigation of *The Lay of the Last Minstrel* (1805) and, tellingly, even in *The Lord of the Isles* (1815). *The Lord of the Isles* is Scott's last long narrative poem, and the picture that has emerged from a textual investigation of it supports the pattern that we have observed for the earlier poems. Although by this point Scott (who was now publishing his novels anonymously) was striving for greater secrecy regarding the details of his unpublished poems, examination of his letters reveals that he continued to discuss his works-in-progress with close friends including Lady Abercorn, Joanna Baillie and Robert Southey. Moreover, examples of revisions between first and second editions that could only have been made by Scott again strengthen the suggestion that he is artistically engaged with the poem after the printing of the first edition.

What this revealed was that not only *Marmion* but all of the poems we examined were undergoing a rapid process of creative evolution during their early editions and that Scott continued to be artistically engaged with the poems, adding to them, altering them, and responding to comments from friends and the wider public both before and after their publication, at least for the first year after their appearance. As one might expect, however, collation also revealed that while Scott may be 'improving' his poems at this early stage, the poems are also simultaneously deteriorating: punctuation, layout and even occasional words

---

[34] *The Lady of the Lake*, 1st edn (Edinburgh: John Ballantyne and Co., 1810), p. lvi, and *The Lady of the Lake*, 2nd edn (Edinburgh: John Ballantyne and Co., 1810), p. 346.

[35] Ibid., II.6.

[36] Ibid., III.7.

[37] Ibid., V.5.

are subject to the 'Chinese whisper' type of corruption that is inevitable as compositors transmit one version of a text to the next.

So what are the implications of this for the textual policy of the EEWSP? First and foremost, it is clear that, by contrast with most of his works of fiction, Scott does not become disengaged with his work after its appearance in print. On the contrary, he remains creatively engaged with it, continuing to respond both to his own imaginative impulses and the suggestions of others. As a consequence we concluded that the first editions of the poems could not necessarily be the end of the line and that the chosen base text for each poem should be that which represents the point at which the poem settles into its earliest fullest articulation. In other words, because of the rapidity at which these early editions are being produced we will consider them to be part of what we might call the initial creative process and, as with *Marmion*, the base text may well be the second, third or even a later edition — whatever is deemed to be the point at which Scott seems to have ceased to be actively engaged in the creative evolution of it, within the early time frame of its production. This decision, however, renders the fact that the texts are simultaneously deteriorating in ways consistent with the transmission of hand-set nineteenth-century editions particularly problematic; our copy texts come under pressure both from what might be seen as authorial improvement and textual deterioration, thus raising particularly interesting questions for legitimate emendation. Our policy, therefore, aims to emend these base texts both where there are obvious misreading or errors from the manuscript and where there is clear deterioration which can be attributed to compositors' errors and blundered attempts at correction, thus capturing both the freshness of the original texts and the adjustments made by Scott and rendering, as far as it can be ascertained, the author's creative vision during the early lifetimes of these poems.

Having reached this position it might be expected that we had made sufficient decisions about the nature of the text itself to move forward but one final issue remained and that is the fraught issue of Scott's own notes to his narrative poems. While the majority of Scott's notes to the novels were introduced as part of the Magnum Opus edition it is important to recall that the notes were *always* intrinsic to the narrative poems; they are an important part of their paratextual dialogue, and, as discussed above, are frequently the feature of them which is textually most unstable. How, though, should the notes be treated? Are they part of the 'text' of the poem or do they function as supplementary and explanatory material, overtaking the need for a modern textual apparatus of annotation? A very cursory look at the notes of any of Scott's longer poems will reveal that they do not serve the function of modern annotation. In fact, rather than being notes as we would now understand them, Scott's notes function to give accounts of his sources, supplementary material, and narratives in their own right. Indeed,

Scott's notes are best understood as a kind of *surplusage*, indicative of a process which he describes late on in his career as an inability to resist the act of story telling, stating in *Reliquiae Trotcosienses* that he could never prevent himself from 'gliding into the true musing style of an antiquarian disposed to "spin a tough yarn"'.[38] Having identified this feature of Scott's notes, then, it became clear that they must be presented as part of the text of his poems, and that further modern annotation, including annotation of the notes themselves, would be required. Along with the text of the poems (which will include Scott's notes), therefore, the Edinburgh Edition of Walter Scott's Poetry will provide an emendation list, an essay on the text, a historical note, explanatory notes, where necessary a glossary and, in some instances, a map. The poetry volumes will therefore follow the pattern of the Edinburgh Edition of the Waverley Novels and provide a companion to it.

At the time of writing (2017), the first volume in the Edinburgh Edition of Walter Scott's Poetry, *Marmion*, edited by Ainsley McIntosh, is about to go to press. Work on the volume to follow, the *Shorter Poems*, edited by Peter Garside and Gillian Hughes, is well under way, as is that on *Poetry from the Waverley Novels and Other Works*, edited by David Hewitt and *The Lady of the Lake*, edited by myself. The aim of the Edinburgh Edition of Walter Scott's Poetry, like that of the Edinburgh Edition of the Novels, is to restore Scott's poems to a form which best reflects his vision during the initial creative process and which is freed as far as possible from the various errors and non-authorial interventions that arose in the course of their publication and successive re-printings. It also aims to facilitate the reading experience of the modern reader by providing supporting editorial material in the form of notes, essays and, where necessary, maps and glossaries. It is the hope of all involved that by doing so the full significance of Scott's poetry will be realized, along with the complexities at work within it and the relevance of the issues with which it deals. We are not blind to the challenge: reading nineteenth-century narrative poetry of the kind that Scott writes, to say nothing of verse dramas, requires a kind of retraining of the mind, perhaps a type of reading that has to some extent been forgotten. It is hoped that a critical edition that provides readers with clear and accurate texts along with the support they need to understand them in a twenty-first-century context will at least encourage a willingness to rediscover and revisit this kind of reading. The rewards are, I would suggest, invaluable.

---

[38] Walter Scott, *Reliquiae Trotcosienses or the Gabions of the Late Jonathan Oldbuck. Esq. of Monkbarns*, ed. by Gerard Carruthers and Alison Lumsden, EEWN (Edinburgh: Edinburgh University Press, 2004), p. 34.

'Land Debateable': The Supernatural in Scott's Narrative Poetry

AINSLEY McINTOSH

London

In his 'Introductory Epistle' to *The Fortunes of Nigel*, Scott famously describes creativity as 'a dæmon who seats himself on the feather of my pen when I begin to write.'[1] This metaphor of supernatural intervention in the writing process can be extended all the way to the 'printer's devils' who turned Scott's manuscripts into books fit for consumption by an eager audience.[2] Scott's choice of metaphor nicely conveys the sense that imagination operates through supernatural power, and suggests the centrality of the supernatural to Scott's writing. Focusing on Scott's major narrative poems, *The Lay of the Last Minstrel* (1805), *Marmion* (1808), and *The Lady of the Lake* (1810), this essay explores some of the various ways in which Scott deploys the supernatural in his poetry and what this contributes to our understanding of Scott as poet.[3]

Of these three texts, *The Lay of the Last Minstrel* appears upon first reading to offer Scott's most unambiguous engagement with magic and the supernatural.[4] Extraordinary events unfold through acts of necromancy (2.17–19), shape-shifting (3.11–12; 3.21), the casting of spells (1.1; 3.9), and communion with spirit deities (1.15–17); and through the actions of fairy tale archetypes including a witch, a sorcerer, and a goblin dwarf. However, the *Lay* registers ambivalence about the power and the effects of use of magic, such that ambiguity becomes a central motif of the poem even as it unfolds along the fixed polarities of the natural and the supernatural, truth and deception, life and death, good and evil.

---

[1] Walter Scott, *The Fortunes of Nigel* (1822), ed. by Frank Jordan, EEWN (Edinburgh: Edinburgh University Press, 2004), p. 10.

[2] The *OED* gives the 1683 definition of 'printer's devil': 'The Press-man sometimes has a Week-Boy to Take Sheets, as they are Printed off the Tympan: These Boys do in a Printing-House, commonly black and dawb themselves: whence the Workmen do Jocosely call them *Devils*'. See *Oxford English Dictionary*, online <http://www.oed.com> [accessed 29 September 2016].

[3] Given the limitations of space, some avenues of investigation have had to be culled from this article. Key among these is the proximity of the supernatural to the sexual, and particularly in relation to constructions of female sexuality and power.

[4] All references to the poem are taken from *Scott's Poetical Works: The Lay of the Last Minstrel* (London: Adam & Charles Black, 1896).

Yearbook of English Studies, 47 (2017), 143–160
© Modern Humanities Research Association 2017

As I shall argue, the *Lay* suggests the limitations of magic, or perhaps more specifically of its adherents, when confronted with the universals of death, love, and fate: the goblin acknowledges that 'his power [is] limited' (3.13) and his spell fails to disguise Cranstoun's true appearance from Margaret (5.12), suggesting the restricted range of his magic; Lady Buccleuch's magical powers similarly appear to be confined to the sphere of her secret bower and she ultimately concedes defeat to 'Fate' (5.26); and even Michael Scott, the poem's most powerful practitioner of magic, succumbs to death. Through its narrative strategies it further challenges belief in the magical events that it relates. This deflation of credulity is achieved through the poem's narrative framing device, which distances both Scott's audience and the minstrel's seventeenth-century listeners from the *Lay*'s mid-sixteenth-century setting. Scott's extensive antiquarian annotation, offering ethnographical commentary on popular superstitious beliefs held in medieval Scotland, creates a further remove for his readers. The suspension of disbelief (to invoke Coleridge's rhetoric) in magic is disrupted moreover through the minstrel's refusal fully to endorse his own tale.[5] To take just a few examples, the minstrel merely reports: 'Men said' and 'bards avow' that Lady Scott of Buccleuch's father practised magic and passed his skill to her (1.11–12). Similarly, ''Tis said' (2.22; 1.12) that William of Deloraine and the Monk hear strange sobs and laughter when they remove the 'mystic Book' (2.14) from its resting place, but the minstrel 'cannot tell how the truth may be; | I say the tale as 'twas said to me' (2.22). Through this use of dissociative language, the minstrel assigns many of the *Lay*'s supernatural elements to superstitious hearsay and invites audience scepticism.[6] This raises questions concerning how we are meant to interpret the tale that is being presented to us, and these questions have broader implications for how we are to interpret texts in general.

Upon closer analysis, then, there appears to be something unsatisfactory about the way in which the supernatural is invoked only to be dismissed. As Alison Lumsden has said, there is something ineffectual about the use made of Michael Scott's book of magic, despite its centrality to the plot.[7] The book is described as 'the treasure of the tomb' (1.22) that will come to the aid of Branksome's chief in his hour of need (2.15), but while its power is described (2.13–14) it is never

---

[5] Coleridge explains that in creating ballads that dwelt upon the supernatural in *Lyrical Ballads* (1798) he was attempting to 'procure for these shadows of imagination [the] willing suspension of disbelief'. See *Biographia Literaria* (1817), ed. by Adam Roberts, The Edinburgh Critical Edition of the Major Works of Samuel Taylor Coleridge (Edinburgh: Edinburgh University Press, 2014), p. 208.

[6] For further examples see also 2.21; 2.31; and 6.5. Similarly, see 6.26, where conflicting eyewitness accounts of what is heard and seen when Michael Scott makes his reappearance from beyond the grave make us question what actually occurred.

[7] Alison Lumsden, *Walter Scott and the Limits of Language* (Edinburgh: Edinburgh University Press, 2010), pp. 62–63.

fully revealed nor utilized during the course of the narrative. It is stressed that the information contained within its pages is dangerous, forbidden even: something that 'should ne'er be known' (2.5). To speak the words in the book 'were a deadly sin', and for even thinking 'them my heart within' (2.13) the Monk has spent sixty years undertaking a 'treble penance' (2.5, 13). Lady Buccleuch warns William of Deloraine that he must not read in this book, for 'If thou readest, thou art lorn! | Better had'st thou ne'er been born' (1.23). Deloraine, however, proves immune to the book's dangerous influence because he cannot read (1.24).

One can only conjecture what the 'Ladye' could achieve with access to this magic, for the book never reaches her. Instead, it falls into the hands of Cranstoun's malevolent goblin-page, Gilpin Horner. The one spell that the goblin gleans from the book has 'much of glamour might, | Could make a ladye seem a knight;' (*Lay* 3.9), and Horner uses this transformative spell primarily to achieve mischief (3.12, 13). However, his actions also function as the catalyst for the union of Cranstoun and Margaret and the resolution of the romance love plot, thereby proving remedial rather than diabolic. The minstrel struggles to account for the goblin's ultimately reconciliatory role (5.13). The ambivalence of his actions mirrors the ambiguous power of the book, with both demonstrating the capacity for good or for evil. By extension, both function as allegorical representations of the ambiguous power of language. The narrator ensures that we take a sceptical view of the supernatural, but this is a scepticism directed towards the apparent events in his historical narrative (for this is what his tale purports to be). In the poem, however, magic and the word are closely associated.

The association of language and magic is established in the *Lay*'s opening verse, where we learn that Lady Buccleuch's tower is equally 'guarded by word and by spell' (1.1) for 'mighty words and signs have power' (6.5). The transformative meaning of 'grammar' (scholarship) to 'glamour' (magic) in early eighteenth-century Scots underlines this relationship in a poem that abounds with associative word play and puns.[8] As Penny Fielding notes in her discussion of the role of this book in Hogg's *Three Perils of Man* (1822), the book, or the text contained within this physical object, appears to wield the 'power of life and death'.[9] Ian Duncan similarly recognizes the juxtaposition of the book to death: it is 'not so much dead as buried alive, undead in fact, waiting for reanimation

---

[8] For a fuller discussion of this aspect of the poem see J. H. Alexander, *The Lay of the Last Minstrel: Three Essays* (Salzburg: Institut für Englische Sprache und Literatur, Universität Salzburg, 1978), p. 37. See also Susan Oliver, *Scott, Byron and the Poetics of Cultural Encounter* (Basingstoke: Palgrave, 2005), pp. 78–79.

[9] Penny Fielding, *Writing and Orality* (Oxford: Clarendon Press, 1996), p. 67.

each time its pages are opened.'[10] This power is latent until the book is recovered and the goblin first reads and then utters its magical words, which suggests the need to disseminate, investigate and then articulate the text contained therein. This establishes the connection between magic and the processes of writing, reading, interpreting and circulating a text.

The proximity of the book of magic to (im)mortality is implied by Michael Scott's state of life-in-death through the suspension of bodily decay which is revealed when Deloraine breaks open his tomb (2.19). The unnatural extension of the life of the Monk who guards this tomb (he has reached the unlikely age of one hundred years (2.4)), and his swift demise when the book is removed from Melrose Abbey (2.28), similarly suggests that proximity to its powerful magic has acted as a life-sustaining force. However, as the deaths of both attest, if the book has the power to sustain life, or the appearance of life, it lacks the power to bestow it. The minstrel's *Lay* concludes with a *Dies Irae* (Day of Wrath), a 'Hymn for the Dead' (6.31): death has the final say, even as it does in the material world. The narrative closes on a scene of mourning rather than of marriage, and the minstrel will tell us 'nought of the bridal' (6.28) that should have formed the conclusion to the plot.

And indeed, the *Lay* operates as both a commemorative act and as a site in which to inscribe memory: the minstrel mourns the loss of his son (4.2) and of the minstrel class, and offers elegiac tribute to the House of Buccleuch ('Introduction', Canto 1; 1.7; 'Conclusion', Canto 4); the poet laments the universality of mutability and death.[11] Nonetheless, further possibilities are opened up by the reappearance in Canto 6 of a 'shape' that Deloraine identifies as Michael Scott (6.26). His materialization from beyond the grave offers an alternative to the closure imposed by death. Similarly, the art of both poet and minstrel is positioned as a partial corrective to the eventuality of death:[12] despite the passage of time and 'fickle fame's' attempts to blot 'from her rolls' the names of heroes long gone, 'this old man's verse | Could call them from their marble hearse' (Conclusion, Canto 4) so that they continue to live 'in the poet's faithful song' (Introduction, Canto 5). If they are inscribed into the oral tradition only, they necessarily die 'a second death' with the poet's 'parting breath' ('Introduction', Canto 5), but by recording their exploits in writing the poet

---

[10] Ian Duncan, *Scott's Shadow: The Novel in Romantic Edinburgh* (Princeton, NJ: Princeton University Press, 2007), p. 200.

[11] In this way, both enact the function of a bard, which is, as Katie Trumpener outlines, to act as 'the mouthpiece for a whole society, articulating its values, chronicling its history, and mourning the inconsolable tragedy of its collapse'. Katie Trumpener, *Bardic Nationalism: The Romantic Novel and the British Empire* (Princeton, NJ: Princeton University Press, 1997), p. 6.

[12] For a compelling argument about language's limited triumph over death see Alison Lumsden, *Walter Scott and the Limits of Language*, pp. 57–61.

ensures that their names live on, potentially in perpetuity. In this way, the 'Book of Might' (2.19) becomes analogous to the biblical 'Book of Life' in which God is said to write down, and also to blot out, the names of those destined for an afterlife in heaven.[13] Being recorded or written into the text assures an afterlife of sorts for its characters. Moreover, the voice of the Minstrel achieves immortality, albeit transformed, in the sound of the river.

By the *Lay*'s conclusion, Michael Scott has reclaimed ownership of the goblin and, we presume, his book of magic, and the Lady has 'Renounced, for aye, dark magic's aid' (6.25–27). This seems to suggest that there is no place for magic in the modern world; however, this interpretation is made problematic by their disappearance rather than their destruction. We end by contemplating the possibility that Michael Scott and his book of magic are still operating in some unseen region. In many ways then, the poem raises more questions than it answers, and thus becomes an allegory for literary ambiguity and the activity of interpretation.

Death and the afterlife are again central preoccupations of *Marmion*. The themes of death and mutability pervade both the narrative and the six inter-polated conversation poems.[14] The narrative chronicles the collapse of the chivalric world, and the framing epistles, although acutely personal in their ruminations, develop the theme of decay, degeneration, and loss to exude a sense of backward longing for a previous age. As with the *Lay*, the tone is predominantly elegiac, and the poem explores mourning at the personal and collective level.

The second canto of *Marmion* opens in gothic detail as a group of nuns sets sail across a sublime seascape on their way to Lindisfarne Priory.[15] Once there, they recount legends of the miracles performed by their saints and of St Cuthbert's restless spirit. Rival narratives of the beliefs held by the Church and those of the fisher folk concerning the afterlife lead into the description of a secret Vault of Penitence that is again surrounded by stories of the 'spirits of the sinful dead' (2.14–17). In this dark dungeon, Constance de Beverley, a perjured nun and one-time lover of the English knight Marmion, is soon to meet a horribly realized end. Brought before a holy tribunal, and following the full confession of her sins, Constance is condemned to death by immurement within the vault's walls. The speaker of the poem has forewarned the reader that she will be

[13] See Isaiah 32. 33; Daniel 12. 1; and Psalms 69. 28 in the Authorised King James Version of The Holy Bible.

[14] All references to the poem are taken from Walter Scott, *Marmion; A Tale of Flodden Field* (1808), ed. by Ainsley McIntosh, EEWSP (Edinburgh: Edinburgh University Press, 2017).

[15] Scott's opening description of the foreboding castles that 'look grimly down' upon the nuns and the 'boiling' sea (2.9) creates an air of gothic suspense, which sets the scene for the dramatic dungeon episode about to unfold.

enclosed 'Alive, within the tomb' (2.25), a phrase that Constance echoes when she warns her executioners to 'dread me, from my living tomb' (2.31). This ominous remark, which is picked up again later in the text (3.15), acquires the 'tone of prophecy' (2.32), recalls Christ's resurrection after three days in the tomb, and finds resonance in de Wilton's 'resurrection'. The setting up of ghost stories at the start of this canto prepares the reader for Constance's disembodied reappearance (of a kind) later in the poem.

As in the *Lay*, reading and writing are of thematic significance, but the book of magic has been replaced by more mundane documents. Constance confesses that she has colluded with Marmion in forging documents that frame another knight, de Wilton. The plot of the poem hinges upon this crime of forgery, so that the narrative is driven by a literary act that presents itself as being authentic when it is in fact a manipulation or subversion of the truth. Correspondingly, Gilpin Horner's magical transformation in the *Lay* is likened to counterfeit, even as the goblin is said to counterfeit, or fake, fear (*Lay* 4.14–15). Deception and disguise are similarly intertwined in *Marmion*: Constance has masqueraded as Marmion's stableboy for three years, de Wilton is disguised as a palmer for most of the action, and Scott dons the guise of bard-like narrator. In this way, forgery constitutes an act of appropriation that finds resonance in the varying appropriations of voice, identity and intention that occur within the text.

The scene of Constance's 'inquisition' (2.4) becomes a metaphor for the interrogation of language and narrative form that takes place within the text. The rival narratives of Constance's verbal and written confession, or her 'guilty packet' (2.27), forces a renegotiation of the authoritative closure implied by the forged documents. However, the authority initially granted to these spurious scrolls, in the sense that their authenticity is accepted and deemed more credible than de Wilton's protestations of innocence, prompts questions about the reliability and authority of all literary fictions. Indeed, the word fiction itself, implying the creative acts both of lying and that of imaginatively constructing a story, illustrates the inherent ambiguity of language and alerts the reader to the need to sift for discursive meaning and truth. The connection between falsehood and fiction is made explicit through Marmion's allusion to the 'lying legend[s]' that 'holy ramblers' purvey (1.25). This suggests the need to establish the reliability of all witnesses, narrators, and mediators within the text. However, it becomes particularly challenging in a Scott text where polyphonic voices and a complex hybrid of narrative forms jostle for attention and supremacy.

The various acts of narrative disclosure that occur, and the forms they take, illustrate the impossibility of locating textual authority definitively in any one discourse. Nonetheless, storytelling and song are granted a special status, each accruing a double value in terms of encoded meaning and performativity. The coded value of music is repeatedly suggested in the text. For example, the tolling of a bell to signify death (2.23; 3.13), the blasting of a bugle-horn to herald the arrival of visitors (1.3), the blowing of trumpets to mark a scene of celebration (1.4), or the braying of war-pipes and the banging of drums to indicate the approach of war (4.24; 5.5). However, it is lyrics that prompt action because they are populated by the meanings attached to them by their listeners and also by the readers of the text.[16]

This can be illustrated by considering the roundelay that is embedded into Canto 3. Marmion and his men have stopped to rest for the night at an inn and Marmion requests that the squire Fitz-Eustace sing a song to alleviate the gloom caused by the palmer's brooding presence. Fitz-Eustace offers to sing Constance's favourite lay, one that she has customarily performed for them. This information is presented directly before the song, ensuring that its connection to Constance is at the forefront of the audience's consciousness; and that audience, of course, includes Marmion. The song tells the tale of a 'traitor' who has ruined and deserted his maiden lover, and concludes:

> Where shall the traitor rest,
>   He, the deceiver,
> Who could win maiden's breast,
>   Ruin, and leave her?
> In the lost battle,
>   Borne down by the flying,
> Where mingles war's rattle,
>   With groans of the dying.
> CHORUS
> *Eleu loro*, &c. There shall he be lying.
>
> Her wing shall the eagle flap
>   O'er the false hearted;
> His warm blood the wolf shall lap,
>   Ere life be parted.
> Shame and dishonour sit
>   By his grave ever;
> Blessing shall hallow it,—
>   Never, O never.
> CHORUS
> *Eleu loro*, &c. Never, O never. (3.11)

Because the reader has been alerted to the fact that the song echoes Marmion's seduction and abandonment of Constance, we are primed to extract a particular meaning from it; to find treachery encoded in the lyrics, awaiting this interpretation. As Penny Fielding argues in relation to Scott's supernatural short story 'Wandering Willie's Tale', through its oral rendition Constance's tale is

---

[16] The poem highlights, nonetheless, that even without lyrics music is open to the subjective interpretation of its listeners: 'Thus clamour still the war-notes [...] | To you they speak of martial fame; | But me remind of peaceful game' (5.24).

further situated as an 'act of memory':[17] the suggestively melancholy air and the associative connections that he makes with the lyrics revives Marmion's memory,[18] which in turn awakens his dormant conscience, remorse and love (3.12–18). Through repetition of its central refrain, the formal structure of the roundelay ensures that it is embedded within the listener's memory and mind. It becomes 'at the same time a performative act and a story with real relevance for the lives of its actants and its hearers'.[19] Again, the reader is not left to infer this connection, because it is made explicit by the poet-narrator.

By means of its performance then, Constance's song accrues a power that extends far beyond the significance of the song itself. This is evident first in its ability to arouse an emotional response in Marmion, and further in the exponential growth of the song's status as the poem progresses, such that it acquires the authority of prophecy. The song warns that the traitor's fate will be to perish in battle, his dying body prey for wild scavengers.[20] Accordingly, Marmion is killed in combat at the Battle of Flodden, and his corpse mutilated by spoilers who arrive, like predatory wolves, to strip and gash the slain. His remains are confused with those of a 'lowly woodsman' (6.36) who has followed Marmion to battle and the peasant's body is interred in the Marmion family crypt while Marmion is left to lie in an unmarked grave on the battlefield.

Constance's song attains a supernatural power as Marmion lies dying on Flodden Field. A Monk desperately tries to read him his last rites, but we are told that Marmion cannot hear him because:

> Ever, he said, that, close and near,
> A lady's voice was in his ear,
> And that the priest he could not hear,
> 　　For that she ever sung,
> *"In the lost battle, borne down by the flying,*
> *Where mingles war's rattle with groans of the dying!"* (6.32)

Despite the all too concrete reality of her physical entombment, Constance's voice reaches out beyond the grave, recalling her warning to the priests that the vaults which enclose her will 'burst open' (2.31). She has been literally suffocated, smothered and silenced, but the performative re-enactment of her story allows her to transcend the silence and resist the closure imposed by death. The salient

---

[17] Penny Fielding, *Writing and Orality*, p. 103.

[18] For a discussion of the positive power of associative memory see Catherine Jones, *Literary Memory: Scott's Waverley Novels and the Psychology of Narrative* (Lewisburg, PA: Bucknell University Press, 2003), pp. 49–53.

[19] Penny Fielding, *Writing and Orality*, p. 106.

[20] There is an onward transmission of this motif from 'The Twa Corbies' in Scott's *Minstrelsy of the Scottish Border* (1802). As Susan Oliver highlights, this ballad both 'embodies a theme of feudal corruption, decay and abandonment', which Scott revisits in *Marmion*, and is an allegory of literary scavenging. See Oliver, *Scott, Byron and the Poetics of Cultural Encounter*, pp. 61–62.

point is not that she has been enclosed alive within the tomb, but that through the re-enactment of her personal narrative she continues to remain alive within the tomb; or, more specifically, her story survives even if she does not. Constance's voice has replaced Michael Scott's book of magic as the thing that is entombed yet still alive and potent. As with the *Lay*, each reading of *Marmion* constitutes a reanimation of the text that creates afterlives for its characters.

Constance's lay sparks a chain reaction of interpolated tales, each of which tells of encounters with revenants or supernatural foes. This allows Scott to continue with his supernatural theme and his exploration of the psychological effects produced by belief in such phenomena. First, 'The Host's Tale' relays the local legend of a martial encounter between Alexander III and a 'Goblin Knight' (3.19–26; see also Scott's Note 3.8), and after hearing it Marmion goes in search of this same 'Elfin Foe' (3.30). This is followed by 'Sir David Lindesay's Tale' in which James IV is warned by 'a ghostly wight' to desist from seeking war with the English (4.12–14; see also Scott's Note 4.7). Listening to the story prompts Marmion to share the details of his moonlight encounter with what he believes to be de Wilton's ghost (4. 16, 17). In turn, this causes Sir David to recount the story of an apparition that appears in Rothiemurchus and the surrounding area that bears the semblance of the Scottish knight Ralph Bulmer (4.18). The series of tales mimics the way in which storytelling itself proceeds, with one story begetting another. Scott joins in, inserting further ghost stories and tales of the supernatural into the notes,[21] so that the sense of enclosure imposed by narrative form is undermined by the way in which narrative spills over into Scott's paratexts. Just as Constance's voice 'bursts' free of the tomb, the text appears to 'burst' free from the prison-like containment imposed by structural form.

The embedded tales also suggest the role played by guilt and superstitious credence in the world of the supernatural. The poem highlights that agency lies in the individual's imagination rather than in actual supernatural occurrences.[22] Marmion's guilt, which has been activated by listening to the lay, causes him to interpret the encounter with de Wilton as a meeting with a 'spectre' (4.17) and he later curses himself when the realization dawns that ''Twas no fay nor ghost, | I met upon the moonlight wold' (6.17). Marmion's guilt and his betrayal of a loved one doubles for James IV's guilt over the betrayal and death of his father, James III (4.12). Tellingly, James IV receives the ghostly warning during Mass on the anniversary of his father's death at Sauchieburn, while he is doing penance for his crime. Sir David Lindesay underlines the connection between debilitating guilt and credence in the supernatural, when he tries to comfort Marmion:

---

[21] For examples of this see *Marmion*, Notes 5.20; 6.6; 6.8.

[22] Compare Coleridge's statement concerning the status of supernatural events, that 'real in *this* sense they have been to every human being who, from whatever source of delusion, has at any time believed himself under supernatural agency', in *Biographia Literaria*, p. 208.

> For seldom have such spirits power
> To harm, save in the evil hour,
> When guilt we mediate within,
> Or harbour unrepented sin. (4.18)

Marmion's guilt causes him to read meaning into ghost stories that he would normally dismiss as the superstitious nonsense loved by 'the vulgar' (3.18). In James's 'conscience burns the sting' (4.12), and in his self-reproach he interprets the messenger as a visitation from heaven. The sixteenth-century Scottish historian Robert Lindsay of Pistcottie, referenced frequently in Scott's annotations to *Marmion*, reads Flodden as the inevitable outcome of licentious rule.[23] This may help us to interpret the final, moralistic 'vision, passing Nature's law' (5.25): the supernatural summons at Edinburgh's Market-cross which foretells that the nobles of Scotland will die with their king at Flodden for each 'deadly sin' and 'brutal lust' they have committed (5.26). This perhaps offers one way to read *Marmion*, mapping Marmion's personal narrative onto Scotland's national narrative of defeat at Flodden, his guilt writ large upon the national scale and psyche, with the supernatural effecting the transformation of personal guilt into national shame.

Scott returns to the issue of national and cultural crisis in 1810, with his third long narrative poem *The Lady of the Lake*.[24] In this poem, the supernatural operates as a spatial variant of Scott's engagement with historical process, by means of which he juxtaposes two competing discourses of political and ideological reality: Lowland versus Highland cultural identity, and ancient feudal rule versus the modernizing forces of centralized government.[25] This allows Scott to address issues of political significance to both the post-Flodden Scotland of the poem's setting and to a post-1745 political landscape, and to explore complex issues surrounding national identity in these periods of profound cultural change and political uncertainty.

In *The Lady of the Lake* Scott sets up a supernatural paradigm through the repeated use of magical imagery to describe the lady Ellen and the land she inhabits; such that, the island setting of the opening stanza becomes itself part of the machinery of the supernatural. Straying over the threshold of this 'strange' and 'wondrous landscape' (1.10) James Fitz-James gazes upon a scene that is carefully described in the terms of an exotic 'fairy dream' (1.12). We are told that he looks upon a landscape where

---

[23] For a fuller discussion of the historical sources in *Marmion* see my 'Historical Note' in *Marmion*.

[24] All references to the poem are taken from Walter Scott, *The Poetical Works of Sir Walter Scott*, ed. by J. Logie Robertson (London: Oxford University Press, 1917).

[25] Andrew Lincoln, *Walter Scott and Modernity* (Edinburgh: Edinburgh University Press, 2007), p. 43.

The rocky summits, split and rent,
Form'd turret, dome, or battlement,
Or seem'd fantastically set
With cupola or minaret,
Wild crests as pagod ever deck'd,
Or mosque of Eastern architect. (1.11)

The dreamlike quality of the language evokes a mysterious otherworldly realm that exists outside the ordinary course of experience. Scott heightens the impression of timeless mystery by comparing the majesty of the scene with the marvels of the ancient world:[26] the pyramids of Egypt, the tower of Babel, and the pagodas and mosques of the East (1.11). The mountains are personified as giants who stand 'To sentinel enchanted land' (1.14). Scott's use of chivalric imagery further aligns Loch Katrine with the regions of medieval romance, and the landscape seems to dance and shimmer in colourful splendour: the glade twinkles with dewdrops; briar roses hang like green streamers; shrubs wave in the wind like banners, and high on the mountain peaks 'glist'ning streamers waved and danced' (1.12). The Loch glitters and gleams in the setting sun like a 'burnish'd sheet of living gold', and its sandy shores shine in the moonlight like a 'silver strand' (1.17). The green and gold landscape represents the heraldic colours of a pastoral, Arcadian realm, and thus evokes a desirable world of magic.[27] Scott further strengthens the impression that Fitz-James has stumbled across the threshold of an 'imaginative golden age in time and space', by locating the scene within a mythopoeic discourse.[28] The title of the poem and its subsequent allusions to Malory's Le Morte d'Arthur (1485) link it structurally and thematically to Arthurian legend.[29] Fitz-James is personally linked to Arthur, the overarching figure of British myth and legend, who in turn is imbued with the mythical quality of Christ.

However, despite the implications of these magical and mythopoeic elements, not a single event that takes place in the poem involves human interaction with supernatural agents. Despite so carefully and deliberately evoking a sense of the supernatural, the descriptors in this passage anchor the action to a densely textured and, analysing the semantic field, exoticized corporeal realm. Scott's magical world is grounded in reality, and its borders are set by the same spatial parameters as those of the natural world. The action of the narrative is set in an

---

[26] For a discussion of how Scott's poetic language renders the Highlands exotic and 'other' see Susan Oliver, 'Crossing "Dark Barriers": Intertextuality and Dialogue between Lord Byron and Sir Walter Scott', in Studies in Romanticism, 47.1 (Spring 2008), 15–35 (pp. 16–17).

[27] Northrop Frye, 'The Mythos of Summer: Romance', in Anatomy of Criticism: Four Essays (Princeton, NJ: Princeton University Press, 1957), pp. 186–205 (p. 200).

[28] Ibid., pp. 188–200.

[29] For a fuller discussion of this aspect of the poem see Nancy Moore Goslee, Scott the Rhymer (Lexington: Kentucky University Press, 1988), pp. 67–94.

identifiable, geographically specified region (the Trossachs and Stirling), and Scott's fictional characters interact with recognizable figures from history. Douglas is the only character who is reported to perform a feat that exceeds the capabilities of human nature when he exhibits such 'superhuman' strength and skill at the pageant that 'The youth with awe and wonder saw | His strength, surpassing Nature's law.' (5.24). However, this event is easily reconcilable with the limits of feasibility, and the poem's movement towards a realist dialectic differentiates it from its medieval and Renaissance romance genre prototypes.

The island is the archetypal motif of a civilization that has been lost, cut off or suspended from everyday reality and Scott's linguistic reconstruction of Loch Katrine as a supernaturally endowed region aptly conveys the sense of the Highlands as a distinct ideological landscape, even it as suggests that the Highlanders negotiate a different cultural, political and legal reality from the rest of Scotland. It is particularly appropriate that Scott locates his magical world in what Susan Oliver has nicely termed the 'Highland margins', sitting as the Trossachs do on the physical boundary between the Lowlands and Highlands of Scotland.[30] Such a setting fittingly conveys a sense of liminality: the island appears to exist *on* the margins of reality, even as its exiled inhabitants exist *at* the margins of society. And, of course, Scott returns to this idea in *The Heart of Mid-Lothian*, suggesting that Effie Deans may escape the law's penalty of exile if she secretly settles on the Duke of Argyle's Highland estate, for 'Living on the verge of the Highlands, she might, indeed, be said to be out of Scotland, that is, beyond the bounds of ordinary law and civilization.'[31]

Canto 2 of *The Lady of the Lake*, which is titled 'The Island', appears to support such an interpretation of Scott's use of the supernatural in the poem: it creates, but then confounds, reader expectations that the narrative will continue to expand upon the secluded magical setting, instead shifting into an allegory of Scotland's fractured political situation. The change is signalled towards the end of Canto 1, at the very moment that Fitz-James crosses the threshold of Ellen's highly feminized floral bower — only to enter instead into a distinctly masculine domain adorned with weapons, hunting trophies and the blood-soaked relics of combat (1.27). This stark contrast, and the sense of destabilization that it produces, reinforces the thematic link between the supernatural and the socio-political in the poem.

In addition to the symbolic use of spatial dynamics, Scott represents the theme of Scotland's intercultural socio-political struggle through the symbolic and supernatural representation of individual characters in the poem. Critics have

[30] Oliver, *Scott, Byron and the Poetics of Cultural Encounter*, p. 89.
[31] *The Heart of Mid-Lothian* (1818), ed. by David Hewitt and Alison Lumsden, EEWN (Edinburgh University Press: Edinburgh, 2004), p. 378.

argued that Scott 'seems determined to erase the body from his texts',[32] but I would suggest that just as the body of the land becomes imbued with interpretative significance, physicality is constructed in ways that are key to our engagement with the poem. Just as there is a blurring between the mythic and the physical in descriptions of the Scottish landscape, there is a mingling of the elemental and the corporeal in Scott's construction of his characters' physical attributes. Significantly, there is also a level of transference of physical qualities between characters. In 'The Mythos of Summer: Romance', Northrop Frye identifies the romance convention of consistent and clear demarcation between the archetypes of protagonist and antagonist. He argues that 'The enemy is associated with winter, darkness, confusion, sterility, moribund life, and old age, and the hero with spring, dawn, order, fertility, vigor, and youth.'[33] Accordingly, as his name indicates, 'Roderick Dhu' or 'Black Sir Roderick' (2.12) personifies the dark forces of nature, being as 'wild as Bracklinn's thundering wave' (2.14). He is the embodiment of uncontrolled passion, such that 'wildly while his virtues gleam, | They make his passions darker seem' (2.14). His eyes flash 'Dark lighting' (5.14) during a heated exchange with Fitz-James, and when Ellen rejects his suit, he acquires a look of preternatural gloom in his wounded pride, appearing terrible 'Like the ill Demon of the night' (2.33). This sense of similitude to a malign supernatural force is reinforced by his comparability to the 'moody Elfin King,' (4.13) in the 'Ballad of Alice Brand'. Like the Elfin King, Roderick resents the intrusion of a 'knight-errant' (1.24) into his magical kingdom. Through the accumulation of this stormy and supernatural imagery he represents an anarchical, chaotic force that challenges the order and legitimacy of Fitz-James's rule.

However, if Roderick is anarchical he is also regal. Furthermore, if he is vindictive he is also generous, if he is jealous he is also faithful, if he is unmerciful he is also liberal, and if he is murderous he is also undeniably brave. Fitz-James views Roderick 'as an outlaw'd desperate man, | The chief of a rebellious clan', who lives a 'robber life' (5.5–6), but Roderick argues that it is the Gael who has been robbed of his birthright in the first place, so that he is now only taking back what is rightfully his, 'To spoil the spoiler as we may, | And from the robber rend the prey' (5.7). At all times Roderick adheres strictly to his Highland code of honour and offers Fitz-James hospitality and protection saying, 'Thou art my guest; I pledge my word' (5.11). Furthermore, Roderick rules over his rough domain with a firm hand, upholding 'honour's laws' (4.31) and 'though outlaw'd hath his hand | Full sternly kept his mountain land' (2.12). Indeed, in this realm

[32] See, for example, the call for papers for the International Scott Colloquium, 'Corporeality and Spirituality in the Works of Sir Walter Scott', held at the Paris-Sorbonne University in 2012 <www.sfee.univ-tours.fr/Scotland/aScott2012.pdf> [accessed 20 September 2016].

[33] Frye, 'The Mythos of Summer: Romance', pp. 187–88.

there exists 'No law, but Roderick Dhu's command' (3.24). His leadership is successful because he demonstrates the desirable traits expected of a clan chief, and in consequence, is beloved by his fiercely loyal men. He is described as 'Clan-Alpine's honour'd Pine' (6.22), and we are told that the rallying power of 'One blast upon his bugle horn | Were worth a thousand men!' (6.18). Roderick is likened to the 'mountain eagle' (3.3), and at his death Allan Bane laments that 'the prison'd eagle dies for rage' (6.22); all of which makes him a worthy rival of Fitz-James the stag King.

There are many points of correspondence between these rival leaders, not least because Fitz-James is also portrayed as a fragmented, flawed character. Roderick describes his rival as a 'tyrant' full of 'vindictive pride', 'So faithless and so ruthless known' (2.28). However, Fitz-James refutes this accusation, defending himself as 'No tyrant [...] though ire and pride | May lay [my] better mood aside' (6.25), and the narrator vouches that, 'A kindly heart had brave Fitz-James' (4.28). Fitz-James proves his courage by boldly declaring himself Roderick's enemy, and by being ready to stand alone against five hundred foes (4.30; 5.9). His offer to remove Ellen to a 'lovely bower' in Stirling is morally ambiguous (4.18), but he displays courteous nobility in the face of her rejection, and maintains his (now brotherly) offer to escort her to safety. Again, his brutal and deceptive dealings with the Border chiefs are questionable to say the least (2.28), but by ultimately bringing peace and order to the Border region they facilitate the desired result of good rule. In critiquing social function through personal identity Scott widens the individualistic scope of the traditional conflict between hero and enemy to a social level. In creating characters full of light and dark, and subject to internal division, he moves them beyond the static polarization of traditional romance types and towards modernity.[34]

Furthermore, the multifaceted presentation of these rival characters allows Scott to explore and express the moral and legal complexity surrounding issues of legitimacy.[35] In *The Lady of the Lake*, this complexity arises partly as a result of the king's personality and personal inclinations. Fitz-James not only wears a physical disguise, but also is not the king that he should be during much of the action of the poem; like Shakespeare's Prince Hal, he tries to escape from the realities and rigours of his role. His conversation with Ellen in Canto 4 shows him to be dismissive of the value of his position, and he expresses greater happiness in his assumed role of knight-errant than that of king (6.28). Like Fitz-Eustace in *Marmion* who 'reads' the Scottish landscape and Clare through

[34] Frye, 'The Mythos of Summer: Romance', p. 187. See also Scott's discussion of flat character types in medieval romance in Walter Scott, 'Essay on Romance', in *The Miscellaneous Prose Works of Sir Walter Scott, Bart.*, 28 vols (Edinburgh: Robert Cadell, 1834), VI, 150.

[35] As in his fiction, Scott revisits this theme in his poetry. *The Lord of the Isles* (1815), for example, explores the legitimacy of Robert the Bruce's rule.

the lens of the 'romantic tome[s]' he is so fond of poring over (*Marmion* 4.4; 5.3), Roderick chooses to filter experience through the lens of his romantic feelings for Ellen. However, while he focuses on a quest to find personal fulfilment, which leads him back to the Highlands to search for Ellen, Roderick Dhu is rallying the clans for rebellion. Charmed by what he sees, Fitz-James fails to realize that civil trouble is brewing and is too late to stop the preparations for battle that take place in Canto 4. Instead it is the Earl of Mar who marches to quell Clan-Alpine's uprising, and Fitz-James concedes, 'Thou warns't me I have done amiss; | I should have earlier look'd to this' (5.32). This acknowledgment of dilatoriness serves as warning against giving oneself up entirely to the seduction of romance, to reading reality through the lens of romance fiction; an idea that Scott returns to in *Waverley*. Fitz-James now realizes that he must correct the passive form of governance that he has been exercising and fully embrace his role of kingship. Scott indicates that Fitz-James has at last acquired true kingly status when he suggests that he is, 'Not like a stag that spies the snare, | But lion of the hunt aware' (4.26). By associating Fitz-James with the lion motif, the ancient emblem of the Kingdom of Scotland, Scott supports his right, and ability, to rule.

In appropriating the materials of myth, magic and legend Scott creates a discourse that supports the legitimacy of Fitz-James's rule and helps to ultimately locate him as a romance hero. To take just one example of this, we can consider the symbolism inherent in the connection between the greenwood motif and the king. Fitz-James revels and lingers in the dreamlike setting of the greenwood, exclaiming, 'Blithe were it then to wander here!' | [...] | A summer night, in greenwood spent, | Were but to-morrow's merriment' (1.16).[36] By clothing Fitz-James in a 'hunting suit of Lincoln green' (1.23), and referring to his similarly clad knights as 'merry men' (5.17; 5.18), Scott sets him up as a Robin Hood figure, which is in part symbolic of his desire for freedom and escape from the constraints of his real role. His desire to be assimilated into the world of faery is implied through his comparability to Roland in the 'Ballad of Alice Brand' when the Elfin King challenges Roland's right to wear 'The fairies' fatal green' (4.13). However, if the greenwood motif signifies freedom and faery it is also the archetypal symbol of fertility, and the verdant land motif is again connected to the issue of Fitz-James's ability to rule. He is both hunter and green man, and by associating Fitz-James positively with these symbols of fecundity and monarchy Scott suggests that he is the strong ruler of a healthy realm. Through gained experience, Fitz-James becomes a wiser man and a better king, which brings

---

[36] Compare this with the opening song of Act II Scene 5 in *As You Like It*, in which Duke Senior similarly extols the virtues of Arcadian ideal freedom over the exercise of courtly responsibility. See William Shakespeare, *As You Like It* (Oxford: Oxford University Press, 2008).

benefits to the subjects of his kingdom. Thus, in Canto 6, Fitz-James's quest terminates successfully in the gain of treasure, which, Frye argues, 'in mythopoeic romance oten means wealth in its ideal forms, power and wisdom'.[37] If any doubts remain concerning the reality of his sovereignty, Fitz-James subdues and ultimately vanquishes his rival Roderick Dhu in single combat (5.15), thereby satisfying chivalric law and romance genre conventions.

Ultimately, Scotland's political issues are not, nor can be, resolved in the supernatural realm represented by the Highlands, as Ralph Stewart concludes in his article 'The Enchanted World of *The Lady of the Lake*'.[38] Instead, Fitz-James resolves matters on his own terms and on his own ground at Stirling. Scott delights with Fitz-James in his illicit forays over the threshold of the enchanting, charming, and 'supernatural' world, but ultimately he returns both Fitz-James and the action of the poem to the mainframe of reality. The suggestive appeal of the supernatural may temporarily seduce both poet and king, but neither can escape from the need for due process and procedure in the natural world. The alternative social reality realized through the islanders is precarious and cannot present a sustained challenge to the dominant political discourse and the inevitability of its progress towards the formation of the modern nation-state. Douglas's appeal to the crowds at the pageant that they adhere to the rule of 'Scotland's law' (5.28) signals recognition of the need for the Highlanders' cultural assimilation if they wish to be brought from the margins and towards the centre of this subsuming discourse. Consequently, the island court is disassembled and its members travel to Fitz-James's seat of power to attain social repatriation and forgiveness from the king. Like Waverley, the self-styled, conjured 'Genius of the Lake', Fitz-James and his equally self-styled Lady of the Lake must leave their enchanted world behind. Just as Waverley laments the loss of the 'realms of fairy bliss',[39] Fitz-James similarly mourns the disruption of his 'idle dream' (6.28). He is 'heart-sick' (6.25) as his Elysian vision dissolves into the ether, but it cannot end any other way.

Structurally, Scott chooses not to present a first-hand account of the 'bloody fray' (6.4) or the collapse of this 'ideal world', filtering it instead through a minstrel's song, like an off-stage action. This inset narrative device perpetuates the separation of reality from romance, so that it is as if the enchanted island continues to exist at some level. Indeed, by turning the motif of a human snatched away to fairyland on its head, so that the inhabitants of fairyland are instead spatially transferred to the 'real' world, Scott ensures that this community

---

[37] Frye, 'The Mythos of Summer: Romance', p. 193.

[38] Ralph Stewart, 'The Enchanted World of *The Lady of the Lake*', *Scottish Literary Journal*, 22.2 (November 1995), 5–13 (p. 6).

[39] *Waverley; Or 'Tis Sixty Years Since* (1814), ed. by P. D. Garside, EEWN (Edinburgh: Edinburgh University Press, 2007), p. 24.

survives. If the poem begins with the king crossing the liminal threshold of the real into the unreal, it ends conversely by transferring the sense of a summertime scene of enchantment to the court at Stirling. If the imagery of fairyland dominates the opening stanza of the poem, it is again invoked in its concluding stanza, as Fitz-James seems to open a magic casement onto a gossamer world of faery, populated by 'Aërial knights and fairy dames' (6.26).

Finally, it is Fitz-James's kingdom that appears to glow in brilliant splendour, encouraging 'fancy' to convert the world of reality into the world of faery. The 'magic' is reconstructed for a moment. If the king paused, 'raptured and amazed' (1.15), a 'wondering stranger' (1.28), as his gaze swept over Ellen's domain, it is now Ellen who is a 'bewilder'd and amazed' (6.26) spectator. Ellen's diminished and relinquished power is mirrored conversely in Fitz-James's adoption of increased power and the newly won (albeit fragile) cohesion of his kingdom. The result is that loss also represents gain: the spatial transference of fairyland allows for political and social reconciliation, which brings peace and stability to Scotland. Furthermore, social reconciliation facilitates the reconstruction of individuals within this community and brings true happiness, as the conclusion of the 'Ballad of Alice Brand' makes clear:

> Merry it is in the good greenwood,
> When the mavis and merle are singing
> But merrier were they in Dunfermline grey,
> When all the bells were ringing. (4.15)

This process has a healing, transformative effect upon Stirling's society, which has been previously depicted as sick, sinful and segregated (5.22; 6.1–2). Fitz-James benefits as much as his subjects from this process of romance transformation, as the warring factions within his own personality appear to be reconciled by the poem's end.

Scott's use of the supernatural in *The Lady of the Lake* implies that, while a trip into the mythopoeic may offer something that prompts resolution in the real world, to ignore the reality of experience may be dangerous. Furthermore, it suggests that while the supernatural is appealing it is simultaneously limited in its potency. Scott establishes a preternatural paradigm in *The Lady of the Lake* in order to explore the institutional, political and social problems of Scotland's multi-cultural society; and the result is the reconciliation of a disparate political body. To invoke Freud's essay on 'The Uncanny', what is initially presented as the unfamiliar, the unnatural and the unlawful, is ultimately revealed as the familiar, the ordinary and even the order-forming.[40]

---

[40] Sigmund Freud, 'The Uncanny', in *The Standard Edition of the Complete Psychological Works of Sigmund Freud, Volume XVII* (1917–1919): *An Infantile Neurosis and Other Works*, trans. by J. Strachey (London: Hogarth, 1919), pp. 217–56.

In conclusion, this essay has argued that the supernatural performs multiple functions in Scott's poetry. Scott uses magical and supernatural imagery to explore the power of superstitious belief and guilt, and the debilitating effects this can have upon an individual. He warns against succumbing to the seductive, ambiguous power of romantic interpretation. He uses supernatural plots and imagery to examine rival discourses of ideological, socio-political and legal power, and to negotiate complex issues surrounding national identity in times of cultural crisis. Finally, and most significantly of all, he uses the instability of the supernatural to express and to explore the power of the imagination. As we have seen, Scott's poems depend for their plots and their affect on a suspension of disbelief that embraces, even if only temporarily, the charm of a supernatural tale. By doing so, I have argued, they exemplify Coleridge's advocacy of the power of such poetry to stimulate thought and feeling without an actual belief in 'magic'. A longer study would read the same poems against the context of another Romantic theory of the imagination: John Keats's concept of 'negative capability', which pleads the case for 'being in uncertainties, mysteries, doubts, without any irritable reaching after fact and reason'.[41] In creating textual spaces in which the entrancing coexists alongside the mundane, Scott invites the reader to share in his imaginative engagement and delight with things beyond our ken.

[41] John Keats, letter to George and Tom Keats, 21 December 1817. <https://www.poetry foundation.org/resources/learning/essays/detail/69384> [accessed 8 January 2017].

The Lay of the Last Minstrel and Improvisatory Authorship

DANIEL COOK

University of Dundee

Scott's first long verse romance, *The Lay of the Last Minstrel* (1805), must have struck early readers as wholly novel and yet comfortably familiar. By this time, a 'minstrelsy complex' had 'moved beyond its origins in antiquarian polemic to take up residence within the heart of poetry and poetics', as Maureen N. McLane has observed.[1] Thomas Gray's *The Bard* (1757) and James Beattie's *The Minstrel* (1771–74), among many poems that focused on British bardic figures, were still being widely reprinted and imitated. Along with many aspiring poets of the period, Scott had been an avid student of Thomas Percy's *Reliques of Ancient English Poetry* (1765) since his youth (from the age of twelve, in his case). So adept at mimicry was Scott as a schoolboy he later recalled with unrelenting anger an old blue-buskined wife accusing him of plagiarizing 'my most sweet poetry'.[2] Like all apprentice poets, he casually reminds us, he had indeed copied out choice words and ideas for later use — a legitimate learning tool misconstrued by his amateur critic as outright theft.

As Susan Stewart has suggested, the *Lay* is not 'properly a ballad imitation' but 'a kind of manifesto, or perhaps parting statement, of the ballad revival spurred by Percy and that revival's concomitant invention of the minstrel figure'.[3] Scott's speaker, 'an ancient Minstrel, the last of the race', has 'caught somewhat aof the refinement of modern poetry, without losing the simplicity of his original model', or so the poem's preface claims.[4] In order to communicate in popular poetry the history of a specific locale, to put it another way, Scott's *Lay* over-

---

[1] Maureen N. McLane, *Balladeering, Minstrelsy, and the Making of British Romantic Poetry* (Cambridge: Cambridge University Press, 2008), pp. 144, 151–52. For extended accounts of improvisation in the period see Erik Simpson, *Literary Minstrelsy, 1770–1830: Minstrels and Improvisers in British, Irish, and American Literature* (Basingstoke: Palgrave Macmillan, 2008) and Angela Esterhammer, *Romanticism and Improvisation, 1750–1850* (Cambridge: Cambridge University Press, 2008).

[2] 'Essay on Imitations of the Ancient Ballad', in *The Poetical Works of Sir Walter Scott, Bart.*, 12 vols (Edinburgh: Printed for Robert Cadell, 1833), IV, 3–78 (p. 54). Unless stated otherwise, I use this edition for Scott's poetry and prose.

[3] Susan Stewart, 'Scandals of the Ballad', *Representations*, 32 (1990), 134–56 (p. 149).

[4] Scott, *Poetical Works*, VI, 39.

Yearbook of English Studies, 47 (2017), 161–185
© Modern Humanities Research Association 2017

writes an ancient metrical romance in predominately modern dress.[5] Francis Jeffrey particularly enjoyed the passages 'in which the antient strain is suspended, and the feelings and situation of the minstrel himself described in the words of the author'.[6] William Hazlitt, by contrast, unpicks what he calls Scott's 'minstrel masquerade' in a damning assertion that he is to the great poet what an excellent mimic is to a great actor.[7] More recently, Marlon B. Ross has critiqued Scott's 'chivalric pose', in which the author 'silences the last minstrel, so that he can take the mantle'.[8] By putting the *Lay* into the mouth of a character, Peter T. Murphy observes, Scott asserts his authorial self while diffusing it at the same time.[9]

Beyond Scott's headline impersonation of the Last Minstrel, modern readers have identified a further voice in the scholarly apparatus. For Gillian Hughes, the notes are a vital part of the poem's larger 'new-old' aesthetic. Wearing an 'antiquarian mask', Hughes suggests, Scott revels in appending supernatural anecdotes and stories often more outlandish than those told in the course of the poem.[10] J. H. Alexander similarly detects in the notes an editorial persona noticeably more sceptical and humane than the minstrel-narrator himself.[11] (Perhaps we should treat the scholarly voice in the notes as itself a patchwork of multiple characters, including the frequently cited Walter Scott of Satchwells, a seventeenth-century genealogist, among others). In addition to heralds and spirits, yet other authorial voices appear in the poem, most obviously the three minstrels who deliver short songs at the wedding feast that is supposed to close the story: Albert Graeme, a simple Border minstrel who sings of love and war; Fitztraver, a courtly harpist who collaborates with the real-life poet Henry Howard, the Earl of Surrey; and Harold of St Clair, an Orcadian bard who delivers a romantic dirge. More broadly, as Alison Lumsden says, there is a mingling of the Last Minstrel's voice with the author's own at the opening and closing of each canto, so that it is not altogether clear whether we as readers are addressed by an early modern bard or a modern author, an experienced

---

[5] See Jane Millgate, '"Naught of the Bridal": Narrative Resistance in *The Lay of the Last Minstrel*', *Scottish Literary Journal*, 17.2 (1990), 16–26.

[6] *Edinburgh Review*, 6 (April 1805), 1–20 (p. 7).

[7] Quoted in McLane, p. 131.

[8] Marlon B. Ross, 'Scott's Chivalric Pose: The Function of Metrical Romance in the Romantic Period', *Genre*, 19 (1986), 267–97 (p. 293). See also Beth Lau, 'Authorial Anonymity and Intertextuality: Scott's *The Lay of the Last Minstrel*, Coleridge, and Keats', *Studies in Scottish Literature*, 40 (2014), 116–33.

[9] Peter T. Murphy, *Poetry as an Occupation and an Art in Britain, 1760–1830* (Cambridge: Cambridge University Press, 1993), p. 146.

[10] Gillian Hughes, 'Pickling Virgil? Scott's Notes to *The Lay of the Last Minstrel*', *Scottish Literary Review*, 7.2 (2015), 51–62 (p. 58).

[11] J. H. Alexander, *'The Lay of the Last Minstrel': Three Essays* (Salzburg: Institut für englische Sprache und Literatur, University of Salzburg, 1978), p. 167.

improviser of songs or an emergent composer of poems.[12] In this respect, Scott builds on the example of a handful of long narrative poems published in the period that make dramatic capital out of shifts of voice and tone. As early as William Lisle Bowles's 1798 blank-verse poem *Coombe-Ellen*, the speaker summons a 'pale minstrel' to the page with an invocation shaped by an emphatic ballad metre:

> Son of the magic song, arise!
> And bid the deep-toned lyre
> Pour forth its manly melodies.
> With eyes on fire.[13]

Working against Scott's Last Minstrel and his impersonated singers, a barely articulate but highly disruptive voice in the *Lay* belongs to Gilpin Horner, a goblin-page appropriated from both oral and written folklore, as Scott repeatedly reminds us in lengthy citations. Entering almost a third of the way into Scott's poem, the goblin-page seeks out a mysterious book of spells that, once gained, would allow him to seize control of the plot as it is being told.[14] He is, as Margaret Russett has argued, not merely a reader but also 'primitively' a 'writer who wins his power to deceive by anointing the volume with the blood of an illiterate', momentarily opening its forbidding iron clasps.[15] For Dino Franco Felluga, the goblin-page epitomizes the paradigmatic shift from a 'cult of the book' to a liberating if perilous 'culture of the text': whereas a book calls attention to itself as a weighty, ornamented object, text is 'endlessly reproducible and readily consumable'.[16] Nancy Moore Goslee argues that the *Lay*'s 'anarchic goblin may represent both an author's imagination escaping all normal restraints and a nightmare vision of the "ideal reader" attracted by such violence'.[17] The goblin-page, for Murphy, fulfils the role of the 'patron of irregularity' who 'runs through the poem disrupting the sense of calm'.[18] I want to extend these claims to suggest the goblin-page represents more specifically the rise of wild, supernatural writing

---

[12] Alison Lumsden, *Walter Scott and the Limits of Language* (Edinburgh: Edinburgh University Press, 2010), p. 51.

[13] See Susan Stewart, 'Romantic Meter and Form', in *The Cambridge Companion to British Romantic Poetry*, ed. by James Chandler and Maureen N. McLane (Cambridge: Cambridge University Press, 2008), pp. 53–75 (p. 69).

[14] For an excellent in-depth discussion of the book as magic object and as discursive text see Penny Fielding, 'Black Books: Sedition, Circulation, and *The Lay of the Last Minstrel*', *ELH*, 81.1 (2014), 197–223.

[15] Margaret Russett, *Fictions and Fakes: Forging Romantic Authenticity, 1760–1845* (Cambridge: Cambridge University Press, 2006), p. 169.

[16] Dino Franco Felluga, *The Perversity of Poetry: Romantic Ideology and the Popular Male Poet of Genius* (Albany: State University of New York Press, 2005), p. 59.

[17] Nancy Moore Goslee, *Scott the Rhymer* (Lexington: University Press of Kentucky, 1988), pp. 18–40 (p. 20).

[18] Murphy, p. 170.

fashionable in the second half of the eighteenth century (including Scott's translations of Gottfried August Bürger's demonic balladry and his own efforts for Matthew Gregory Lewis's somewhat maligned *Tales of Wonder* [1801]), against the ancient, hard-won improvisatory skills of the Last Minstrel and his poetic brethren.

When writing to Lady Dalkeith, who had commissioned a poetic retelling of the curious folk tale of Gilpin Horner, Scott conceded that the poem 'has drawn itself out to such a length that it cannot be received into the third volume of the *Minstrelsy*'.[19] The *Lay*, in other words, spilled out of Scott's ever-expanding *Minstrelsy of the Scottish Border* (1802–03), where he had been attempting to impose order on the common stock of popular poetry in the region. In *Minstrelsy* he divides the contents into three broad categories: historical ballads, which largely uphold martial and patriotic ideals; romantic ballads, which rely on wild, supernatural, or sentimental elements, and erode the morality underpinning chivalric ideals; and imitation ballads, with which he seeks to reverse what he perceives to be the debauchery of the 'romantic' style.[20] In what follows I want to trace what only superficially appear to be contradictions in the improvisatory authorship of the *Lay*. Scott seeks to dramatize in a modern printed poem anchored by historical notes the spontaneous and occasional remit of traditional minstrelsy. The story itself, moreover, turns on actions that are notionally unforeseen (*improvisus*) for an uninitiated reader of romantic ballads.

Scott's Poetical Character: A Retrospective

Seemingly from memory, Scott, through his surrogate compositional voices, refashions (while only selectively referencing) a range of poetic and scholarly materials from a common stock and from the corpora of others, including — controversially — an as-then unpublished but widely recited fragment by Coleridge. Reining in his plot by the closing of the text, Scott asserts his authorial control over the poem as it exists on the page and yet still maintains in a kind of living archive the open-endedness of improvised minstrelsy. As Meredith Martin reminds us, a lay is a transcription of a song, a recording of a performance and therefore a fantasy of communal creating and recreating.[21] Scott's *Lay* is not merely a poem; as Celeste Langan has demonstrated, it was a prolonged 'media event'.[22]

---

[19] Quoted in Edgar Johnson, *Sir Walter Scott: The Great Unknown*, 2 vols (London: Hamish Hamilton, 1970), I, 200.

[20] See Susan Oliver, *Scott, Byron, and the Poetics of Encounter* (Basingstoke: Palgrave Macmillan, 2005), pp. 60–64.

[21] Meredith Martin, '"Imperfectly Civilized": Ballads, Nations, and Histories of Form', *ELH*, 82.2 (2015), 345–63 (p. 352).

[22] Celeste Langan, 'Understanding Media in 1805: Audiovisual Hallucination in *The Lay of the Last Minstrel*', *Studies in Romanticism*, 40.1 (2001), 49–70. See also Peter J. Manning, '"The

With the copyright of the *Lay* due to run out in 1833, Scott took the opportunity to write an extended introduction in which he could concretize in print an appropriative, collaborative authorship ideal that had been undermined by a highly persistent, slow-burning allegation of plagiarism from which the poem has never really recovered.[23] Whereas in the 1805 edition he merely outlined his aim to illustrate life in the Borders through a modernized impersonation of minstrelsy, in the later introduction (written in April 1830 and revised in the autumn of 1831) he shifts the focus to an account of his burgeoning career in verse and its attendant pitfalls. Quickly noting the popularity of the first edition of *Minstrelsy*, he admits that the second did not sell as well, particularly in England, where, he claims, readers would have been put off by poems left 'in the rude garb of antiquity' and accompanied by obscure notes. More than that, he makes an extraordinary claim about a seeming lack of public interest in balladry: 'the practice of ballad-writing was for the present out of fashion, and [...] any attempt to revive it, or to found a poetical character upon it, would certainly fail of success'. 'The ballad measure itself, which was once listened to as to an enchanting melody', he continues, 'had become hackneyed and sickening, from its being the accompaniment of every grinding hand-organ'. To please his target audience he considered using the measured short line common in English, but soon conceded that it leads to 'slovenly', formulaic composition. Feeling intimidated, as he puts it, he also avoided the octosyllabic verse that, in recent years (and after Scott produced his major verse romances), had been used to great effect by Byron.

Such considerations set us up for an important if quickly abandoned revelation: Scott heard, from his friend John Stoddart, recitations of a handful of unpublished poems by the Lake School poets, including Coleridge's as-yet unpublished *Christabel* (1816).[24] Coleridge, for his part, noted in 1807 that the *Lay* had 'no dishonourable or avoidable resemblance to *Christabel*'.[25] But the appearance in print of Byron's sideswiping claim that the *Lay* was heavily 'indebted' to Coleridge, without whom Scott's poem 'would never have been thought of', forced Scott to respond in some way.[26] Among the 'specimens'

Birthday of Topography": A Response to Celeste Manning', *Studies in Romanticism*, 40.1 (2001), 71–83, and Nick Bujak, 'The Form of Media History: Narrator-Space and *The Lay of the Last Minstrel*', *Studies in English Literature, 1500–1900*, 54.3 (2014), 697–716.

[23] Scott, *Poetical Works*, VI, 5–31.

[24] Earl Griggs suggests that Coleridge gave a copy of *Christabel* to Stoddart, who recited it to Scott in 1802: *Collected Letters of Samuel Taylor Coleridge*, ed. by Earl Griggs, 6 vols (Oxford: Clarendon Press, 1956–71), II, 1191–1202.

[25] *Collected Letters of Samuel Taylor Coleridge*, II, 1191.

[26] Thomas Medwin, *Conversations of Lord Byron: Noted during a residence with his lordship at Pisa, in the years 1821 and 1822*, 2nd edn (London: Henry Colburn, 1824), pp. 249–50.

recited by Stoddart, Scott admits that he was most struck by *Christabel*, noting its appropriateness as a model for an unusual commission with which he had been grappling, namely a poetic retelling of a goblin story for Lady Dalkeith: 'the singularly irregular structure of the stanzas, and the liberty which it allowed the author to adapt the sound to the sense', Scott writes, 'seemed to be exactly suited to such an extravaganza as I meditated on the subject of Gilpin Horner'. Openly acknowledging Coleridge's direct influence on him as that of 'the pupil to his master', Scott nevertheless cagily downplays Coleridge's proprietary claims over an unfinished work. He even lambasts Coleridge for habitually dashing 'unfinished scraps of poetry' off his pen, defying the skill of his 'poetical brethren to complete them'.

Having skirted around the plagiarism allegation, Scott continues what Jane Millgate has called his 'fable of composition'.[27] First, he did not immediately begin 'my projected labour' (drawing our attention to the originality of his work). Second, he shared some early stanzas with learned friends, who had little to say in answer to what they had heard. Scott responded by throwing his manuscript into the fireplace, thereby invoking a common topos in antiquarian editing: the perishable manuscript. Percy, for example, had famously claimed he had personally retrieved from a fire many of the poems later included in his *Reliques*. Decades later, Scott mimics the elusive, textually unstable outpourings of the Coleridgean poet but also moves his own work within the stabilizing remit of recovered balladry. Taking this further, he announces his friend's suggestion that he should add Spenserian prologues to explain his work in a pseudo-antiquarian style. After all, Scott tells us, this friend had made little comment on the *Lay* because he had not yet heard 'a poem so much out of the common road', another indication of its uniqueness. Scott instead added 'the Old Minstrel, as an appropriate prolocutor'. Having been vetted by critics as 'fit for the market', the poem was soon finished at about the rate of a canto per week. Now the writer, 'who has been since so voluminous', could lay claim to be considered 'an original author' intensively labouring over his materials.

It is also important to note that the new introduction to the *Lay* is, as Scott mentions towards the beginning, a sequel of sorts to two important articles included in a revised edition of *Minstrelsy*: 'Introductory Remarks on Popular Poetry, and on the Various Collections of Ballads in Britain, Particularly those of Scotland' and 'Essay on Imitations of the Ancient Ballad'. Traditional balladry has fallen into disrepute, he claims in the first essay, because the popular pieces have congealed into 'a joint stock for the common use of the profession'.[28]

---

[27] Jane Millgate, *Walter Scott: The Making of the Novelist* (Edinburgh: Edinburgh University Press, 1984), p. 15.

[28] Scott, *Poetical Works*, I, 5–91.

Habitual imitation, in this context, undermines the practising poet's work: lazily appropriating from the worn-out stock makes his immediate task easier but ultimately degrades his art, his value-added labour. Scott extends his treatment of revivifying authorship in 'Essay on Imitations of the Ancient Ballad' with an account of his early pieces 'Glenfinlas' (an imitation from the Gaelic) and 'The Eve of St John', both of which he treats as poetic experiments that were not entirely successful: 'I shook hands with criticism, and reduced my ballads back to their original form, stripping them without remorse of those "lendings" which I had adopted at the suggestion of others'.[29] These pieces had appeared in Lewis's *Tales of Wonder*, an anthology of old and new works cruelly dubbed *Tales of Plunder* by parodists. Rather than gloss over this period of his career, Scott instead showcases it as a formative experience by appending extensive extracts from his correspondence with his grumbling editor.[30]

This establishes a counter-narrative, in which Lewis's treatment of Scott's poems ought to be taken as a decisive influence on his style, in the sense that Scott adopts some of his editor's observations and publicly rejects others. Lewis, for one, favours a traditional ballad metre: 'Observe, that, in the Ballad, I do not always object to a variation of metre; but then it ought to increase the melody, whereas, in my opinion, in these instances [in Scott's poems], it is diminished'. In the *Lay*, Scott largely moves away from the old ballad praised by his editor here, and instead employs an irregular rhyme scheme (other than an impersonation of the four-line ballad quatrain within Canto Sixth), though he does use some internal rhyme and repetition. He also varies his prosodic structuring, much more so than Coleridge, from whom he supposedly took his metre. Even though Coleridge did not explicitly claim in his preface that his metre had been plagiarized, he did insist on the importance of his innovation:

> I have only to add, that the metre of the Christabel is not, properly speaking, irregular, though it may seem so from its being founded on a new principle: namely, that of counting in each line the accents, not the syllables. Though the latter may vary from seven to twelve, yet in each line the accents will be found to be only four.[31]

One of the most respected bards of the time, Thomas Moore, tried to put Coleridge straight: 'the monstrous assurance of any man coming forward coolly at this time of day, and telling the readers of English poetry, whose ear has been

---

[29] Ibid., IV, 3–78 (p. 71).

[30] Ibid., IV, 79–87.

[31] Samuel Taylor Coleridge, *The Collected Works of Samuel Taylor Coleridge: Poetical Works I, Poems (Reading Text): Part 1*, ed. by J. C. C. Mays (Princeton, NJ: Princeton University Press, 2001), pp. 482–83. As Brennan O'Donnell points out, the weight of the lines varies from four to fourteen syllables; and not all lines have four stresses. See O'Donnell, 'The "Invention" of a Meter: *Christabel* Meter as Fact and Fiction', *Journal of English and Germanic Philology*, 100.4 (2001), 511–36.

tuned to the lays of Spenser, Milton, Dryden, and Pope, that he make his metre "on a new principle!" but we utterly deny the truth of the assertion'.[32] Spenser had used a four-stress line for extended passages throughout *The Shepheardes Calender* (1579). Chatterton, Burns, and Blake, more recently, had used accentual metre. In fact, Scott's *Minstrelsy* is replete with poems comprising four-stress lines of anywhere between eight and ten syllables. In the *Lay*, Scott uses an accentual metre in the very opening sections of what is a very long, multifaceted poem, but only occasionally thereafter. Throughout the cantos he flits in an appropriately improvisatory manner between accentual verses, traditional ballad metres, conventional octosyllabic couplets, and even, in the mouth of a sophisticated minstrel, the Spenserian stanza. Furthermore, as P. B. Anderson shows, Scott had used accentual metre far more extensively in 'St John' than he does in the *Lay*.[33]

So the *Lay* is an extension — and arguably a culmination — of Scott's prior experimentation with traditional and modern poetics. I now wish to trace some points of influence and reworking across the six cantos of the *Lay*. Sometimes Scott alludes to specific texts, both authored and traditional, for local comparison. Elsewhere, he follows the example of others in order to recreate or even unsettle certain expectations. And in other places he attempts to expunge their work from his own as he strives to establish his 'poetical character' at the outset of his career.

Framing the First Canto

The framing narrative of the *Lay* establishes a decrepit minstrel with a death-wish, compelled — like Coleridge's Ancient Mariner — to keep telling tales:

> The last of all the Bards was he,
> Who sung of Border chivalry;
> For, welladay! their date was fled,
> His tuneful brethren all were dead;
> And he, neglected and oppress'd,
> Wish'd to be with them, and at rest. (Introduction, 7–12)

Scott suggests the songs have grown heavy while also reminding us of their former elegance: 'No more on prancing palfrey borne, | He caroll'd, light as lark at morn'. Not only does the modern age fail to appreciate his sound, it evinces an egregious prejudice against the 'harmless art':

---

[32] *Edinburgh Review*, 27 (September 1816), 58–67 (p. 64). Well into the 1830s, however, critics continued to laud the originality of Coleridge's prosody: 'Some new form of verse seems wanting to modern poetry', wrote John Abraham Heraud, 'and this of Coleridge's invention might have been more generally adopted with advantage', *Fraser's Magazine*, 10 (Oct 1834), 379–403 (p. 394).

[33] P. B. Anderson, 'Scott's *The Eve of St John* and the "Influence" of *Christabel* on *The Lay of the Last Minstrel*', *Philological Review*, 35.1 (2009), 1–10.

> Old times were changed, old manners gone;
> A stranger fill'd the Stuarts' throne;
> The bigots of the iron time
> Had call'd his harmless art a crime. (Introduction, 19–22)

Formerly adored at court, he has become a 'wandering Harper, scorn'd and poor' begging 'his bread from door to door', thereby conforming to Joseph Ritson's depiction of the minstrel figure as a lowly itinerant retelling the degraded wares of others. Gladdened by the kindness of the Duchess and her circle, 'his minstrel pride' returns to him as he talks of great earls 'dead and gone'.[34] However, with the stage set for a revival among a captive audience more suited to Percy's account of the minstrel figure — a professional court poet and dignified inventor of songs — he falters:

> For, when to tune his harp he tried,
> His trembling hand had lost the ease,
> Which marks security to please;
> And scenes, long past, of joy and pain,
> Came wildering o'er his aged brain —
> He tried to tune his harp in vain! (Introduction, 65–70)

Perhaps Scott wanted to confront the naïve praise of song-making in Percy's *The Hermit of Warkworth* ('All Minstrels yet that ever I saw, | Are full of game and glee') and Beattie's *The Minstrel* ('As ever as he went some merry lay he sung'). Or perhaps he had in mind Spenser's celebratory lines in *The Faerie Queene* (1590–96):

> And forth he comes into the commune hall,
>> Where earely waite him many a gazing eye,
> To weet what end to straunger knights may fall.
>> There many Minstrales maken melody,
>> To driue away the dull melancholy,
>> And many Bardes, that to the trembling chord
>> Can tune their timely voyces cunningly,
>> And many Chroniclers, that can record
> Old loues, and warres for Ladies doen by many a Lord. (I.V.iii.1–9)[35]

Spenser's minstrels appear confident and artful, a standard that Scott's faltering minstrel struggles to achieve. The poise of the narrator's speech in the *Lay* is belied by the intrusion of a triplet (*pain, brain, vain*) within a 100-line proem largely made up of couplets. The variation conveys, and is arguably affected by, the minstrel's fumbling. Elsewhere in the proem Scott uses triplets to similar effect:

---

[34] For a pertinent discussion of the debate between Percy and Ritson, see McLane, pp. 146–51. See Oliver for a discussion of Scott's literary response to the dispute: pp. 33–38, 53–61.

[35] Edmund Spenser, *The Faerie Queene*, ed. by Thomas P. Roche, Jr (London: Penguin Books, 1987), p. 92.

> When kindness had his wants supplied,
> And the old man was gratified,
> Began to rise his minstrel pride:
> [...]
> And then, he said, he would full fain
> He could recall an ancient strain,
> He never thought to sing again. (Introduction, 45–47, 75–77)

These last two examples capture the Last Minstrel's feelings in the moment, whether he is overwhelmed by sudden kindness or toying with the idea of singing a controversial 'long-forgotten melody'. Towards the close of the proem, as we prepare for Canto First, Scott introduces a faulty triplet:

> Amid the strings his fingers stray'd,
> And an uncertain warbling made,
> And oft he shook his hoary head. (Introduction, 84–86)

These lines translate the minstrel's oral failures into print: *strayed* and *made* rhyme perfectly well, despite their appearance on the page, whereas *head* is at best a half rhyme, at worst a twinless one. However, at this point the Last Minstrel comes alive in a noticeably Coleridgean manner:

> But when he caught the measure wild,
> The old man raised his face, and smiled;
> And lighten'd up his faded eye,
> With all a poet's ecstasy! (Introduction, 87–90)

In the authorial narrative outlined in the 1830 introduction to the *Lay*, Scott took pains to state, categorically, that he had not parodied Coleridge. But surely many readers would have seen Scott's Last Minstrel (here, at least) as a potential variation of the enchanted storytellers we find in Coleridge's narrative poems, particularly the glittering-eyed Ancient Mariner, rather than, say, Beattie's 'long-robed minstrels' who with 'mellow breath the martial pipe inspire' or the 'sad eyes' of Gray's wearied bard. Moreover, the opening verse paragraph of Canto First relies heavily on a technique favoured by Coleridge and oral poets alike: incremental repetition. And, in the following lines, it mimics the octosyllabic couplets used in *Christabel*:

> The way was long, the wind was cold,
> The Minstrel was infirm and old;
> His wither'd cheek, and tresses gray,
> Seem'd to have known a better day;
> The harp, his sole remaining joy,
> Was carried by an orphan boy. (Introduction, 1–6)

Against, for example, the sprightly opening of Percy's well-known Northumberland ballad *The Hermit of Warkworth*, the leaden, 'limp march of these lines',

John Sutherland suggests, aptly captures the minstrel's weariness.[36] Soon enough, though, the poem springs into life over lines of varying syllabic length, each with four or five spread-out, insistent and energetic stresses:

> The feast was over in Branksome tower,
> And the Ladye had gone to her secret bower;
> Her bower that was guarded by word and by spell,
> Deadly to hear, and deadly to tell—
> Jesu Maria, shield us well!
> No living wight, save the Ladye alone,
> Had dared to cross the threshold stone. (I.i.1–7)

Not only is this the shortest verse paragraph in the canto (the longest runs over seventeen lines), it is the only one that directly contains a line from Coleridge ('Jesu Maria, shield us well!), in what amounts to a brief, pointed pastiche of Coleridge's improvisatory, stuttering style ('[…] her secret bower; | Her bower […]'), cacophonous use of rhyme in short lines (*spell, tell, well*), and abundant assonance (particularly the open *o* and *ea*). The lifted line is even marked out as a line 'deadly' to hear and to tell, perhaps a criticism of the demonization of the poetic voice in post-bardic writing.

Certainly the second verse paragraph shifts abruptly to other imitated voices, that of Spenser and Goldsmith, seemingly in a move to expunge demonic poetics from the page (at this point, at least). Whereas the first paragraph leaves the Ladye in her secret bower, the second remains in the hall:

> The tables were drawn, it was idlesse all;
>   Knight, and page, and household squire,
> Loiter'd through the lofty hall,
>   Or crowded round the ample fire:
> The stag-hounds, weary with the chase,
>   Lay stretch'd upon the rushy floor,
> And urged, in dreams, the forest race,
>   From Teviot-stone to Eskdale-moor. (I.ii.1–8)

The stanza is sprinkled with Spenserian coinage ('idlesse') and an uncommon word used in Goldsmith's 'The Hermit, or Edwin and Angelina' ('rushy', as in 'my rushy couch, and frugal fare, | My blessing and repose'). And we move from the couplets of *Christabel* to the alternate rhyming of *The Faerie Queene*, albeit in a far less sophisticated, prolonged execution. More importantly, perhaps, it sets up a Spenserian tone of 'deepe darkness dred', particularly in the seemingly banal, descriptive sixth verse paragraph:

---

[36] John Sutherland, *The Life of Walter Scott* (Oxford: Blackwell, 1995), p. 102.

> Why do these steeds stand ready dight?
> Why watch these warriors, arm'd, by night?—
> They watch, to hear the blood-hound baying:
> They watch, to hear the war-horn braying;
> To see St. George's red cross streaming,
> To see the midnight beacon gleaming:
> They watch, against Southern force and guile,
>   Lest Scroop, or Howard, or Percy's powers,
>   Threaten Branksome's lordly towers,
> From Warkworth, or Naworth, or merry Carlisle. (I.vi.1–10)

This is the closest we get to a Spenserian stanza in the *Lay*'s first canto. A fairly fixed form, discounting for a moment deliberate deviations, the Spenserian stanza contains nine lines in total: eight lines in iambic pentameter followed by a single alexandrine line in iambic hexameter (a-b-a-b-b-c-b-c-c). Here, by contrast, we have ten lines made up of eight or nine syllables each, aside from a final twelve-line alexandrine, rhyming a-a-b-b-b-b-c-d-d-c. Aside from an occasional archaism ('dight'), the diction is thoroughly modern. And Scott's rigidly end-stopped lines here make little attempt to emulate the wavy pattern of caesurae employed to such musical effect by Spenser. But the use of an alexandrine and an overzealous reliance on present participle verbs and compound nouns as favoured (but used fairly sparingly) by Spenser ('devouring speare', 'steele-headed'), and the impending threat in the tone, suggest *The Faerie Queene* (particularly the Redcrosse Knight) had a shaping influence on Scott, certainly when set against the intensive, invasive mimicry of Coleridge at the opening.

One might wonder why Scott adopts the label of an Anglo-Italian canto over the Scottish fytte, bearing in mind his *Minstrelsy* takes the latter term. After all, the first two cantos of the *Lay* in particular recall the ballads defined as historical and romantic in *Minstrelsy*. As Susan Oliver suggests, the Ladye — Janet Scott of Buccleuch — for one, represents 'excessive passion' along with an effeminized martial tradition that had become associated with 'romantic' writing.[37] More specifically, Janet's small son takes us back to the ballad of Johnie Armstrang:

> Until, amid his sorrowing clan,
>   Her son lisp'd from the nurse's knee—
> 'And if I live to be a man,
> My father's death reveng'd shall be!'— (I.ix.11–14)

With hardly a word altered, these are the concluding lines of the Jacobite song 'Johny Armstrong's Last Good-Night' published by Joseph Ritson.[38] Scott chose

---

[37] Oliver, p. 76.

[38] 'If ever I live to be a man, | My fathers death reveng'd shall be': Joseph Ritson, *A Select Collection of English Songs*, 3 vols (London: J. Johnson, 1783), II, 322–26 (p. 326).

not to use these lines in his own version of that ballad in *Minstrelsy*, almost certainly because they fostered revolutionary sentiments.[39] In the new context, the *Lay*, Scott sets the scene for a survivor of the rebellions, the Last Minstrel, to refocus our attention on the emotional fallout of war for mothers or lovers. He follows the borrowed lines, and closes the stanza, with a Coleridgean couplet:

> Then fast the mother's tears did seek
> To dew the infant's kindling cheek. (I.ix.15–16)

By 'Coleridgean' I refer more specifically to a spurious sequel that appeared in print, ironically, before *Christabel*, but after *Lay*:

> But now returning beauty warms
> Her lips, and her kindling cheek so well,
> She looks like the lovely Christobell. (23–25)[40]

Perhaps Scott had a popular line from James Beattie in mind: 'Quick o'er the kindling cheek, the ready blush; | And from the smallest violence to shrink' (*The Seasons* [1726–30]).[41] In any case, Scott liked the phrase as he repurposed it in *Rokeby* (1813): '[…] bended brow, and glance of fire, | And kindling cheek, spoke Erin's ire'. Thomas Moore, too, uses it in 'The Philosopher Aristippus to a Lamp which was given him by Lais' ('And I shall mark her kindling cheek, | Shall see her bosom warmly move'). Scott perhaps does directly borrow from Coleridge at this point in the poem as the line 'burning pride and high disdain' clearly echoes the second part of *Christabel* ('words of high disdain'). The ensuing verse paragraph more faintly mimics Coleridge, again, in its brevity and repetition ('All loose her negligent attire, | All loose her golden hair'), as well as in its rapid rhyming at the close:

> And well she knew, her mother dread,
> Before Lord Cranstoun she should wed,
> Would see her on her dying bed. (I.x.15–17)

Of the whole *Lay*, one might suggest, the first canto seems to have the widest array of allusions, thereby establishing the free-ranging, improvisatory tone.

Other borrowings in Canto First seem to rely on a decent knowledge of the common stock of songs. A good example is the seemingly throwaway conclusion to the twenty-seventh verse paragraph — 'Ambition is no cure for love!' — which

---

[39] Scott, *Poetical Works*, I, 392–413.

[40] Often attributed to Anna Jane Vardill, the poem was published in the *European Magazine* in April 1815. See Donald H. Reiman, 'Christobell; or, The Case of the Sequel Preemptive', *Wordsworth Circle*, 6.4 (1975), 283–89 (p. 286).

[41] William Scott, a teacher in Edinburgh, included the passage in *Lessons in Elocution* (Edinburgh: C. Elliot; London: T. Longman, 1779), p. 271. The passage was also excerpted in the periodical press in such publications as *The Lady's Magazine* and *The Student*.

gains more meaning if the reader is familiar with Sir Gilbert Elliot's song 'Amynta' (*The Charmer* [1749]), a favourite at concerts throughout the eighteenth century: 'No more for Amynta fresh garlands I wove; | For ambition, I said, would soon cure me of love'. A song about regret ('Oh, what had my youth with ambition to do? | Why left I Amynta? Why broke I my vow?') and failure ('moments neglected return not again') has been used in the *Lay* as a warning to William of Deloraine as he rides, unchallenged, through the Borders. Spurning pastoral convention, and arguably Coleridgean enchantment, Scott's new-old romance seeks new ground:

> In bitter mood he spurred fast,
> And soon the hated heath was past;
> And far beneath, in lustre wan,
> Old Melros' rose, and fair Tweed ran. (I.xxxi.1–4)

A version of Coleridge's Aeolian harp threatens to stir, but ultimately it meets silence:

> The sound, upon the fitful gale,
> In solemn wise did rise and fail,
> Like that wild harp, whose magic tone
> Is waken'd by the winds alone.
> But when Melrose he reach'd, 'twas silence all. (I.xxxi.9–13)

A thin black line pierces the page, like the break in a dramatic text, and the Last Minstrel stops, seeking the approval of his audience. Indifferent to 'present praise', he instead

> spoke of former days,
> And how old age, and wand'ring long,
> Had done his hand and harp some wrong. (I, Conclusion, 8–10)

Rejecting Coleridge's modern poetics and pushing against Elliot's regional pastoral, however much he admired both, Scott suggests the old songs, and the old ways of playing, will remain popular when delivered with an animated, fluid performance. Duly captivated by the minstrel's talent, the Duchess and her daughters 'long'd the rest to hear'.

Lengthening the Tale

The epilogue to Canto Second, however, suggests the Last Minstrel's overly ambitious, 'lengthened tale' has already drained his talents. This canto takes on a gothic and fantastical turn as we welcome to the page, through an assortment of related vignettes, a series of new characters, including the long-dead Michael Scott, whom we learn in a story told by the solemn Monk of St. Mary's had been an inspiring wizard; the fairest maid of Teviotdale, Margaret; and Lord Cranstoun's goblin-page, who is described as 'waspish, arch, and litherlie', despite his apparent lack of words ('Lost! Lost! Lost!', he mutters). Indeed, the account of the goblin-page interrupts a mooted love story between Deloraine and Margaret in a standout moment of meta-minstrelsy that provides a miniature version of the unsaid tale along formulaic yet enticing lines:

And now, fair dames, methinks I see
You listen to my minstrelsy;
[...]
Ye ween to hear a melting tale,
Of two true lovers in a dale;
And how the Knight, with tender fire,
To paint his faithful passion strove;
Swore he might at her feet expire,
But never, never cease to love;
And how she blush'd, and how she sigh'd,
And, half consenting, half denied,
And said that she would die a maid; —
Yet, might the bloody feud be stay'd,
Henry of Cranstoun, and only he,
Margaret of Branksome's choice should be. (II.xxix.1–16)

Over the ensuing four verse paragraphs the minstrel instead prefers to leave the canto with a mob of Scotts burning St. Mary's chapel in a rage, while the goblin-page, the Knight and the Lady flee the scene in a curiously lackadaisical denouement. Aside from a strategic, pointed use of Gothic pastiche, the canto as a whole is largely descriptive, often needlessly so. The account of Melrose Abbey at the opening has long been popular ('For the gay beams of lightsome day | Gild, but to flout, the ruins grey'), but the introduction of Margaret is couched in cloying and repetitive imagery:

The sun had brighten'd Cheviot grey,
The sun had brighten'd the Carter's side;
And soon beneath the rising day
Smiled Branksome Towers and Teviot's tide.
The wild birds told their warbling tale,
And waken'd every flower that blows;
And peeped forth the violet pale,
And spread her breast the mountain rose.
And lovelier than the rose so red,
Yet paler than the violet pale,
She early left her sleepless bed,
The fairest maid of Teviotdale. (II.xxv.1–12)

When discussing Michael Scott, the Last Minstrel — through the character of the Monk — carefully avoids bedevilling words:

to speak them were a deadly sin;
And for having but thought them my heart within,
A treble penance must be done. (II.xiii.11–13)

However, when Deloraine takes the Mighty Book from the 'cold hand' of the dead wizard, Gothic terror ('He thought, as he took it, the dead man frown'd'), excess ('The night return'd in double gloom') and multivocality ('Loud sobs, and laughter louder, ran, | And voices unlike the voice of man') unravel the Last Minstrel's song, which he now disowns ('I cannot tell how the truth may be; | I say the tale as 'twas said to me').

Canto Third opens with an emphatic continuation of the minstrel's notional rejection of pastoral love as ill-suited to his style: 'How could I to the dearest theme, | That ever warm'd a minstrel's dream', he says, 'So foul, so false a recreant prove!' He further acknowledges the ubiquitous dominance of love as a popular topic in 'the court, the camp, the grove'. Seemingly sharing this assumption, Lord Cranstoun 'pondering deep the tender scene' is interrupted by the goblin-page who 'shouted wild and shrill'. The appearance of the latter coincides with a noticeably grittier realism that distracts us from the abstract loveliness of pastoral: 'That warrior's steed, so dapple-gray, | Was dark with sweat, and splash'd with clay'. Furthermore, the realism abruptly gives way to violent fantasy, a step further away from gentle nature writing: 'Their very coursers [...] snorted fire'. Cranstoun, facing Deloraine, becomes anxious, as indicated in the clunky repetitiveness of the description:

> He sigh'd a sigh, and pray'd a prayer;
> The prayer was to his patron saint,
> The sigh was to his ladye fair. (III.v.2–4)

Bombast returns to the text — 'The meeting of these champions proud | Seem'd like the bursting thunder-cloud' — in a manner reminiscent of Scott's efforts in Lewis's *Tales of Wonder*, specifically 'The Fire-King' ('His breath it was lightning, his voice it was storm'), or even *Fingal* (1762) and many other Ossian poems ('Lightning pours from their sides of steel'). Cranstoun nevertheless quickly defeats his foe with a delicate image in our minds: his lance pierced 'like silk, the Borderer's mail'. He asks his page to 'stanch the wound' — a phrase that Scott tells us in the scholarly notes is taken from *Pieces of Ancient Popular Poetry* (1791) ('And with some kind of words he staunched the blood') and used on two more occasions in the *Lay* — thereby establishing his adherence to the chivalric code of the historical ballad. The goblin-page, seeing the Mighty Book, instead 'thought not to search or stanch the wound, | Until the secret he had found', thereby corrupting that code. The book, however, resists him:

> The iron band, the iron clasp,
> Resisted long the elfin grasp:
> For when the first he had undone,
> It closed as he the next begun.
> Those iron clasps, that iron band,

> Would not yield to unchristen'd hand,
> Till he smear'd the cover o'er
> With the Borderer's curdled gore;
> A moment then the volume spread,
> And one short spell therein he read,
> It had much of glamour might,
> Could make a ladye seem a knight;
> […]
> And youth seem age, and age seem youth—
> All was delusion, nought was truth. (III.ix.1–18)

With this snatched spell acquired the goblin-page is able to impersonate the young heir of Buccleuch, stolen by an English yeoman, who himself appears to be an inadvertent, or perhaps parodic, copy of Spenser's Redcrosse Knight, in appearance at least ('His coal-black hair, shorn round and close, | Set off his sunburn'd face'). Meanwhile, it is the noble Ladye who successfully attends to the injured Deloraine: 'with a charm she stanch'd the blood' (a more exact, legitimate borrowing from the 1791 poem). This seems to allow a pastoral love theme to re-enter Scott's *Lay* as the Last Minstrel dwells at length, at this point, on fair Margaret alone in her turret. Whereas the gothicized goblin-page wrestles with the iron clasp of the book, in the case of Margaret we see

> Her golden hair stream'd free from band,
> Her fair cheek rested on her hand,
> Her blue eyes sought the west afar,
> For lovers love the western star. (III.xxiv.13–16)

However, Margaret is an experienced enough reader to know that 'yon red glare' in the sky is a beacon of impending death; and the warder also watching it 'blazing strong' duly 'blew his war-note loud and long'. The rest of the canto looks ahead to the battle scene that makes up Canto Fourth. The song of war trumps the momentarily dominant song of love, just as it does in Percy's *Hermit* ('And deeds of arms and war became | The theme of every tongue').

Canto Fourth of the *Lay* opens with a fond reminiscence of the days of battle long past:

> The glaring bale-fires blaze no more;
> No longer steel-clad warriors ride
> Along thy wild and willow'd shore. (IV.i.2–4)

The lament takes a personal turn as the Last Minstrel remembers 'The hour my brave, my only boy, | Fell by the side of great Dundee'. Quickly dismissing the aside — 'Enough—he died the death of fame' — he refocuses our attention on the battle scene, or rather its cultural significance. After a lengthy catalogue of the knights involved, as well as a detailed account of the background of the disputes, in the thirty-fourth verse paragraph the Last Minstrel discusses the influence of Rattling Roaring Willie and ancient minstrelsy at large. He is fully aware of the expectations placed on war songs:

> I know right well, that, in their lay,
> Full many minstrels sing and say,
>   Such combat should be made on horse. (IV.xxxiv.1–3)

However, he openly refuses to follow their example:

> Why should I tell the rigid doom,
> That dragg'd my master to his tomb;
>   How Ousenam's maidens tore their hair,
> Wept till their eyes were dead and dim,
> And wrung their hands for love of him,
>   Who died at Jedwood Air?
> He died!—his scholars, one by one,
> To the cold silent grave are gone;
> And I, alas! survive alone,
> To muse o'er rivalries of yore,
> And grieve that I shall hear no more
> The strains, with envy heard before;
> For, with my minstrel brethren fled,
> My jealousy of song is dead. (IV.xxxv.1–14)

Left alone, like Beattie's Minstrel or Gray's Bard, Scott's singer grieves for the lost songs that were forged in a competitive environment such as is described in Percy's *Hermit*:

> The Minstrels of thy noble house,
>   All clad in robes of blue,
> [...]
> The great atchievements of thy race
>   They sung [...].[42]

Canto Fifth of the *Lay* extends the disquisition on the legacy of dead poets given in the previous canto with two contrasting verses. The first offers a conventional pastoral elegy in which nature mourns the poet who has praised it:

> Call it not vain:—they do not err,
>   Who say, that when the Poet dies,
> Mute Nature mourns her worshipper. (V.i.1–3)

Initially suggesting that 'mountains weep in crystal rill', the Last Minstrel curtails his claims with an emphatic 'Not that, in sooth, o'er mortal urn | Those things inanimate can mourn'. An isolated bard cut off from his creative community, he has free rein over genre.

---

[42] Thomas Percy, *The Hermit of Warkworth. A Northumberland Ballad* (London: T. Davies, 1771), p. 20.

Ill would it suit your gentle ear,
Ye lovely listeners, to hear
How to the axe the helms did sound,
And blood pour'd down from many a wound;
[...]
But, were each dame a listening knight,
I well could tell how warriors fight! (V.xxi.1–8)

Despite claiming that he won't focus on the fight between 'Deloraine' (who, in fact, is Cranstoun in disguise) and Richard of Musgrave, he is compelled to give in miniature the lurid highlights using the present tense:

'Tis done, 'tis done! that fatal blow
Has stretch'd him on the bloody plain;
He strives to rise—Brave Musgrave, no!
Thence never shalt thou rise again!
He chokes in blood. (V.xxii.1–5)

Canto Fifth certainly rounds off the story of the poem, from one perspective at least. Towards the end, in the twenty-seventh verse paragraph, Scott inserts a plot summary ('[...] as they left the listed plain, | Much of the story she did gain'), though Cranstoun, so the Last Minstrel observes, 'half his tale [...] left unsaid'. As the author of his own narrative, the baron naturally turns it into a martial song that celebrates his achievements, downplaying the goblin-page's wild, 'romantic' intentions:

How Cranstoun fought with Deloraine,
And of his page, and of the Book
Which from the wounded knight he took;
And how he sought her castle high,
That morn, by help of gramarye;
How, in Sir William's armour dight,
Stolen by his page, while slept the knight,
He took on him the single fight. (V.xxvii.3–10)

The Ladye, meanwhile, suppresses the fantastical elements of her own story — 'Cared not the Ladye to betray | Her mystic arts in view of day' — and even plots to close it off:

But well she thought, ere midnight came,
Of that strange page the pride to tame,
From his foul hands the Book to save,
And send it back to Michael's grave.— (V.xxvii.15–18)

At the demarcating long dash the minstrel refers to another unfinished story, that is the declaration, with regards to Margaret and Cranstoun, that he 'Needs not these lovers' joys to tell: | One day, fair maids, you'll know them well'. Here, the narrator and the Ladye have dismissed from the *Lay* supernatural and pastoral balladry, though the latter is retained for a possible spin-off. Even though this would be a satisfying conclusion, in the context of Scott's attempts to stabilize his form, three further verse paragraphs and a framing section follow.

Deloraine suddenly awakens 'from his deathlike trance' in a paragraph that largely comprises rapid-fire couplets ('Hence, to the field unarm'd, he ran, | And hence his presence scared the clan'), before it winds into a quick but poignant lament shaped by a rhyming quatrain and a faintly rhyming, unobtrusive couplet:

> And so 'twas seen of him, e'en now,
>> When on dead Musgrave he look'd down;
> Grief darken'd on his rugged brow,
>> Though half disguised with a frown;
> And thus, while sorrow bent his head,
> His foeman's epitaph he made. (V.xxviii.22–27)

His epitaphic interjection occupies the ensuing verse paragraph. Similar in form to the previous sections, its prosody is noticeably clunky and the sounds sloppy and sluggish: 'if I slew thy brother dear, | Thou slew'st a sister's son to me'. Largely favouring elegantly end-stopped lines in this canto and elsewhere, here Scott's speaker delivers stalling lines with needless syntactic interruptions:

> long months three,
> Till ransom'd for a thousand mark,
> Dark Musgrave, it was long of thee. (V.xxix.6–8)

An acknowledged borrowing from Michael Drayton's *Poly-Olbion* (1612–22) — 'The lands, that over Ouse to Berwick forth do bear, | Have for their blazon had, the snaffle, spur, and spear' — seems oddly forced in the middle of Deloraine's triplet:

> In all the northern counties here,
> Whose word is Snaffle, spur, and spear,
> Thou wert the best to follow gear! (V.xxix.15–17)

After Deloraine's lament for his fallen foe, the Last Minstrel, in the next verse paragraph, closes Musgrave's story by having Lord Dacre's men carry his body away in a suitably militaristic manner:

> And laid him on his bloody shield;
> On levell'd lances, four and four,
> By turns, the noble burden bore. (V.xxx.4–6)

Another minstrel (within the story) delivers a 'plaintive wail', which is followed by a requiem sung 'for the warrior's soul' by four priests and, finally, an escorted journey to Leven's shore, where Musgrave's body is laid in his father's grave. Although this offers yet another neat ending to the canto, Scott (or an authoritative poet figure of some kind, at least) interrupts with what amounts to a blurred extension of the Last Minstrel's conclusion:

> The harp's wild notes, though hush'd the song,
> The mimic march of death prolong;

> Now seems it far, and now a-near,
> Now meets, and now eludes the ear;
> Now seems some mountain side to sweep,
> Now faintly dies in valley deep;
> Seems now as if the Minstrel's wail,
> Now the sad requiem, loads the gale;
> Last, o'er the warrior's closing grave,
> Rung the full choir in choral stave. (V, Conclusion, 1–10)

Above all of his self-sabotaging attempts, it is this inconclusive, prolonging insertion that finally unsettles the Last Minstrel's lay, placing it far and near, at the mountainside and in the valley, in the wind and over the grave, in ever-shifting levels of audibleness. It is left to the three now-dead sixteenth-century singers of the sixth canto to bring minstrelsy back to the fore.

The Extraneous Canto

'The sixth canto is altogether redundant', Scott confessed, 'for the poem should certainly have closed with the union of the lovers, when the interest, if any, was at an end. But what could I do? I had my book and my page still on my hands, and must get rid of them at all events'.[43] To be sure, the subject of Canto Sixth, a feast to celebrate the marriage of Margaret and Cranstoun, is both an extension of the apparently concluded story of the previous cantos (the union of two families in the face of external challenges) and a rerun of earlier formal and generic disruptions. Read in the context of meta-minstrelsy, needless to say, this 'extra canto' finally defeats the wild writing that Scott sought to overturn in his recent collection of *Minstrelsy*, and champions, under pressure, his authorial ideal of improvisatory recreation. The wedding feast is honoured by three very different and seemingly incidental songs by Albert Graeme, a Border minstrel; Fitztraver, a courtly poet; and Harold of St Clair, an Orcadian bard. As Scott states in his note to the eleventh verse paragraph, Graeme's 'simple song' in ballad quatrains reworks an old Scottish song, which begins:

> She lean'd her back against a thorn,
>   The sun shines fair on Carlisle wa':
> And there she has her young babe born,
>   And the lyon shall be lord of a'.[44]

Graeme Anglicizes (that is, linguistically 'stabilizes') this stanza, and foregrounds a marital — and national — union in keeping with the occasion:

[43] Scott to Anna Seward (21 March 1805), *The Letters of Sir Walter Scott*, ed. by H. J. C. Grierson, 12 vols (London: Constable, 1932–37), I, 242–43.
[44] Scott, *Poetical Works*, VI, p. 197.

> It was an English ladye bright,
> (The sun shines fair on Carlisle wall,)
> And she would marry a Scottish knight,
> For Love will still be Lord of all. (VI.xi.1–4)

Ostensibly a call for peace in the Borders, Graeme's song is quickly marred by tragedy as the bride's brother poisons her: 'That wine she had not tasted well, | [...] | When dead, in her true love's arms, she fell'. Read on its own, the ballad looks fundamentally conventional in its form and theme. Canto Sixth at large opens with an anatomy of Border minstrelsy: for one, it is inspired by the wildness of the terrain ('O Caledonia! stern and wild, | Meet nurse for a poetic child!'). War and love are interrelated, even interchangeable themes ('Whisper'd young knights, in tone more mild, | To ladies fair'), as Scott also suggested in the opening of his earlier ballad, 'The Fire-King': 'Bold knights and fair dames, to my harp give an ear, | Of love, and of war, and of wonder to hear'.[45] But, contextually, Graeme's song comes at the Dame's request in response to the ill-behaviour of the goblin-page, whom we have come to identify with the wild imagination. Before Graeme steps forth, the 'wily page, with vengeful thought' molests the guests with 'bitter gibe and taunting jest', causing a riot in the hall, before cowering in a dark nook, grinning and muttering 'Lost! lost! lost!' Seemingly defeated — temporarily, at least — the page's actions introduce violence into the hall ('With bodkin pierced him to the bone'), which is repeated in the song ('He pierced her brother to the heart'). In Graeme's version, importantly, the Knight, having killed the murderous brother, dies off-page during the Crusades in Palestine for the sake of his bride, returning us to the minstrels' song in Percy's *Hermit*, where Lord William

> gain'd a fair young Saxon bride
> With all her lands and towers.
>
> Then journeying to the Holy Land,
> There bravely fought and dy'd.[46]

Chivalry can still shape the triumphant message of Graeme's song, in spite of the disruption going on around the minstrel.

The second singer, Fitztraver ('a bard of loftier port'), extends the chivalric theme in a seemingly more sophisticated measure. Heralded as Lord William's 'foremost favourite [...] | And chief of all his minstrelsy', Fitztraver has frequently collaborated with the 'gentle' Henry Howard, the Earl of Surrey and a respected real-life poet. Couching his tale in neatly knit Spenserian stanzas, albeit with a noticeably high number of trochaic and anapaestic inversions, Fitztraver is

---

[45] Matthew Gregory Lewis, *Tales of Wonder*, ed. by Douglass H. Thomson (Ontario: Broadview, 2010), pp. 92–97 (p. 92).

[46] Percy, p. 21.

inspired by Surrey's 'raptured line' that conjures forth 'That fair and lovely form, the Lady Geraldine'. But, references to Surrey and Spenser aside, it is the modern bard Coleridge who really haunts this song: Scott's imagery, like that seen in *Christabel* and elsewhere, is atmospherically vague ('Cloudy and indistinct, as feverish dream'), and his lines, again like those in Coleridge's poem, build up internal repetition for a vivid visual effect ('And part by moonshine pale, and part was hid in gloom'). Scott's Geraldine is certainly closer to Coleridge's Geraldine than to Surrey's. Although feted in some circles as worthy rivals to the ultimate poetic couple, Petrarch and Laura, Surrey only wrote one piece that was certainly in the honour of his 'Geraldine' (Elizabeth Fitzgerald): a pleasing, praising sonnet ('Her beauty of kinde, her vertues from above, | Happy is he, that can obtaine her love'). In Coleridge's poem Christabel rescues 'fair Geraldine', whom she discovers had been attacked by five unnamed warriors. Wearied on their subsequent journey, the women lay down to sleep, at which point (the abrupt ending to Part I) Christabel catches a glimpse of Geraldine's bosom and half her side, which is evasively described as a 'Sight to dream of, not to tell!', the 'Mark of my Shame, this Seal of my Sorrow'. A hundred or so lines into Part II, by which time Sir Leoline has declared he will avenge his daughter's new friend, Christabel again shudders at the sight of Geraldine's body: 'Again she saw that Bosom old, | Again she felt that Bosom cold'. This and a later, more revealing glimpse, some 583 lines into the poem, level a psychological terror at the form of Geraldine:

> A Snake's small Eye blinks dull and shy;
> And the Lady's Eyes they shrunk in her Head, [...]
> At Christabel she look'd askance! —
> One moment — and the Sight was fled! (583–88)[47]

In the *Lay*, Fitztraver's song covers forty-five taut lines and therefore cuts well short of Coleridge's slow reveal of the false lady's true nature. But readers of both poems, after 1816, might have picked up on a similar sense of impending threat in the knowing sexualization of Scott's outwardly coy description of the vision of his Geraldine: 'O'er her white bosom stray'd her hazel hair, | Pale her dear cheek, as if for love she pined'. Whereas Coleridge's poem ends with Sir Leoline, mesmerized, abandoning his daughter for the bewitching lady, Scott's much more rushed song ends in sudden violence — the sort of violence Geraldine claims to have evaded in *Christabel* — 'The gory bridal bed, the plunder'd shrine, | The murder'd Surrey's blood, the tears of Geraldine!' The charming sacrifice of the doomed Knight in Graeme's ballad has given way to the 'wild caprice' and murderousness we associate with the goblin-page. The hitherto courtly Fitztraver has passively imitated — or unconsciously plagiarized, to use Dorothy

---

[47] Coleridge, *Poetical Works I.1*, p. 501.

Wordsworth's phrase — the goblin-page, a beguiling impersonator like Coleridge's Geraldine, as he recomposes his song in response to the terrors around him.[48]

By the time we hear the third song, a 'secret horror' has taken over the feast as the goblin-page has 'Found! found! found!' what he has been looking for: the resurrected wizard Michael Scott. Seemingly oblivious, Harold of St Clair, an Orcadian bard, weaves a tale of love, a major theme of Border minstrelsy as understood by Scott, and pointedly rejects the theme of war as it is inappropriate for his audience: 'No haughty feat of arms I tell; | Soft is the note, and sad the lay'. At the outset we learn that the dirge mourns Rosabelle who, we discover at the end, has drowned. Marked by death, the poem is filled with supernatural or, at the very least, eerie imagery:

> Seem'd all on fire within, around,
>   Deep sacristy and altar's pale;
> Shone ever pillar foliage-bound,
>   And glimmer'd all the dead men's mail. (VI.xxiii.37–40)

Harold's poised song in praise of the noble family members buried with 'candle, with book, and with knell' jars with the creeping dread that 'chill'd the soul of every guest' at the feast itself. Reality becomes far more fantastical than the minstrelsy that punctuates it as, 'Then sudden, through the darken'd air | A flash of lightning came'. Scott noticeably quickens the pace of the writing, baldly invokes Spenser ('levin-brand', a thunderbolt), mixes short ('flash'd') and long sounds ('smouldering'), and uses repetition to enact a mood of puckish villainy:

> So broad, so bright, so red the glare,
>   The castle seem'd on flame.
> Glanced every rafter of the hall,
> Glanced every shield upon the wall;
> Each trophied beam, each sculptured stone,
> Were instant seen, and instant gone;
> Full through the guests' bedazzled band
> Resistless flash'd the levin-brand,
> And fill'd the hall with smouldering smoke,
> As on the elvish page it broke. (VI.xxv.3–12)

The vividness of this verse paragraph unravels in the ensuing one, where the guests at the feast perceive the scene before them in starkly different ways: 'Some saw an arm, and some a hand, | And some the waving of a gown'. Although rendered 'speechless, ghastly, wan', Deloraine becomes our surrogate storyteller

---

[48] For a discussion of 'passive imitation' in *Christabel* and other poems see Tilar J. Mazzeo's *Plagiarism and Literary Property in the Romantic Period* (Philadelphia: University of Pennsylvania Press, 2007), pp. 27–35.

as he attempts to articulate for the 'anxious crowd' who 'trembling heard the wondrous tale' of the ghostly vision before him:

> At length, by fits, he darkly told,
> With broken hint, and shuddering cold —
>   That he had seen, right certainly,
> *A shape with amice wrapp'd around,*
> *With a wrought Spanish baldric bound,*
>   *Like pilgrim from beyond the sea;*
> And knew — but how it matter'd not—
> It was the wizard, Michael Scott. (VI.xxvi.18–25)

In response the listeners turn to new authority figures, in prayers to various saints and blessed patrons. The happy ending wrought by the wedding has been firmly overwritten (''twere vain | To wake the note of mirth again'). This is in turn followed by a communal 'Hymn for the Dead' sung by the holy fathers at the close of the Last Minstrel's downbeat lay. But the larger poem does not end there. Rather, Scott provides an extensive epilogue in which we learn of the Last Minstrel's post-*Lay* life. Fled is the supernatural imagination that frightened the courtly eyes and ears. Instead, the old tales of chivalry find an audience of stray guests who, so we're told, delight in the unending storytelling of the newly established poet-in-residence:

> The aged Harper's soul awoke!
> Then would he sing achievements high,
> And circumstance of chivalry,
> Till the rapt traveller would stay,
> Forgetful of the closing day. (VI, Conclusion, 21–25)

The unending lay was continued — or simply written again, according to Jeffrey — when Scott turned his hand to *Marmion* (1808). After that, parodies by younger contemporaries, James Kirke Paulding's *The Lay of the Scottish Fiddle* (1813) and John Roby's *The Lay of the Poor Fiddler* (1814), picked over Scott's material, returning it to the marketplace in a mocking mixture of dialects and stanza forms. By then, a sort of minstrel fatigue had crept into mainstream poetry. In *The Excursion* (1814), Wordsworth's Pastor, for one, rails against the declining art of improvisatory minstrelsy ('Listen who would, be wrought upon who might, | Sincerely wretched hearts, or falsely gay'). But the *Lay*, meanwhile, reached its fifteenth edition in 1816, a little over a decade since its first publication. When they fell out of copyright in the 1830s, Scott's long poems appeared in attractively rebound editions at affordable prices for diverse readerships: if you looked in the right bookshops in 1839 you could still buy the *Lay*, *The Lady of the Lake*, and *Marmion* for less than a shilling apiece.

SECTION IV

History and Sites of Conflict

Sir Walter Scott's *The Antiquary* and the *Ossian* Controversy

NIGEL LEASK

University of Glasgow

Although *The Antiquary* was a personal favourite of Sir Walter Scott's, he worried that it was more concerned 'to describe manners minutely, than to arrange [...] an artificial and combined narration'; and regretted that he had been 'unable to unite these two requisitions of a good Novel'.[1] Critics have largely endorsed this view, especially when compared to *Waverley* and *Guy Mannering*, Scott's first two novels. Penny Fielding describes *The Antiquary* as 'an unhistorical historical novel', while Ian Duncan notes that for 'a work composed mere months after Waterloo [it's striking that it] unfolds its epiphany of national solidarity through the mock-heroic narration of a conflict that does not take place'. Duncan refers here to the French invasion scare that turns out to be a false alarm at the novel's conclusion.[2] Reflecting on Scott's sense of imbalance, David Punter suggests that *The Antiquary* is more concerned with the making of history than with history itself.[3] He describes the rather stagey gothic plot as a 'peg on which to hang a series of characters and a set of views on the central issues raised by the cultural phenomenon of the "antiquary"' (p. xiv), which seems absolutely right.

But what exactly is at stake regarding these 'central issues'? The late Susan Manning argued that in its obsession with material particularities, antiquarianism was 'the "other" of Enlightenment historiography, the double agent on its boundaries', obsessed by the flotsam and jetsam of the past, yet lacking the connectivity that made for grand historical narrative.[4] Scott's own comments on *The Antiquary* seem to acknowledge that: for all the satire levelled at Jonathan Oldbuck and his character type, he had himself succumbed to a kind of literary

---

[1] *The Antiquary*, intro. by David Punter, ed. by David Hewitt (Harmondsworth: Penguin, 1999), p. 3. (Pagination hereafter given in the text.)

[2] Penny Fielding, *Scotland and the Fictions of Geography: North Britain, 1760–1830* (Cambridge University Press, 2008) p. 120; Ian Duncan, *Scott's Shadow: The Novel in Romantic Edinburgh* (Princeton, NJ: Princeton University Press, 2007), p. 139.

[3] David Punter, intro. to *The Antiquary*, p. xiv.

[4] Susan Manning, 'Antiquarianism and the Scottish Science of Man', in *Scotland and the Borders of Romanticism*, ed. by Leith Davis, Ian Duncan and Janet Sorenson (Cambridge: Cambridge University Press, 2004), pp. 57–76 (p. 67).

Yearbook of English Studies, 47 (2017), 189–202
© Modern Humanities Research Association 2017

antiquarianism in preferring the description of manners to narrative. More-over, in 1836, John Gibson Lockhart noted that, despite laying false trails for identifying Oldbuck's real-life prototype, '[Scott] could hardly [...] have scrupled about recognizing a quaint caricature of the founder of the Abbotsford Museum, in the inimitable portraiture of the Laird of Monkbarns'.[5]

In focusing on one of these antiquarian debates in particular, namely the controversy following James Macpherson's publication, in the early 1760s, of what he claimed were his 'translations' of the poems of the third-century Gaelic bard Ossian, I might initially seem to be making a mountain out of a molehill, given that in plot terms, sustained discussion of *Ossian* is limited to a single chapter (volume III, chapter 1). There it serves the limited purpose of dramatizing the relationship between Oldbuck and his hot-headed nephew Hector MacIntyre. *The Antiquary*'s more extensive concern with Roman and medieval antiquities better reflects Oldbuck's own scholarly tastes: and we even learn that the unworldly Lord Glenallan has never heard of *Ossian* (p. 277). Neither does the Gaelic world of *Ossian* seem particularly relevant to the novel's Lowland setting in 'Fairport' (most likely situated on the north-east coast of Scotland, somewhere like Montrose or Arbroath), geographically distinct from the Highlands of *Waverley*, *Rob Roy*, or Scott's Highland verse romances.

Nevertheless, in Scott's time, Macpherson's *Ossian* poems and the controversy they aroused played an important role in the debate about Scottish history, literature, and identity. This was true even in the years after the Highland Society of Edinburgh had published its largely damning report on *Ossian* in 1805 (the subject of a long essay by Scott in the *Edinburgh Review*, which I will discuss below); that is to say, a decade before the composition of *The Antiquary*. Scott elsewhere admitted that he had 'devoured rather than perused' *Ossian* as a boy, and in the 1830 Preface to his *Poems* acknowledged that Macpherson had first persuaded him that 'writings on Highland subjects were qualified to interest the reader'.[6] Strange then that (despite their Ossianic imagery), absolutely no direct reference is made to *Ossian* (or to James Macpherson) in either *The Lady of the Lake* (1810) or *The Lord of the Isles* (1815), both of them set in the Highlands, and both accompanied by voluminous antiquarian notes. So how does one explain the sudden obtrusion of *Ossian* in *The Antiquary*? In this essay I'll explore the relationship of *Ossian* with some of the novel's other antiquarian preoccupations, as well as its construction of Scottish identity, concluding with a suggestion that Macpherson's poem may even have inspired elements of the often-maligned plot of *The Antiquary*.

---

[5] Quoted in Caroline McCracken-Flesher, *Possible Scotlands: Walter Scott and the Story of Tomorrow* (Oxford: Oxford University Press, 2007), p. 33.

[6] *Poetical Works*, ed. by J. Logie Robertson (London: Henry Froude, 1913), p. 274.

At stake here was more than just a question of 'authenticity', namely Macpherson's claim that *Fragments of Ancient Poetry*, or his epics *Fingal* and *Temora* were 'translations' of ancient Gaelic poetry. Just as contentious was his boldly revisionist account of Scottish history presented in the poem's introductory dissertations, footnotes and appendices. Here he sought to promote, in Colin Kidd's words, 'the continuity of Scottish liberty and national identity from hazy Caledonian roots'.[7] Rejecting George Buchanan's 'Dalriadan' account of early Scottish history, Macpherson proposed that the modern Highlanders, 'are the genuine descendants of the antient Caledonians, and not a pretended colony of Scots [from Ireland], who settled first in the north, in the third or forth century'.[8] He gravely offended Irish opinion by representing the Irish as descended from Scottish colonizers (the reverse of the established view represented by Buchanan), and in his epic *Fingal* depicting them and their leader Cuchullin as vulnerable and enfeebled, dependent upon the Scottish 'Fingal, King of Morven' to rescue them from invading Norsemen.[9] It is now widely accepted that *Ossian* presented its readers with an ideologically as well as aesthetically doctored version of genuine Gaelic tradition.[10] But the extent to which Fingal is the offspring of Galgacus (the heroic leader of the Caledonians at the battle of Mons Graupius in AD 43, in Tacitus's *Agricola*) has never been adequately grasped by commentators. *Fingal* asserted Scotland's flagging national pride during the crisis of the Bute administration, when it was still smarting from the debacle of Culloden, and government-enforced military impotence in the face of the renewed threat of foreign invasion.

In first half of the eighteenth century, travelling antiquaries like Alexander Gordon (author of the 1726 *Itinerarium Septentrionale*, the weighty tome which Oldbuck is clutching in the Queensferry Diligence, in the opening scenes of Scott's novel), obsessively tracked the Scottish sites of Roman camps and battles in search of the material traces of Roman conquest. But after 1760, the publication of *Ossian* reinvented the Highland landscape as the scene of Fingalian

[7] Colin Kidd, *Subverting Scotland's Past: Scottish Whig Historians and the Creation of Anglo-British Identity, 1689–1830* (Cambridge: Cambridge University Press, 1993), p. 235.

[8] James Macpherson, 'A Dissertation' (1763), in *The Poems of Ossian, and Related Works*, ed. by Howard Gaskill, intro. by Fiona Stafford (Edinburgh: Edinburgh University Press, 1996), p. 207.

[9] See Clare O'Halloran, *Golden Ages and Barbarous Nations: Antiquarian Debate and Cultural Politics in Ireland, c. 1750–1800* (Cork: Cork University Press, 2004), pp. 97–124.

[10] Richard Sher has read *Ossian* in the context of the 'Poker's Club's' campaign for a Scottish Militia in the 1760s, as a response to the threat of French invasion during the Seven Years' War, one aspect of Macpherson's nationalistic bid to bolster the myth of Caledonian resistance to foreign invaders. See *Church and University in the Scottish Enlightenment* (Princeton, NJ: Princeton University Press, 1985), pp. 242–61; Kidd, *Subverting Scotland's Past*, pp. 219–39. For Macpherson, Ossian's third-century setting permitted Fingal to be represented as the leader of Scotland's Iron Age tribes against the Roman *imperium* in the figure of 'Caracul, the son of the *King of the World*' (*Ossian*, p. 47), a metaphor for Hanoverian triumphalism.

resistance, rather than Roman triumph, quite possibly because the military threat of Jacobitism had been defeated, and once-rebellious Gaels drafted into Britain's military struggle against France. The famous boulder burial in Perthshire's 'Sma' Glen', for example, was initially identified as a 'Roman' tomb by Hanoverian soldiers constructing General Wade's road network in the 1730s, but sometime after 1760 it was named (or renamed) 'Clach-Ossian' or 'Ossian's Grave', and it became an obligatory site on the eighteenth-century *petit tour*, inspiring Wordsworth's 1805 poem 'Glen-Almain': 'In this still place, remote from men, | Sleeps Ossian, in the NARROW GLEN', even if the poem remains agnostic about the authenticity (or otherwise) of Macpherson's poem.[11]

But let us turn to Scott's novel. The central character of *The Antiquary* is not of course the mysterious but insipid southern hero 'Mr Lovel', but the eponymous antiquary Jonathan Oldbuck, Laird of Monkbarns, whose good-humoured foibles and learned wit permeate the novel. Oldbuck's antiquarian obsessions are shared by his neighbour and sparring partner, the near-bankrupt landowner Sir Arthur Wardour. But it is not Wardour so much as the bluecoat beggar Edie Ochiltree who shares centre stage with Oldbuck, and both characters prove to be crucial agents in unfolding Scott's plot. Their relationship is dramatized in the famous episode early in the novel when Oldbuck is showing off his property of the 'Kaim of Kilprunes' to Lovel, which he claims to be the site of Agricola's camp before the Battle of Mons Graupius, where the Romans had defeated the Caledonians in AD 84. Oldbuck's claim is founded upon his discovery of a Roman altar stone bearing the inscription A.D.L.L., which he interprets as an acronym for *Agricola Dicavit Libens Lubens* ('Agricola willingly and happily dedicated this'). But Oldbuck's antiquarian dreams of the Roman praetorium are shattered by Edie's brutal interjection 'I mind the bigging o't'. The beggar insists that the inscription ADLL stands for 'Aiken Drum's Lang Ladle' (p. 31), recalling how, just twenty years before, he and some friends had built the shelter for Aiken's bridal ceremony.

Yet while Scott explodes antiquarian illusions here, he hardly promotes the cause of scepticism: Caroline McCracken-Flesher rightly points out that 'Edie tells a lie that should have been obvious to Scott's readers'.[12] Far from being an old pal of Edie's, Aiken Drum is the protagonist of a well-known and entirely

---

[11] *William Wordsworth: The Poems*, ed. by John O. Hayden, 2 vols (Harmondsworth: Penguin, 1977), I, 638. A similar 'Fingalization' of Highland topography occurred across the whole region as part of the pre-romantic transformation of Scotland, although after 1810 Walter Scott's fictional protagonists would replace the ghostly *dramatis personae* of *Ossian* in giving imaginative life to the emptying glens of the Highlands (as of the Lowlands and Borders), for a new generation of romantic tourists. Thanks to Margaret Bennett for pointing out to me that although no evidence survives, *Clach Ossian* was in all likelihood the stone's traditional name in this part of the Perthshire *Gàidhealtachd* long before its identification as a 'Roman tomb'.

[12] McCracken-Flesher, *Possible Scotlands*, p. 41.

fantastic children's song, 'He played upon a ladle, a ladle, a ladle [...] and his name was Aiken Drum'. Edie's 'correct' version of historical memory turns out to be based on a scrap of playground verse. Ian Duncan writes that 'frauds and hoaxes proliferate throughout the novel's texture of allusion as well as its plot'.[13] Oldbuck's 'praetorium' is probably fraudulent, just like Edie's claim that exposes it: so is the historicity of Oldbuck's planned epic *The Caledoniad* (which I'll compare with Macpherson's *Fingal*, another 'fraudulent epic'), or the genealogy of the early kings of Scotland contested by Wardour and Oldbuck. Hoaxes punctuate the plot as well: Dousterswivel's 'salted mine' of non-existent treasure; the malicious claim that Lord Glenallan's marriage is incestuous, or that the mysterious protagonist Lovel/Neville is illegitimate. A thin line divides the fraudulent from factual history for Scott, that great writer of historical fiction, who, we might recall, failed to deliver his own planned *History of Scotland* about the same time as he was composing *The Antiquary*. In this connection, McCracken-Flesher reminds us of 'Hume's caveats about how meaning is made: there is no "history" without data, and the meaning that is identity — personal, communal, national — is made in the gaps and from the clashes arising from the circulation of equivalent, fragmentary stuff'.[14]

If the Lovel/Neville plot centres on contested genealogy, the question of Scotland's (and by extension Britain's) national genealogy looms large in the antiquarian clashes between Oldbuck the Whig, and his Tory (and formerly Jacobite) neighbour, Sir Arthur Wardour. Oldbuck is descended from a line of Protestant German printers who had been exiled at the start of the Reformation for printing the Augsberg Confession, and like his father he strongly identifies with the Hanoverian dynasty and the Protestant succession. In 1745, Oldbuck senior, as provost of Fairport, had arrested the young Sir Arthur and his Jacobite father, and had them committed to the Tower for the duration of the uprising; but as we learn in chapter 5, historical enmity has mellowed into antiquarian sparring between the two neighbours. Oldbuck the Gothicist is firmly convinced that Scandinavia is the '*officina gentium*, the mother of modern Europe, the nursery of those heroes, "Stern to resolve, and stubborn to endure, | Who smiled in death?"' (pp. 242–43). Wardour disagrees, preferring a story of Irish and Celtic antecedents.

The debate about Scottish origins is introduced in volume I chapter 6 in the form of an after-dinner disagreement about the authenticity of the Fergusian regal lists,[15] leading to a dispute about the ethnicity of the Picts. After a tasty

---

[13] Duncan, *Scott's Shadow*, p. 139.

[14] McCracken-Flesher, *Possible Scotlands*, p. 40.

[15] The Stuart royal genealogy, based on the medieval and early modern histories of John of Fordun and Hector Boece, which dated the Scottish kings back to Fergus MacFerquard in 330 BC. For further discussion, see Kidd, *Subverting Scotland's Past*, pp. 26–29, 101–07.

dinner of undercooked 'Solan Goose' (gannet) at Monkbarns, the two antiquaries press the respective claims of Celts and Goths, witnessed by the bemused Lovel, the ladies having wisely retired. Each party invokes a battery of antiquarian authorities: Oldbuck summons the authority of Sir Robert Sibbald, Alexander Gordon, and 'the learned [John] Pinkerton' in support of the Gothic origin of the Picts, while Wardour evokes Father Thomas Innes, George Chalmers, and Joseph Ritson in favour of the Celtic. Problematically, the sole surviving word of the Pictish language (*penval*), can be interpreted to support either party, and Penny Fielding rightly observes that 'language breaks down as the key to ethnic origins, ancient history and property rights'.[16] As Colin Kidd has shown, the real-life debate was racially toxic. In his *Dissertation on the Origin and Progress of the Scythians or Goths* (1787), John Pinkerton (himself notorious for forging medieval Scottish ballads) argued for the superior Gothic origins of the Picts, and characterized the Celts as 'a weak and brutish people [...] savages since the world began [...] their personal manners are nasty and filthy, as they were in ancient times when they washed their bodies and cleaned their teeth with urine'.[17] In only slightly milder vein, Oldbuck dismisses the Celtic genealogy of the Pictish kings as 'sprung from the tribe of Macfungus — mushroom monarchs every one of them; sprung up from the fumes of conceit, folly, and falsehood, fermenting in the brains of some mad Highland seannachie' (p. 49). (In contrast, by 1830 Scott had made up his own mind — *contra* Oldbuck — that both Scots and Picts were 'by descent a Celtic race'.)[18] But it is a social rather than racial pedigree that turns the debate sour in this particular exchange, as Sir Arthur sneers at Oldbuck as 'descendant of a Westphalian printer' (p. 50), and Oldbuck retaliates by reminding Wardour of the blot of illegitimacy on his family's escutcheon. Knockwinnock storms out of the house with his daughter Isabella, both nearly losing their lives to high tides on Halket-Head, but for the timely appearance of Lovel and Edie, who rescue them from a watery death.

The subject of *Ossian* is first raised in a breakfast conversation after Lovel's disturbed night in the haunted Green Chamber, when Oldbuck offers to 'show [him] the controversy upon Ossian's Poems between Mac-Cribb and me — I hold with the acute Orcadian — he with the defenders of the authenticity — the controversy began in smooth, oily, lady-like terms, but is now waxing more sour and eager as we get on — it already partakes somewhat of old Scaliger's style' (p. 84). As his name suggests, in addition to his Gaelic patronymic, 'Mac-Cribb'

---

[16] Penny Fielding, *Scotland and the Fictions of Geography*, p. 114.

[17] Quoted by Patrick O'Flaherty, *Scotland's Pariah: The Life and Work of John Pinkerton, 1758–1826* (Toronto and London: Toronto University Press, 2015), pp. 46–47.

[18] Walter Scott, 'Essay on Popular Poetry', in *Minstrelsy of the Scottish Border*, ed. by John Gibson Lockhart (1833), vols I–IV of *The Poetical Works of Sir Walter Scott*, 12 vols (Edinburgh, 1861), I, 27.

is something of an antiquarian magpie, and we elsewhere learn that he has walked off with Oldbuck's cherished 'Syrian medal' in his pocket. He comes up again later, when Oldbuck is lamenting the destruction of his 'lachrymatory from Clochnaben' by Hector's dog Juno, 'the main pillar of my theory [...] in despite of the ignorant obstinacy of Mac-Cribb, that the Romans has passed the defiles of these mountains' (p. 239).

Although 'Mac-Cribb' is a fictional composite of the Gaelic partisans for *Ossian* (scholars like the Revs Donald MacNicol, Donald MacQueen, James MacLagan), Oldbuck's 'acute Orcadian' is a real character, the Scottish historian Malcolm Laing. Influenced by Pinkerton, Laing had attacked the authenticity of Macpherson's *Ossian* in his *History of Scotland* (1800) and again, with a rather obsessive display of critical energy, in an edition of Macpherson's poems published in 1805, which tracked every one of Macpherson's supposedly 'ancient' allusions and metaphors to a modern literary source, thereby proving to his satisfaction that the poems were forged. Notably, Laing also published Macpherson's juvenile poetic efforts, *The Hunter* and *The Highlander*, alongside the Ossianic corpus, to expose some telling similarities between the plots of his own verse and the supposedly 'traditional' epic *Fingal* — Laing noted that in both, a mysterious Scottish hero of indeterminate paternity rescues Gaeldom from foreign invasion, a point to which I will return.[19]

Walter Scott wrote in 1805 to the Lichfield poet Anna Seward: 'as for the great [Ossian] dispute, I would be no Scottishman if I had not very attentively considered it at some point in my studies'.[20] That same year, in July 1805, he published a lengthy review of the Highland Society's *Report on Ossian*, and of Malcolm Laing's edition, in the *Edinburgh Review*.[21] Scott's review opens with a facetious worry that 'by mingling in the approaching storm, we run the risk of a chance-blow from a Highland claymore, or an Orcadian battle-axe' (*ER* 429). He demolished one of Macpherson's partisans for explaining away Laing's critique on the grounds that it was inspired by resentment at the 'severe checks given by the ancient Caledonians to [his] predatory Scandinavian predecessors', which had 'raised prejudices not yet extinct' in the Orcadian historian (*ER* 436). Scott protested that the same individual (Rev. Andrew Gallie) claimed to have heard oral recitations in Gaelic of the Ossian poems that corresponded *verbatim*

---

[19] Scott facetiously commented that Laing's edition would have been more correctly entitled "The Poetical Works of James Macpherson, &c., containing The Poems of Ossian', *Edinburgh Review*, 6 (July 1805), 433.

[20] Scott also confessed here that he had 'devoured rather than perused' Ossian as a boy, before his maturing taste grew tired of 'the eternal repetition of the same ideas and imagery' that he felt characterized Macpherson's English *Ossian*, J. G. Lockhart, *Life of Sir Walter Scott* (London: Adam & Charles Black, 1893), p. 128.

[21] *Edinburgh Review*, 6 (July 1805), 429–62. (Hereafter abbrev. *ER*).

to Macpherson's translations, when the latter was still a child. But the poem's partisans refused point blank to countenance scepticism about the translations: as Scott put it in the letter to Seward, 'when once the Highlanders had adopted the poems of Ossian as an article of national faith, you would far sooner have got them to disavow the Scripture than to abandon a line of the contested tales'.[22] The question of ethnic prejudice lies at the roots of the antiquarian dispute that Scott would explore a decade later in *The Antiquary*, illustrating his view of the need to get beyond what we might (anachronistically) call an 'Old Firm' mentality in theorizing Scottish identity.[23]

The often quoted conclusion to Scott's review ('let us therefore hear no more of Macpherson') (*ER* 461), would seem to foreclose the whole issue: but given that twenty-seven new editions of the English *Ossian* were published between 1801 and 1830, this seems to have been far from the case.[24] In fact, Scott's review is more ambivalent than his summary verdict allows, in acknowledging that Macpherson was the first Scottish poet to have reached an international audience, and that he had after all drawn on some genuine Gaelic sources. Macpherson's fault was not so much in 'embellishing' traditional material — Scott must have been conscious that he had done something similar in 'mending and polishing' traditional ballads in *Minstrelsy of the Scottish Border*. (As late as 1830, he praised Macpherson as 'an excellent poet rather than a faithful editor and translator', and confessed that the English *Ossian* was the model for his first original poem, 'Glenfinlas'.)[25] Rather, the problem lay with what Eric Gidal has marvellously described as 'Ossianic unconformity': that is to say, Macpherson had mixed up the sequential stages of history, superimposing modern manners — chivalry and romance — upon Iron Age Celts, whose savagery Scott compared to that of modern-day Tahitians or Indians. To that extent, he insisted, Macpherson's English Ossian poems bore no more resemblance to authentic Gaelic *finaigecht* ballads than John Home's 'Tragedy of Douglas does to the Ballad of Gil Morris' (*ER* 462). He hoped that the Highland Society would publish an authoritative collection of ancient Gaelic poetry in translation, together with the original text in an appendix, on the model of Charlotte Brook's *Reliques of Irish Poetry* (1789).

---

[22] Lockhart, *Life*, p. 128.

[23] Referring to the collective title for Glasgow's Rangers and Celtic football clubs which dominate the Scottish sporting scene, whose supporters are often associated (respectively) with Protestant and Catholic sectarianism.

[24] Dafydd Moore, 'The Reception of Ossian in England and Scotland', in *The Reception of Ossian in Europe*, ed. by Howard Gaskill (London: Thoemmes Continuum, 2004), p. 30.

[25] 'Essay on Imitations of the Ancient Ballad', *Minstrelsy*, IV, p. 66. See Nigel Leask, '"A Degrading Species of Alchymy": Ballad Poetics, Oral Tradition, and the Meanings of Popular Culture', in *Romanticism and Popular Culture in Britain and Ireland*, ed. by Philip Connell and Nigel Leask (Cambridge University Press, 2009), pp. 51–71.

And because Macpherson had failed to do any such thing, or to produce any material or textual evidence of his Gaelic sources, Scott found him guilty as charged.

During his 1814 cruise around the Highlands and Islands on the *Pharos*, Scott had a chance to conduct some of his own Ossianic fieldwork. Following Thomas Pennant and other authorities, he recorded Ossianic place names in Skye,[26] and reported that 'a tacksman of Macleod's, called Grant, recite[d] the celebrated Address to the Sun; and another person [...] repeat[ed] the description of Cuchullin's car. But all agree to the gross infidelity of Macpherson as a translator and editor'.[27] (Both these passages occur in Macpherson's *Fingal*, and whatever the local opinions reported by Scott here concerning Macpherson's fidelity, they underlined the authenticity of his Gaelic sources. In a balanced treatment of the questions, while finding much evidence of fabrication by Macpherson, the modern Gaelic scholar Derick Thompson argues that Malcolm Laing 'goes too far with his method, as when he compares the description of Cu Chulainn's chariot to that of Solomon's, although the obvious parallel is the description [...] in Scottish and Irish sources'. We should note that Scott concurred, in his *Edinburgh Review* essay of 1805.)[28] Significantly, however, when Scott visited the most celebrated of all Ossianic landmarks on the Isle of Staffa, purportedly 'discovered' by Joseph Banks in 1772, he referred only to 'the celebrated cave', rather than 'Fingal's Cave'.[29] Curiously, Scott regretted how little poetic tradition survived in the Hebrides, 'considering how lately the bards and genealogists existed as a distinct order', but proceeded to fill the gap with the creations of his own imagination, especially in his 1815 poem *The Lord of the Isles*.[30]

Scott's major fictional engagement with Ossian occurs at the start of volume III of *The Antiquary*, in a comic dialogue between Oldbuck and Hector MacIntyre. After Hector's dog Juno has smashed the 'lachrymatory from Clochmaben', Hector quickly placates his uncle by offering him a beautiful Egyptian cameo ring bearing Cleopatra's head, which he had procured 'from a French savant to whom I rendered some service after the Alexandria affair'.

---

[26] Actually based on a spurious etymology linking the Cullins to the Ossianic hero Cuchullin.

[27] *The Voyage of the Pharos: Walter Scott's Cruise around Scotland in 1814*, intro. by Brian Osborne (Edinburgh: Scottish Library Association 1998), pp. 82–83, 96.

[28] Derick S. Thomson, *The Gaelic Sources of Macpherson's Ossian* (Aberdeen: Oliver and Boyd, 1952), p. 3. See also Donald E. Meek, 'The Gaelic Ballads of Scotland', in *Ossian Revisited*, ed. by Howard Gaskill (Edinburgh: Edinburgh University Press, 1991), pp. 19–48. Scott discussed the disputed authenticity of the 'Address to the Sun' in his *Edinburgh Review* article, and in the end defended the claims of 'Mr Macdiarmid' that it was genuine against Malcolm Laing's criticism, which imputed that it was based on 'Satan's address to the Sun in Paradise Lost' (*ER* 441–42).

[29] *The Voyage of the Pharos*, p. 96.

[30] Ibid., p. 83.

(Given that the Battle of Alexandria, in which Hector's regiment the Black Watch had played a particularly distinguished role, occurred on 21 March 1801, this allusion represents a flagrant breach of chronology in a novel purportedly set in 1794.) Strolling down to Steenie Meiklebackit's funeral, Hector mentions to his uncle how the soldiers of the 42nd celebrate their father's fame in order to raise their martial spirit:

> 'I used often of an evening to get old Rory MacAlpine to sing us songs of Ossian about the battles of Fingal and Lamon Mor, and Magnus and the spirit of Muirartach.'
>
> 'And did you believe,' asked the aroused Antiquary, 'did you absolutely believe that stuff of Macpherson's to be really ancient, you simple boy?'
>
> 'Believe it, sir? — how could I but believe it, when I have heard the songs sung from my infancy?'
>
> 'But not the same as Macpherson's English Ossian — you're not absurd enough to say that, I hope?' said the Antiquary, his brow darkening with wrath.
>
> But Hector stoutly abode the storm; like many a sturdy Celt, he imagined the honour of his country and native language connected with the authenticity of these popular poems, and would have fought knee-deep, or forfeited life and land, rather than have given up a line of them. (p. 243)

Although retracing well-trodden territory, Scott's dialogic reworking of the arguments here is actually quite balanced in exposing the prejudices aired by both parties. When Hector insists that it is reasonable that he should admire 'the antiquities of my own country more than those of the Harolds, Harfagers, and Hacos you are so fond of', Oldbuck rebuffs him angrily in Pinkertonian vein: 'Why those, sir, — these mighty and unconquered Goths, — were your ancestors! — the bare-breeched Celts whom they subdued [...] were but their Mancipia and Serfs!' (p. 244). Unsurprisingly, Hector bridles at this, insisting that 'such names are very improperly applied to Scotch Highlanders', and proclaiming the antiquity of his Celtic pedigree. But Oldbuck's folkloristic curiosity — and his better nature — gets the better of Pinkertonian prejudice as he asks Hector if he can recall any of the Ossianic poems recited by the regimental piper Roderick MacAlpine.

Hector obliges, while remonstrating that his uncle 'does not understand the Gaelic': this forces him to translate one fragment of verse from its original, 'a dialogue between the poet Oisin, or Ossian, and Patrick, the tutelary saint of Ireland', which he runs over 'well garnished with *aghes, aughs,* and *oughs,* and similar gutterals'. The exchange between the pagan Oisin and the Christian saint turns out to be just as bad-tempered as that which has just ensued between Oldbuck and Hector:

> 'Upon my word, son of Fingal [says Patrick]
> While I am warbling the psalms,
> The clamour of your old women's tales
> Disturbs my devotional exercises.'

Oisin answers 'Dare you compare your psalms, | You son of a —' (glossed by Hector as 'female dog'), followed by 'Do you compare your psalms | To the tales of the bare-armed Fenians?'

Oldbuck is quick to compare the racy Gaelic originals with Macpherson's anodyne translation: and Hector is obliged to concede that 'If you are sure of that […] [Macpherson] must have taken very unwarrantable liberties with his original'. The exchange concludes with Oldbuck's surmise that the epithet 'bare-armed Fenians' is a mistranslation of 'bare-arsed Fenians': 'I should have thought the nudity might have been quoted as existing in a different part of the body' (alluding to David Hume's 'bare-arsed banditti'). At this point, in a wonderful mock-heroic passage, Hector is sidetracked by the sight of a seal upon the beach, which arouses his sporting instincts. Snatching his uncle's walking stick, he sallies to the attack, only to be worsted in the conflict by the aggrieved *phoca*. He picks himself up off the rocks, 'just […] in time to receive the ironic congratulations of his uncle, upon a single combat, worthy to be commemorated by Ossian himself' (p. 246). As well as parodying Hector's identification with Ossianic 'mighty hunters', this incident comically foreshadowing the more serious 'single combat' fought between Hector and Lovel (at the instigation of the former) over Isabella Wardour, in which the Highlander again comes off worst.

As David Hewitt indicates in his notes to the Edinburgh edition, the poem recited here by Hector is not actually contained in Macpherson's Ossianic corpus, but is quoted from a 'Dialogue between St Patrick and Ossian', a translation by the English ballad collector Thomas Hill of 'Oisin agus an Clerich', published in the *Gentleman's Magazine* in 1783, and said to be 'taken down from the recitation of a Highland blacksmith' in Glenorchy.[31] Hill (who unlike Macpherson often published the Gaelic originals alongside his translations) was happy to acknowledge that many of the *finagaicht* ballads which he had collected on his field trips had an Irish source, a fact hotly denied by Macpherson, who had in fact assiduously airbrushed out any reference to St Patrick in his English Ossian.[32] Although never mentioned by Scott in his 1805 review, it seems highly likely that Hill's articles in the *Gentleman's Magazine* had an important influence on his perceptions of the Ossian controversy. Hill's Ossian poems, in contrast to

---

[31] Although Hill made three tours, visiting Perthshire and Strathspey as well as the West Highlands, he concluded that 'the songs relating to the Feinne, and their chieftain, Fion-mac-Coul […] are wholly confined to Argyleshire, and the Western Highlands, where the scene of their action is supposed to have lain'. 'New Light on the Ossian Controversy', *Gentleman's Magazine*, 52 (December 1782), 570–71. This western geographical location, near Ireland, encouraged Hill to suggest that the poems were of Irish origin.

[32] Macpherson insisted that the original poems pre-dated Christianity, and were in any case of Scottish, not Irish provenance, thereby suppressing any links with a medieval Catholic popular culture common to Ireland and Gaelic Scotland, a fact which played well with Presbyterian ministers like Hugh Blair and Andrew Gallie, who were among his staunchest supporters.

Macpherson's, were in a sense 'the real thing', revealing all the directness of expression (and, as we've seen, comic vulgarity) of a folk poetry passed down through oral tradition, revealingly described by Scott in his 1830 'Essay on Popular Poetry' as a 'degrading species of alchymy, by which the ore of antiquity is deteriorated and adulterated'.[33] Above all, Hill's versions of Gaelic ballads does not threaten the narrative of stadial history cherished by Scott, mixing up the chivalric manners of a more advanced age with the barbarism of primitive folk-heroes like Fingal and his Fianna in the manner of Macpherson's 'translations'.

In this respect, it is appropriate that Scott should put these authentic Ossianic verses into the mouth of Hector, who for all his faults (and stereotypical Gaelic impetuosity) is intended as a more acceptable embodiment of the modern Gael than anything invented by Macpherson.[34] As a Captain in the Black Watch, Hector represents the ancient martial spirit of Fergus MacIvor, redeemed from the rebellious taint of Jacobitism, and pressed into the service of the British state. (We might recall that Edie Ochiltree, although no Highlander, is also a veteran of the 'Forty-twa', who had served at Prestonpans and Fontenoy.) As William Donaldson notes, the gallantry of Highland soldiers at Quebec, Ticonderoga and Seringapatam (not to mention Alexandria, and more recently, given the publication date of *The Antiquary*, Waterloo), 'enabled even the staunchest Whig to accept them as the latter-day standard bearers of the ancient military ideals of the Scots, and they played a key role in the continuous redefinition of national stereotypes in the century following the Union'.[35] Scott may have known that the martial virtues of Fingal and his Fianna has been employed in the 1790s by the Gaelic poet Duncan Ban MacIntyre (another loyalist MacIntyre) to promote anti-Jacobin and anti-French propaganda, in contrast to a very different, rebellious trajectory in 'Fenian' Ireland, as Luke Gibbons has argued.[36]

[33] *Minstrelsy of the Scottish Border*, 4 vols (Edinburgh: Black, 1861), I, 22.

[34] One of the most impressive collections of eighteenth-century Ossianic verse in Gaelic was made by the Rev. James MacLagan, who was chaplain to the Black Watch in the 1770s and '80s before he became minister at Blair Atholl. Much of it was gathered by MacLagan from Highland soldiers while campaigning in North America, Ireland or Europe: currently located in Glasgow University's Special Collections, it was also ransacked by James Macpherson (and possibly annotated by him) while preparing his English Ossian in 1760. In this sense, Scott's characterization of Hector MacIntyre as a regimental transmitter of an authentic Gaelic version of Ossian coincides exactly with the historical record, give or take a few anachronisms.

[35] William Donaldson, *The Jacobite Song: Political Myth and National Identity* (Aberdeen: Aberdeen University Press, 1988), p. 70.

[36] See Nigel Leask, 'Fingalian Topographies: Ossian and the Highland Tour', *Journal for 18th Century Studies*, 39.2 (June 2016), 183–96 (p. 187); Luke Gibbons, 'From Ossian to O'Carolan: The Bard as Separatist Symbol', in *From Gaelic to Romantic: Ossianic Translations*, ed. by Fiona Stafford and Howard Gaskill (Amsterdam and Atlanta, GA: Rodopi, 1998), pp. 226–51.

In conclusion, I want to return to an earlier passage of the novel where Oldbuck attempts to persuade Lovel (whom he believes to have poetic talents) to compose an epic poem, for which he will supply the antiquarian notes:

'I'll supply you with a subject — The battle between the Caledonians and Romans — The Caledoniad; or, Invasion Repelled — Let that be the title — It will suit the present taste, and you may throw in a touch of the times.'

'But the invasion of Agricola was not repelled.'

'No, but you are a poet — free of the corporation, and as little bound down to truth of probability as Virgil himself — You may defeat the Romans in spite of Tacitus.' (p. 107)

Taking a leaf out of Macpherson's book, Oldbuck's rewriting of history is justified by the 'present taste' (in 1794) for a patriotic epic that will imagine the repulsion of foreign invasion. In so doing, Oldbuck boasts that 'I'll annihilate Ossian, Macpherson, and Mac-Cribb' (p. 108). Although the plot of *The Caledoniad* might sound distinctly Fingalian in representing ancient Caledonians defeating a foreign invasion, we should recall that Oldbuck was convinced that the aboriginal Scots were Goths not Celts, so his response to Macpherson is to rewrite Scottish patriotism in a Gothic idiom.

As we've seen, the threatened French invasion at the conclusion of *The Antiquary* turns out to be a hoax, but Lovel's restoration as the legitimate Lord Geraldin (converted from ancestral Catholicism to the Protestant faith) permits his acceptance by Isabella Wardour, representing a *Waverley*-like marriage/ union. The historical false alarm is an opportunity not only for resolving the fictional plot, but also provides an opportunity for a display of Highland martial pomp, as Glenallan's tenants form 'a regiment of five hundred men, completely equipped with the Highland dress, whom he had brought down from his upland glens, with their pipes playing in the van'. Forced to swallow his anti-Celtic animus, Oldbuck is pleased to note how 'the ancient military spirit of [Glenallan's] house seemed to animate and invigorate the decayed frame of the Earl, their leader'; and as it turns out, this military apparition of feudal loyalty is to be Lovel/Neville/Lord Geraldin's inheritance (p. 351). By 1816, it might have been relatively easy for Scott to write off the French invasion scares of the 1790s in a mock-heroic vein: but there's nothing mocking about the neo-feudal tartan pageantry evoked here, which totally eclipses Oldbuckian scepticism about 'bare-arsed Fenians', and offers a preview of Scott's management of the 'King's Jaunt' in 1822, when Edinburgh was literally wrapped in tartan. Moreover the exposure of Dousterswivel as a German *illuminatus* and conman does little to promote Pinkertonian or 'Gothicist' claims, as Oldbuck is forced to concede. Scott's eirenic vision of Britain resolves ethnic conflict between Goths and Celts in the interest of national unity.

We saw Oldbuck speaking of 'annihilating' Macpherson by rewriting his Celtic epic *Fingal* as *The Caledoniad*. I'll close with a very tentative suggestion that Scott might have pursued a similar goal in borrowing a markedly Macphersonian plot for his novel, hackneyed as that plot has seemed to critics. In the 1805 review of Malcolm Laing's edition, he glossed the plot of Macpherson's earlier pre-Ossian poems, *The Hunter* and *The Highlander*: 'An unknown youth arrives at the Scottish camp, when the Danes have made good a descent upon the coast. It will be readily anticipated that he becomes the principal hero in the ensuing battle; is discovered to be the lawful heir of the Scottish crown; marries a beautiful princess, and reigns in peace and glory'.[37] Fiona Stafford's analysis of this rather stale romance plot offers a bit more nuance:

> Macpherson examines the idea of the prince raised in obscurity, proving his worth through deeds rather than merely inheriting his power. In both, the military interest of Scotland being close to defeat but emerging victoriously is mingled with a romantic tale of love and marriage.[38]

Stafford also notes that the young Macpherson was here drawing on the narrative of the authentic Gaelic 'Magnus Ballad', which told the story of the King of Lochlin's invasion of Ireland, providing the plot outline of *Fingal*:

> [The] tale of the unknown nobleman discovering his true birth and atoning for the death of his father has much in common with the legend of Finn MacCumhail [...] [whose] father was traditionally slain by Goll MacMorna at the battle of Cnuch, so that the orphaned boy had to be brought up in obscurity. Eventually, the son discovers his true identity and reclaims his father's position as head of the militia, reconciling the two warring factions of Clan Baiosgne and Clan Morna.[39]

Seen in this light, several episodes of *The Antiquity* might be read as mock-heroic re-workings of Macpherson's plot, with Wardour and Lord Glenallan as the 'failed guardians' of Uillin, MacIntyre as the flawed hero Cuchullin, and Lovel as a mysterious Fingalian commander. Lovel reappears at a crucial point in the narrative in the guise of the conquering hero Major Neville to repel invasion, after fighting a duel with MacIntyre for the hand of the heroine. Scott doubtless intended *The Caledoniad* to ironize the relation between epic (whether neo-classical or Ossianic), and *The Antiquary*'s modern, mock-heroic narrative, where nothing of world-historical importance ends up happening, but which quite literally exposes 'history in the making' between facts and frauds. But if I am correct, Scott's novel might have owed rather more to Macpherson's 'fraudulent' *Ossian* than he was willing to acknowledge.

---

[37] *ER* 458.

[38] At one point, Alpin, the hero of Macpherson's *Highlander*, raises his clansmen to meet the threat of invasion: 'The mountain-chiefs, in burning arms incased, | [...] | To guard their homely huts, though mountains rose; | Yet feeling Albion in their breasts, they dare | From rocks to rush, and meet the distant war'. Fiona Stafford, *The Sublime Savage* (Edinburgh: Edinburgh University Press, 1988), pp. 68–71 (pp. 68–69).

[39] Stafford, p. 69.

'This right of mercy': The Royal Pardon in *The Heart of Midlothian*

TARA GHOSHAL WALLACE

George Washington University

In July 1736, John Porteus, Captain of the Edinburgh City Guards, was convicted and sentenced to hang for having fired into a restive crowd during the execution of the smuggler Andrew Wilson. In early September, at the request of local authorities, he won a royal reprieve, but was dragged out of the Tolbooth prison and hanged by an incensed and well-organized mob, an insurrection interpreted as anti-government rebellion by Queen Caroline (serving as Regent during George II's absence in Hanover) and the Parliament in Westminster. In May 1738, Isobel Walker, a young Scots countrywoman, was condemned to death for having concealed her pregnancy and murdered her baby, but was pardoned by a royal warrant, perhaps due to the exertions of her sister Helen Walker, who, according to Scott's source, walked to London from near Dumfries in order to beg the intercession of the Duke of Argyle. It is Scott's great achievement in *The Heart of Midlothian*, as almost every critic notes, to bring together, in 1818, the stories of these two royal reprieves to construct a narrative that illuminates a significant aspect of post-Union history and gives us a heroine who, in winning a pardon from Queen Caroline, has won the hearts of readers for two hundred years.[1]

Jeanie Deans not only overcomes the Queen's spleen against the Scots for 'the gross insult and outrage done in your capital city to the royal authority', but also supplies the occasion, desired on both sides, for a political rapprochement between the Duke of Argyle and his royal masters.[2] The resolution provides a

---

[1] See, for example, Ann Rigney, who compares Scott's procedure to curating a museum collection: 'The two episodes are historical in the sense that they are documented, but it is the novel that brings them together for the first time as part of Scottish history [...] mutually reinforcing meaning [...] organizing events into poetic patterns', in *The Afterlives of Walter Scott: Memory on the Move* (Oxford: Oxford University Press, 2012), p. 30. Catherine Jones calls Scott's Magnum Opus introduction 'a misleading account of the novel's genesis that makes no reference to Scott's most significant innovation to his initial source: his combining of the private story of Helen Walker/Jeanie Deans with the publicly known case of Porteous'. See Catherine Jones, *Literary Memory: Scott's Waverley Novels and the Psychology of Narrative* (Lewisburg, PA: Bucknell University Press, 2003), p. 54.

[2] *The Heart of Midlothian*, ed. by David Hewitt and Alison Lumsden, EEWN (Edinburgh: Edinburgh University Press, 2004), p. 336. All further references are to this edition.

Yearbook of English Studies, 47 (2017), 203–223

closure so emotionally satisfying that many readers have decried Scott's decision to continue the narrative into a fourth volume. Some deprecators have followed the lead of the anonymous reviewer in the *British Review*, who complained that 'It [the ending] is a poor device for so great an author' — to write, for the sake of money, 'the trash, of which he has composed the latter part of his work', while others have questioned Scott's aesthetic judgment.[3] More forgiving readers have ascribed the long denouement to Scott's personal and authorial impulses: Mary Lascelles, for example, though she faults the episodes beyond the pardon as being 'false to the tragic tone and historical context', attributes the lapse to 'His generous heart, his pleasure in giving satisfaction to his readers' as well as 'the necessity he had incurred of filling a fourth volume', while Harry Shaw finds no evidence of mercenary padding, noting instead 'Scott's delight in Jeanie Deans' and 'unfinished business' regarding the political evolution of David Deans.[4]

Recent critics have produced a wide-ranging and nuanced body of work rehabilitating the despised fourth volume, placing it within a historical context that positions Scott as either nostalgically resisting or complicit in the post-Union modernization of Scottish society. James Kerr and Ian Duncan refer to a 'romance' or 'fable' of 'national regeneration' worked out in the idyllic but decidedly fictional world of the Duke of Argyle's estate, Roseneath, that Highland Arcadia which serves as an imaginary solution to the fragmented and turbulent post-Union polity represented in the early episodes set in Edinburgh, while Andrew Lincoln and Regina Hewitt point to the way in which Roseneath demonstrates the 'substitution of a private solution for a public one', which 'allows Scott to explore the kinds of interactions that promote structural flexibility and integrative control'. For Charlotte Sussman, the 'continuation of Jeanie's story long after it has lost any dramatic interest' signals Scott's participation in the demographic politics that replaces 'a useless population [...] with a productive one' at the same time that it 'reveals that the novel is not perfectly aligned with the project of forging a modern, imperialist state'. And, in

---

[3] Unsigned Review, *British Review* (November 1818) in *Walter Scott: The Critical Heritage*, ed. by John O. Hayden (London: Routledge, 1970), p. 169. Twentieth-century critics who accuse Scott of venality or artistic lapses include Eric Quayle, *The Ruin of Sir Walter Scott* (New York: Clarkson N. Porter, 1958), p. 121, Dorothy Van Ghent, *The English Novel: Form and Function* (New York: Harper & Row, 1953), p. 115, Robert C. Gordon, *Under Which King? A Study of the Scottish Waverley Novels* (New York: Barnes & Noble, 1969), p. 94, and Patricia Mayer Spacks, *Desire and Truth: Functions of Plot in Eighteenth-Century English Novels* (Chicago, IL: University of Chicago Press, 1990), p. 231.

[4] Mary Lascelles, *The Story-Teller Retrieves the Past: Historical Fiction and Fictitious History in the Art of Scott, Stevenson, Kipling, and Some Others* (Oxford: Clarendon Press, 1980), p. 102; Harry E. Shaw, *The Forms of Historical Fiction: Sir Walter Scott and his Successors* (Ithaca, NY: Cornell University Press, 1983), pp. 241–42. Robin Mayhead, in 'The *Heart of Midlothian*: Scott as Artist', *Essays in Criticism*, 5.6 (1956), 266–77, argues that 'Scott's most serious interest ends almost exactly half way through the novel, with the conclusion of the trial of Effie Deans' (p. 267).

a provocative study arguing for Scott's subversive (and pervasive) Scottish nationalism, Julian Meldon D'Arcy locates in Roseneath not a vindication of Union, but 'a more grimly pessimistic picture of eighteenth-century Scotland: the individual Scotsman could gain all the profits of the British Empire, but the Scottish nation had lost its soul'.[5]

Scott anticipates and incorporates into his text a reading of Roseneath as pastoral fantasy, devising a gently mocking moment when Jeanie indulges her imagination, becoming, if you will, a kind of pedestrian Waverley: impatiently awaiting Argyle's permission to leave London, 'Jeanie's fancy, though not the most powerful of her faculties, was lively enough to transport her to a wild farm in Northumberland, well stocked with milk-cows, yield beasts and sheep; a meeting house hard by, frequented by serious presbyterians, who had united in a harmonious call to Reuben Butler to be their spiritual guide [...] herself, with the maiden snood exchanged for a matron's curch' (p. 357). Jeanie attains her fantasy, but the fourth volume that rewards her virtues serves, I argue, as an extended revaluation of the climactic pardon scene that has resonated with so many readers. This essay considers the agenda of the final volume through the institution of the royal pardon itself, addressing Scott's strategy of manipulating entrenched judicial practices not only to enable the novel's plot but also to examine the effects of the royal prerogative itself. Scott's view of the royal right to pardon comprises a range of complexity that reaches the level of contradiction, of a kind that elicits the familiar assessment of Scott as simultaneously a nostalgic romancer and a hard-headed, even 'greasily obsequious' propagandist for the Hanoverian regime.[6] The Heart of Midlothian emphasizes the problematics surrounding the 'mercy' of the Hanoverians, bringing into prominence questions of biopolitical sovereign power discussed in Foucault's The History of Sexuality and recently debated by Giorgio Agamben and Roberto Esposito.[7] Like the

---

[5] James Kerr, *Fiction against History: Scott as Storyteller* (Cambridge: Cambridge University Press, 1989), p. 64; Ian Duncan, *Modern Romance and the Transformations of the Novel: The Gothic, Scott, Dickens* (Cambridge: Cambridge University Press, 1992), p. 154; Andrew Lincoln, *Walter Scott and Modernity* (Edinburgh: Edinburgh University Press, 2007), p. 177; Regina Hewitt, *Symbolic Interactions: Social Problems and Literary Interventions in the Works of Baillie, Scott, and Landor* (Lewisburg, PA: Bucknell University Press, 2006), p. 119; Charlotte Sussman, 'The Emptiness at *The Heart of Midlothian*: Nation, Narration, and Population', *Eighteenth-Century Fiction*, 15.1 (October 2002), 103–26 (pp. 121, 124); Julian Meldon D'Arcy, *Subversive Scott: The Waverley Novels and Scottish Nationalism* (Reykjavik: University of Iceland Press, 2005), p. 162. See also Anne Frey, in *British State Romanticism: Authorship, Agency, and Bureaucratic Nationalism* (Stanford, CA: Stanford University Press, 2010), p. 107 and Rigney, in *Afterlives*, p. 31.

[6] John Sutherland uses the term in *The Life of Walter Scott: A Critical Biography* (Oxford: Blackwell, 1997), p. 209.

[7] Michel Foucault, *The History of Sexuality*, Vol. 1: *An Introduction*, trans. by Robert Huxley (New York: Vintage Books, 1990); Giorgio Agamben, *Homo Sacer: Sovereign Power and Bare Life*, trans. by Daniel Heller-Rouzen (Stanford, CA: Stanford University Press, 1998); Roberto Esposito,

pardons coerced from the Duke of Cumberland in *Waverley* and backed by military threat in *Redgauntlet*, the royal pardons depicted in *Midlothian* construe Hanoverian clemency as reluctant, arbitrary, and self-serving. At the same time, the novel ultimately argues, especially in its final chapters, what Scott explicitly urges in his *Life of Napoleon* — the danger of 'wresting from the crown [...] this right of mercy.'[8] The sovereign's legitimate right of mercy, however capriciously or ineffectively exercised, trumps a subject's arrogation of that right, since the exercise of pardon by unauthorized agents in no way ameliorates the disarray precipitated by the sovereign power's failure to protect the body politic.

* * *

An overview of the way Scott manipulates standard judicial protocols governing the crime of infanticide and the granting of royal pardons will help demonstrate my argument. The 1690 Scottish statute that condemns Effie was based on a similar English law, but with precise conditions requiring the Crown to prove that the accused was guilty of 'concealing pregnancy, giving birth alone, and having no living child to show'.[9] The reasons behind this highly unusual infringement of the principles of common law and *habeas corpus* were, as scholars on the subject tell us, social and ideological, meant to curb a practice 'detrimental to population and to the country', and to discipline the bodies of women and the lower classes.[10] Scott's Bartholine Saddletree, explaining Effie's vulnerability to prosecution for 'murder presumptive, that is, a murder of the

Immunitas: The Protection and Negation of Life, trans. by Zakiya Hanafi (Cambridge: Polity, 2011). Both Anne Frey in *British State Romanticism*, p. 6 and Evan Gottlieb in *Walter Scott and Contemporary Theory* (London: Bloomsbury, 2013), pp. 76–85, draw on Foucault's lectures on governmentality to read *The Heart of Midlothian*.

[8] *The Life of Napoleon Bonaparte, Emperor of the French. With a Preliminary View of the French Revolution*, 2 vols (Honolulu: University Press of the Pacific, 2003; rpt. of 1846 edn), I, pp. vi, 72.

[9] Deborah A. Symonds, *Weep Not for Me: Women, Ballads, and Infanticide in Early Modern England* (University Park: Pennsylvania State University Press, 1997), p. 128. Leon Radzinowicz notes that the statute was among the eight listed for repeal by a committee established in 1771 to consider the excessive number of capital crimes, but the recommendation was rejected by the House of Commons and remained in force until 1803, when 43 Geo.3, c.58, s.3 changed it to conform to 'general principles of English criminal jurisprudence'. See *A History of English Criminal Law and its Administration from 1750: The Movement for Reform, 1750–1833* (New York: Macmillan, 1948), pp. 431, 436.

[10] Radzinowicz, p. 435. See also Evan Gottlieb, '"Almost the Same as Being Innocent": Celebrated Murderesses and National Narratives in Walter Scott's *The Heart of Midlothian* and Margaret Atwood's *Alias Grace*', in *Scottish Literature and Postcolonial Literature: Comparative Texts and Critical Perspectives*, ed. by Michael Gardiner, Graeme MacDonald and Niall O'Gallagher (Edinburgh: Edinburgh University Press, 2011), pp. 30–42. Ian Ward states that 'The only justification for such barbaric laws as the Infanticide law is pragmatic and immediate; stop the lower classes from running amuck [*sic*], having sex, breeding bastards or worse still aborting them', in 'The Jurisprudential Heart of Midlothian', *Scottish Literary Journal*, 24.1 (1997), 25–39 (p. 34).

law's construing or construction', observes that 'it being a statute made by our sovereign Lord and Lady [...] the crime is rather a favourite of the law, this species of murther being one of its ain creation' (p. 47). The law that condemns Effie precisely enacts what Agamben, discussing a fragment from Pindar, calls

> a scandalous unification of the two essentially antithetical principles [...] violence and justice [...] The sovereign is the point of indistinction between violence and law, the threshold on which violence passes over into law and law passes over into violence.

Indeed, it derives from both forms of 'power over life' outlined by Foucault: the 'body as machine' liable to technologies of discipline and the 'species body, the body imbued with the mechanics of life and serving as the basis of the biological processes' subject to 'regulatory controls'. It also participates in the immunatory function of law that Esposito characterizes as 'a logical reversal between guilt and condemnation. Life is not condemned because it is guilty, but rather *in order to make it* guilty.' Effie's body, having slipped out of regulatory controls, must be construed as guilty because it has been condemned by a law founded on 'perpetuating life through the sacrifice of the living'.[11]

In practice, the 1690 law was applied both sparingly and unpredictably: J. H. A. Macdonald's *Practical Treatise* informs Scottish lawyers that accused women were exempt from the statute covering concealment even if they responded to queries with denial, 'if it was given in a jocular manner or otherwise, so as to lead to the conclusion that in reality she admitted to the fact', a directive so vague as to allow great elasticity to the defence. Leon Radzinowicz notes that juries often required proof that a child was born alive, and Deborah A. Symonds's research shows that 'trials in which the child's body had not been recovered were extremely rare. Statute or no statute, the demand for direct evidence remained fairly constant in the courtroom'. Marilyn Francus points to the case against Ann Halle in 1717, in which, although the 'court was able to prove she was guilty of concealment', the accused was acquitted for lack of sufficient proof of murder.[12] Francus further notes that women who were 'docile' in court or were considered to be of good character were usually exonerated, and both Symonds and Julie Kipp cite the royal accoucheur William Hunter, who proposed that women in labour suffered from a temporary mental incapacity that cancelled legal liability.[13]

---

[11] Agamben, pp. 31–32; Foucault, p. 139; Esposito, pp. 32–33.

[12] J. H. A. Macdonald, *A Practical Treatise on the Criminal Law of Scotland*, 2nd edn (Edinburgh: William Green & Sons, 1877), p. 147; Radzinowicz, p. 434; Marilyn Francus, 'Monstrous Mothers, Monstrous Societies: Infanticide and the Rule of Law in Restoration and Eighteenth-Century England', *Eighteenth-Century Life*, 21.2 (May 1997), 133–56 (pp. 142, 134); Symonds, p. 154. According to Symonds, of the 347 women 'investigated for murdering their children at birth, after attempting to hide their pregnancies', fifty were executed' (pp. 2–5).

[13] Francus, pp. 134, 143; Symonds, p. 147. Julie Kipp, *Romanticism, Maternity, and the Body Politic* (Cambridge: Cambridge University Press, 2003), pp. 127–28.

As a practising lawyer, Scott would have known that Effie meets prevailing criteria for exoneration on multiple grounds.[14] Daughter of a family 'held in high regard' by the community (p. 93), she responds 'with bitter sarcasm, and [...] sullen denial' to the taunts of neighbours who register 'her disfigured shape, loose dress, and pale cheeks' (p. 92), a response that could be construed as indirect admission. Unlike in the case of Isobel Walker, no infant's body provides irrefutable proof of murder. Witnesses were called to testify to her character: 'All gave her an excellent one' (p. 207) and her demeanour in court exhibits all the shame and contrition required to signal docile submission. And even Jeanie seems to know enough about precedent to plead for Argyle's intercession on the grounds that Effie 'canna be proved to be a murderer [...] She has not been proved guilty' (pp. 321–23). But Effie must be found guilty in order to activate the plot culminating in the royal pardon, so Scott proposes an explanation based on a disturbing rise in numbers. Both Middleborough (the magistrate investigating the case) and the presiding judge cite the need for judicial rigour in the face of an increasing rate of infanticide. Middleborough anticipates that she will hang because 'The crime has been too common, and examples are become necessary' (p. 116). Scott's anomalously passive judge instructs the jury that they must proceed 'according to the laws as they stood'; scrupulously complying with the letter of the law, he ascribes its rigour to 'the alarming progress of a dreadful crime' (p. 214). A dozen chapters later, Argyle invokes numbers to explain Effie's fourteen-year banishment from Scotland : 'within the course of only seven years, twenty-one instances of child murther had occurred in Scotland' (p. 352).[15] In fact, as the editors of the recent Edinburgh edition of the novel note, 'there is no evidence of an increase in the crime in the 1730s [...] There is no evidence in the 1730s that there was any change in policy on the administration of the 1690 Act; of the twenty-four cases prosecuted between

[14] David Marshall, in *Sir Walter Scott and Scots Law* (Edinburgh: William Honge and Co., 1932), traces Scott's legal career; Jane Millgate, 'Scott and the Law: *The Heart of Midlothian*', in *Rough Justice: Essays on Crime in Literature*, ed. by M. L. Friedland (Toronto: University of Toronto Press, 1991), pp. 95–114, shows 'how thorough and continuous was his immersion in the legal life of Scotland, and how familiar he was with every aspect of the practice of law' (p. 98). Indeed, Scott's essay opposing Lord Grenville's proposals to align Scottish law more closely with English jurisprudence demonstrates his deep engagement with the history and politics of legal practices which, in Scotland, have 'attained a point of perfection unknown to any other country in Europe'. See 'View of the Changes Proposed and Adopted in the Administration of Justice in Scotland', in *Sir Walter Scott's Edinburgh Annual Register*, ed. by Kenneth Curry (Knoxville: University of Tennessee Press, 1977), p. 175. In *Heart of Midlothian*, Scott pointedly contrasts superior practices in Scottish criminal procedure, which included 'advocates, whom the humanity of the Scottish law (in this particular more liberal than that of the sister country), not only permits, but enjoins, to appear and assist with their advice and skill all persons under trial' (p. 195).
[15] The Edinburgh edition notes that Argyle uses figures from Hugo Arnot's 1785 compilation, which covers the period from 1700 to 1706 (p. 698).

1730 and 1739, three of the accused were hanged, the rest either released or banished' (pp. 590–91).

The supposed increase in infanticide, then, provides a rationale for the unusually inflexible application of the law. Similarly, the Porteous affair is deployed to justify the Court's reluctance to adhere to the system of almost automatic royal pardon obtaining by the middle of the eighteenth century, thereby enabling a plot that requires Jeanie to seek direct monarchical intervention and enact what R. F. Fisher has characterized as a movement from the 'inferno' of the journey to the 'purgatory' of Argyle's intercession to the 'paradise of the pardon'.[16] Legal historians have traced the evolution of the royal prerogative of pardon from its early investiture in the kings of Wessex in the seventh to tenth centuries to William the Conqueror who 'brought from Normandy the view that clemency was an exclusive privilege of the king', to its statutory delimitation by the Habeas Corpus Act in 1679, the Bill of Rights in 1689, and the Act of Settlement in 1701. As Stanley Grupp puts it, 'by the close of the seventeenth century and the early eighteenth century the power of pardon was still a special prerogative of the Crown but a prerogative which had been encroached upon by both custom and statute', especially after Parliament was granted similar powers in 1721. By the eighteenth century, judges wielded considerable influence: J. M. Beattie notes that 'the king virtually never refused to spare someone nominated by the judge who had presided at the trial [...] Judges were told they need not even justify their decisions; they simply sent in the names of those they thought deserving and they would be granted the king's mercy'.[17] Moreover, the protocols for granting pardon were simultaneously well established and mysterious: a petitioner appealed through the Secretary of State to the judge, usually with the help of 'someone of social and political eminence' and employed the services of an attorney who could couch the plea in the required formal language and proper form, an apparently transparent system that was, according to Douglas Hay, made opaque by secret pardon-dealing that 'went on at the highest levels only' so that 'the royal prerogative of mercy could be presented as something altogether more mysterious, more sacred and more absolute in its determinations'. But even the hidden machinations behind some

[16] P. F. Fisher, 'Providence, Fate, and the Historical Imagination in Scott's "The Heart of Midlothian"', *Nineteenth-Century Fiction*, 10.2 (September 1955), 99–114 (p. 112).

[17] Stanley Grupp, 'Some Historical Aspects of the Pardon in England', *The American Journal of Legal History*, 7.1 (January 1963), 61–52 (pp. 55–58); J. M. Beattie, 'The Royal Pardon and Criminal Procedure in Early Modern England', *Historical Papers/Communications Historiques*, 22.1 (1987), 9–22 (p. 13). Regina Hewitt's research shows 'how Scottish professionals embraced discretion and flexibility [...] and how they used them to decrease their imposition of death sentences without crisis or legislation [...] Discretionary power was thus institutionalized within the Scottish system' (*Symbolic Interactions*, pp. 51–52).

royal reprieves followed established patterns; as Peter King notes, 'The pardoning system usually enabled those at the very apex of the social hierarchy to demonstrate that they had the favour of the King or of his key ministers'. The heroic exertions of Jeanie (and of her putative avatar Helen Walker) are thus highly unusual, amounting to what James Kerr calls a social transgression in 'daring to seek justice and mercy from her superior'.[18]

* * *

In order to set Jeanie's feet and his central plot in motion, Scott turns to the Porteous affair as the key to the royal animosity that obstructs Effie's access to standard policies regarding pardons. As the always pedantic but often well-informed Mr. Saddletree tells his neighbours, 'The king and queen is sae ill pleased with that mistak about Porteous, that de'il a kindly Scot will they ever pardon again, whether by reprieve or remission, if the hail town o' Edinburgh suld be a' hanged on ae tow' (p. 220). Argyle, too, warns Jeanie that 'the late disorders in Edinburgh have executed a prejudice in government against the nation at large, which they think can only be managed by measures of intimidation and severity' (p. 320), and both character and narrator ascribe Argyle's diminished influence at Court to his open opposition to the government's harsh reprisals against Edinburgh, an assessment Scott repeats in *Tales of a Scottish Grandfather* when he writes that Queen Caroline 'considered the commotion, and the impunity with which it was followed, as an insult to her personal authority', so that her resentment led to a bill 'prepared and brought into Parliament for the punishment of the city of Edinburgh, in a very vindictive spirit'.[19] As with the statistics regarding infanticide, Scott skews chronology here to bring together the political and personal plots of *Midlothian*, but he also accurately represents the very real tensions between the government in London and violently rebellious populations in Scotland. As examples of mob violence, Kenneth J. Logue, in *Popular Disturbances Scotland, 1780–1815*, lists the Porteous riots among uprisings that include 'Anti-English feelings' behind the1705 lynching of English sailors (wrongly charged with piracy and murder in an attack on a Scottish ship), riots against the Union in 1706, riots in Glasgow against the Malt tax in 1725, as well as food riots, anti-recruitment riots and political riots on the King's birthday later in the century. Logue concludes that 'The popular disturbance [...] was [...] a widely distributed and frequently recurring

---

[18] Beattie, pp. 14–16; Macdonald, p. 549; Douglas Hay, 'Property, Authority and the Criminal Law', in *Albion's Fatal Tree: Crime and Society in Eighteenth-Century England*, ed. by Douglas Hay and others (New York: Pantheon Books, 1975), pp. 17–63 (p. 47); Peter King, *Crime, Justice, and Discretion in England, 1740–1820* (Oxford: Oxford University Press, 2000), p. 326; Kerr, p. 70.

[19] *Tales of a Scottish Grandfather*, intro. by George Grant, 4 vols (Nashville, TN: Cumberland House, 2001), IV, 134.

expression of popular will in the period' and that 'The Edinburgh people were notorious for the ease with which they formed themselves into a crowd to take direct action'.[20] In the novel, Scott recalls the Edinburgh guard's 'skirmish with the rabble on the king's birth-day' (p. 28), repeated uprisings 'against the government' (p. 34), and a general anti-Hanoverian bias, which causes the 'mob of Edinburgh' to be 'jacobitically disposed, probably because that was the line of sentiment most diametrically opposite to existing authority' (p. 194). In this atmosphere of general hostility to the centre, the pardon of Porteous, which Duncan considers 'a breach of statute',[21] confirms disaffected Scots' suspicion that the monarchy represents neither justice nor legitimate sovereignty: even the respectable matron Mrs. Howden exclaims, 'Deil that they were back at their German kale-yard [...]' (p. 220). The Queen's fury against the Edinburgh rioters, though in fact occurring two years before the case of Isobel Walker, enables Scott to construct the extreme circumstances that require Jeanie's journey, so that she can accomplish what popular opinion in Edinburgh declares to be impossible: 'reach the length o' Lunnon' (p. 37).[22]

Legal and political manoeuvrings in *The Heart of Midlothian* culminate in the personal encounter between Jeanie and Queen Caroline that some read as Scott's nostalgia for 'the intimacy of a rude past', a 'journey into the communal identity of the nation in which the king and queen participate'.[23] But this touching and central episode, while it packs the emotional punch of virtue rewarded and the uplifting spectacle of authority yielding to compassion, provides, at the same time, the occasion for a profound interrogation of the rationales behind and consequences of the royal right of pardon. It is not necessary here to rehearse in detail what many critics have pointed out: Queen Caroline's carefully calculated move to repair the dangerous breach with Argyle and to make a dramatic gesture that confirms the notion of Hanoverian mercy toward subjects. As James Carson suggests, 'Jeanie's principles lead to a happy outcome only by means of the Queen's policy', one which recognizes the government's dependence on Argyle

[20] Kenneth J. Logue, *Popular Disturbances in Scotland, 1780–1815* (Edinburgh: John Donald Publishers, 1979), p. 1. Margaret Criscuola, 'The Porteous Mob: Fact and Truth in *The Heart of Midlothian*', *English Language Notes*, 22.1 (1984), 43–50, attributes the deliberate distortions in Scott's depiction of the Porteous riot to his desire to foreground 'the importance of national character and the value of particularity, of being true to one's origins' (p. 48).

[21] Duncan, p. 155.

[22] Jane Millgate, in *Walter Scott: The Making of the Novelist* (Toronto: University of Toronto Press, 1984), points out that 'the abolition of the Scottish parliament continued to be felt as a national injury, cutting off the Scottish people from direct contact with their rulers' (p. 157).

[23] Daniel Cottom, *The Civilized Imagination: A Study of Ann Radcliffe, Jane Austen, and Sir Walter Scott* (Cambridge: Cambridge University Press, 1985), p. 179; John P. Farrell, *Revolution as Tragedy: The Dilemma of the Moderate from Scott to Arnold* (Ithaca, NY: Cornell University Press, 1980), p. 111.

to keep surly Scots in line.[24] Indeed, Scott leaves little for critics to tease out, supplying three closely written pages of political context, which he says 'will be found necessary to understand the scene which is about to be presented to the reader' (p. 333). His background information consists of a delineation of Caroline's influence over George, which she retains by sometimes painful submission to his desires and tastes, even to the extent of 'endangering her life [with cold baths when suffering from the gout] that she might be able to attend the king in his long walks' (p. 332). Although he gives George II more credit for appreciating his wife's talents than the courtier does, Scott's description of Caroline closely follows Lord Hervey's characterization of a woman habitually balancing internal warring elements — 'her predominant passion was pride, and the darling pleasure of her soul was power; but she was forced to gratify the one and gain the other, as some people do health, by a strict and painful régime, which few besides herself could have had patience to support, or resolution to adhere to'.[25] Scott's historically grounded portrait of Caroline prepares the reader for the rapid shifts of mood and affect we witness in the dramatic encounter between Queen and country-girl.

The pardon scene plays out both the pride and self-discipline limned by Hervey: injured pride causes her to lash out at Argyle's 'humble petition', angrily exclaiming 'I, at least, have had enough of Scot pardons' (p. 336) and to indulge in bitter sarcasm when she tells Jeanie that 'if the King were to pardon your sister [...] I suppose your people of Edinburgh would hang her out of spite' (p. 339); habitual discipline makes her 'ready at repairing any false step of this kind' (p. 334), smoothly glossing over her hasty insult to the Duke and Scotland. Queen Caroline's political wisdom determines her to 'retain some hold over so important a personage as the Duke of Argyle', just as she routinely extends her considerable 'personal address' toward 'the reclaiming from their political heresy many of those determined tories, who, after the reign of the Stuarts had been extinguished in the person of Queen Anne, were disposed rather to transfer their allegiance to her brother the Chevalier de Saint George, than to acquiesce in the settlement of the crown on the Hanover family' (p. 331). The desire to bind wavering loyalties induces Caroline to placate Argyle, despite Horace Walpole's record of royal vexation that Argyle's 'powers were uncontrolled in Scotland'.[26] The knowledge of that power compels Queen Caroline, in a chronologically

[24] James P. Carson, *Populism, Gender, and Sympathy in the Romantic Novel* (New York: Palgrave Macmillan, 2010), p. 65. See also Bruce Beiderwell, *Power and Punishment in Scott's Novels* (Athens: University of Georgia Press, 1992), p. 79; A. O. J. Cockshut, *The Achievement of Walter Scott* (New York: New York University Press, 1969), p. 186; Kipp, p. 150; D'Arcy, p. 156; William J. Hyde, 'Jeanie Deans and the Queen: Appearance and Reality', *Nineteenth-Century Fiction*, 25.1 (June 1973), 86–92 (pp. 89–91).

[25] *Lord Hervey's Memoirs*, ed. by Romney Sedgwick (London: B. T. Batsford, 1963), p. 254.

[26] Walpole, p. 185.

convoluted moment, to reprise, in an 1818 text set in 1736, the episode in an 1814 text about 1745 when Colonel Talbot coerces a pardon from her son (the Duke of Cumberland) by invoking his family's support for the Hanoverian government, and finally, 'as a last resource', threatening to resign his commission.[27] What Alexander Welsh construes as the Queen's romantic agency, 'the intuitive compassion of one human being who *is* sovereign',[28] thus becomes implicated in a complex network of power relations which require both sovereign and subject to negotiate shifting ascendancies in order to sustain an unstable centre.

Scott's preparatory matter also 'humanizes' the Queen, figuring Caroline's sexual jealousy as an impetus for being ready to hear Jeanie's plea. Once again using Hervey's and Walpole's accounts of Caroline's shrewd management of Lady Suffolk, he recounts how the queen manipulates the unlucky paramour to 'unite in her own person the two apparently inconsistent characters of her husband's mistress, and her own very obsequious and complaisant confidante [...] if she submitted to the mortification of being obliged to connive at her husband's infidelity, she was at least guarded against what she might think its most dangerous effects, and was besides at liberty, now and then, to bestow a few civil insults upon "her good Howard"' (p. 333).[29] Since Jeanie unknowingly provides the insult, Caroline can simply acknowledge the hit 'with a smile, which marked that she enjoyed the triumph' (p. 339). In this case, the Queen's two bodies tactically collude to position sovereign power in a posture of dignified royal clemency.

It is a mark of Scott's narrative genius that his readers, primed to be cynical by 'remarks [...] necessary to understand' the pardon scene, are still mesmerized and moved by the encounter. With Argyle, we gasp when Jeanie, ignorant of the toxic relations between their Majesties and their heir (a recent biographer of the family writes that 'They treated Frederick with a venom that exceeded any legitimate political frustration, and conceived a hatred for him that became almost pathological in its intensity'[30]), makes an ill-advised reference to mothers who 'are unkind to their own flesh and blood', and we sigh with relief when her equally inadvertent insult to Lady Suffolk regarding 'breaking the seventh commandment' wins the Queen's approbation because 'her Majesty had not so

---

[27] *Waverley*, ed. by P. D. Garside, EEWN (Edinburgh: Edinburgh University Press, 2007), pp. 333–34.

[28] Alexander Welsh, *The Hero of the Waverley Novels* (New Haven, CT: Yale University Press, 1963), pp. 131–32.

[29] Hervey sympathetically portrays Lady Suffolk as a powerless mistress who 'had the mortification of knowing the Queen's influence so much superior to hers, that the little show of interest she maintained was only a permitted tenure dependent on a rival who could have overturned it any hour she pleased' (p. 13).

[30] Janice Hadlow, *A Royal Experiment: The Private Life of King George III* (New York: Henry Holt and Co., 2014), p. 58.

lost the feelings of a wife in those of a Queen, but what she could enjoy a jest at the expence of "her good Suffolk"' (pp. 338–39). We applaud Jeanie's shrewd rhetoric in denying any direct connection with the Porteous mob, in invoking at least one Scotsman (her 'broken hearted' father) who prays day and night that 'his Majesty might be blessed with a long prosperous reign' and in proclaiming her confidence 'that baith town and country wad rejoice to see his Majesty taking compassion on a poor unfriended creature' (pp. 339–40), thus appealing to the Hanoverian desire to bury what Lincoln calls 'the record of violence and atrocities that looms so large in the history of Scotland'.[31] Jeanie's moving invocation of the Queen's own 'hour of trouble [...] hour of death' when her compassion for Effie 'will be sweeter' than any memory of royal revenge, even carries literary resonances, recalling Jane Shore's impassioned prayer in Nicholas Rowe's 1714 tragedy 'That heav'n will pay you back when you most need | The grace and goodness you have shown to me'.[32] The emotional power of Jeanie's exchange with the Queen carries us so far beyond the reasons of state that Scott has conscientiously described that even so attentive a reader as Robert Gordon is moved to consecrate the scene as one in which 'one vessel of grace confronts another, and justice is done'.[33]

* * *

The final volume of *The Heart of Midlothian* reminds us, despite Jeanie's idealized domesticity in Argyle's Highland Arcadia, how little grace and justice follow directly from the royal pardon so compellingly narrated at the end of Volume III. As Jane Millgate cogently points out, Jeanie's first experience as Argyle's privileged protégée is as witness to the hanging of Meg Murdockson and the brutal mob violence inflicted on Madge Wildfire at Carlisle:

---

[31] Lincoln, p. 170. Gottlieb expands this reading: 'by publicly granting clemency to a poor Scotswoman who is guiltless of any actual crime, the British monarchy can with a single stroke save an innocent life and help repair its relationship with its Scottish subjects' ('"Almost the Same"', p. 33).

[32] Nicholas Rowe, *The Tragedy of Jane Shore*, ed. by Harry William Pedicord (Lincoln: University of Nebraska Press, 1974), Act II, ll. 169–70.

[33] Gordon, p. 93. Jeanie's allusion to grateful prayers of the populace echoes the words of the judge John Comyn when he appeals for royal mercy on behalf of Anne Milborne, convicted of infanticide in 1728: 'I think it my duty [...] not only to raise in the minds of the people a reverence and veneration towards his Majesty and Administration on account of his Justice but to engage their love and affection towards him on account of his Goodness and Mercy in cases of hardship and compassion' (Beattie, p. 17, fn 17). For analyses of Jeanie's rhetoric see Raymond F. Hillyard, *Ritual Violence and the Maternal in the British Novel, 1740–1820* (Lewisburg, PA: Bucknell University Press, 2010), pp. 220–21; Susan Morgan, 'Old Heroes and a New Heroine in the Waverley Novels', *ELH*, 50 (1983), 559–85 (p. 581); Francis R. Hart, *Scott's Novels: The Plotting of Historic Survival* (Charlottesville: University Press of Virginia, 1966), p. 143; and Alison Lumsden, *Walter Scott and the Limits of Language* (Edinburgh: Edinburgh University Press, 2010), p. 128.

She has moved unmolested through the world of crime to arrive in the presence of the Queen herself, and there in an act of single moral combat she has wrested the life of her sister from the sovereign's grasp by the force of her own impassioned speech [...] It is hard for Jeanie or the reader to feel completely comforted by the restoration of the laws of natural justice in the pardoning of Effie, when that pardon is undercut by an episode such as this.[34]

On a national canvas, popular unrest and political uprisings demonstrate the inefficacy of the Hanoverian tactic of pacification through strategic clemency. The monarchs in *Midlothian* do not win the general approbation of 'baith town and country' as Jeanie had predicted. Indeed, even as Jeanie approaches Argyle's domains, her party skirts the environs of Glasgow where 'Some temporary causes of discontent had occasioned tumults' which might, Argyle's steward Archibald fears, escalate in unpredictable ways: 'as our Duke is in opposition to the court, perhaps we might be too well received; or they might take it in their heads to remember that the captain of Carrick came down upon them with his highlandmen in the time of Shawfield's mob in 1725, and then we would be too ill received' (p. 370). And while many critics have rightly noted the novel's glaring compression or evasion of 1745 and its aftermath, Scott's readers, both in 1818 and now, would be well aware of how imperfectly Hanoverian mercy, whether general as in the aftermath of 1715 or particular as in Effie's case, managed to quell Scottish opposition and unrest.

At the level of plot, Scott goes to some lengths to show that the consequences to Effie herself are, at the very least, problematic. Effie's life subsequent to the precious reprieve, which Van Ghent reads as 'preferable to Jeanie's reward',[35] comprises social success but personal and domestic misery, scarred by barrenness and constant fear of exposure, which she says would cause her now status-conscious husband to 'hate me — he will kill me' (p. 418). Moreover, Effie's royally redeemed but blighted life has no effect on a spirit that Scott characterizes as 'naturally impatient and petulant' (p. 391) and that from early youth 'possessed a little fund of self-conceit and obstinacy' (p. 86). Her narcissism not only contributes to her secret liaison with Staunton but also causes her to fantasize melodramatically about audience reaction to her hanging and to reject, with bitter recrimination, Jeanie's sympathy: 'What signifies coming to greet over me, when you have killed me? [...] me that wad hae wared body and soul to save your finger from being hurt' (pp. 190, 224). The 'English impudence' to which Duncan Knockdunder attributes Lady Staunton's serene appropriation of the

---

[34] Millgate, 'Scott and the Law', pp. 104–05. Millgate adds that Effie's pardon does not change the law regarding infanticide (p. 106), a point Sutherland takes a step further when he writes that in *The Heart of Midlothian* there is 'no perceptible sentiment [...] that the cruel and stupid *law* should be changed' (p. 215).

[35] Van Ghent, p. 122.

Butlers' Roseneath home and her dismissive rudeness to 'shentlemens as if they were pounden servants' (p. 437) attests to the 'smothered degree of egotism' that Jeanie detects in Effie's letter:

> We should have heard little about her [...] but that she was feared the Duke might come to learn wha she was [...] but Effie, puir thing, aye took her ain way, and folks that do that think mair o' themselves than of their neighbours. (p. 420)

Effie's continuing focus on self effectively undermines the legal fiction of reclaimable 'good character' which constitutes a predictive rationale behind the granting of royal pardons and which both Beattie and King list as a primary category in appeals for clemency.[36]

In Volume IV, the (non)effects of the pardon on Effie's character remind us of the similar point made about Porteous early in Volume I, when the man with 'a wild and irreclaimable propensity to dissipation [...] a hot and surly temper [...] a character void of principle' (pp. 26–28) wins a royal reprieve. In his case, the stay of execution is granted not to the character but to the function Porteous represents: given that his violent actions, while possibly illegal and certainly ill-advised, were undertaken in the service of the state, 'to visit it with a capital punishment would render it both delicate and dangerous for future officers [...] to act with effect in repressing tumults' (p. 34) that might imperil the peace of the realm.[37] In the government's reasoning, the pardon of Porteous constitutes part of the sovereign power's role as what Foucault terms 'managers of life and survival, of bodies and the race [...] the biological existence of a population' entrusted to its authority. But on the same biopolitical grounds, the populace of Edinburgh registers it as contravening the sovereign power's right and *duty* to inflict death. Completing his analysis of the new polity, Foucault adds:

> How could power exercise its highest prerogatives by putting people to death, when its main role was to ensure, sustain, and multiply, life, to put this life in order? For such a power, execution was at the same time a limit, a scandal, and a contradiction. Hence capital punishment could not be maintained except by invoking less the enormity of the crime itself than the monstrosity of the criminal, his incorrigibility, and the safeguard of society. One had the right to kill those who represented a kind of biological danger to others.[38]

---

[36] Beattie, p. 15; King, pp. 299–300. While Cockshut describes Effie as a 'clear, white, courageous figure' at her trial (p. 184), Hart condemns her 'caprice, lack of integrity, a selfish disregard for others, secrecy, a corrupting desire for social status' (p. 135), and Duncan concludes that neither Effie nor Staunton is really saved, so that 'The pardon comes to seem more and more of a formality' (p. 164).

[37] Susan Broomall and David G. Barrie, in 'Changing of the Guard: Governance, Policing, Masculinity, and Class in the Porteous Affair and Walter Scott's *Heart of Midlothian*', *Parergon*, 28.1 (2011), 69–90 (pp. 66, 84, 74, 65) argue that Porteous represents the kind of 'male governance gone wrong' that led to Act 11. George III.C36 in 1771, which established more professional policing.

[38] Foucault, pp. 137–38.

For the citizens of the city, character and biopolitical responsibility precisely denote the grounds on which Porteous deserves to die. Comparing him with the smuggler Wilson,

> 'This man', they said,—'the brave, the resolute, the generous, was executed to death without mercy for stealing a purse of gold [...] while the profligate satellite, who took advantage of a trifling tumult, inseparable from such occasion, to shed the blood of twenty of his fellow-citizens, is deemed a fitting object for the exercise of the royal prerogative of mercy. Is this to be borne?' (pp. 35–36)

Whether read through a Hobbesian model of covenant or a Foucauldian model of governmentality, the pardon of Porteous, to the Edinburgh mob, constitutes a derogation of responsibility that dissolves the contract between sovereign and voluntary subject, between authority and internalized techniques of discipline. Interpreted according to Esposito's medico-linguistic framework, the prophylactic pardon of the sovereign's functionary, attacked 'in the exercise of a trust delegated to him by the lawful civil authority [...] and, in finally repelling force by force', acting in 'self-defence' (p. 24), becomes

> an immune mechanism that has gotten out of hand because of the continuous strengthening of its core [...] like a machine that has to produce more and more order, it loses contact with the disorder that establishes its confines and provides its material, eventually becoming prey to it.[39]

Unlike Effie, whose conviction can be construed as a species of the classical sacrifice to legal, political, civic and biopolitical health,[40] Porteous becomes transformed into what Agamben calls *homo sacer*, a man who can be killed with impunity because he 'is the one with respect to whom all men act as sovereigns'.[41] And, as if to confirm the populace's view of his character, Porteous, supremely confident of his invulnerability and 'Habituated [...] to despise and overawe the rabble of the city' (p. 56), arrogantly refuses to seek official safety in Edinburgh Castle and celebrates his reprieve with a drunken carouse in the Tolbooth, behaviour which Scott figures in language borrowed from *Hamlet*, thus aligning the Captain with a sinful and unrepentant Claudius, whose illicit power and life must be destroyed before the health of the realm can be re-established.

If Porteous's unregenerate bravado precipitates the plot that leads to the climactic pardon scene, Effie's restless selfishness sets in motion events culminating in Staunton's murder at the hands of his son and in the Whistler's subsequent escape from justice. In Roseneath, bored with the 'homely accommodations of her sister's house', Effie finds Romantic solace in nature (the

---

[39] Esposito, pp. 108–09.

[40] Hillyard suggests that 'Effie Deans's pivotal symbolic role in the social order is underscored by her being a public cynosure, a spectacle', and that Staunton 'has the function of villain-sacrificer' who 'expresses ambivalence toward the persecuted heroine' (pp. 210–11).

[41] Agamben, pp. 82, 84.

narrative quotes from Wordsworth's 'The Brothers' in describing her pleasure), among the most picturesque scenes in the Highlands.[42] Compulsively 'Bent [...] on gratifying her curiosity' about 'the utmost recesses' of a particularly spectacular waterfall, she recklessly endangers both her own life and that of Jeanie's son David, first by insisting that he conduct her to a terrifyingly precarious crag, and then by exposing them to the homicidal greed of the outlaw Donacha Du (pp. 440–45). Donacha Dhu, who had 'neither forgotten the Whistler's report of the gold he had seen in Lady Staunton's purse, nor his old vow of revenge against the minister', determines to 'break into Butler's peaceful habitation, and flesh at once his appetite for plunder and for revenge' before fleeing the country (p. 464), thus bringing about the confrontation that ends with his own death, parricide, and the capture of the Whistler. In a horrifyingly circular irony, Effie almost commits the infanticide for which she was wrongly convicted, *and* she almost causes the death of a child born to the sister whose exertions saved her from execution. Queen Caroline's mercy toward Effie repeats the fatal consequences attendant upon her openly political pardon of Porteous.

Hanoverian mercy in *Heart of Midlothian*, multiply compromised by strategic or petty personal agendas, proves to be both politically ineffective and conducive to dire consequences for Effie's family. Argyle's implicit promise to Caroline that the pardoning of Effie 'is a business [...] which I am convinced may be highly useful in conciliating the unfortunate irritation which at present subsists among his Majesty's good subjects in Scotland' (p. 335) fails to avert violence on either local or national scales; even the rather cursory allusion to the 1745 rebellion reminds us that not only do his Majesty's good subjects remain poised to turn against the dynasty but also that the uprising and its suppression create further disarray and criminality. Although the text makes a point of noting that Donacha Dhu does not belong to the ranks of dispossessed Highlanders, his marauding career flourishes in a time 'when all police was disorganized by the civil war' (p. 426). Nor, importantly, does gratitude and loyalty engendered by the pardon prevent Jeanie from participating in what Saddletree calls 'these [...] kittle times [...] when the people take the power of life and death out of the hands of the rightful magistrate' (p. 108). Jeanie's action in freeing the Whistler has been interpreted as both an act of grace and as one tainted by personal motives. Austin, for example, attributes Jeanie's appropriation of the right to pardon to her new-found emotional and cultural empathy with 'Highlanders who suffered so much after the 1745 rebellion, to brigands, thieves, smugglers, gypsies and tinkers', defining it as 'a moral act that reverses her failure of sympathy for Madge and

---

[42] See Shaw, who characterizes Effie's appreciation of natural landscapes as part of her 'self-division', 'finding in them a compensation for worldly sorrows, instead of being unconsciously part of them' (p. 244).

Scotland's dispossessed', while Fleishman characterizes it as 'Mercy, at the expense of retributive justice'; but her action also aligns with a polity in which 'rough justice' continues to be administered by those outside the legitimate juridical order, to claim for herself the sovereign 'state of exception' which for Agamben 'is the originary structure in which law refers to life and includes it in itself by suspending it'.[43] As Millgate notes in completing her reading of the post-pardon world in which Madge becomes a victim of mob violence, 'It is scarcely less disturbing that Jeanie should carry out as her final major action in the novel the release of her nephew, the parricidal Whistler'.[44] Indeed, Jeanie's arrogation of the right to pardon doubly opposes legitimate authority. If, as Kerr and Duncan have suggested, Argyle represents 'the paternal authority which the Deanses and Butlers have lacked for so long', if he is 'a monarch of private property and local genius of divine right',[45] then Jeanie's decision to over-ride Knockdunder's determination that summary justice should be exacted when 'a shentleman, friend to the Duke, was killed in his country' (p. 465) can be construed as a form of civil disobedience. And when she 'resolve[s] [...] to avert, at least to delay, the fate which hung over her nephew [...] if [...] she should see any hope of his being brought to better temper', she both replicates and distorts the established paradigms for granting reprieves: she appropriates the office of the judge who requests clemency as well as the prerogative of the sovereign who grants it, but she also ignores the condition of repentance and reform essential within the system, freeing him even after he expresses his determination to join a band of outlaws and to 'revenge Donacha's death on all and sundry' (pp. 465–66). Conflating the complex network of petition and pardon, Jeanie telescopes the whole system into a single moment of genealogical and speculative reasoning: 'he is my sister's son [...] our flesh and blood [...] There may be good in him yet [...] I will try fair play with him' (p. 466).

Scott's narrative, approaching its end, dismisses the consequences of Jeanie's extra-judicial action in one short paragraph, which informs us that the Whistler, sold into slavery in America by the 'avaricious shipmaster' who was to convey him beyond the reach of British law, heads 'a conspiracy in which his inhuman master was put to death' and subsequently joins a 'tribe of wild Indians. He was

---

[43] Agamben, p. 28.

[44] Austin, p. 633; Avrom Fleishman, *The English Historical Novel: Walter Scott to Virginia Woolf* (Baltimore, MD: Johns Hopkins University Press, 1971), p. 99; Millgate, 'Scott and the Law', p. 105. For Hillyard, freeing the Whistler 'provides a final example of the mercy she had successfully persuaded Queen Caroline to grant' (p. 225). Beiderwell distinguishes the 'providential punishment' in Volume IV from 'the self-interest, passion, and uncertainty' of 'human justice' evident in the first three volumes (pp. 73, 65). My reading is congruent with D'Arcy's argument that Jeanie's act of 'aiding and abetting the escape of a murderer' (p. 161) represents a general breakdown of legal constraints imposed from the centre.

[45] Kerr, p. 65, Duncan, p. 166.

never more heard of; and it may therefore be presumed that he lived and died after the manner of that savage people, with whom his previous habits had well fitted him to associate' (p. 467). The narrative delivers the Whistler into an almost mythic space outside history, just as Geordie Robertson disappears from view, and eventually into legend.[46] The boy's fate, however, resonates well beyond this curt dismissal from the text. The violence the son perpetrates in the New World exactly matches that of his father, who led the Edinburgh conspirators against another local tyrant while 'disguised apparently with red paint and soot, like an Indian going to battle' (p. 125) and remains both unrepentant and vengeful, threatening the magistrate with retaliation if Effie, like Wilson, should suffer the rigours of the law (p. 165). We remember, too, that presumptions about the Whistler's death have been erroneous before, because another Scotswoman had taken pity on him, although there is some narrative confusion about which one: either Madge Wildfire, prompted by a confused combination of pity and identification, spared the life of Effie's baby and handed him over to 'a female stroller', or Meg herself had sold 'that most unfortunate child' to one Annaple Bailzou, who had in turn sold him to Donacha Dhu (pp. 432, 447,463). In any case, all during Effie's trial and Jeanie's pilgrimage, during the Stauntons' bitter social triumphs and Jeanie's comfortable domesticity, the Whistler's body has been in circulation as both commodity and outlaw, marked by both disposability and immense value, existing, like Agamben's colossus, 'on a threshold that belongs neither to the world of the living nor to the world of the dead'. Jeanie's act of mercy once again sets his unregulated body in motion, and the text can only exile him from the narrative, reinstating his status as mobile bandit, so that he 'can save himself only in perpetual flight or a foreign land'.[47]

Of course, freeing the Whistler does not represent the first time that Jeanie has usurped the royal prerogative to pardon, constructing her own version of what constitutes ethical citizenship. She resolves not to buy Effie's life by sacrificing that of Staunton, destroying the documentary proof presented to her by 'the most active conspirator in the Porteous mob' on the grounds that the 'crime for which he was amenable to the laws—was a crime against the public indeed, but it was not against her', thus removing herself from a communal body politic. Shifting from the ethical to the politico-juridical realm, she re-casts the nature of the crime itself, linking it 'with the idea of ancient national independence', which exempts it from retributive justice, in accordance with

---

[46] A children's illustrated version of the novel makes an astute revision to Scott's text when it ends with the Whistler's narrative, which has him declare that 'No white man would ever hear of him again' and gives him an undetermined future which carries with it memories of Madge Wildfire's dying song. See *Heart of Midlothian*, retold by Margaret Elphinstone, illustrated by Ken Laidlaw (Stroud, Gloucestershire: Real Reads, 2012), pp. 52–54.

[47] Agamben, pp. 99, 183.

what Grupp observes 'was once common practice [by government] [...] during times of "riots and popular movements"'.[48] But, as in the case of Whistler, self, to quote Elizabeth Bennet, will intrude. Jeanie dreads being branded a traitor even more than she doubts the righteousness of bartering Staunton's life for Effie's: 'Jeanie trembled at the idea of her name being handed down to posterity with that of the "fausse Monteith," and one or two others, who having deserted and betrayed the cause of their country, are damned to perpetual remembrance and execration among its peasantry' (p. 314).[49] Ethics, patriotism, and concern for her own historical reputation coalesce into a jumble of motives no less suspect than Queen Caroline's complex web of political and personal reasons to grant Jeanie's appeal.

Judith Wilt posits that in *The Heart of Midlothian* there is a pattern of women pardoning men, arguing that 'the crucial topos of this novel [...] is that woman must save, may not kill, man', so that 'Jeanie, Effie, and Madge protect George Staunton'.[50] She might have added Meg Murdockson, who, despite her fury against Staunton, cannot bring herself to betray him because 'I have nursed him at this withered breast' (p. 269). But we need to add at least one male to the list of those who provide Staunton with a reprieve: activated by a conscience he barely knew he had, the criminal turned lawman Ratcliffe not only refuses to help the procurator-fiscal pry information out of Effie but also manipulates Madge into singing the coded words that alert the fugitive to a trap set by Sharpitlaw (pp. 152–60). Late in the fourth volume, Ratcliffe disavows his incipient perception that 'the representative of Sovereignty, covered with lace and embroidery' may indeed be 'the plebeian convict, that, disguised in the rags of Madge Wildfire, had led the formidable rioters to their destined revenge' (pp. 446, 452). Impelled by their own reasons, these very different members of a polity supposedly subservient to a central system of sovereign power grant Staunton the series of reprieves that enables him (and, by extension, Effie) to impersonate legitimate wielders of class-based political authority. Indeed, Effie, blithely obtuse to irony, boasts that she can advance the military ambitions of a young Butler since 'we have always supported government, and never had occasion to trouble ministers' (p. 439). And indeed, she exerts her influence to acquire a commission for young David Butler, thus functioning as an agent for sovereign bio-power, transferring a 'private' body to the control of state

[48] Grupp, p. 59; quoted from *The Attorney General's Survey of Release Procedures, Pardon, Volume III.*

[49] Jeanie has reason to anticipate long Scottish memories. Walpole recounts General Anstruther's complaint in 1751 that 'he had undergone a long persecution from his countrymen, who all hated him for having been the only Scot that on Porteous's affair had voted for demolishing the Nether Bow at Edinburgh' (p. 28).

[50] Judith Wilt, *Secret Leaves: The Novels of Sir Walter Scott* (Chicago, IL: University of Chicago Press, 1985), p. 126.

apparatus. In another manifestation of ironic circularity, the Stauntons, who owe their lives to a series of reprieves obtained through the efforts of unempowered outsiders who have both enlisted and resisted Hanoverian authority, become influential agents of that sovereign power.

In *The Heart of Midlothian*, the royal right to pardon animates the plot and provides the occasion for a climactic episode which resonates so deeply with readers' desire for an emotionally satisfying resolution that it seems to bring closure to the vexing post-Union politics of sovereignty. Jeanie's success in confronting and winning over Queen Caroline validates all sorts of wishful dreams about Hanoverian clemency, about the ability to speak truth to power, about compassion, about sisterhood, and about the possibility of individual, moral action overcoming institutional injustice. At the same time, the royal prerogative is shown to be deeply implicated in the consolidation of sovereign bio-power; as Foucault puts it, 'As soon as power gave itself the function of administering life, its reason for being and the logic of its exercise — and not the awakening of humanitarian feelings — made it more and more difficult to apply the death penalty'.[51] But the Hanoverian strategy of affirming its legitimacy through the exercise of the right to mercy proves both politically ineffectual (as evident in the Jacobite rebellion of 1745 and continuing local uprisings) and self-defeating as a form of immunization: the pardon of Porteous neatly fits Esposito's category of

> immunotherapy, which in acting to defend the body ends up weakening it [...] As in all areas of contemporary social systems, neurotically haunted by a continuously growing need for security, this means that the risk from which the protection is meant to defend is actually created by the protection itself.[52]

The mercy granted to Effie not only fails to immunize Hanoverian authority against Scottish disaffection but also exposes the limit point of state power over the bodies that constitute sovereign identity, whether as agents, allies, or criminals subject to juridical control. Yet if we are tempted to read the novel as an endorsement of a democratic dispersal of the royal prerogative, we encounter covert appropriations of power that unleash their own threats to the body politic. The Whistler, set free by Jeanie's illicit and unacknowledged act of mercy, carries the infection of violent sociopathology to the New World. Staunton, reprieved by the internal impulses of his various protectors and so deeply entrenched within the Hanoverian establishment that he walks 'at the right-hand of the representative of Sovereignty' in Edinburgh (p. 446), carries hidden on his body the very infection the regime was summoned to combat, 'the crucifix, the beads, and the shirt of hair which he wore next his person [...] the dogmata of a religion,

---

[51] Foucault, p. 138.
[52] Esposito, p. 141.

which pretends, by the maceration of the body, to expiate the crimes of the soul' (pp. 462–63). Covert Catholicism, like political uprisings and violent criminality, survive and flourish despite both Hanoverian efforts at immunization through the royal prerogative of pardon and individual acts that appropriate the state of exception by 'wresting [...] this right of mercy' from officially constituted sovereign power.

Sir Walter Scott and the Caribbean: Unravelling the Silences

CARLA SASSI

University of Verona

Since 2007, the year that marked the bicentenary of the abolition of the transatlantic slave trade in the UK, a remarkable number of TV and radio programmes, events, exhibitions, literary and artistic works, as well as scholarly studies, have unearthed and brought to the attention of the larger public Scotland's involvement with the Atlantic slave trade and the exploitation of slaves in the Caribbean.[1] A central concern in the ongoing investigation of this chapter of Scotland's colonial history has been what I term an '(un)willed amnesia'[2] — a forgetfulness that appears more radical in Scotland than in other European countries also involved in the exploitation of slavery in the Caribbean, among which are England, France, Holland, Portugal and Spain. My choice of the term 'amnesia' represents an attempt to convey the endemic nature and extensive proportions of such forgetfulness, while by defining it as '(un)willed' I propose that different levels of responsibility can be identified, and that an ethical distinction should be made between those who witnessed the events, or historians of later generations who were at least partly aware of them, and nonetheless repressed its memory, and the 'common wo/men' of the post-emancipation eras, who hardly had the means and competence to retrieve, or to imagine, a long-buried past.

---

[1] As recent historiography has revealed, Scots engaged in the imperial enterprise as British subjects but also, even though mostly cryptically, as members of their own nation. Scotland's status of stateless nation, in fact, did not prevent it from firmly privileging and protecting its economic and political interests. See, among others, *Scotland and the British Empire*, ed. by John M. MacKenzie and T. M. Devine (Oxford: Oxford University Press, 2011). In the Caribbean in particular, as Douglas J. Hamilton observes, Scots created powerful networks 'to buttress their imperial activities' employing 'connections among their families and friends', but also developing 'fictive bonds' that allowed them to be especially responsive to local circumstances. See Douglas J. Hamilton, *Scotland, the Caribbean and the Atlantic World, 1750–1820* (Manchester: Manchester University Press, 2005), p. 27.

[2] Carla Sassi, 'Acts of (Un)willed Amnesia: Dis/appearing Figurations of the Caribbean in Post-Union Scottish Literature', in Giovanna Covi, Joan Anim-Addo, Velma Pollard and Carla Sassi, *Caribbean-Scottish Relations: Colonial and Contemporary Inscriptions in History, Language and Literature* (London: Mango Publishing, 2007), pp. 131–98.

Yearbook of English Studies, 47 (2017), 224–240
© Modern Humanities Research Association 2017

'Recovering Scotland's slavery past' — to use T. M. Devine's phrase[3] — is in fact a complex task. At least two obstacles to such recovery are familiar to scholars in the wider field of Atlantic slavery studies. The first concerns the defectiveness of archives that have preserved mainly non-narrative documents (newspaper advertisements regarding slave auctions or runaways, laws pertaining to slavery, bills of sale etc.); abolitionist literature, often marred by a narrow ideological perspective;[4] or slave narratives, relatively rare and often questioned with regard to their authenticity.[5] The second, and partly related, problem is represented by the resistance of national historiographies and narratives to full assimilation of the history of slavery. Transnational studies on slavery today are numerous and engaging, but they have made relatively little or no impact on national historiographies, which still tend to exclude or marginalize events that threaten to undermine the moral self-esteem of the nation.

The specific problem with Scotland's amnesia, however, is more complex. It arguably has its deepest roots in the teleological philosophy of history conceived and diffused by the Scottish Enlightenment, according to which 'the analysis of the past [is] not on its own terms, but in the light of what it could contribute to an account of progress towards the present'.[6] In the nineteenth century especially, the practice of slavery across the Atlantic dramatically conflicted with Enlightenment principles of 'civility' and 'liberty', which were closely associated with the idea of 'progress'. Even though exploited for economic profit and 'justified' by racist ideologies, slavery remained a morally questionable, if not downright unacceptable, and 'primitive' practice.

Scotland's removal of the memory of slavery, however, is certainly also related to the mechanisms of construction and transmission of national history in a stateless nation, taking place largely outside the boundaries of (or in open antagonism with) institutional historiography. In Scotland's case, in Murray G. H. Pittock's words, lack of independence went along 'with a lack of independent means of securing one's own history',[7] and ultimately led to a mythologized, or

---

[3] *Recovering Scotland's Slavery Past: The Caribbean Connection*, ed. by T. M. Devine (Edinburgh: Edinburgh University Press, 2015).

[4] On the limits of abolitionist representations of slavery, see Marcus Wood, *Blind Memory: Visual Representations of Slavery in England and America* (New York: Routledge, 2000), and Brycchan Carey, *British Abolitionism and the Rhetoric of Sensibility: Writing, Sentiment, and Slavery, 1760–1807* (New York: Palgrave Macmillan, 2005).

[5] A meaningful and well-known example is represented by *The Life of Olaudah Equiano* (1789), whose complex in/authenticities have been investigated at least since the 1990s. See, among others, Katalin Orban, 'Dominant and Submerged Discourses in "The Life of Olaudah Equiano" (or Gustavus Vassa?)', *African American Review*, 27.4 (1993), 655–664.

[6] Murray G. H. Pittock, 'Historiography', in *The Cambridge Companion to the Scottish Enlightenment*, ed. by Alexander Broadie (Cambridge: Cambridge University Press, 2003), pp. 258–79 (p. 258).

[7] Murray G. H. Pittock, *The Invention of Scotland: The Stuart Myth and the Scottish Identity, 1638 to the Present*, Routledge Revivals (London: Routledge, 2014), p. 5.

iconified version of national history, long assessed as a lack, or a failure,[8] and only recently appropriately re-evaluated as a form of 'protest history' or 'underground history'.[9] It is in such a fluid and problematic context that the tension revealed by contemporary theorists of history, at least since Hayden White's *Metahistory* (1973), between two contradictory directions — history as a knowledge based on traces and signs, and history as rhetorical mode/art of telling — takes on a new level of complexity.

The work of Sir Walter Scott — staging an elaborate dialogue between history and romance, and functioning as a powerful source of alternative historiography — can be seen as placed at the confluence of all these tensions, and thus as epicentral also in the field of Caribbean-Scottish studies. Like Robert Burns, Scott did not join the ranks of abolitionists. The regrettable truth is that the works of the two most iconic and popular Scottish writers bear only fleeting references to an issue that took centre-stage in the debates of the time. But while Burns's silence has been interrogated by critics in the past decade,[10] no doubt also in virtue of the Bard's lasting status of icon of Scottishness — that of an 'archetype for every other Scot to aspire to'[11] — Scott's reticence has on the whole been neglected. And yet, Scott's silence appears both as more striking and more impactful, given his crucial and complex role as historiographer and myth-maker in nineteenth-century Scotland. Scott, indeed, 'stands central to the cultural work that is Scotland',[12] as Caroline McCracken-Flesher points out; 'precisely because his influence is both admitted and resisted Scott is in fact a site of contestation producing the nation today'.[13]

The present essay makes no claim to exhaustiveness in the coverage of Scott's vast literary production, but rather aims, by drawing especially from recent narratological theories, to interrogate, through the discussion of a selection of exemplary texts, Scott's literary silences as a form of communication in their own right. By revealing the invisible maps of meaning of the unsaid and 'unnarrated', especially in his fiction, I also propose critically to rethink the problems and possibilities of engaging with Caribbean slavery in British and other European nineteenth-century fiction. The first necessary step, however, is to account for the actual intersections between Scott's own world and colonial Caribbean history.

[8] See, for example, Marinell Ash, *The Strange Death of Scottish History* (Edinburgh: Ramsay Head Press, 1980).

[9] Pittock, *The Invention of Scotland*, p. 5.

[10] See Michael Morris, 'Robert Burns: Recovering Scotland's Memory of the Black Atlantic', *Journal for Eighteenth-Century Studies*, 37.3 (2014), 343–59; and Michael Morris, *Scotland and the Caribbean, c. 1740–1833: Atlantic Archipelagos* (New York: Routledge, 2015), pp. 115–17, 120–27, 128–31.

[11] Alan N. Bold, *A Burns Companion* (New York: St Martin's Press, 1991), p. 157

[12] Caroline McCracken-Flesher, *Possible Scotlands: Walter Scott and the Story of Tomorrow* (Oxford: Oxford University Press, 2005), p. 4.

[13] McCracken-Flesher, p. 5.

Scott and the Caribbean: Chronologies and Intersections

Scott's social background and education, and even his life span (1771–1832) placed him at the very centre of what was, from the last decades of the eighteenth century to at least the Slavery Abolition Act in 1833, a high-profile and emotional debate, in Scotland as much in the rest of the United Kingdom. As a resident of the New Town in Edinburgh (before moving to Abbotsford in 1812), he lived next door to many fellow countrymen who were variously involved in the slave trade.[14] As a lawyer, he was in an ideal position to follow and understand the legal implications of the many parliamentary debates on slavery. His knowledge of national and colonial history, and his interest in and grasp of economic issues,[15] no doubt enabled him to be fully aware of the scope and implications of Caribbean slavery. As a freemason, and a member of the prestigious St David's Lodge, he was no doubt in privileged contact with a host of notable and important people,[16] including representatives of that city's mercantile elite who, in the same period, thrived on the labour of African slaves in the West Indies. He must have been well aware of the many initiatives of the Edinburgh Committee for the Abolition of the Slave, 'the oldest and by far the strongest in Scotland'.[17] Interestingly, Ian Whyte lists Scott among the prominent subscribers to the Committee's reprint, in 1790, of the anti-slavery petitions previously published by the Presbytery and the Chamber of Commerce.[18]

Scott had also relatively close family ties to the West Indian world. Of the four brothers who lived to adulthood, three pursued military or administrative careers in the British Empire. Thomas (1773–1823) expected for a while a West Indian appointment, which never came;[19] he was instead sent to Canada, where he died. Two other brothers, the eldest and the youngest, did travel to the Caribbean, and were both deeply affected by their experiences there. Robert (1767–1787) took part in the naval Battle of the Saintes (1782), where Lord Rodney defeated the French fleet, restoring British naval supremacy in the West Indies. Robert's stories 'about Rodney's battles and the haunted keys of the West Indies' inspired

---

[14] An interactive 'Edinburgh Slavery Map', part of an ongoing UCL-based project, has begun charting the city's legacy of slave-ownership by identifying the addresses of slave-owners on the basis of compensation claims following the Slavery Abolition Act 1833 <http://www.scotland slaverymap.com/> [accessed 3 December 2017].

[15] Alexander Dick, 'Scott and Political Economy', in *The Edinburgh Companion to Sir Walter Scott*, ed. by Fiona Robertson (Edinburgh: Edinburgh University Press, 2012), pp. 118–29.

[16] Among these, his future publishers James and John Ballantyne. See Adam Muir Mackay, *Sir Walter Scott as a Freemason*, rev. edn (Fort William: Temple-Arch Publishers, 1999), pp. 3, 7–8.

[17] Iain Whyte, *Scotland and the Abolition of Black Slavery, 1756–1838* (Edinburgh: Edinburgh University Press, 2006), p. 87.

[18] Whyte, p. 88.

[19] Letter to Tom, 1 November 1810, in *The Letters of Sir Walter Scott*, ed. by Sir Herbert Grierson, 12 vols (London: Constable, 1932–37), VII, 453.

many passages in *The Pirate* (1821).[20] Daniel (1776–1806), the 'black sheep' of the family, died after returning from a voyage to Jamaica, where he had been sent, thanks to Scott's connections, to make a new life. Here, 'ordered to subdue a revolt among a band of rebellious Negroes', as Edgar Johnson informs us, 'he showed the white feather and was dismissed in disgrace'. He returned home to die, and Scott refused to attend his funeral, suffering, in later years, a sense of guilt for turning his back on his frail youngest brother.[21] One is left to wonder whether the source of Scott's intense shame was merely confined to his brother's cowardice, or was possibly amplified by its dark colonial context.

Scott would have been definitely too young to form an opinion on the momentous 1778 *Knight* v. *Wedderburn* case, where Joseph Knight, an African slave, was granted the freedom to leave the employment of his Scottish master, John Wedderburn, in the Court of Session, Scotland's supreme civil court.[22] However, other crucial moments of the national debate on slavery unfolded in his lifetime. William Wilberforce (1759–1833), for example, was his contemporary, and Scott witnessed his long battle, which culminated in the 1807 Parliamentary abolition of the slave trade, leading ultimately to the Slavery Abolition Act in 1833. We know that Wilberforce admired and was inspired by Scott's works,[23] and we also know that the two men had a pleasant dinner in Battersea Rise in February 1821.[24] Scott died in 1832, in the same year when Scottish advocate and historian Archibald Alison (1792–1867) issued a dramatic warning to the UK on the catastrophic consequences of abolishing slavery.[25] On a global level, the Haitian Revolution (1791–1804), often described as the largest and most successful slave rebellion, led by former slave Toussaint L'Ouverture (1743–1803), was an event that shook France, whose colonial power was for the first time overturned from the inside, and the whole Western world. Given Scott's interest in French history, and in particular in the French Revolution (whose

[20] John G. Lockhart, *Memoirs of the Life of Sir Walter Scott: In Three Volumes* (Paris: Baudry's European Library, 1837), I, 89.

[21] Edgar Johnson, *Sir Walter Scott: The Great Unknown* (New York: Macmillan, 1970), p. 257. Cited in Tony Inglis, 'Re-writing Origins in *The Heart of Midlothian*', in *Scott in Carnival: Selected Papers from the Fourth International Scott Conference, Edinburgh, 1991*, ed. by J. H. Alexander and David Hewitt (Aberdeen: Association for Scottish Literary Studies, 1993), pp. 216–31 (p. 226).

[22] See 'Feature: Slavery, freedom or perpetual servitude? The Joseph Knight case', The National Archives of Scotland <http://www.nas.gov.uk/about/071022.asp> [accessed 3 December 2016].

[23] See Anne Stott, *Wilberforce: Family and Friends* (Oxford: Oxford University Press, 2012), pp. 12, 174, 230, 258.

[24] See John S. Harford, *Recollections of William Wilberforce, Esq., M.P. for the County of York During Nearly Thirty Years* (London: Longman, Green, Longman, Roberts, & Green, 1865), p. 111. For a comment, see also Stott, p. 222.

[25] Catherine Hall, '"The Most Unbending Conservative in Britain": Archibald Alison and Pro-Slavery Discourse', in *Recovering Scotland's Slavery Past*, ed. by Devine, pp. 206–24.

principles had inspired the slave rebels), one would imagine this was an event that troubled Scott as much as it affected the larger public.

Such rare references to the contemporary reality of the West Indies as do appear in Scott's letters are accompanied by little or no detail — they were evocations of a reality that did not require much explanation, and with which his correspondents were already acquainted. He informs Miss Seward, for example, that Mrs Jackson's 'sons are prospering in the West Indies',[26] but worries at the thought that his own son Walter might have to travel there.[27] Elsewhere, he evokes the unfavourable conditions of life in the Caribbean by describing a heat wave at Abbotsford as 'West Indian', 'exceeding in oppression any thing which I ever felt'.[28] Scott indeed does not differ substantially in his use of colonial clichés from many of his contemporaries. The few references to the West Indies, however, always imply an extreme situation — extreme wealth, extreme danger, extreme heat. There is no room for 'normality'.

The Caribbean does occupy a place of prominence in Scott's ambitious account of Scotland's history, *Tales of a Grandfather* (1828–31), which contains his most extended discussion of Scottish–Caribbean colonial relations. Scott offers here a detailed account of 'the disastrous history of the Darien colony'[29] and of the complex political and economic reasons that bring this venture to failure. The focus is firmly patriotic and Scoto-centric (that is, concerned with the welfare and future of Scotland as a nation), and colonial — Darien is the 'Other place', a mere 'object' of conquest, and irredeemably so.

Literary Silences

'History is what hurts',[30] according to Fredric Jameson, who challenged poststructuralist theories of History-as-text by pointing out that even though History is an absent cause, its painful consequences can be felt in the present. History is then for Jameson not simply a process that we can recount, but also a limit, or a consequence that we inevitably feel and experience. In my investigation of the gaps and silences in Scott's *oeuvre* in reference to Caribbean slavery I propose to follow an eclectic method, focusing both on pragmatic/narratological theories of silence, or the 'unnarratable', and on sociological/cultural investigations of collective remembering and forgetting, especially in relation to

---

[26] Letter to Miss Seward, in *Letters*, II, 52 (23 April 1808).

[27] Letter to Lady Compton, in *Letters*, V, 244 (1818).

[28] Letter to Lord Montagu, in *Letters*, VI, 216 (1820).

[29] Walter Scott, *Tales of a Grandfather. Being Stories Taken from Scottish History*, 2 vols (Exeter, NH: J. & B. Williams, 1833), II, 249, and *Tales of a Grandfather. Being Stories Taken from Scottish History, second series* (London: Gowans and Gray, 1923), p. 412.

[30] Fredric Jameson, *The Political Unconscious: Narrative as a Socially Symbolic Act* (Ithaca, NY: Cornell University Press, 1981), p. 102.

traumatic historical events. I also intend to borrow and adapt Jameson's idea of History as something that cannot be entirely organized into a narrative, as an open wound that defies words.

The idea that a conscious silence within an utterance (be it common speech or historical narrative) may bear meaning and become a 'metaphor for communication'[31] has emerged in the past two decades across a vast body of scholarship. Silence in fact occupies a position at the crossroads of 'diverse communicative phenomena: linguistic, discoursal, literary, social, cultural, spiritual and meta-communicative',[32] and studies on silence have inevitably developed in an interdisciplinary direction. In what follows, I will briefly discuss some of the concepts that I intend to deploy to frame Scott's literary silences.

In a pragmatic framework, long silences, produced consciously, 'acquire meaning from their particular position, length, etc. And on the other, cast light on the verbal utterance produced': a deliberate abstention from talk in a conversation may either signal consideration for the interlocutor or, on the contrary, hostility.[33] Remaining silent can thus 'be a manifestation of either negative, positive or off-record politeness'.[34] Silence, then, functions like speech, insofar as it 'enables people to communicate both polite and impolite messages'. However, 'it is not talk or silence *per se* which lead[s] to such implications', but rather 'the absence of what is conventionally anticipated'.[35]

Along similar lines, some recent approaches to narrative treat gaps and silences as an author's conscious strategy to imply without saying — to gesture towards the object of a text's avoidances and unstated assumptions. Investigations of the unnarratable in fiction have highlighted how literary silences can be rife with meaning. Gerald Prince, for example, introduced the concept of the 'disnarrated', as a category of the unnarratable, to describe specifically 'all the events that do not happen though they could have and are nonetheless referred to (in a negative or hypothetical mode) by the narrative text'.[36] Among recent theorizations, Robyn R. Warhol, in her development of Prince's concepts, identifies four categories of the unnarratable: the 'subnarratable', unworthy of narration; the 'supranarratable', that which defies narrative, the ineffable; the 'antinarratable', violating social conventions; the 'paranarratable', transgressing

---

[31] Adam Jaworski, 'Introduction: An Overview', in *Silence: Interdisciplinary Perspectives*, ed. by Adam Jaworski (Berlin: Mouton de Gruyter, 1997), pp. 3–14 (p. 3).

[32] Ibid., p. 3.

[33] Maria Sifianou, 'Silence and Politeness', in *Silence: Interdisciplinary Perspectives*, ed. by Jaworski, pp. 63–84 (pp. 64–65).

[34] Sifianou, p. 72.

[35] Ibid., p. 79.

[36] Gerald Prince, *Narrative as Theme: Studies in French Fiction* (Lincoln: University of Nebraska Press, 1992), p. 30.

the laws of a specific literary genre.[37] Warhol focuses especially on the last two categories as more problematic, and points out how they may generate two different types of literary silences: a truly complete absence of information as opposed to an inexplicit presence. Warhol also observes how the laws of literary conventions seem more inflexible than laws of social convention and 'have led throughout literary history to more instances of unnarratability than even taboo has led'.[38] She also usefully points out how an author's conscious silences may be interpreted pragmatically as a form of 'politeness' — a desire to meet the reader's expectations that plays a central role in the choice to include or exclude specific subjects or information. Indeed, as Ruth Rosaler has more recently observed, 'authors' writings are likely to be affected by their perceptions of what they think their audience will approve'.[39]

Rosaler further develops the notion of disnarration by introducing the concept of 'implicature' — 'a deliberate refusal of explicitness' that can characterize fiction, a way of communicating 'narrative propositions without explicitly stating them'.[40] Implicature does not simply describe lack of information, but identifies a 'conspicuous silence', which acquires and generates meaning through the interaction of text and context, and represents a form of communication in its own right, placing 'more emphasis on the listener's powers of inference than on his or her ability to decipher the information linguistically encoded in the utterance'.[41] Implicature, then, allows a writer to 'narrate implicitly rather than explicitly', thus 'maintaining presentational politeness while discussing an impolite topic',[42] and can be realized through a number of textual strategies, from allusions to symbols, from metaphors to negative statements, or by implicitly communicating knowledge or feelings that are shared by writer and reader, but of which characters are unconscious or only partly conscious.

Finally, substantial scholarship focusing on the political, ideological, and psychological forces producing literary silences has been produced in the fields of postcolonial, trauma, and holocaust studies in the past two decades or so. At the crossroads of these fields, silences and gaps in narratives of Atlantic slavery have also received special attention. From abolitionist descriptions, slave memoirs, planters' journals or travellers' accounts in the eighteenth and nineteenth centuries, to the many recuperative fictional narratives written in the

[37] Robyn R. Warhol, 'How to Render the Unnarratable in Realist Fiction and Contemporary Film', in *A Companion to Narrative Theory*, ed. by James Phelan and Peter J. Rabinowitz (Oxford: Blackwell, 2005), pp. 220–31 (pp. 222–26).

[38] Warhol, p. 226.

[39] Ruth Rosaler, *Conspicuous Silences: Implicature and Fictionality in the Victorian Novel* (Oxford: Oxford University Press, 2016), p. 35.

[40] Ibid., p. 2.

[41] Ibid., p. 3.

[42] Ibid., p. 63.

twentieth and twenty-first centuries, accounts of Atlantic slavery are deeply haunted by the unsaid and the unsayable. Silences may be produced by the impossibility of conveying the deeply traumatic experience of slavery and/or by the limitations posed by a white readership in the case of slave narratives, by a reluctance to come to terms with the historical responsibilities of slavery in the case of planters' journals and travellers' accounts, or by an internalized apprehension about disclosing shocking details and of offending one's audience in the case of abolitionist literature. Silences may also become a conscious and powerful mnemonic tool in the hands of modern and contemporary writers that trace and decode them in eighteenth- and nineteenth-century narratives, in order to re-create the suppressed texts and concealed stories in their works.[43]

The Caribbean in Scott's Fiction: Invisible Maps of Meaning

There is a conspicuous imbalance between what Scott evidently knew about his fellow countrymen's long-standing involvement in the colonization of the Caribbean, from the Darien scheme onwards, and the place that the reality of slavery and Caribbean colonialism occupies in his literary work. Such a gap may be explainable by the fact that the Caribbean connection was a subject that neither belonged to a remote and sealed past, nor fitted into the "'tis sixty years since' formula of shortest safe distance from the facts narrated, but instead extended controversially and troublingly into the present. This, however, can only work as a partial explanation, since Scott does indeed engage with the history and progress of empire, and on the entanglements of nationalism and imperialism in the nineteenth century. Ian Duncan agrees with Martin Green in saying that Scott should be identified as the father of 'imperial romance', and argues that while he 'made the *internal* imperial formation of the modern secular national state his great theme, the canonical topic of "history"', the Waverley novels also provide a pioneering representation 'of the imperial matter of military and commercial penetration outside the national boundaries of European civilisation'.[44] References to colonial realities surface in several novels by Scott, either as 'casual' terms of comparison, as in *Waverley* (1814), where Highlanders are compared to 'American Indians', 'Esquimaux' and 'African Negroes', or as more complex representations, as in *Guy Mannering* (1815) and in *The Surgeon's Daughter* (1827), that engage with the experience of empire in India. While Scott's main concern is always national (British and/or Scottish) history, it is correct to state that for him history is, 'to a great extent, the story of how Britain

---

[43] See, among others, Lars Eckstein, *Re-membering the Black Atlantic: On the Poetics and Politics of Literary Memory* (Amsterdam: Rodopi, 2006).

[44] Ian Duncan, 'Scott's Romance of Empire: *The Tales of the Crusaders*', in *Scott in Carnival*, ed. by Alexander and Hewitt, pp. 370–79 (p. 370).

comes to manage the legacies of those other worlds'[45] — indeed, in Andrew Lincoln's words 'Scott's work [...] suggests that nations and empires are manifestation of the same process of political and cultural consolidation'.[46]

Given the central role played by the imperial theme in Scott's historical fiction, and the historical and economic relevance of the Caribbean connection, it seems all the more striking that he avoided engaging with it in any substantial way. There is an evident difference, for example, in substance and length, between the detailed account of the colonial reality of the East Indies in *Guy Mannering*, and the fleeting and elliptical reference to Glasgow's West Indian source of wealth in *Rob Roy* (1817),[47] Scott's most 'radical' reference to Scotland's colonial exploitation of the Caribbean colonies. The East Indian connection, well visible and explicit in Scott's *oeuvre*, has solicited an investigation of Scott's understanding of India, a country he had not visited but that had nonetheless attracted his attention and kindled his imagination.[48] The few passages in *Rob Roy* that evoke the West Indies, and that will be analysed further on, have, unsurprisingly, invited so far only a few considerations on the reasons for Scott's 'deeply ingrained reticence'[49] in the context of the recent re-assessment of Caribbean–Scottish relations, more as an example of Scotland's 'willing amnesia', than as critically relevant material.

There are, however, at least two reasons why Scott's reticence should be considered more carefully — more carefully than I myself did in my 'Acts of (Un)willed Amnesia' article. One is more general, and pertains to the meaningfulness of conscious literary silences, especially in relation to traumatic or shameful contexts, as discussed in the previous section. The second pertains to Scott's complex approach to writing and his metanarrative and metalinguistic concerns. These have been recently explored by Alison Lumsden, who has pointed out how Scott's creativity has 'at its very heart an awareness of the limits (and problematics) of language as a tool for communication'.[50] Such awareness,

[45] Samuel Baker, 'Scott's World of Wars', in *The Edinburgh Companion to Sir Walter Scott*, ed. by Roberston, pp. 70–81 (p. 73).

[46] Andrew Lincoln, *Walter Scott and Modernity* (Edinburgh: Edinburgh University Press, 2007), p. 90.

[47] For an analysis of *Rob Roy*'s engagement with the West Indies, see Carla Sassi, 'Acts of (Un)willed Amnesia', pp. 146–47; and Michael Morris, 'Yonder Awa: Slavery and Distancing Strategies in Scottish Literature', in *Recovering Scotland's Slavery Past*, ed. by Devine, pp. 41–43.

[48] Among these, see Iain Gordon Brown, 'Griffins, Nabobs and a Seasoning of Curry Powder: Walter Scott and the Indian Theme in Life and Literature', in *The Tiger and the Thistle: Tipu Sultan and the Scots in India, 1760–1800*, ed. by Anne Buddle, Pauline Rohtagi, and Iain Gordon Brown (Edinburgh: National Gallery of Scotland, 1999), pp. 71–79; Claire Lamont, 'Scott and Eighteenth-Century Imperialism: India and the Scottish Highlands', in *Configuring Romanticism*, ed. by Theo D'haen, Peter Liebragfe, and Wim Tigges (Amsterdam: Rodopi, 2003), pp. 35–50.

[49] Sassi, p. 146.

[50] Alison Lumsden, *Walter Scott and the Limits of Language* (Edinburgh: Edinburgh University Press, 2010), p. 15.

according to Lumsden, generates a distinctive anxiety, often surfacing in Scott's writing, in relation to the possibility of recovering the past. 'The unreliable and slippery nature of language', in fact, prevents meaning from being tied to — or closed by — the speaking or writing subject,[51] and thus hinders historical construction. It is within this metalinguistic uneasiness that silence takes on a 'compensative' and communicative role in Scott's poetry and fiction. Lumsden observes how 'silence, or what might be called "negative narration," can be found throughout Scott's earlier work'. In *The Lady of the Lake* (1810), for example, the whole plot appears to rely 'upon what is not said rather than what is said'.[52] In later works, the use of silence takes on even more extreme features, as in *Peveril of the Peak* (1823), where 'characters are repeatedly rendered speechless at key moments of crisis and conflict'. Here the author's awareness 'of the fissuring and distorting nature of language' seems to lead to 'a realisation that, at times of crisis, the only option available may, indeed, be silence'.[53]

In what remains of this essay, I shall explore Scott's silence as a writer, as well as the silences enacted by implied authors and characters in his fiction. I will also try to set my investigation against a nineteenth-century ideological backdrop, taking into account readers' expectations, writers' concerns, genre demands/limitations, as well as genre insubordination, that is, the possibility of over-stepping conventions, by introducing new narratorial strategies leading to what Warhol calls a 'neonarrative'.[54]

The first observation concerns the genre privileged (and shaped) by Scott, described by Ann Rigney as 'hybrid' — Scott's brand of historical realism indeed 'calls into question any easy separation of fictional narrative and historical fact, of invention and representation, at the same time as it suggests a certain tension between them'.[55] That a conflict of, or a tension between, discourses and genres is a distinctive trait of Scott's fiction has been reiterated by several scholars. Among these, Fiona Robertson, besides highlighting the complex interplay of styles and genres in Scott's fiction, has also observed how a fluid authorial presence further complicates the narrative form — the 'inbuilt plurality in the identity of the "Author of Waverley"'[56] would be an example — and how his novels take on an extreme polyphonic form, through the continuous release of new voices, as well as of paratextual discourses.

---

[51] Ibid., p. 96.

[52] Ibid., p. 64.

[53] Ibid., p. 161.

[54] Warhol, p. 221.

[55] Ann Rigney, *Imperfect Histories: The Elusive Past and the Legacy of Romantic Historicism* (Ithaca, NY: Cornell University Press, 2001), p. 16.

[56] Fiona Robertson, *Legitimate Histories: Scott, Gothic, and the Authorities of Fiction* (Oxford: Clarendon Press, 1994), p. 117.

A question we should ask ourselves at this point is: could this complexity have accommodated an openly critical representation of Caribbean slavery, if this had been — and quite obviously it was not — what Scott had at heart? The reply is in all probability no, not in the nineteenth century. Today, his novels' polyphonic complexity and relativism represent an ideally sensitive instrument for the retrieval of the traumatic and fragmented memory of Atlantic slavery. Caryl Phillips's *Cambridge: A Novel* (1991),[57] for example, recounting the fictional story of an African slave in an eighteenth-century Caribbean plantation, owes a lot to Scott's method — from its deployment of different, conflicting and intersecting voices, to its hybridization of different genres and use of a paratextual apparatus. The problem here is rather that the distinctive features of Scott's historical novel appear to be incompatible with the tenets of abolitionist literature (or indeed of any 'propagandist' literature), as it was defined in the second half of the eighteenth century in Britain. British abolitionism, voiced across different genres (novels, poetry, tracts, newspaper articles, journals, pamphlets, political speeches etc.), was in fact structured around a distinctive rhetoric of sensibility. Brycchan Carey has observed how 'a number of loosely connected rhetorical tropes and arguments [was] available for the rhetorician to choose from when attempting to persuade an audience that a person or group of people are suffering and that that suffering should be diminished or relived entirely'. Abolitionist literature was then deeply animated by 'a belief in the power of sympathy to raise awareness of suffering, to change an audience's view of that suffering, and to direct their opposition to it'.[58] Within this context, it would be unproductive to adopt a black and white perspective in assessing Scott's work, and to equate simplistically his silence to a downright acceptance of the practice of slavery.

There are, in fact, specific ways in which Scott's texts engage with Caribbean history, which are worth addressing. Direct references to the Caribbean — as a land of adventure and opportunity, of plentiful natural resources, of lawless buccaneers, of unnamed threats and horrors, and as the theatre of colonial conflicts and naval wars — surface, almost unnoticeable, throughout Scott's literary work. Such references may be regarded as little more than an evanescent series of fleeting, apparently accidental allusions — they are never the central object of the narration, and represent, at best, a second-degree subtext. And yet, their sum, in a macro-textual perspective, evokes a subtle filigree — a cryptic map of the 'West Indian' connection that is very much in line with colonial discourses at Scott's time.

The poem 'Rokeby' (1813) provides an interesting illustration of this. Set in England, at Rokeby Park in County Durham, during the Civil War (1642–51)

---

[57] Caryl Phillips, *Cambridge: A Novel* (London: Bloomsbury, 1991).
[58] Carey, p. 2.

just after the Parliamentarian victory at Marston Moor (1644), its plot is advanced through the clash between Parliamentarian Oswald Wycliffe and Royalist Lord Rokeby. Among the characters, both Philip Mortham, a former associate of Oswald Wycliffe, and the villainous Bertram Risingham have returned as rich men after a spell of piracy in the Caribbean. The poem discloses glimpses of the violent, dark, and adventurous life of buccaneers, while a rich series of notes in the 'Appendix' provide a structured and detailed account of legal and technical aspects related to piracy in the Caribbean in a historical perspective. Susan Oliver, inquiring into Scott's choice of 'a tale of buccaneers and their plunder, and of the bringing home of experience gained from encounters with native Americans, at this particular point in his writing career', has observed that 'Scott's characterization of Risingham is unmistakably anxious, for the latter's devious nature (we learn late in the poem that in his youth he was a Borders reiver, or cattle rustler) has been exaggerated as a result of his foreign experiences'.[59] Risingham's ferocious nature is indeed presented by Scott as the outcome of his 'going native', of embracing the ways of 'Caribbean and American Indians'.[60] I wish to suggest that a possible way of interpreting both the choice of this subject, and its 'anxious' framing, is that of treating them as the outcome of a conspicuous 'implicature' — a refusal to engage with the antinarratable, that is with the horrors of slavery, still practised in the Caribbean at the time of writing the poem, and under growing political and social pressure after the abolition of the slave trade in 1807. The buccaneers' dark world of the seventeenth century, marginally evoked in the poem, would then act as a metonymic gesture towards a closer, unnameable reality, well-known to both writer and reader. Furthermore, the hybrid form of 'Rokeby', split between poetic text and denotative paratext, may suggest a paranarratable plot closure, exposing the limitations of the long poem to articulate by itself the repressed history of violent colonial encounter.

The inexplicit presence of Caribbean slavery is nowhere closer to an actual presence than in *Rob Roy*. Set around the time of the 1715 Jacobite rising, and developing across four 'regions' — London, Northumberland, Glasgow and the Scottish Highlands — this is a novel that engages with the complexities of the United Kingdom at the dawn of Union but also with the unsettling realities of the expanding Empire. The historical context invoked by the novel is closely and directly connected, politically and economically, to that in which Scott lived. As Ian Duncan has argued, in *Rob Roy* 'historical romance [is] a medium for viewing, not the past, but the unrecognizable forms of the present'.[61] This is also

---

[59] Susan Oliver, 'Crossing "Dark Barriers": Intertextuality and Dialogue between Lord Byron and Sir Walter Scott', *Studies in Romanticism*, 47.1 (2008), 15–35 (p. 24).

[60] Ibid., pp. 24–25.

[61] Ian Duncan, 'Introduction', *Rob Roy*, ed. by Ian Duncan (New York: Oxford University Press, 1998), p. xi.

a novel haunted by a deep sense of anxiety that remains unredeemed to the end
— from the protagonist and narrator's sense of guilt and inadequacy (Frank
Osbaldistone is indeed 'frank'/'honest', but largely unable to trace and convey
information reliably), to the many dark, gothic happenings that take centre-stage
and remain troublingly unsolved.[62] It is Frank who introduces the West Indian
theme, by offering insight into the recent origins of Glasgow's present affluence:
'the Union had, indeed, opened to Scotland the trade of the English colonies',
Frank observes, and the 'immense fabric of commercial prosperity' witnessed by
Scott's contemporaries depended on 'an extensive and increasing trade with the
West Indies and American colonies'.[63] Frank elides Caribbean slavery from the
enticing picture of Glasgow's growing prosperity: his mention of the West Indies
can thus be considered as a subtle implicature — he leaves to the reader the not-
so-difficult task of fill in the missing information. More meaningful, however,
are the elisions enacted by Glasgow magistrate and merchant Nicol Jarvie, whose
confidence in the progressive and prosperous future brought about by the
imperial enterprise, pragmatism, and competence in the matters of law and
commerce make him a much more reliable source of factual information than
Frank. Not only does he omit reference to Caribbean slavery, but he suppresses
— twice, in the course of the novel — the name of the region where this takes
place, 'euphemizing' the West Indies into a vague direction in space — 'west-
awa' yonder' and 'yonder awa''.[64] As Morris has pointed out, Jarvie almost slips
into a direct mention of slavery at least once, when, celebrating the quality of a
West Indian liquor, he observes that 'good ware has aften come frae a wicked
market'.[65] Morris observes that here 'contemporary readers would be likely to
hear the echo of the apology for slavery — the needs justifies the means', and
that indeed, slavery 'hangs like a shadow over the scene, present only in the
readers' knowledge of historical context'.[66] It is worthwhile to further interrogate
the structure and function of Jarvie's implicatures. The first ('yonder awa'') clearly
elides euphemistically a name that for Jarvie is evocative of, or metonymically
contiguous to, something shameful or embarrassing. There is of course no
specific need to suppress the name of the 'West Indies', which is actually used
by the narrator in the same passages. The only plausible function of the
euphemism here seems to be that of highlighting and making *visible* the moral
friction that is the source of Jarvie's embarrassment — the fact that slavery may

[62] See, among others, Fiona Robertson's discussion of *Rob Roy* in *Legitimate Histories*, pp. 177–87.
[63] Walter Scott, *Rob Roy*, ed. by David Hewitt, EEWN (Edinburgh: Edinburgh University Press, 2008), p. 155. For a more articulated commentary on this passage, see Sassi, pp. 146–47, and Morris, 'Yonder Awa', pp. 42–43.
[64] *Rob Roy*, ed. by David Hewitt, pp. 205, 221.
[65] Ibid., p. 205.
[66] Morris, 'Yonder Awa', p. 43.

be regarded as acceptable, but certainly not morally commendable. Seen in this light, the euphemism can be seen as a form of gentle indictment of Jarvie's hypocrisy. The second implicature goes in the same direction, and further foregrounds the ambiguity of Jarvie's moral stance: while many readers, and in all probability Scott himself, subscribed to the magistrate's ruthlessly pragmatic philosophy, the friction between the pleasure of drinking that 'excellent liquor' and the 'wicked' practice behind it is nonetheless exposed. Scott's silence, even in this case, is a complex one, and reveals a more nuanced stance than a firmly pro- or anti-slavery one.

In the relatively few references to the Caribbean in Scott's fiction, the most recurrent allusion is that to a place of darkness and danger. 'My uncle is the best man in the world, and in his way the kindest; but rather than hear any more about that cursed *phoca* ['seal'], as he's pleased to call it, I would exchange for the West Indies, and never see his face again',[67] mutters Hector McIntyre, the Antiquary's nephew in the eponymous novel (1816). As a captain engaged in the war in Flanders, his ironic suggestion that the Anglo-French naval conflict in the Caribbean (culminating with the victory of Britain in 1794) would represent a lighter option than his uncle's company in fact reinforces the stereotypical idea of the West Indies as a hellish world — a cliché shared by Scott and his readers. What actually makes the Caribbean a fearful destination, even for a soldier, is figured here (and in several other examples across Scott's work) as the antinarratable — as belonging beyond the bounds of what can be represented and said. The horror is here actually neutralized or deferred by the ironic inversion — a sort of narrative exorcism.

A similar association, more tied to the advancement of the plot and thus more consequential, but not less cryptic, can be traced in *The Heart of Mid-Lothian* (1818), where the villain, George Staunton, the son of the Rector of Willingham, is born in the West Indies. His childhood story is briefly but meaningfully evoked by the narrator:

> The father of George Staunton had been bred a soldier, and during service in the West Indies, had married the heiress of a wealthy planter. By this lady he had an only child, George Staunton, the unhappy young man who has been so often mentioned in this narrative. He passed the first part of his early youth under the charge of a doting mother, and in the society of negro slaves, whose study it was to gratify his every caprice. His father was a man of worth and sense; but as he alone retained tolerable health among the officers of the regiment he belonged to, he was much engaged with his duty.[68]

---

[67] *The Antiquary*, ed. by David Hewitt, EEWN (Edinburgh: Edinburgh University Press, 1995), p. 305. See also fn 305.9, p. 514.

[68] *The Heart of Mid-Lothian*, ed. by David Hewitt and Alison Lumsden, EEWN (Edinburgh: Edinburgh University Press, 2004), pp. 314–15.

It is of course striking that the narrator chooses to qualify the limitations of Mrs Staunton as a mother, but remains silent as to the nature of the 'negro' slaves' negative influence on the boy's personality. This is only implied by the narrator, unsayable, and yet 'known' to (or rather imaginable by) Scott's readers. Within the same silent 'complicity' between writer and reader, it is also possible to locate Mrs Staunton's personality — as a member of the plantation society, she appears as a gentler offshoot of the same, wider moral degradation. Her (moral) weakness as a mother is in fact pitted against her husband's soldierly and 'rational' solidity: his 'tolerable health', in the context of a highly unhealthy climate (and social milieu) may indeed symbolize his distance from and resistance to a world he inhabits but he does not belong to. Scott's recurrent father–son theme takes on here, then, a specific colonial and Caribbean colouring. The antinarratable seems to shade over into the paranarratable, as the historical romance itself appears not to be able to accommodate any further representation of and comment on the Caribbean plantation world. Interestingly, however, later on, some insight into Atlantic slavery is indeed offered by the narrator, who this time describes it and denounces it, deploying the framework of a typically nineteenth-century discourse of sympathy, making extensive use of that language of feeling that in the same period permeated abolitionist discourse.[69] The episode in question concerns the shady dealings of Donacha dhu na Dunaigh, a bandit and a trafficker in human beings, in the troubled times about 1745. 'Black Duncan' is a man 'to whom no act of mischief was unknown' and is 'occasionally an agent in a horrible trade then carried on betwixt Scotland and America, for supplying the plantations with servants, by means of *kidnapping*, as it was termed, both men and women, but especially children under age'.[70] While Scott's fiction includes passionate and open indictments of the practice of slavery — from *Ivanhoe* (1820) to *The Talisman* (1825) — all at a safe remove, geographically or chronologically, from the contemporary Caribbean scene, *Heart of Mid-Lothian* is unique in accommodating these two very different approaches to two almost identical aspects of the same system of exploitation.

Conclusion

While ongoing historical research may reveal further intersections between Scott and the Caribbean, what we can infer from the nuanced silences in his fictional writings — more, in fact, than those I have been able to discuss in the present essay —is nonetheless very valuable. These reveal a complex and fluid 'map', straddling the conventional categories of anti- or pro-abolitionist literature of

---

[69] See Evan Gottlieb, '"To Be at Once Another and the Same": Walter Scott and the End(s) of Sympathetic Britishness', *Studies in Romanticism*, 43.2 (2004), 187–207 (pp. 189–98).

[70] *The Heart of Mid-Lothian*, p. 463.

the time. Scott himself seemed to inhabit, like many of his contemporaries, a 'grey' area, between a degree of abhorrence for what could not but be considered as an inhumane practice, and a pragmatic attachment to the economic and political certainties of imperial politics. It is not his personal stance — not commendable, for sure — that makes his work relevant in a Caribbean–Scottish studies perspective, nor can what he tells us about the West Indian world strike us as original and innovative. His silences, however, complex at least as his polyphonic, uneasy narratives, tell us of social and literary conventions in the nineteenth century, and usefully point to their contradictions, ambiguities and hybridities. They also speak of that History that, in Jameson's words, 'hurts', as shame, fear, anger, or trauma, that cannot be entirely organized into a narrative, and that yet seeks and demands expression.

SECTION V

Literary Geographies and Ecocriticism

'All that is curious on continent and isle': Time, Place, and Modernity in Scott's 'Vacation 1814' and *The Pirate*

PENNY FIELDING

University of Edinburgh

The islands of Britain and Ireland form a scattered archipelago in which it is tempting to trace forms, shapes, borders and continuities. We have tended to think of the geography of early nineteenth-century Britain as part of a historical process of assimilation. In Linda Colley's influential model Britons came to identify themselves as people of an island nation, increasingly homogenized under a banner of 'liberty'.[1] In a more sophisticated formulation, Franco Moretti's analyses of the geographies of the historical novel show how the genre turned its attentions to the internal borders of nations, a point where history and geography can be seen to produce each other, but with the final design 'to represent internal unevenness, no doubt; and then, to abolish it'.[2] In this essay I pursue Moretti's general point about the way the time and space of the historical novel meet on imagined internal borders, but I also focus on how this cultural process generates a surplus of space that prolongs both the indeterminacy of specific places and the difficulty of absorbing them into larger cultural wholes. The formation of a national geography around a political centre (England or Edinburgh) or by a dominant cultural figure (in my case, Walter Scott) will always leave unresolved spaces that cannot quite be accommodated by the taxonomic geographic decisions that borders require (urban/rural, centre/ periphery, Anglophone/Gàidhealtachd and so on).

Some spaces fit awkwardly into national structures, or remain incompletely assimilated — not fully subject to the processes of national acculturation. These may be different from more familiar spaces that claim to be resistant to historical incorporation or to be threatened by what Saree Makdisi describes as a process of modernization. Such heterotopias (which for Makdisi includes Scott's Highlands as well as Wordsworth's spots of time) are examples of a 'hitherto untransformed enclave that, when discovered and colonized by the outside

---

[1] Linda Colley, *Britons: Forging the Nation, 1707–1837* (New Haven, CT: Yale University Press, 1992).

[2] Franco Moretti, *Atlas of the European Novel* (London: Verso, 1998), p. 40.

Yearbook of English Studies, 47 (2017), 243–262
© Modern Humanities Research Association 2017

world, is seen to experience a fall which erases or, rather, rewrites it, by weaving it tightly into the history of the outside world'.[3] Rather, I want to look at a location which in the early nineteenth century had been neither idealized as a natural space nor constructed as a bearer of national history, and to see what happens to it when it is visited by that great instrument of historicization, Walter Scott.

My subject is Scott's two visits, first in person and then in fiction, to Orkney and Shetland, the Northern Isles of Great Britain, and their place in his literary-historical geography. The first took place in the summer of 1814, when Scott accepted an invitation from the lighthouse engineer Robert Stevenson to accompany the Commissioners of the Northern Lights on their annual inspection of the lighthouses around the coast of Scotland. Then, in 1821, he revisited the unpublished diary he had kept on this voyage to compose his novel *The Pirate*, set on Shetland and Orkney. These encounters allow us to think about the meeting points of place, time, and narrative more generally — the relation between the accumulated cultural forms that give places their historical contours and the contingencies and demands of the present. Both of Scott's narratives, seemingly excursions into history, turn out to be permeable in unexpected ways by their immediate contexts in which history becomes mediated by disruptive forms of present temporality.

1814: Europe

In 1814 the Northern Islands were not firmly etched on the literary landscape. Four years after Scott's visit, Orkney would feature briefly in *Frankenstein* as the embodiment of that most negative and formless aspect of the Burkean sublime — privation. Deflected from his aesthetic tour with Henry Clerval, Victor Frankenstein decides upon one of the most remote of the Orkney islands to work on his female creature:

> It was a place fitted for such a work, being hardly more than a rock whose high sides were continually beaten upon by the waves. The soil was barren, scarcely affording pasture for a few miserable cows, and oatmeal for its inhabitants, which consisted of five persons, whose gaunt and scraggy limbs gave tokens of their miserable fare. [...]
> In this retreat I devoted the morning to labour; but in the evening, when the weather permitted, I walked on the stony beach of the sea to listen to the waves as they roared and dashed at my feet. It was a monotonous yet ever-changing scene.[4]

---

[3] Saree Makdisi, *Romantic Imperialism: Universal Empire and the Culture of Modernity* (Cambridge: Cambridge University Press, 1998), p. 12.

[4] Mary Shelley, *Frankenstein: The 1818 text*, ed. by Marylyn Butler (Oxford: Oxford University Press, 1992), p. 136. In 1822 (and having recently read *The Pirate*) Byron also seems unconcerned about the exact location of the islands. Torquil, hero of his poem *The Island*, is described as 'The fair-hair'd offspring of the Hebrides, | Where roars the Pentland with its whirling seas,' despite the

Geographically, Britain's Northern Islands were not, in 1814, on what James Buzard has called 'the beaten track' — the institutionalization of travel that awards to places authentic cultural identity and to individual travellers a concomitantly authentic experience of travel.[5] In practical terms, the islands were hard to reach — the journey to Orkney from the north coast of Scotland meant crossing the dangerous Pentland Firth, and even the mail service from Leith (Edinburgh's port) was intermittent. Despite their long interactions with Scandinavia, the Northern Islands seemed to have slipped away from literature and history. Arthur Edmonston, a Shetlander and author of the most widely read early nineteenth-century account of the islands, regrets the loss of historical record:

> There were few to describe [Shetland's early history]; and in an illiterate age, many important events take place, of which posterity receives no intelligence. As the pronunciation of the names, both of individuals and of places, is subjected to the ignorance of the inhabitants and the caprice of foreigners, it is liable to frequent changes, and but a few places retain long their first appellations. These causes operate, no doubt, more or less in every country, but their effects will be the most conspicuous in rude societies, where language having been reduced to no fixed standard, is liable to perpetual variation.[6]

It was to these unfamiliar islands that Scott set off in 1814. That summer was a time of waiting. For Scott, the waiting was for the reception of *Waverley*, published on 7 July. By the time he left with Robert Stevenson on 29 July, the novel had already gone into a second edition, and notices were appearing in the Edinburgh press, but he was yet to see the reviews in the London journals. Europe was also in a state of political anticipation. Napoleon had arrived on Elba on 30 May, and European politicians were anticipating the Congress of Vienna, which would open on 18 September, ten days after Scott's return to Edinburgh. The political map of Europe remained in suspension as the victors in the Napoleonic wars were yet to meet to redraw its territorial divisions.

The temporality of politics can be imbricated with that of narrative. Mary Favret has shown how times of war introduce their own experience of duration: 'wartime is an affective zone, a *sense* of time that, caught up in the most unsettled sort of present, without knowledge of its outcome, cannot know its own borders. It indicates a dislocation of the bounded terrain usually associated with war and

---

Pentland Firth in fact being the stretch of water that separates Orkney from Scotland. Lord Byron, *The Complete Poetical Works*, ed. by Jerome McGann, 7 vols (Oxford: Oxford University Press, 1993), VII, 40.

[5] James Buzard, *The Beaten Track* (Oxford: Oxford University Press, 1993), p. 6.

[6] Arthur Edmondston, *A view of the ancient and present state of the Zetland Islands: including their civil, political, and natural history; antiquities; and an account of their agriculture, fisheries, commerce, and the state of society and manners*, 2 vols (Edinburgh: James Ballantyne, 1809), I, 71.

the extension of war into a realm without clear limits'.[7] In 1814 the Napoleonic Wars were, it was assumed, over, yet the 'unsettled sort of present' that Favret describes was far from becoming settled. She demonstrates how, in the case of *Persuasion* (published in 1816 and set in 1814), that disrupted wartime temporality of painful waiting and anxiety is translated into the plot of a domestic novel. And we can trace another kind of unexpected connection in the relation of the apparently distant Northern Islands — seemingly on the edge of Europe — with European post-war dislocations at the time of Scott's visit.

Peter Fritzsche's account of the period following the French Revolution describes an affective temporality that he calls the feeling of being 'stranded in the present'. He starts from the familiar position that the Revolution inaugurated a form of modernity that radically cut the present away from a past history that could be narrated on a grand scale by a public class of individuals or institutions called 'historians'. Displaced physically by war, and socially by political upheaval, all sorts of people now come into conversation with each other and, faced with the anxiety of a radically cut-away past and an unknown future, they create new, multiple, imaginative, and spontaneous forms of history:

> Insofar as the present moment was characterized by the new, the past appeared increasingly different, mysterious, and inaccessible. Cut off from the present, the past turned opaque, which invited a new, more subtle scholarship to take its measure. More aware of the distinctiveness of their own contemporary present, men and women came to invest the past with their own historicity and to understand it in terms of 'time' and 'place'. This enlarged the scope of history to include the most ordinary artefacts and the most undistinguished subjects that reflected a particular 'spirit of the age'.[8]

This is a Europe of exiles and fractured communities where common experience was no longer easily recordable; or, if it was, that experience was one of being estranged from one's own time and dispossessed from history. Fritzsche follows James Chandler's argument in *England in 1819* where Chandler identifies in a proliferation of historically self-conscious works around that year a complex and often self-contradictory version of *zeitgeist*. In the move to identify the new concept of a distinct and homogenous 'Spirit of the Age', a specific present different from the past, writers in fact produce a literature that addresses differences and incongruities, and tackles the problem of history as a 'case' to which there may be exceptions.[9] That is, the foundation of modernity as a

---

[7] Mary A. Favret, *War at a Distance: Romanticism and the Making of Modern Wartime* (Princeton, NJ: Princeton University Press, 2010), p. 18.

[8] Peter Fritzsche, *Stranded in the Present: Modern Time and the Melancholy of History* (Cambridge, MA: Harvard University Press, 2004), p. 7.

[9] James Chandler, *England in 1819* (Chicago, IL: University of Chicago Press, 1998), Chapters 1 and 2.

universally recognizable present simultaneously generates a historicism of multiple and often contradictory actors.

Against these fractures and uncertainties new forms of historicism were — sometimes literally — erected. Britain, with its territorial borders intact during the war years, was particularly adept at visualizing this geographical stability in historical terms. Ann Rigney has documented the historical monuments constructed in the year 1814 to give a visual object for the public memory of history and to arrange that history into coherent or sequential events.[10] Just before Scott left Edinburgh, the 500th anniversary of the Battle of Bannockburn was commemorated with a statue of William Wallace at Bemersyde, close to Scott's own home at Abbotsford. While he was away, an extensive historical pageant in celebration of Nelson's 1798 victory at the Battle of the Nile, timed to coincide with the centenary of the Hanoverian succession, was held in Hyde Park in London. Scott was himself to include an account of it in the *Edinburgh Annual Register* for 1814.[11]

Other forms of historicism adapted themselves to the sense of history in ruins by rendering the narrative of history as partial or fragmented. Fritzsche argues that antiquarian objects no longer indicated a generalized pre-historic past but were drawn back into a narrative of history that could reimagine something of the national stories that seemed to have been occluded or fractured in war-torn Europe. Just as the discourse of the present resided in the coming-together of individual subjects, so the past could be summoned in the fragment remains of pasts that had not entered into formal historical narratives: 'The work of archaeological recovery in this period aimed at the reconstruction of the multilayered contexts that historical victories had effaced.'[12] This, then, offers us both a historical and a historiographical context for Scott's lighthouse voyage — a journey that was to prove an encounter with forms of the present that could not be easily assimilated into temporal rationalizations — structures such as improvement, progress, or the stabilizing of the past in tangible antiquarian objects.

With the publication of *Waverley*, Scott had nominated his own act of historical commemoration, subtitling his account of the Jacobite rising *'Tis Sixty Years Since*. In doing so, he places his lighthouse narrative squarely in its year when he heads his diary with the title 'Vacation 1814'. But the diary is far from an act of historical recollection; rather, it explores the experience of the present, even when it seems to call upon an ancient past. The title refers partly to the legal

[10] Ann Rigney, 'Making Publics in 1814: *Waverley* and the Culture of Commemoration', paper given at *On or About 1814: A Symposium on Literature in History*, University of California, Berkeley, 2014. I am grateful to the author for a copy of this paper.

[11] *The Edinburgh Annual Register*, 7 (January 1814), 104–22.

[12] Fritzsche, *Stranded in the Present*, p. 104.

period of vacation when the law courts do not sit — another period of suspended time. 'Vacation' also carries the sense of vacancy or emptiness, and 'to vacate' has another legal meaning of removal from legal validity. Freed from legal and official regulation the diary announces its own emptiness and its own status as a voyage into the unknown and unregulated newness of time and space. Scott's temporal experience is, in this sense, one of a continuous present that finds its expression in the form of a journal in which events are encountered in an expected sequence without a recognizable narrative form. A diary proceeds in episodic steps, recorded at short intervals that are not always plotted on a predetermined line. The trip had a clear purpose for the Commissioners of the Northern Lights, but not an obvious one for Scott. He had the idea of collecting material for his next poem, *The Lord of the Isles*, but that was for the return trip down the west coast — a much more familiar land- and seascape which Scott saw as already historicized. There is no indication that Scott already had any idea that he was going to write *The Pirate* eight years later — and in fact, as we shall see, that novel was brought about by a rather different set of circumstances. Scott was not going to Orkney and Shetland for any particular reason other than to go *on vacation*, and the language of his diary has often the feeling of an experience that is simply unfolding itself in the present.

In all these senses — his own literary career and that of the novel as a genre, the political state of Europe, and the form of the diary — Scott is in a state of suspension. And he finds himself in a strange kind of historical present when he reaches the islands which themselves seem to him to lack a clear position in linear or incremental history. Temporally adrift in two ways, the Northern Islands cannot be understood through written history, nor do they seem properly inserted into Scottish Enlightenment ideas about historical progress. Faced with the apparent lack of historical inscription and the precedent of cultural representation, Scott's two most abiding interests — improvement and antiquarianism — fail to provide the temporal and historical narrative that they are called upon to serve.

Scott's loosely optimistic account of the islands is predicated on a suspended temporality of things always just about to happen. Agriculture should be improving, given the progressive views of the landowners he encounters, but Scott finds it hard to chart such improvement on the Enlightenment map of historiography. Instead of a nicely progressive or stadial model in which one form of subsistence gives way to another (herding to farming to commerce), all of these are mixed up on the islands. Scott complains that the people live an undifferentiated lifestyle that confuses the categories of economic progress. This is the case both spatially and temporally. The ownership of land is not, for Scott, sufficiently demarcated — 'there are several obstacles to improvement, chiefly the undivided state of the properties' — and the labouring people 'are often absent at the proper times of labour'.[13] This latter problem Scott ascribes to the amphibious character of Shetland's workforce who appear to him to move indiscriminately between fishing and farming. In Smithian terms, the division of labour is lacking not only within trades but also between them. The clear separation of these labouring practices is necessary to place Shetland in the course of progress, and Scott hopes that this will happen, even though, in the diary's characteristic temporality, it has not quite happened yet and awaits an unspecified future:

> The improvement of the arable land, on the contrary, would soon set them beyond the terrors of famine with which the islanders are at present occasionally visited; and, combined with fisheries, carried on not by farmers, but by real fishers, would amply supply the inhabitants, without diminishing the export of dried fish. This separation of trades will in time take place, and then the prosperous days of Zetland will begin. (p. 154)

If the agricultural condition of Shetland makes the future a conjecture without immediate security in the present, then the past fails to reveal itself in the way an antiquarian visitor to the islands might expect. Or perhaps more accurately, Scott's antiquarian expectations are subject to the particular insecurities of war-time temporality.

Scott's interest in collecting was piqued by war. The following year he was to travel to Belgium — his first journey outside Britain — to acquire items from the field of Waterloo. He covered one wall of his house, Abbotsford, in the most ferocious military hardware. Fritzsche argues that nineteenth-century antiquarianism is both inspired by war and an attempt to ward off its dislocations. The revolutionary conflicts of the late eighteenth century renewed European interest in the religious wars of the seventeenth century, and offered a way of thinking through a violent present by revisiting these disruptive energies from history. Antiquarianism can become the modern mode of historicism, when modernity seeks ways of rendering its own fractured and unstable temporality as objects. It offers the lure of access to the objects of the past that can be experienced as empirical and tactile, but that simultaneously acknowledges the unavailability of historical continuity. Antiquarian objects are uprooted from the past, are often fractured or incomplete, and signify the gaps and interruptions of history rather than its inevitable progress. Modern antiquarianism takes up this doubled and paradoxical position, on the one hand seeking the reassurance that the temporality of history can return the subject to something that has already been experienced (the antiquarian object or practice),

---

[13] 'Vacation 1814: Voyage in the Lighthouse Yacht to Nova Zembla, and the Lord knows Where', in John G. Lockhart, *Memoirs of the Life of Sir Walter Scott, Bart.*, 7 vols (Edinburgh: Robert Cadell, 1837), III, 136–277 (pp. 143 and 244). Further references are given following quotations in the text.

while on the other hand announcing the temporal gulf that separates us from that past.[14]

Thus deracinated, antiquarian objects are themselves exiled from the very historical, tangible or empirical moment they are supposed to represent. Scott knew quite a lot about old Nordic literature: 1814 saw not only the publication of *Waverley* but also his retelling of the Icelandic *Eyrbyggja Saga*.[15] Yet he finds that the things and the cultural performances that he seeks to collect are vexingly unavailable, just on the cusp of living memory, always somewhere else, on some other island, just out of reach. Here is his account of the Shetland sword dance, which he believes to be the only surviving example of 'the warlike dances of the northern people' (p. 163) and therefore a way of anchoring Shetland in a Northern European history:

> At Scalloway my curiosity was gratified by an account of the sword-dance, now almost lost, but still practised in the Island of Papa, belonging to Mr. Scott. [...]. Some rude couplets are spoken (in *English*, not *Norse*), containing a sort of panegyric upon each champion as he is presented. They then dance a sort of cotillion, as the ladies described it, going through a number of evolutions with their swords. One of my three Mrs. Scotts readily promised to procure me the lines, the rhymes, and the form of the dance. I regret much that young Mr. Scott was absent during this visit; he is described as a reader and an enthusiast in poetry. Probably I might have interested him in preserving the dance, by causing young persons to learn it [...]. (p. 162)

We witness Scott reaching for continuities that constantly elude him. The ritual is 'almost lost' but can still be found on an island that is at once a distant, primitive location and the property of a modern landowner. The dance is on the verge of disappearing from history, but the modern ladies have described it as 'a sort of cotillion' — a recognizable social function. These contemporary friends have promised Scott a transcript of the performance, but he has yet to receive it. And if only Scott could have met with 'young Mr Scott' (unrelated to him) then a line of continuity could have affected the progress of the ancient ritual into the modern world. Scott remains in a present whose promises are a gamble on an uncertain future that may or may not revive an ancient past.

Scott is eager to discover traces of the Picts, the supposed aboriginal people of Scotland and the subject of a continuing debate over their language and

---

[14] See also Philip Shaw, *Waterloo and the Romantic Imagination* (Basingstoke: Palgrave Macmillan, 2002), p. 63 for a study of post-Waterloo writing as a way of confronting a moment that tested the limits of national self-definition. Shaw traces in Scott's *The Antiquary* 'illusions redeemed and rechannelled in the service of the state'.

[15] See Julian D'Arcy and Kirsten Wolf, 'Sir Walter Scott and *Eyrbyggja Saga*', *Studies in Scottish Literature*, 22.1 (1985), 30–43. For Scott's knowledge of Nordic culture see Andrew Wawn, *The Vikings and the Victorians: Inventing the Old North in Nineteenth-Century Britain* (Cambridge: D. S. Brewer, 2000), pp. 60–83.

ethnicity. He ascribes a number of artefacts and buildings to Pictish origin. But he also includes a story, narrated to him by Robert Stevenson, of a visit Stevenson had earlier made to the island of South Ronaldsay when Stevenson is invited by the islanders to give his opinion on a man whom they claim to be an 'ancient Pecht' (p. 195). On meeting this individual, Stevenson finds that he is in fact an ironmonger whom he had known in Edinburgh — the imagined ancient origin is a modern arrival.

Not only is Scott's experience mediated by an uncertain temporality, the geography of the Northern islands turns out to be less homogenous, and less isolated, than he might have expected. Just before leaving Edinburgh Scott had written to his friend J. B. S. Morritt that he hoped the tour would present him with 'all that is curious on continent and isle',[16] evoking a fractal archipelago in which islands and continents do not form a clear hierarchy. In the story of the ancient Pecht, the supposedly ancient origin turns out to be outsider, washed up on the shores of Orkney, and the fractal geometries of Orkney and Shetland start to mimic curiously a Europe of displaced persons where the rules of hospitality and practices of cosmopolitanism are no longer in harmony with each other. The islands are a much more international locality than Scott expects, and their population more transient. Instead of Picts, he finds a mobile community of disparate nations — Dutch, Norwegians, Danes. These people disrupt any idea of the rude primitivism of the native Shetlanders, by importing luxury goods into their diet 'the proportion of foreign luxuries seems monstrous, unless we allow for the habits contracted by the seamen in their foreign trips. Tea, in particular, is used by all ranks, and porridge quite exploded' (p. 147). This is again the work of what we might think of as a kind of antiquarian sociology: when confronted with hybridity, Scott looks for continuities and origins which turn out not to be fully realizable.

Shetland bears more traces of the political present that Scott might have supposed. He records the presence of foreign sailors who have been marked by the war with France, as if they were refugees: 'They seemed very poor, and talked of having been pillaged of everything by the French, and expected to have found Lerwick ruined by the war' (p. 182). The number of foreign vessels around the archipelagos gives rise to frequent shipwrecks, often of Dutch or Scandinavian vessels, and the local legends tell of ships of the Spanish Armada that foundered on the rocky coastlines in the sixteenth century. Far from being the primitive racial origin that the Picts were supposed to stand for, Shetland bears traces of the wrecked cosmopolitanism of the rest of the Europe where to be a citizen of no particular nation means to be in exile as much as on a Grand Tour. And in

[16] *The Letters of Sir Walter Scott*, ed. by H. J. C. Grierson, 12 vols (London: Constable, 1932–37), III, 477 (28 July 1814).

these wrecks Scott comes up against the edge of what it means to be human. He is shocked by the pillaging of wrecks by the locals, and the superstition that to save a drowning man will end with the rescued man doing his saviour some harm or injury. He has become an exile in his own nation, unable to understand its customs through the familiar enlightenment routes of sympathy or historical progress:

> Several instances were quoted to-day in company, in which the utmost violence had been found necessary to compel the fishers to violate this inhuman prejudice. [...] It may seem strange that the natives should be so little affected by a distress to which they are themselves so constantly exposed. But habitual exposure to danger hardens the heart against its consequences, whether to ourselves or others. (p. 156)

Scott is now dependent on the past as bricolage — not so much history as romance, but rather as a disparate conversation between people who may not share the same forms of historical knowledge. The vacation that the diary fills up is not so much a journey into a romance past as into a set of diverse ways of understanding the present.

1821: Empire

In 1821 Scott had the opportunity to revisit Orkney and Shetland. Perhaps mindful of the huge success of Byron's *The Corsair* in 1814, Scott's publisher, Archibald Constable, tried to persuade his best-selling author to write a book on a piratical theme. Constable's idea was for a novel entitled *The Buccanier* set in the aftermath of the Restoration that would follow the adventures in America of three of the regicides of Charles I. Scott rejected the title, but the idea of piracy seems to have turned his thoughts to John Gow, a notorious Orkney pirate about whom he had heard just before he left the islands. *The Pirate* was composed throughout 1821 (a long time for Scott to spend on a novel) and published right at the end of that year (although the colophon bears the date 1822). Scott turned back to the 1814 diary, but seems to have felt that his first-hand experience of the islands did not provide the historical and topographical heft that he needed for a whole novel. He conducted further researches into the history and present agricultural state of the islands, and corresponded with his friend William Erskine, Sheriff Depute of Orkney and Shetland, commenting 'I want to talk to you about the locale of Zetland, for I am making my bricks with a very limited allowance of straw'.[17] The brick-making metaphor points backwards to the gaps I have already discussed in the diary and also raises the question of the form and structure that Scott used to construct his fictional edifice, *The Pirate*. In this section I explore Scott's revisiting of the

---

[17] *Letters*, VII, 12 (27 September 1821).

Northern Isles in novel form, and look at the ways in which the fractured present of his first visit is replayed in fiction.

The Pirate bears some signs of the national tale, and of narrative patterns established in Scott's early novels to explore the political geographies of the nation.[18] As in *Waverley*, the hero moves to an outlying region where he must choose between a dark, dangerous proponent of regional independence, and a more nationally compliant fair woman whose father agrees to the marriage when

> his Norse blood gave way to the natural feeling of the heart, and he comforted his pride while he looked around him, and saw [...] that as well 'his daughter married the son of an English pirate, as of a Scottish thief'.[19]

But this resolution, with its national tale telos, is not quite a summary of the topographical trajectory of the characters. Mordaunt Mertoun, the hero (though not the titular character) is the geographical reverse of Scott's earlier heroes who set out to explore the wider world, and although he 'eagerly longed to see more of the world than his lonely situation had hitherto permitted' (p. 81), Mordaunt never gets further than Orkney.

The principal incomer to Shetland is not the hero (Mordaunt is a child when he arrives), but the hero's father, Basil Mertoun, who arrives with no obvious identity. He is a stranger, but the antithesis of the outsider who is an object of local curiosity: 'No one asked him whence he came, where he was going, what was his purpose in visiting so remote a corner of the empire, or what was likely to be the term of his stay' (p. 7). Basil himself, spokesman for global homogeneity, rejects the entire basis in climate of Enlightenment geographical determinism. Montesquieu's careful formulation of the production of national character through the somatic-social reaction to climate means nothing to him. Invited to his neighbour's house, where the air is said to be better, he declaims: 'I am indifferent to climate; if there is but air enough to fill my lungs, I care not if it be the breath of Arabia or of Lapland' (p. 11).

Basil's atopical expansion is at odds with Scott's request to Erskine for information on the local and the specific — the peculiarities of the 'thick description' of localities and costumes that create a sense of topical realism in the national tale. The novel gives Scott the opportunity to revisit his antiquarian interests from his diary (he is this time able to imagine the absent Sword Dance).

---

[18] Shetland had been the subject of a solitary national tale published earlier in 1821 when Dorothea Campbell's *Harley Radington* tested the limits of a form usually set in the much more culturally inscribed regions of Ireland and the West of Scotland. See Penny Fielding, 'Genre, Geography and the National Tale: D. P. Campbell's *Harley Radington*', *European Romantic Review*, 23.5 (2012), 593–611.

[19] Walter Scott, *The Pirate*, ed. by Mark Weinstein and Alison Lumsden, EEWN (Edinburgh: Edinburgh University Press, 2001), p. 389. Further references are given following quotations in the text.

But *The Pirate*'s sense of spatiality continually pulls away from these anchors in a particular time and place. Even more than the diary, the novel is set in a fictional present — dissolving history and geography, opening out its perspectives to global space and a-chronological time. As Scott was writing *The Pirate*, Napoleon died on the very distant island of St Helena. British focus was now less in Europe than in its global territories. And Scott, as Ian Duncan has noted, is in the midst of an 'intermittent but decisive widening of scope across [his] career, from the philosophical domain of national history to that of world history'.[20]

As Scott widens his geographic lens, *The Pirate* marks a strange focal point in his return to the Northern Islands. On the one hand, the islands mark the extreme point of Britain, an outlier waiting to be drawn back into the national geography. But on the other, as they were on Scott's first encounter, they remain unfixed, porous, and elusive in their historical positioning. *The Pirate* resists its own opportunities to be a story about Britain. Scott provocatively sets the events in 1689 against a historical background, as Minna Troil reminds us, 'the Highlands against the Lowlands — the Williamites against the Jacobites — the Whigs against the Tories' (p. 210), but the novel pays very little attention to these developments. Instead, Scott turns the national tale's British perspective outwards to a global one. Minna and Norna plan a kind of violent Zetland Independence movement that will restore the past glories of Norway, which Minna sets in an imperial context:

'My father is a Zetlander, or rather a Norwegian,' said Minna, 'one of an oppressed race, who will not care whether you fought against the Spaniards, who are the tyrants of the New World, or against the Dutch and English, who have succeeded to their usurped dominions. His own ancestors supported and exercised the freedom of the seas in those gallant barks, whose pennons were the dread of all Europe.' (p. 210)

Minna articulates Shetland's independence on an imperial rather than a national stage — a claim that the novel undercuts with a certain dramatic irony, for Shetland is already part of a global empire based not on military conquest but on the commercial expansion of modern imperialism.

The story of imagining Orkney and Shetland in global terms had started before Scott arrived on the archipelagos, but where to situate them in relation to the empire was not clear. In his 1809 account of Shetland, Arthur Edmonston (one of Scott's sources of information) worries about how to place them in relation to larger geographies. The islands, he complains, are not faring well in

---

[20] Ian Duncan, 'The Trouble with Man: Scott, Romance, and World History in the Age of Lamarck', in *Romantic Frictions*, ed. by Theresa M. Kelley, special issue of *Romantic Circles* (November 2011), online at <www.rc.umd.edu/praxis/frictions/HTML/praxis.2011.duncan.html> [accessed 23 November 2016]. See also Evan Gottlieb, *Romantic Globalism: British Literature and Modern World Order, 1750–1830* (Columbus: Ohio State University Press, 2014), p. 13 for an account of Scott's 'novelistic negotiation of Britain's post-Napoleonic role as a world power'.

the public consciousness, as even more distant outposts of Empire are being added to the map of the world:

> while the most trivial observation respecting New Holland, and those isles which lie scattered in the Pacific Ocean, is read with interest, and remembered with satisfaction, many valuable and useful communications, which relate to our native country, are soon overlooked and forgotten.
>
> The Zetland Islands, although they have long constituted an integral part of Great Britain, and their utility to it, especially in a maritime point of view, be obvious and acknowledged; yet their productions, resources, and internal economy, are less generally known than those of the most distant colony of the empire.[21]

Edmonston's geographical frame makes the Shetland Islands both more and less familiar. These islands can be understood by means of comparison with other islands in the British Empire, but the latter's' newly discovered status serves to diminish Shetland's older position as archetypically British. Instead of acting as the origin of national-spatial identity, Shetland is *terra incognita*, waiting to be discovered and to find a place in Britain's expanding global reach.

The Pirate exploits the islands' apparently free-floating spatiality to conjure up a version of Empire cut free of its political and historical anchors. The pirates in *The Pirate* have their origin in the Caribbean. Basil Mertoun was formerly the owner of a plantation on the West Indian island of Tortuga. When their estate is raided by the Spanish, Basil and his older son (Mordaunt's half-brother) become pirates. Both men, after conflicts with their respective crews, are marooned on different islands and, by very different routes and at different times, end up in Shetland. But the piratical localities are very thinly drawn in the novel. *The Pirate* is set mainly on Shetland, with its later chapters on Orkney, and although the pirates have been plying their trade around the West Indies these distant locations are not directly realized geographically or ethnographically.[22] The novel makes almost no mention of slavery. Rather, the world beyond the islands is represented by the circulation of commodities seemingly unsecured to any regular origin or route and driven by an extra-legal — or piratical — economy of smuggling and *ad hoc* trading.[23]

---

[21] Arthur Edmonston, *View of the Zetland Islands*, I, pp. v–vi. The South Shetland islands in the South Atlantic were not so named until 1819. By contrast, the Western Isles of Scotland were already established in colonial toponymy: James Cook had named the 'New Hebrides' (now Vanuatu) in 1774.

[22] For the differences between Shetland and Orkney in the novel see Mark Ryan Smith, *The Literature of Shetland* (Lerwick: Shetland Times, 2015), pp. 32–37.

[23] Arnold Schmidt identifies in *The Pirate* a more immediate condemnation of slavery: 'the hypocrisy evident in the novel mirrors contradictions in 19th-century British society, where the civic virtues of a seemingly ethical society conflict with the imperial economy that makes that society possible'. 'Walter Scott's *The Pirate*: Imperialism, Nationalism and Bourgeois Values', in *Fictions of the Sea*, ed. by Bernhard Klein (Aldershot: Ashgate, 2002), pp. 89–103 (p. 91).

The Shetland islands are globally permeable and the lives of their inhabitants intersect with the commodities of empire in unofficial capacities — the Shetlanders trade with the Dutch, the local pedlar has Spanish items on offer, cane sugar is in plentiful supply, and the local hostelry serves rum because of 'the commerce of the Zetlanders with foreign vessels, and homeward bound West Indiamen' (p. 128). Magnus Troil owns

> a punch-bowl of uncommon size, the gift of the captain of one of the Honourable East India Company's vessels, which, bound from China homeward, had been driven north-about by stress of weather into Lerwick-bay, and had there contrived to get rid of part of the cargo, without very scrupulously reckoning for the King's duties. (p. 127)

This energetic economy of black-marketeering and the improvised acquisition of goods is something different from the local pursuits of fishing and farming that Scott notes in the diary. The islanders, alert to their economic opportunities, combine an ancient primitivism with the commodity-based, globalized modernity that makes them more, not less, advanced than mainland Britain:

> with the foreign delicacies of tea, coffee, and chocolate; for, as we have already had occasion to remark, the situation of these islands made them early acquainted with various articles of foreign luxury, which were, as yet, but little known in Scotland. (p. 154)

These deracinated commodities stand in sharp contrast with the antiquarian objects that the novel promises to deliver to its readers. The antiquarian object should anchor history as a visible or tangible confirmation of the reality of the past as it was lived in a particular locality, thus calling on the specificity of place — the local habitation of the object — to illuminate time. But although Scott does include a number of the Norse or 'Pictish' discoveries he either made or narrowly missed on the 1814 tour, they often evade the role of acting as this kind of historical evidence. Scott repeats from his diary the idea that the 'Stones of Stenniss', an apparently druidical monument, have 'no rival in Britain, excepting the inimitable monument at Stonehenge'. But our attention, focalized by Clement Cleveland (the titular pirate), is almost immediately diverted as Cleveland is 'less interested by this singular monument of antiquity' (p. 359) than he is by the prospect of being reunited with his ship. A discovery of old silver coins leads to a discussion of their financial value and taxable status as treasure trove rather than any antiquarian interest.

The novel repeats a move of enfolding a supposedly primitive past into commercial modernity in a way that removes its temporality from linear, incremental or causal history. Its most extreme example is the meeting point between Norna, self-styled seer and Zetland nationalist, with the novel's motif of global commerce. At a number of points, The Pirate associates Norna's attempts to control events by magic with the modern discourse of capitalism —

the market, the price of labour, buying and selling — as in this exchange between the landowner Magnus Troil and Claude Halcro:

'She bade me begone about my business, and told me that the issue would be known at the Kirkwall Fair; and said just the like to this noodle of a Factor — it was all that either of us got for our labour,' said Halcro.

'That is strange,' said Magnus. 'My kinswoman writes me in this letter not to fail going thither with my daughters. This Fair runs strongly in her head; — one would think she intended to lead the market, and yet she has nothing to buy or to sell there that I know of.' (p. 285)

Magnus's trope of creating a market out of nothing substantial is dramatically voiced by Basil Mertoun as he discourses on Norna's claim to be able to control the winds through supernatural powers. Basil makes no distinction between the allegedly superstitious, primitive practice of selling favourable winds to sailors to assist them out of the port and modern, global commerce in which the natural world itself is subsumed in an economy where everything is for sale:

Every thing in the universe is bought and sold, and why not wind, if the merchant can find purchasers? The earth is rented, from its surface down to its most central mines; — the fire, and the means of feeding it, are currently bought and sold; — the wretches that sweep the boisterous ocean with their nets, pay ransom for the privilege of being drowned in it. What title has the air to be exempted from the universal course of traffic? All above the earth, under the earth, and around the earth, has its price, its sellers, and its purchasers. In many countries the priests will sell you a portion of heaven — in all countries men are willing to buy, in exchange for health, wealth, and peace of conscience, a full allowance of hell. (p. 65)

Basil absorbs Shetland's local economy of fishing into a totalizing state of universal buying and selling in which everything melts into air, in this case wind. His nightmare vision imagines a fully monetized globe where all places are alike in a sort of hypermodern global commercialism whose temporal and spatial homogeneity removes local or national distinctions altogether. Again the origin and materiality of commodities evaporate into a generalized economy.

We might further note that Norna represents one of the novel's very few (albeit lateral) acknowledgements of African slavery. Clement Cleveland (the pirate of the title) describes her as a practitioner of Obeah, a form of West Indian folk magic or medicine: 'a person whom I had frequently seen while in Zetland, and to whom they ascribe the character of a sorceress, or, as the negroes say, an Obi woman' (p. 297). The novel glances at the political realities of an empire built on trade, only to absorb them back into a world in which modern global commerce takes on the insubstantial character of 'primitive' superstition and all enslaved of marginalized subjects disappear from view.

Of particular relevance here is Ian Baucom's exploration (amid a very extensive and multiple study) of what happens in the history of Atlantic slavery when the liberal abolitionist discourse of humane sympathy tries to engage with the abstracting, evaluating force of capital. For Baucom, the example of Scott illustrates what is at stake in the adoption of liberal sympathy as a modern position that is really a kind of transaction with the past. Such a move exchanges the spectator's sympathetic investment in the past for a performance of sympathy itself, and relegates the lessons of that engagement *to* the past: 'Scott figures any time but the time of cosmopolitan capital as wounded and dying, worthy, finally, of no more than a passing expression of sympathy and an honorable burial'.[24] *The Pirate*, as it picks at the fissures of Enlightenment progress, demonstrates continuities between a modern world of abstract commercialism and the primitive superstition that to rescue a drowning person brings bad luck to the rescuer. Acknowledgement of the suffering of the dying or injured is, in *The Pirate*, another Enlightenment ideal squeezed between the twinned forces of the primitive and the modern in which both require a calculated interestedness that excludes the suffering subject.

Such radical interventions of non-chronological time or undivided space haunt the novel and push against the containment of literary form. Arthur Edmonston's complaint that Shetland has not been taken as seriously as more distant islands in the empire identifies a weak point in a strand of imperial writing that calls up the archipelagic structure of Great Britain in order to imagine a global empire linked by patterns of islands. In his study of imperial georgic poetry of the late eighteenth century, Markman Ellis uses this geographical structure to show how the georgic themes of cultivation and civilization underpin economic networks of empire. Ellis points to the way in which geographic homologies came into use to define the continuities between Britain and its empire — the figure of archipelago at the imperial centre could duplicate itself hierarchically across the globe: 'As well as elaborating the individual insularity of the Caribbean islands, this poetry explores ways in which the sugar islands cohere together. This sense of the imperial organization of discrete entities might be described as the archipelagic trope, conceptualizing the empire as a collection of islands in relation to each other.'[25]

As we have seen, the archipelagic structure of Shetland in *The Pirate* is porous and unstable. Rather than tracing geographical patterns, or establishing trade routes, the islands benefit from the haphazard para-economy in which the goods of empire arrive by chance, singular encounters, or extra-legal activities. The pedlar Bryce Snaelsfoot sums up this situation as an unpredictable but providential force that delivers goods, without any seeming material causality at

---

[24] Ian Baucom, *Specters of the Atlantic: Finance Capital, Slavery and the Philosophy of History* (Durham, NC: Duke University Press, 2007), p. 282.

[25] Markman Ellis, '"The Cane-Land Isles": Commerce and Empire in Late Eighteenth-Century Georgic and Pastoral Poetry', in *Islands in History and Representation*, ed. by Rod Edmond and Vanessa Smith (London: Routledge, 2003), pp. 43–62 (p. 55).

all, as he moves through the novel on his 'quiet walk round the country, in the way of trade — making the honest penny, and helping myself with what Providence sends on our coasts' (p. 73).

The Shetland Islands' refusal in *The Pirate* to be incorporated into a fixed geography of world trade echoes Scott's eroding of the generic forms of literature. The novel fits awkwardly into the plot- and character-structure of the national tale, and the genre of the imperial georgic that had underpinned Britain's island empire now becomes the object of scrutiny in a way that robs it of its traditional poetic functions. Georgic traces a movement from the material conditions of working the land, through the metonymic expansion of this labour as economic value, to its metaphoric confirmation as an act of literary cultivation. Studies of Romantic-period georgic cover a wide field in which the mode is either rejected, absorbed into new forms, or allowed to work as a disruptive presence literature.[26] Most immediately relevant here is Samuel Baker's identification of a 'maritime Georgic' that traces the Virgilian synthesis of husbandry and poetic reflection from the eighteenth century into new poetic forms and cultural functions for Britain's maritime empire. Baker argues that Romantic georgic requires a new abstraction that allows writers to transfer the mastery of land into the space — made possible by the technologies of modern navigation — of the global extent of oceans and in doing so 'characterised literary work as in its own right a national tradition of production, one that evoked the land all the more ardently because it spanned the seas'.[27]

The generic home of georgic is poetry and the examples Baker discusses in his study of the absorption of the local in the maritime global are poetic.[28] *The Pirate* takes a step back from exercising the cultural labour of georgic itself to offer a critique of the cultural force of literature from within the structures of the historical novel as it adapts the influences of the national tale. More precisely,

[26] Kevis Goodman argues that eighteenth-century georgic self-consciously mediates the work it represents. The act of reading does not duplicate the labour it describes, but rather generates forms of affect that disrupt access to history; it gives rise to experiences that take place in the present but that cannot be fully articulated as historical experience. Goodman's emphasis on the reading experience is beyond the scope of this essay, but it is relevant that georgic, for Goodman, is another kind of troubled present, one that she calls 'the presentness of ongoing history beyond lived experience, or phenomenological verification'. *Georgic Modernity and British Romanticism: Poetry and the Mediation of History* (Cambridge: Cambridge University Press, 2004), p. 64.

[27] Samuel Baker, *Written on the Water: British Romanticism and the Maritime Culture of Empire* (Charlottesville: University of Virginia Press, 2010), p. 83.

[28] Later commentators have rarely taken up Ralph Cohen's 1974 contestation that 'georgic form becomes a literary genre for exploring man's experience, and it leads to prose works such as the novel [...] that embody the exploratory variety of the new georgic'. *Literature and History: Papers Read at a Clark Library Seminar* (Los Angeles: William Andrews Clark Memorial Library, 1974), p. 5. Gabrielle Starr discusses the relationship between the novel and georgic, but in terms of the movement of the novel into poetry. *Lyric Generations: Poetry and the Novel in the Long Eighteenth Century* (Baltimore, MD: Johns Hopkins University Press, 2004), pp. 177–79.

Scott re-imagines and puts under scrutiny georgic as a once-classical and universal mode that harmonizes land, literature and cultivation to assess its uses in the contemporary genre of the national tale. In *The Pirate*, Scott undercuts the national tale's interest in the improvement of the land by filtering it through the lens of georgic.

The Pirate is shot through with Virgilian references, but ones which work against the associated harmonizing of agriculture, sea-faring, and the sphere of literature. The twinned georgic forms of agricultural and artistic meditation are comically pulled apart and represented by two different characters. Triptolemus Yellowley, a factor or land agent on the islands, is an improver, named after the classical inventor of the plough and given to 'thumbing his old school-copy of Virgil' (p. 40), but one whose efforts bear very little fruit, despite his having learned the *Georgics* off by heart. He complains that no one makes any money out of improvement and all his schemes for better roads, new horticulture and modern agricultural implements come to nothing. He mismanages his Virgilian notion of importing bees into Shetland (they all die), a motif that operates in the novel on at least three levels. In a literal sense, it works against the forward historical momentum of improvement driven by the importation of knowledge to the margins from a metropolitan centre. And this is underscored by the association with Mandeville's *Fable of the Bees* with its early Enlightenment ideas about openly cooperative commercial societies and legible economic structures, both of which are notably weak in *The Pirate*'s Shetlandic society. More widely, the isolation of georgic as a comic object within *The Pirate* presses up against the novel's own status as a literary artefact.

We are reminded again how *The Pirate* plays with its own historiography, and uses its 'marginal' geography not to bind the outlying parts of Britain to its centre in the present, but to disrupt its own relation to the historical past. It is set in a period that had been of considerable interest to Scott, who had edited the complete works of Dryden, published in 1808 with a second edition appearing in 1821 as he was composing *The Pirate*. In the 'Life of Dryden' that introduced the edition Scott identifies the period around 1688 as a new opportunity for literature to become absorbed into civic life:

> Instances began to occur of individuals, who rising at first into notice for their proficience in the fine arts, were finally promoted for their active and penetrating talents, which necessarily accompany a turn towards them.[29]

In *The Pirate* no such 'necessary' turn is evident. Although Dryden does feature in the novel as the obsession of the local self-appointed bard, Claude Halcro, this preoccupation, like Triptolemus's interest in Virgil, has no homologous correspondence with the novel itself. That is, instead of exemplifying

---

[29] 'Life of Dryden', in *Works of John Dryden*, 18 vols (London: William Miller 1808), I, 386.

ways in which literature and social development are coterminous and mutually supportive, the literary instances from the seventeenth century remain isolated and functionless. Halcro's knowledge of Dryden has no agency in the novel, and he is soon co-opted by the other characters to address Norna in her pseudo-runic verse that testifies to her madness. Georgic, the genre which should gather and repair all the novel's inconstancies (the relation of land to sea and, and of both to literary contemplation) is overwhelmed by a crazed version of Romance.[30]

In more general terms, a clear historico-political discourse cannot take root in the novel because the time, in Shetland, is out of joint. As we have seen with its early adoption of global commodities, Shetland is both more ancient and more modern than the rest of Scotland. And the principal spokesman for the linear, forward-looking temporality of improvement, Triptolemus Yellowley, is himself caught in a strange form of dislocated time. Yellowley expresses the intention 'to introduce into the *Ultima Thule* of the Romans, a spirit of improvement, which at that early period was scarce known to exist in Scotland itself' (p. 29). In his own words, he collapses three different temporalities into each other and the narrator explicitly tells us that Triptolemus is premature, embodying modernity as a kind of living anachronism who has 'come into the world a century too soon':

> it is plain that Triptolemus Yellowley had been shaken out of the bag at least a hundred years too soon. If he had come on the stage in our own time, that is, if he had flourished at any time within these thirty or forty years, he could not have missed to have held the office of vice-president of some eminent agricultural society, and to have transacted all the business thereof under the auspices of some noble duke or lord. (p. 35)

Modernity here is not the product of gradual, stadial change but of ruptures and discontinuities.[31] Triptolemus is not only ahead of his own time, he would also, the narrator insists, seem a strikingly modern figure at the time of the novel's publication. Fictional time, it seems, is not subject to the incremental progress of Enlightenment historical time, and this brings us to the kind of novel that *The Pirate* represents: one that works against literary ways of containing its geographical and temporal fluidity. If we accept that the novel as a genre has a crucial role in proposing, repeating, and testing the space of the nation, then *The Pirate* has a complex relation to British national temporality. As we have seen,

---

[30] Chad T. May's reading of the novel moves away from the distinction between history and romance to identify its historiography as a traumatic resurrection of the past in the present, figured particularly in treatment of Norna's own violent past. '"The Horrors of My Tale": Trauma, the Historical Imagination and Sir Walter Scott', *Pacific Coast Philology*, 4.1 (2005), 98–116.

[31] Catherine Jones argues that the novel provides 'a case study of a society that is still at an early stage of development, before the division of labour and before allodial tenures are converted into feudal' but that this stadial approach is disrupted by popular memory. *Literary Memory: Scott's Waverley Novels and the Psychology of Narrative* (Lewisburg, PA: Bucknell University Press, 2003), p. 91.

the novel does not easily accommodate itself to the spatial-historical dimensions of a chronotope at all. A chronotope, involving the organization of time and space and their mutual dependency in fictional narrative, should be governed by genre and vice versa, but where the generic contours of a work of fiction are as unstable as they are in *The Pirate* no clear space-time world emerges. Britain's northernmost islands slip out of the containing frame of the nation as they do from the narrative structures of the historical novel and its associate form, the national tale, to form wider and less fixed allegiances with other parts of the world. Scott's visits, in person and fiction, both inhabit shifting temporalities or presents that integrate only unevenly — if at all — the causal past of history or the telos of the historical novel that knows the future of its own narrative. As he recalls his own imperfect investment in past antiquities and future improvement from the Lighthouse Diary, Scott reinvents the incommensurable as a form of fictional temporality.

Scott, India and Australia

GRAHAM TULLOCH
Flinders University

In 1822 Walter Scott wrote to Lord Montagu:

> In giving up Indian appointments Lord Mellville consults admirably for his own convenience but I scarce see how it is compatible with his situation as minister for Scotland. Our younger children are as naturally exported to India as our black cattle were sent to England before the Southron renounced eating roast-beef which seems to be the case this year.[1]

This is only one of many references to India in the context of imperial patronage to be found in Scott's letters and indeed he had expressed the same idea in almost the same words to the same correspondent the year before.[2] Against this we might set one of the few comments in his letters concerning Australia, made to his friend Adam Ferguson in 1819: 'By the bye Old Kennedy the tinker swam for his life at Jedburgh and was only by the sophisticated & timid evidence of a seceding Doctor [...] saved from a well deserved gibbet. He goes to Botanize for fourteen years.'[3]

We might be tempted to see these comments, in both their content and tone and in their degree of frequency in his correspondence, as reflecting a great difference between India and Australia in Scott's personal connections with the two places. However, somewhat surprisingly, even taking into account the fact that India was not, like New South Wales, a penal colony, and the further fact that the British had been in India for centuries whereas they had colonized Australia within Scott's own life time, Scott's personal relations with India and Australia are remarkably similar in kind, though not in quantity. They take place in the same context of patronage and influence that we see so clearly in his comment about Lord Melville. On the other hand when we turn to Scott's imaginative involvement with the two countries through his writing we find a very different picture: India figures quite prominently in his fiction with one novel, *The Surgeon's Daughter*, set in part there, and two others, *Guy Mannering* and *Saint Ronan's Well*, with important characters who have returned from

---

[1] Scott to Lord Montagu, *Letters of Sir Walter Scott*, ed. by H. J. C. Grierson, 12 vols (London: Constable, 1932–1937), VII, 185 (June 1822).

[2] Scott to Lord Montagu, *Letters*, VI, 489 (1 July 1821).

[3] Scott to Adam Ferguson, *Letters*, V, 356 (16 April 1819).

Yearbook of English Studies, 47 (2017), 263–278
© Modern Humanities Research Association 2017

India. But in all Scott's published writing I have found only one passage on Australia, curiously enough tucked into his account of Scottish history in his *Tales of a Grandfather.*

A number of critics have written about various aspects of Scott's imaginative and personal engagement with India.[4] By contrast very little has been written about Scott's engagement with Australia.[5] In this article I propose to compare Scott's well documented and discussed engagement with India with his almost totally ignored engagement with Australia. My discussion begins with India and then proceeds to Australia before offering some comments on the similarities and differences between the roles played by the two places in Scott's life and works.

First, India. Scott had very strong personal connections with India from early in his life. His brother-in-law Charles Carpenter lived and died in India and he had a number of other relatives who went there. He even contemplated going there himself, writing to his brother: 'were Dundas to go out Governor to India & were he willing to take me with him in a good situation I would not hesitate'.[6] However, there is no better example of Scott's personal engagement with India than the case of the poet and oriental scholar John Leyden.[7] Indeed, as Brown has noted, it is not only 'instructive' but also 'moving'.[8] Thus in June 1801 Scott writes to his friend George Ellis that 'Some prospect seems to open for getting Leyden out to India, under the patronage of Mackintosh, who goes as chief of the intended academical establishment at Calcutta', and six months later tells

---

[4] Iain Gordon Brown, 'Griffins, Nabobs and a Seasoning of Curry Powder: Walter Scott and the Indian Theme in Life and Literature', in Anne Buddle with Pauline Rohangi and Iain Gordon Brown, *The Tiger and the Thistle: Tipu Sultan and the Scots in India, 1760–1800* (Edinburgh: National Gallery of Scotland, 1999), pp. 71–79; Peter Garside, 'Meg Merrilies, the Gypsies, and India', in *Scott in Carnival*, ed. by J. H. Alexander and David Hewitt (Aberdeen: Association for Scottish Literary Studies, 1993), pp. 154–71; Claire Lamont, 'Scott and Eighteenth-Century Imperialism: India and the Scottish Highlands', in *Configuring Romanticism: Essays Offered to C. C. Barfoot*, ed. by Theo D'haen (New York: Rodopi, 2003), pp. 35–50 and 'Historical Note to "The Surgeon's Daughter"', in Walter Scott, *Chronicles of the Canongate*, ed. by Claire Lamont, EEWN (Edinburgh: Edinburgh University Press, 2000), pp. 444–55; and Tara Ghoshal Wallace, 'The Elephant's Foot and the British Mouth: Walter Scott on Imperial Rhetoric', *European Romantic Review*, 13 (2002), 311–24. (Brown in particular covers some of the same territory as the first half of the present article.)

[5] For discussion of some aspects of Scott's involvement with Australia see Graham Tulloch, 'Scott and Australia', *Bulletin of the Edinburgh Sir Walter Scott Club* (2007), 16–27, and Graham Tulloch, 'Scott, the Bushranger, and the Bandit', in *'Whaddaya Know?' Writings for Syd Harrex*, ed. by Ron Blaber (Mile End, SA: Wakefield Press, 2015), pp. 14–26.

[6] Scott to Thomas Scott, *Letters*, VII, 452 (1 November 1810).

[7] The case of Leyden is more fully documented than any other and it was one that was particularly close to Scott's heart. For this reason I follow Brown's lead in treating Leyden's case as the preeminent example of Scott's personal engagement with India: see his 'Griffins, Nabobs and a Seasoning of Curry Powder', pp. 75–76.

[8] Brown, 'Griffins, Nabobs and a Seasoning of Curry Powder', p. 75.

Ellis that 'Mr. William Dundas was so good as to promise his interest to get him appointed Secretary to the Institution', and then finally another two months later, the original plan having fallen through, he writes 'I am pleasantly interrupted by the post; he brings me a letter from William Dundas, fixing Leyden's appointment as an assistant-surgeon to one of the India settlements'.[9] Having used his influence with Dundas, Scott then proposes to use it in another direction, telling Leyden, now in Madras, 'Lord Minto is finally to go out as Governor General [of India]. You know that he is one of my most intimate friends in that rank of life. I intend to press your pursuits and person very strongly on his notice before he leaves Europe. He is a man of taste & literature; so pray arrange matters so as to keep in his way'.[10] No letter of this tenor to Lord Minto survives but Scott clearly did write to him, since in January 1809 Minto reported to Scott that

> I am particularly happy in having fixed Leyden by my side, and am enjoying with equal admiration, though of different kinds, his extraordinary talents and his spirited, independent, and estimable character. I have taken the best care I can of his fortunes, and hope one day to see his wandering staff planted in some Teviot haugh, and the wanderer himself under its shade in resting his age amongst the 'Scenes of Infancy.' Those scenes are the object to both our longings [...] though it is not wise to strain either eyes or wishes at distant prospects. I shall hope to find you still haunting and singing those streams which are to me more sacred than the waters of the Ganges to their Hindoo votaries.[11]

Scott had in the meantime heard news of Leyden but not received a letter: in December 1808 he had written to Ellis that

> a gentleman recently arrived from India has brought us most pleasing news of John Leyden with two characteristick remembrances for me. A book on the Indo-Chinese tribes [...] & a Malay cris beautifully mounted & embrued [...] in poison as fatal as that of the Upas. No letter however, but very pleasant accounts both of the wild sage's fortune & reputation.[12]

Despite fretting over not hearing directly from Leyden, Scott did receive one letter written in January 1810 from Calcutta. Leyden writes that he is not sending a full letter but 'merely a note to accompany a Dissertation on the Chinese language by Mr Marshman, one of the missionaries of Serampore'. He reports that Minto's patronage was crucial in having the book published and tells Scott that 'Lord Minto has gained himself immortal glory here by patronizing with energy every useful species of literature, and is generally admitted to be the finest

[9] Scott to George Ellis, *Letters*, I, 116, 124, 133 (10 June 1801; 8 December, 1801; 14 February 1802).

[10] Scott to John Leyden, *Letters*, I, 309 (5 July 1806).

[11] Lord Minto to Scott, *Familiar Letters of Sir Walter Scott*, ed. by David Douglas, 2 vols (Edinburgh: David Douglas, 1894), I, 157–58 (12 January 1809).

[12] Scott to George Ellis, *Letters*, XII, 308–09 (13 December 1808).

private character of a Governor that India ever saw'. He also tells Scott that he has been 'digging away like a Turkish galley-slave in the Oriental mines [...] and I have great progression in a history of Persian poetry'.[13] There can be no doubt of Scott's pleasure in receiving such reports of his protégé's success and such a glowing testament to the activities of his own childhood friend. However, not content with his success in India, Leyden moved on to Penang and eventually died in a British attack on Batavia (modern Jakarta). Even after his death the theme of patronage continues with Scott writing, this time to his brother-in-law, that 'Lord Minto has done great credit to himself by patronizing poor Leyden while alive & honouring his memory when no more'.[14]

Elements of this story which are typical of Scott's personal engagement with India include his active involvement in finding Leyden a place in India and then promoting his career with a letter to the governing powers, his receiving letters from Leyden and the Governor-General, the arrival of presents sent by Leyden from India, and the final unhappy ending to Leyden's story. Features of this story are replicated in others. For instance, it was the successful use of his influence that procured positions for his nephew (another Walter Scott), for his cousin, Patrick Meik, and for the poet Allan Cunningham's two sons, and as regards gifts of Indian origin he received from David MacCulloch, formerly a merchant in Bengal, the gift of a sword which was claimed to be that of Tipu Sultan.[15] Sadly, his letters also record the deaths in India of Richard Lockhart, his son-in-law's brother, and of the brothers Hugh and John Scott (sons of Francis Scott of Beechwood and his distant cousins) who died in India within a month of each other, as well as the death on his way back from India of the eldest son of his friend William Adam of Blairadam.[16]

Given all this it is perhaps not surprising that Scott had mixed feelings about India as a destination for Scotland's sons (and daughters). When his elder son, Walter, hoped to go to India with his regiment Scott opposed it resolutely:

> in the Kings service [...] you can get neither experience in your profession nor credit nor wealth nor anything but an obscure death in storming the hill fort of some Rajah with an unpronounceable name [...] or if you live it is but to come back 20 years hence a lieutenant or captain with a yellow face a diseased liver and not a rupee in your pocket to comfort you for broken health.[17]

---

[13] John Leyden to Scott, *Familiar Letters*, I, 161, 163 (10 January 1810).

[14] Scott to Charles Carpenter, *Letters*, III, 341 (3 September 1813).

[15] Scott to David MacCulloch, *Letters*, IX, 103, 104n (3 May 1825). For a discussion of the collection of Tipu memorabilia after his defeat, including the sword given to Scott, see Maya Jasanoff, *Edge of Empire: Lives, Culture, and Conquest of the East, 1750–1850* (New York: Knopf, 2005), pp. 177–96.

[16] Scott to Anne Scott, *Letters*, X, 214 (18 May 1827); Scott to the Duke of Buccleuch, *Letters*, V, 353 (15 April 1819); Scott to Sir William Knighton. *Letters*, IX, 327 (7 December 1825).

[17] Scott to Walter Scott (his son), *Letters*, VI, 433 (1 May 1821).

When his other son Charles was offered a place as a lawyer in India Scott promptly had the offer postponed and ensured that Charles never went, and when the daughters of his dead friend William Erskine planned to go to India Scott offered only reluctant approval because he could not see any other path for them.[18] Evidently the experience of so many deaths amongst those he had sponsored to go there had cooled his enthusiasm for India as a place of opportunity.

On the other hand, while Leyden and others died in the East, others returned and meeting them provided Scott with another kind of personal engagement with India. Even in his early life he would have met William Russell, his uncle, who returned from India in 1783 when Scott was twelve. Later in life he records meeting 'Mr Impey, son of that Sir Elijah celebrated in Indian history' who 'has himself been in India' and 'the fine old veteran General Gowdie: he lives about three miles from us' (and was in India until 1812) as well as mentioning 'the return of our cousin Colonel Russell from India overland' and, most important of all, the arrival from India of James Ferguson, brother of his friend Adam: James, 'an excellent importation [...] to Tweedside' was later to provide him with information for *The Surgeon's Daughter*.[19]

So much for Scott's personal relations with India; his literary engagement also began in his early years. In his memoir of his early life he tells us that he delighted in romances and poetry but also in military history and, when he was at the age of fifteen forced to remain silent in bed,

in this dreary and silent solitude I fell upon the resource of illustrating the battles I read of by the childish expedient of arranging shells and seeds and pebbles so as to represent encountering armies. [...] I fought my way thus through Vertot's Knights of Malta, a book which as it hovered between history and romance was exceedingly dear to me and Orme's interesting and beautiful history of Indostan where copious plans aided by the clear and luminous explanations of the author rendered my imitative amusement peculiarly easy.[20]

Orme's *History of the Military Transactions of the British Nation in Indostan* (1763) provided Scott, as its title suggests, with a British imperial view of India concentrating on the achievements of British soldiers but significantly it also began with 'A Dissertation on the Establishments made by Mahomedan Conquerors in Indostan' which introduced him to the earlier triumphs of the Mughal emperors. However, as Claire Lamont points out in her edition of *The Surgeon's Daughter*, Scott had relatively few books on India in his library. One

[18] Scott to Alexander Young, *Letters*, x, 327 (5 December 1827).

[19] See *The Journal of Sir Walter Scott*, ed. by W. E. K. Anderson (Oxford: Clarendon Press, 1972), p. 191; Scott to Charles Carpenter, *Letters*, III, 151 (4 August 1812); Scott to Mrs Thomas Scott, *Letters*, IX, 282 (6 November 1825); Scott to Lord Montagu, *Letters*, VIII, 50 (17 July 1823).

[20] *Scott on Himself*, ed. by David Hewitt (Edinburgh: Scottish Academic Press, 1981), pp. 34–35.

book that he did possess was the anonymous *Narrative Sketches of the Conquest of the Mysore, effected by the British Troops and their Allies, in the Capture of Seringapatam, and the Death of Tippoo Sultaun* published in 1800. Tipu's death seems to have fascinated Scott (in this he was not alone) and he admired the 'dogged spirit of resolution which induced Tippoo Saib to die manfully upon the breach of his capital city with his sabre clenched in his hand'.[21] Later, as we have seen, Scott came into possession of Tipu's sword.

When Scott came to write *The Surgeon's Daughter* he could draw on all these resources but, as Lamont suggests, 'it may be a mistake to put too much stress on reading' as he had substantial oral resources at hand.[22] In creating the plot of *The Surgeon's Daughter*, he combined two stories from oral tradition. The germ of the novel was a story told to him by his regular informant Joseph Train. Train recorded that he had 'related to Sir Walter at his table in North Castle Street, the story of a Fifeshire Surgeon's daughter, which pleased him so much that the said, "Well, Mr Train you never run out of excellent stories"'.[23] The story was of a young man of Fife who brought his fiancée out to India intending to hand her over to 'a native rajah [who] was waiting the arrival of the fair maid of Fife, with whom he had fallen deeply in love, from seeing her miniature likeness'.[24] However Scott combined Train's story with another story — that a portrait of Elizabeth Welwood, wife of Allan Maconochie, Lord Meadowbank, was found in Tipu's bedroom after his defeat and death. Lord Meadowbank's son was Scott's friend, and the man who allegedly found the portrait, Sir David Baird, was Scott's son's commanding officer.[25] It seems likely that Scott heard this story from his friend or possibly, through his son, from Baird. Another important source was Colonel James Ferguson who, after his return from India, in 1823, had settled in Scotland at Huntlyburn, a house on Scott's Abbotsford estate. As he approached the end of *The Surgeon's Daughter* and the scene shifted from Britain to India, Scott felt he needed Ferguson's help: 'I cannot go on with the tale without I could speak a little Hindhanee, a small seasoning of curry powder — Fergusson will do it if I can screw it out of him'.[26] Ferguson duly provided some written material that Scott, describing it as 'highly picturesque', incorporated directly into his novel.[27]

---

[21] Scott to Robert Southey, *Letters*, III, 451 (17 June 1814).

[22] Lamont, 'Historical Note to "The Surgeon's Daughter"', p. 452.

[23] Quoted in Lamont, 'Historical Note to "The Surgeon's Daughter"', p. 445.

[24] From Train's written narrative; quoted in Lamont, 'Historical Note to "The Surgeon's Daughter"', p. 445.

[25] See Lamont, 'Historical Note to "The Surgeon's Daughter"', p. 451.

[26] *Journal*, p. 343.

[27] *Journal*, p. 354. For a discussion of Scott's use of Ferguson's material see Lamont, 'Historical Note to "The Surgeon's Daughter"', pp. 453–54.

The novel as finally completed falls very much within the world of influence and patronage and the export of Scotland's sons and daughters to India which I have described as being Scott's own world of personal connection with India. The hero, Adam Hartley, wins a place in India as a surgeon on an East India Company ship through a cousin of his mother and the villain, Richard Middlemas, goes to India under the sponsorship of a General who formerly served there. They enter the world of British India, so familiar to Scott through the accounts of family and friends. The familiarity of this world is further reflected in the preliminary matter where the supposed author of the novel, Chrystal Croftangry, who of all Scott's fictional narrators is the one most closely aligned with him, is told by the supposed source of the story, the lawyer Fairscribe, that he should choose an Indian subject for his story, or as Fairscribe puts it, echoing Scott's own words,

> I think you might do with your Muse of Fiction, as you call her, as many an honest man does with his own sons in flesh and blood. [...] Send her to India [...]. That is the true place for a Scot to thrive in; and if you carry your story fifty years back, [...] [t]hen, for great exploits, you have in the old history of India, before Europeans were numerous there, the most wonderful deeds, done by the least possible means, that perhaps the annals of the world can afford.[28]

To which Croftangry enthusiastically responds, this time himself echoing Scott, 'I remember in the delightful pages of Orme, the interest which mingles in his narratives, from the very small number of English which are engaged. Each officer of a regiment becomes known to you by name, nay, the non-commissioned officers and privates acquire an individual share of interest'.[29]

All this is familiar. But Scott added another element. Joseph Train's original story, it will be recalled, was of 'a native rajah'. The term *rajah* is neutral as to religion but might suggest a Hindu more than a Muslim. By combining Train's narrative with the story of the portrait found in Tipu's bedroom, he identifies the ruler specifically as Tipu, a Muslim. There is nothing particularly unhistorical or inappropriate about Scott portraying India as a world dominated by Muslims — he was writing, after all, of a time when the Muslim Mughal emperor in Delhi was still a significant figure in the north of India and Tipu and his father Haider Ali were dominant Muslim rulers in the south. Nevertheless, as Claire Lamont has pointed out, having his Scottish protagonists enter a Muslim India allowed Scott to introduce one of his recurrent preoccupations, the confrontation of Christian and Muslim.[30] He had already explored the contrast of Christians and

---

[28] Scott, *Chronicles of the Canongate*, ed. by Lamont, p. 155.
[29] Ibid.
[30] As Lamont notes, 'Scott does not deploy the contrasts which became the hallmark of Anglo-Indian fiction: the triangular relations between Hindu, Muslim and Westerner. [...] Scott was therefore able to write within the tradition of Christian-Muslim writing since the Renaissance,

Muslims in *The Talisman* by having Richard Coeur-de-Lion meet Saladin and he was to explore it again by setting the Grand Master of the Knights of St John against Mustapha Pacha, the commander of the Ottoman forces, in his last, unpublished, novel *The Siege of Malta*, which incidentally drew heavily on the other book he remembered, along with Orme, from his childhood days of 'dreary and silent solitude'—Vertot's history of the Knights of Malta. In both cases Scott presents sympathetic Muslims, as he now did in *The Surgeon's Daughter*. By using a setting in Muslim India he is able to view his story through this familiar lens and present his outrightly Christian hero in contrast to a wily but ultimately honourable Muslim adversary. In this way he expands the original rather limited tale to take in a theme of much wider significance. At the same time he ends his novel very much within the world of British India which he knew so well. After the execution of Middlemas under the foot of an elephant, perhaps the most dramatic (or melodramatic) death in his writing, Scott has the perfect opportunity to end his story, as he did so many of his novels, with the marriage of the hero with the maiden he has saved, in this case from the harem of an Eastern monarch. Instead he sends her safely home to Scotland where she never marries and has the hero Hartley die a few years later 'a victim to his professional courage, in withstanding the progress of a contagious distemper, which he at length caught, and under which he sunk'.[31] Like so many of those Scott had seen go out to India, including Leyden, Hartley does not return. Perhaps it was in tribute to Leyden's fate that Scott chose this ending.

If Hartley does not return, several returned 'Indians' feature prominently in Scott's writing, most notably Guy Mannering and Harry Bertram in *Guy Mannering* and Peregrine Touchwood in *Saint Ronan's Well*. While his varying portrayal of these figures reveals much about Scott's attitudes to the imperial enterprise in India, as Tara Ghoshal Wallace in particular has argued, they are not of immediate concern here since my focus in this article is on Scott's direct representation of India itself.[32]

Let us turn now to Australia. Scott's personal connections with Australia were at all levels: he corresponded with two governors, Lachlan Macquarie and Sir Thomas Brisbane (the latter married to his fourth cousin), and received letters from two convicts and from two free settlers whom he had sponsored. No one case can illustrate all aspects of Scott's involvement with Australia but the story of George Harper has several typical features, including Scott's active sponsorship in writing to the governor of the colony, Harper's letters from Australia with reports on his success and praise of the governor, and gifts of Australian

acknowledging that they are both worthy belief systems, which uphold justice and moral ideals' ('Scott and Eighteenth Century Imperialism', p. 40).

[31] *Chronicles of the Canongate*, ed. by Lamont, p. 285.

[32] Wallace, 'The Elephant's Foot and the British Mouth'.

curiosities. These features parallel many in Scott's India experience but without the tragic ending of so many of the Indian stories.

In 1820 Harper set off for New South Wales as a free settler with a parcel of Scott's books and a letter of introduction for Governor Macquarie. Scott's letter to Macquarie has not survived but it is evident from Macquarie's reply that Scott had asked Macquarie if he could procure him a copy of the life of the Tasmanian bushranger Michael Howe, published in Hobart in 1818. Macquarie thought the small booklet he was sending Scott was a poor recompense for a box of books by the most widely read novelist of the time:

> I cannot express to you how much I feel pleased and flattered by your kind remembrance of me; and I feel particularly obliged and gratified by the honor you have done me in sending me a Present of your valuable and most interesting Works which I greatly prize, and hope one day [to] ornament my Library with *in the Isle of Mull* where I should be most happy and proud to receive and welcome their Author. —
>
> I regret I have not now any thing to send you in return for this kindness that would be acceptable; but since you have asked for it, I now do myself the pleasure of sending you herewith the History of Michael Howe the Bush Ranger of Van Diemen's Land; but I hope soon to be able to collect for you a better History of him and the Bush-Ranging System in that Island.[33]

Ironically, *Michael Howe, the last and worst of the Bush Rangers of Van Diemen's Land: Narrative of the Chief Atrocities committed by this Great Murderer and his Associates, during a Period of Six Years, in Van Diemen's Land*, printed by Andrew Bent in Hobart in 1818, is now an extremely rare book (only four copies, including Scott's, are known to exist) and its current value far exceeds what Scott sent to Macquarie. The incident closely parallels one from Scott's dealings with India: in writing to Lord Minto in 1808 to recommend his brother-in-law, Charles Carpenter, Scott had sent him a copy of *Marmion* which was due to appear a few days later.[34] Evidently Scott felt that copies of his books were a useful tool for encouraging patronage for his protégés.

Soon after arriving in New South Wales Harper reported to Scott, 'I have Dined several times at Government House and I always experience great kindness both from the Governor and Mrs Macquarie'. According to him 'this is certainly a very fine country and an excellent opportunity for any young man who is sober and Industrious but an awful place I am sorry to say for Theives and Vagabonds'. Finally he asks Scott to 'accept a few Australian seeds which may perhaps be a rarity in Sco[tland]'.[35] Interestingly, Scott describes the seeds

---

[33] Lachlan Macquarie to Scott, NLS MS 3893, fols 165ʳ–66ʳ (24 November 1821).

[34] Scott to Lord Minto, NLS MS 11149, fols 8–9 (16 February 1808). For the publication of *Marmion* see William B. Todd and Ann Bowden, *Sir Walter Scott: A Bibliographical History, 1796–1832* (New Castle, DE: Oak Knoll Press, 1998), p. 87.

[35] George Harper to Scott, NLS MS 3893, fols 41ʳ–42ʳ (14 August 1821).

as having been 'sent me in gratitude by an honest gentleman who had once run some risque of being himself pendulous on a tree in this country' suggesting that Harper had been in some trouble before leaving Scotland.[36] Six months later Harper tells Scott that he has 'received a Grant of Land of Four hundred acres in a beautiful part of the Country which I have named Abbotsford', and makes an offer: 'I should feel great pleasure in Sending you a Brace of Black Swans, Emus or Kangaroos either of which I can procure for you.'[37]

Five years later Harper returned to Scotland with a present, to the great consternation of Scott who immediately wrote to his publisher, Robert Cadell:

> One Mr Harper who went as a settler (not at government expence) to New South Wales thinking himself more obliged to me than perhaps he really was has brought over two Emusses for my special use and acceptance. Now I knew [no] more what an Emuss was like than what a Phoenix was like but supposed them some sort of large parrots & thought they would hang well enough in the hall amongst the armour. But they prove to be six feet high and being akin [...] to your ostrich may be cursedly mischievous besides expence & trouble. [...] Do for gods sake [...] try to get me free of the Emusses.[38]

Eventually Cadell relieved Scott of this exotic burden by passing them on to the Duke of Buccleuch. By contrast, Scott was much happier with a gift from a 'friend from the famous settlement of New South Wales', consisting of 'a little parrot [who] has for a parrot a very soft voice [and] whistles especially when Anne takes the harp or guittar'.[39]

In his dealings with Australia we once again see Scott operating within the context of imperial patronage, although in a less fully developed system than in India. Several features of Harper's story are replicated in other cases of Scott's dealings with Australia. For instance, though his letter does not survive, he evidently also wrote to Macquarie about a convict, Ebenezer Knox, who had been convicted of possessing forged notes and had been sentenced to transportation for fourteen years. Like Harper, Knox sent his thanks to Scott from 'New South Wails' (as he spells it) but in very different style:

> I am gratly to blame in not acknowg the happiness I enjoy through your humane letter in my favour to the Governor Macquarie who is like you a gentleman distinguished for humanity to the unfortunate, permit me Sir to return you the thanks of a gratful heart for all your goodness [...] I am the Principal Suptd of an Agricultueral establishment of Govt three miles from Sydney the Captial of this collney in discharge of that duty by introducing im-Provements in the above

---

[36] I assume that the 'Botany Bay plants & seeds' that 'have had wet on the voyage' and which Scott offered to forward to Lady Montagu were Harper's. See Scott to Lord Montagu, *Letters*, VII, 99 (14 and 15 March 1822). Scott's receipt of them in mid-March 1822 would fit with Harper sending the seeds in August 1821.

[37] George Harper to Scott, NLS MS 3894, fol. 59ʳ (14 February 1822).

[38] Scott to Robert Cadell, *Letters*, x, 255–56 (12 July 1827).

[39] Scott to Jane Scott of Lochore, *Letters*, x, 378 (8 February 1808).

branch I have given every satisfaction to those in pour which is aknoleged to surpass any thing of that kind seen in this Collney before, But my situation is more respectable then Luctrive, I have a very small Selery for the extensive business I have to manage but I expect to get that mended soon by a free Pardon which the Governor has promised me before he leves this cuntrey and that is expected very soon as we here that Sir Thos. Brisbane is appointed Governor here, and is expected shortley If this shoud reach you before he leves England a letter from you to him would be of infinet service to me. [...] This is a plisent cuntrey there is no winter and [...] every thing that Grows in Europe thrives well here.[40]

Not content with writing to Macquarie on Knox's behalf, Scott took up Knox's hint and also wrote to his successor, Brisbane, describing himself as uncertain 'whether to condole or congratulate you upon your lonely reign so much exceeding in extent that of many monarchs famed in history' and telling him that

[t]here is in your dominions [...] one Ebenezer Knox [who] found his way to Australasia at the governments expense having been guilty of accession to forgery. He is a very good farmer and [of] a very clever family and if his moral obligations have been put to rights by the new situation in which he is placed and inclined him as the sailors say to take a fresh departure I think you will find him a very useful person.[41]

Evidently Brisbane had some doubts about Knox and replied to Scott that 'in regard Ebenezer Knox the least said soonest mended'.[42] Brisbane's doubts were well founded: Knox was convicted of cattle theft in 1835 and died while serving a life sentence in 1847.

Scott's support for another convict, the poet Andrew Stewart, provides us with a parallel to his support for the poet John Leyden. Stewart had published several poems in the *Scots Magazine* before falling into poverty and robbing the home of a calico merchant as an accomplice to his brother and another man. He was condemned to death and wrote to Scott pleading for help. Scott intervened and Stewart's sentence was commuted to transportation to New South Wales for life. A much less distinguished poet than Leyden, Stewart followed him in writing poetry once he had left Scotland and even managed to publish a couple of poems in the *Hobart Town Gazette*. Unlike Leyden, however, Stewart lived into his sixties rather than dying at a tragically early age.[43]

---

[40] Ebenezer Knox to Scott, NLS MS 3892, fols 146^r–47^r (1 June 1821).

[41] Scott to Thomas Brisbane, State Library of New South Wales, Sir Thomas Makdougall Brisbane Papers 1818–1849, Volume 1A: Correspondence Mainly Letters Received 1818–1841, pp. 90–91 (15 July 1824).

[42] Thomas Brisbane to Scott, NLS MS 3900, fol. 286^r (25 June 1825).

[43] Another convict supported by Scott was John Smith who wrote to Scott in November 1825 thanking him for his help in obtaining a pardon. Scott endorsed the letter as from Andrew Stewart but the date of the pardon and the handwriting suggest this is not from Stewart. For more information see Graham Tulloch, 'Andrew Stewart, Poet and Convict', *Studies in Hogg and his World*, 25–26 (2015–16), 66–82.

The case of Andrew Murray is slightly different in that Scott helped him earlier in his career and was not directly responsible for his reception in Australia. However it was Scott's initial support that set him on a career path that led ultimately to Australia. Harper's gift of seeds is paralleled in a similar gift from Murray, as Scott recorded in his journal in September 1826:

> Received a box of Australian seeds forwarded by Andrew Murray, now Head-Gardener to the governor, whom I detected a clever boy among my labourers in 1812, and did a little for him. It is pleasant to see men thrive and be grateful at the same time, so good luck to Andro Mora, as we calld him.[44]

The 'little' which Scott had done was in fact to write to Lord Somerville seeking a position for Murray. Somerville replied that Murray might find employment with 'Gibbs the great Seedsman in London [...] a capital Gardiner and Florist' and 'two years employ in his House might qualify Murray to earn a more cert[tai]n livelihood because he will then have two strings to his bow Farming and Gardining'.[45] Murray took the position and wrote from London to thank Scott; on receiving his letter Scott endorsed it: 'I sent this young man to London to be out of bad family example. Mark if he cross the proverb "A hawk of a bad nest"'.[46] He also replied to Murray, carefully explaining how Murray should behave in the context of the patronage Scott had obtained for him (just as he had enjoined Leyden to 'arrange matters so as to keep in Lord Minto's way'):

> You ought to call on Lord Somerville when you conveniently can & let his servant know that you come to return your thanks & pay your duty to his Lordship for the interest he has been pleased to take in your outset in life. You are indebted to his Lordship & not to me for Mr. Gibbs patronage'.[47]

The letter also reveals that Scott had given Murray funds for his outfit, a typically practical piece of support alongside his working of the patronage network.

Evidently, as Somerville had predicted, Murray learnt the skills that would ultimately forward his career in New South Wales. When he sent his gift of seeds to Scott with Sir Thomas Brisbane on Brisbane's return from his stint as governor of New South Wales, he described himself in the accompanying letter as 'an obscure individual who has been a partaker of your beneficence' and recalls 'the lively interest you took on my behalf at my first outset in life'. He sends the seeds 'as the only sensible token of my gratitude in my reach' but offers to send 'anything else the produce of this colony which you would wish to obtain and

---

[44] *Journal*, p. 193.
[45] Lord Somerville to Scott, NLS MS 3883, fol. 150^v (7 December 1812).
[46] Andrew Murray to Scott, NLS MS 3884, fols 284^r and 285^v (6 November 1813).
[47] Scott to Andrew Murray, State Library of New South Wales, MLMSS 4799/Box 2/Item [3], fol. 1^r (12 November 1813).

which I can procure'. He reports that he has been in New South Wales for eight years and that he came out with 'a Mr McArthur whom I served four years' and that

> on the arrival of our much lamented Governor Sir Thomas Brisbane I had the honour to be appointed to the charge of His Excellency's Garden Here where I have continued to the present time where I am now left to lament the loss of one of the most aimiable and condescending masters that ever servant served.

He ends by reporting that Brisbane 'has conferred upon me a considerable grant of Land, more perhaps than I desire and I am sure more than I had any claim for but I am aware that had I had your interest it would perhaps have been more'.[48] Whatever Murray meant by this somewhat cryptic final comment, it is clear testimony on his part to the effectiveness of Scott's patronage. Murray's 'Mr McArthur' is no less than John Macarthur, one of the most important figures in the colony at the time and the founder of the Australian merino wool industry. With this favourable start Murray went on to a successful career in Australia and died in Sydney in 1858 at the age of 65. However all of this was only possible because Murray's career had been put on the right track by Scott's early intervention seeking patronage for him.

As with India, Scott met various people who had returned from Australia, notably Barron Field, a controversial figure who had been judge of the Supreme Court of Civil Judicature in New South Wales and whose collection called *First Fruits of Australian Poetry* Scott had in his library. Thus, although smaller in quantity and spread over a shorter length of time, Scott's personal connections with Australia were very similar in kind to his connections with India. Also as with India, Scott sends and receives letters (including to relatives by marriage), promotes the interests of young men going out to the country in a context of imperial patronage, and receives gifts from those he has sponsored. However, there are some significant differences. Firstly, Australia was quite simply a much healthier country for Britons than India and none of the stories of Scott's protégés in Australia ends with tragic early death like so many did in India. Secondly while Scott dealt with governors in Australia as he had with the governor-general in India, his Indian dealings offer no parallels with his Australian dealings with convicts. Nevertheless despite these differences, there are striking similarities about his personal dealings with both countries.

On the other hand, when we turn to Scott's literary engagement with Australia we find it is substantially different to his literary engagement with India. Scott did have a number of books about Australia in his library including the account of the life of Michael Howe sent to him by Macquarie, and he had Macquarie's own *Letter to the Right Honourable Viscount Sidmouth* refuting various charges

---

[48] Andrew Murray to Scott, NLS 3901, fol. 163[r-v] (22 November 1825).

made against him,[49] as well as a batch of issues of the *Sydney Gazette* from November 1821 to February 1822 which covered the period of changeover between Governors Macquarie and Brisbane and which he received from George Harper.[50] He would also have encountered in the *Quarterly Review* of January 1828 a review of *Two Years in New South Wales* by Peter Cunningham, the brother of his already mentioned friend Allan.[51] There was enough here to give him a reasonable picture of colonial Australia to add to what he had gleaned from his correspondents and from meeting with people returned from the country. However I am not aware of Scott reading any books dealing specifically with Australia in his childhood, and indeed the colony was not established until he was seventeen. The biggest difference from India lies not in the information he had available to him but in the amount of his literary engagement with Australia. Even his interest in the book about Michael Howe may have owed more to its being described in the *Quarterly Review* as 'the first child of the press of a state only fifteen years old' and '*rarissimus*'[52] than to his recognition that Australian bushrangers provided a parallel to the outlaws of Scotland in whom he had been interested since his early days of hearing their stories in the Border ballads. In fact I have found only one short passage on Australia in all his published work. As already noted, it comes from *Tales of a Grandfather* and is so short that it can be quoted in full along with the preceding sentences to set it in context. In a chapter headed 'Progress of Civilization in Society', Scott describes how human communities come into being:

> [I]t usually happens, that children feel no desire to desert their parents, but remain inhabitants of the same huts in which they were born, and take up the task of labouring for subsistence in their turn. One or two such families gradually unite together, and avail themselves of each other's company for mutual defence and assistance. This is the earliest stage of human society; and some savages have been found in this condition so very rude and ignorant, that they may be said to be little wiser or better than a herd of animals. The natives of New South Wales, for example, are, even at present, in the very lowest scale of humanity, and ignorant of every art which can add comfort or decency to human life. These unfortunate savages wear no clothes, construct no cabins or huts, and are ignorant even of the

---

[49] Lachlan Macquarie, *A letter to the Right Honourable Viscount Sidmouth, in refutation of statements made by the Hon. Henry Grey Bennet M.P. : in a pamphlet 'On the transportation laws, the state of the hulks, and of the colonies in New South Wales'* (London: Richard Rees, 1821). See *Catalogue of the Library at Abbotsford* (Edinburgh, 1838), p. 31.

[50] See *Catalogue of the Library at Abbotsford*, p. 265; according to the catalogue of the Advocates Library in Edinburgh some issues are signed 'G. Harper' above the masthead and in Harper's letter to Scott of 14 February 1822 he writes 'I have sent your honor a few Sydney Gazettes' (NLS 3894, fol. 59ᵛ).

[51] Review of Peter Cunningham, *Two Years in New South Wales*, *Quarterly Review*, 37 (1828) 1–32.

[52] Barron Field, Review of *Michael Howe, the Last and Worst of the Bush Rangers of Van Diemen's Land*, *Quarterly Review*, 12 (1820), 73–83.

manner of chasing animals or catching fish, unless such of the latter as are left by the tide, or which are found on the rocks; they feed upon the most disgusting substances, snakes, worms, maggots, and whatever trash falls in their way. They know indeed how to kindle a fire—in that respect only they have stepped beyond the deepest ignorance to which man can be subjected—but they have not learned how to boil water; and when they see Europeans perform this ordinary operation, they have been known to run away in great terror.[53]

Leaving aside the question of the gross inaccuracy of this statement, it is clear that the Aboriginal people had figured in Scott's mind as somewhat less than noble savages, even though some early depictions of them do set them in this mould. Equally Scott is not describing here the part of Australian society with which he had personal connections — the world of the governors, convicts and free settlers. This contrasts with his writing about India where he was able to write about the British-Indian world with which he had such intimate connections. For Scott the world he is describing here is more deeply Other than even the Muslim world of India. Nor does it derive in any way from the books he loved as a child. In fact Scott's most likely source is a passage in the review of Cunningham's *Two Years in New South Wales* where the reviewer, not Cunningham, presents a very similar picture of Aboriginal society.[54]

Differing as it does so much in quantity and personal knowledge and engagement, is there any way in which this can be seen as parallel to Scott's imaginative engagement with India? There is perhaps one similar aspect. If we return to the context in which this passage appears it is obviously one in which Scott is describing to his grandson the various stages of the development of human society. This view of the progress of civilization permeates all Scott's work although he rarely reaches back to this first stage, being much more interested in the later feudal stage. As many critics have pointed out, this stadial view of history is fundamental to the Enlightenment's philosophical history, which Scott had encountered in his years at University — that is, at much the same age as when he was reading and re-enacting Orme on his sickbed since, like his contemporaries in Scotland, Scott began attending university in his early teens. Just as in presenting the otherness of non-British India Scott resorted to the grand narrative of the confrontation of Muslims and Christians which he had known from his childhood, so in considering the otherness of non-British Australia he resorted to another grand discourse which he had known since his young years, the Enlightenment narrative of the rise of civilization from stage to stage over the centuries. In short, in coping with the alterity of the outer reaches

---

[53] Walter Scott, *Tales of a Grandfather* (London: Adam and Charles Black, 1911), p. 369. The chapter in which this passage occurs was originally the first chapter of the Second Series of *Tales of a Grandfather*.

[54] Review of Peter Cunningham, *Two Years in New South Wales*, pp. 29–30.

of Empire, Scott looked to views of the world which had coloured his imagination from his early years. In writing about India he turned back to Orme and in writing, much more briefly, about Australia he drew on his early involvement with Enlightenment ideas. In this one respect only is Scott's writing about Australia similar to his writing about India. By contrast, his personal engagement with the two countries runs along parallel lines in every respect: in India and Australia Scott reaches out through the network of empire to the high and the low and receives in return gifts as well as information about these distant lands. Small as it is by comparison, Scott's personal involvement with Australia nevertheless shows notable similarities to his personal involvement with India.

Trees, Rivers, and Stories:
Walter Scott Writing the Land

SUSAN OLIVER

University of Essex

Land Ethics

Walter Scott has probably contributed more than any writer to perceptions of Scotland as a land of mountains, moorlands, heather, mists and water. Does his writing look beyond such a stereotypical terrain to demonstrate an agency arising not just from the human histories that form the basis for his plots, but also from the land itself? To what extent did he write about woodlands, rivers, soil and mountains as phenomena existing outside the control of, or manifesting resistance to, the interventions of modern society? Is there anything in his poetry and fiction that advocates or supports what we might call a land ethic? I refer here to something understood as 'a limitation on freedom of action in the struggle for existence', specifically relating to humankind's 'relation to the land', as first proposed by Aldo Leopold in the late 1940s.[1] The relevance of Leopold's land ethic, published 117 years after Scott's death, is its basis in something of primary importance to Scott: the necessary relationship of communities with the land and environment. For Leopold, a land ethic 'enlarges the boundaries of community to include soils, waters, plants, and animals, or collectively: the land'.[2] He proposes responsible land management (not the exclusion of humans) in which love and sympathy exist among people for everything that comprises the ecology of an area.[3] Scott certainly loved the land in ways that valued it beyond its potential to generate economic wealth. His writing makes the case time and again for a sympathetic and collectively responsible approach by people to place. However, whether he evinces a philosophy of land relations that is willing to

Acknowledgement: this essay was produced with the support of the British Academy and the Leverhulme Trust. I am also grateful to the Faculty of Advocates Abbotsford Collection Trust, which has kindly given permission for me to read, quote from, and comment on Scott's MS unpublished planting journal, *Sylva Abbotsfordiensis: Memoranda concerning the woods and plantations at Abbot's Ford. Commenced 1st January 1819.*

[1] Aldo Leopold, 'The Land Ethic', in *A Sand County Almanac and Sketches Here and There* (New York: Oxford University Press, 1949), pp. 201–26 (pp. 202–03).

[2] Ibid., p. 204.

[3] Ibid., pp. 223–25.

Yearbook of English Studies, 47 (2017), 279–300
© Modern Humanities Research Association 2017

relegate human interests to the survival of vulnerable non-human elements is a complex matter requiring further investigation.

Other questions arise: was Scott mostly concerned with a Romantic pastoral Scotland, nostalgic for a time when a mainly rural society had closer ties to the land than to cities, such as would support the maintenance of a strong local as well as national communal identity? Does his representation of environmental issues, including concerns about state and commercially motivated deforestation, planting policies, changes in land use, and his own intervention to preserve stocks of fish in rivers, provide a counterpoint to identity politics based in political economy? These are pertinent questions for readers in the twenty-first century, when it is difficult to imagine a Scotland unaffected by climate change, acid rain, habitat and species loss, and without debates about how to balance an economy based upon exploitable resources (oil and gas, in particular) with the demands for access made by the tourist industry and the lobby for conservation. They are also questions that draw attention to the scale and significance of the contribution that Scott's writing has made to the environmental historiography of Scotland, as a nation always needing to mediate and address the effects of changing land use.

As a self-styled Borders 'minstrel', 'Wizard of the North', and latter-day 'Rhymer', Scott was a storyteller of the environment as much as a writer about social history.[4] All three sobriquets have literary geographical roots in which words derive at least part of their power from an uncanny strangeness associated with the soil: for example, from the Borders lowlands and moorland in which lie buried medieval poets, popular heroes, and travellers who returned from Italy and the Middle East with knowledge of alchemy and occult science gained during foreign travel. His stories are written as ballads, long narrative poems, fiction and verse dramas, but many are also incorporated into letters or essays published in periodicals. Others are found in his journals, notebooks and in contributions to the proceedings of associations such as the Tweed Commissioners, founded in 1805 with the aim of implementing managed stewardship of the overall ecology of the River Tweed. Scott's first long poem, *The Lay of the Last Minstrel* (1805), establishes a connection with Scotland's rivers for everything that he subsequently writes. The minstrel of the poem's title chooses to live his last days beside the River Yarrow, a tributary of the Tweed, and the poem closes with a merging of the living sound of the running river with the dying minstrel's song: 'And Yarrow, as he rolled along | Bore

---

[4] These names that Scott used of himself are based in the peripatetic British and European ballad tradition of medieval minstrels, the travelling scholarship of mathematician and astrologer Michael Scotus (1175–*c*. 1232), and the legend of Borders poet Thomas of Erceldoune, known as Thomas the Rhymer (*c*. 1220–1298).

burden to the Minstrel's song.'[5] The idea that sounds from the land (a river) synthesize with those from literature (the song of the poet) might well be interpreted as part of a conventional ideology of national identity: but an ecologically responsible approach to the non-human environment is necessary if memory and ongoing creativity are to remain possible.

That Scott was caught in some contradiction by today's standards when it comes to land ethics cannot be ignored. He contributed to the rise in the early nineteenth century of Scotland's carbon economy, through involvement in the oil and coal extraction industries. That episode tells a story of Scott's interest in the conversion of fossil fuels into sources of energy, albeit with concern for economic viability alongside some awareness of environmental responsibility. One of the first people to use gas central heating in his home, in 1823 he also literally bought into what he described as the 'mania of the day' by taking shares in the Edinburgh Oil and Gas Company, the aim of which was to light the city of Edinburgh with gas manufactured from oil. Within a year, he was the company's Chairman. The venture failed financially, and five years later the Oil and Gas Company was bought by its rival the Edinburgh Coal Gas Company.[6] Scott lamented in a letter to John Gibson Jr. in January 1828 that he would never see a financial return on his investment.[7] Meanwhile, the location of the oil gas works at Tanfield, Inverleith, next to the Experimental Garden of the Caledonian Horticultural Society (now the Edinburgh Royal Botanical Garden) was creating an environmental controversy. First the distillation plant and then the proposed transfer to coal gas production generated complaints about air pollution that was already affecting health in residential areas as well as damaging trees and plants at the Experimental Garden. Coal was already understood to be a dirtier fuel than oil, as Scott points out in a Statement to Parliament supporting the Edinburgh New Gas-Light Bill in 1827.[8] The same document argues that the Oil Gas Company was controlling lime, tar, and ammonia disposal in environmentally responsible ways, using its dry lime by-product for agricultural manure and taking more secure measures than the Coal Gas company to avoid smells and gas escape.[9] By contrast, the Coal Gas Company was a major polluter,

---

[5] *The Lay of the Last Minstrel*, 2nd edition (London: Longman, Hurst, Rees, and Orme, 1805), 6. 586–87, p. 202.

[6] *The Letters of Sir Walter Scott*, ed. by H. J. C. Grierson et al., 12 vols (London: Constable and Co., 1832–37), IX, 56. Letter to Daniel Terry, dd. March/April 1825.

[7] *Letters*, X, 335.

[8] *Edinburgh New Gas-Light Bill. Statement for Sir Walter Scott, Bart. Chairman, the other Directors, and the Proprietors of the Edinburgh Oil Gas Company, applying for a repeal of a Prohibition in their Act of Parliament to make Gas from Coal*. Sess. 1827. National Library of Scotland.

[9] *Considerations Relative to Nuisance in the Coal-Gas Works with Remarks on the Principles of Monopoly and Competition, as Applicable to those establishments* (Edinburgh: John Anderson,

disposing of its liquid lime effluent directly into common drains and rivers. With that contrast as one of his arguments, Scott travelled to London in a bid to persuade Parliament to allow the Oil Gas Company to use its improved methods of production to make their own coal gas to light the city. The bid was unsuccessful. Scott recorded in his Journal on 4 June 1828, 'By the way, we have lost our Coal Gas Bill. Sorry for it, but I can't cry.' The case for oil as less wasteful of energy than coal was supported by thermo- and electrochemist Michael Faraday.[10]

In 1825, Scott nevertheless had staked a substantial £1500 in the development of a railway that would more cheaply than previously bring coal and lime to Abbotsford, not least to supply cheaper coal for the gas plant that he was using to light and heat his home, but also in order that lime from the process could be used to enrich the soil of the estate on which he claimed to have planted a million trees. His method of using dry lime was indeed efficient in turning an energy by-product into manure, and lay behind the plans for the oil gas lighting bill. Planting trees as an offset to the footprint of carbon fuel consumption is a trade-off in our own time that controversially gestures towards a land ethic. Scott could not have known that he was living during the emergence of a carbon-driven anthropocene epoch associated with the rise of technology deriving from chemist and engineer James Watt's improvements to the steam engine in the 1760s.[11] The Grangemouth oil refinery on the banks of the Forth and twenty-first century arguments over fracking for shale gas in Edinburgh, the Lothians and other Lowland areas of Scotland seem a relatively short step from the oil gas and coal gas production that Scott helped to finance.[12] However, Scott's writing shows him to have been concerned two centuries ago about forms of violence towards

1828). The comparative benefits and nuisances arising from oil and coal gas production were debated in the periodical press, mostly with a concern for economic efficiency. See 'Gas-Lights', *The Literary Gazette: A Weekly Journal of Literature, Science, and the Fine Arts*, 384 (29 May 1824), 345–46. A version of this article was published in the *New Monthly Magazine* (September 1824), pp. 393–94. See also 'On the Illuminating Power of Coal and Oil Gas', *Monthly Magazine, Or, British Register*, 60 (1825), 106–08.

[10] Faraday was one of several scientists whose experiments and findings were used in letters of support for the Oil Gas Light Company's tender. He is particularly invoked as an authority on cleaner types of gas for lighting. See *Letter from Edward Turner, M. D. Lecturer on Chemistry, Edinburgh, and Robert Christison, M. D. Professor of Medical Jurisprudence in the University of Edinburgh* to the Directors of the Edinburgh Oil Gas Light Company dated 9 September 1824; Letter from Dr. D. Brewster, F. R. S. &c &c. to the same, dated 14 September 1824; and Letter from John Pollock, Esq. Secretary to the Oil Gas Company, Dublin to the same, dated 21 September 1824. All at the National Library of Scotland.

[11] Paul Crutzen and Eugene Stoermer, 'The "Anthropocene"', *International Geosphere-Biosphere Programme Newsletter*, 41 (2000), p. 17; Crutzen, 'Geology of Mankind', *Nature* (3 January 2002), p. 23.

[12] On 1 June 2016, the Scottish Parliament voted in favour of a ban on fracking. The Scottish National Party abstained from the vote. See <http://www.bbc.co.uk/news/uk-scotland-scotland-politics-36422083> [accessed 24 June 2016].

the land and towards society resulting from changes in energy policies and farming practice.

Aesthetics

Most scholarship on Scott's storytelling has prioritized his treatment of people, social systems facing crisis, and events from human history. Books and journal essays have explored his development of literary genres from early translations of poems by Goethe and Bürger, to the ballad anthology *Minstrelsy of the Scottish Border*, to the three-volume novel. Studies of his use of narrative methods ranging from framing devices, voice, language, constructions of character, and techniques such as the *entrelacement* of storylines, have shown how he developed original ways of writing from older points of departure, bringing together British and European literature from high and popular cultural sources. Where Scott focused on the natural, non-human environment, critical enquiry over two centuries has investigated how he integrates memory with place and establishes a social politics rooted in landscape aesthetics. Those aesthetics are framed by a combination of Edmund Burke's *A Philosophical Enquiry into the Origin of Our Ideas of the Sublime and Beautiful* (1757), Uvedale Price's *An Essay on the Picturesque, as Compared with the Sublime and the Beautiful* (1794), and William Gilpin's many essays on painting and picturesque landscapes (1768 to 1809), together with numerous other works that develop and critique those theories. Since Scott was educated in the schools of the Scottish Enlightenment and wrote throughout the Romantic period, such a context would be expected. However, his acceptance of parts of Burke's aesthetic philosophy alongside an idiosyncratic alteration of the standard viewpoint implied in the 'picturesque in scenery' requires deeper enquiry.

Burke's argument that the land has an innate capacity to generate feelings of fear and pleasure is given a degree of counterpoint in Price's and Gilpin's recourse to a visual language of knowledge based on how land can be understood through an appreciation of art. Scott's copy of Burke's *Philosophical Enquiry*, in the Library at Abbotsford now owned by the Faculty of Advocates Abbotsford Collection Trust, contains a dedication dated 1789. He was then aged eighteen. He also owned an 1810 copy of Price's *Essay on the Picturesque*[13] and several books of socio-geographical tourism by Thomas Pennant, including a 1790 fifth

---

[13] Edmund Burke, *A Philosophical Enquiry into the Origin of Our Ideas of the Sublime and Beautiful: With an introductory discourse concerning taste, and several other additions.* New edition (London: J. Dodsley, 1787). There is a manuscript dedication on endpapers to Walter Scott Junr from Jane Russell, dated July 13th 1789. Faculty of Advocates Library, Edinburgh. The Faculty of Advocates Library also holds Scott's copy of Price's *Essays on the Picturesque: as compared with the sublime and the beautiful; and, on the use of studying pictures, for the purpose of improving real landscape*, 2 vols (London: Mawman, 1810), with brief marginal notes.

edition of his *A Tour in Scotland, and Voyage to the Hebrides in 1769*.[14] In a letter to Joanna Baillie dated March 1813, eighteen months before he published *Waverley* (1814), Scott attributes to Price's theories his taking of land at Abbotsford out of cereal farming for the purpose of planting trees: 'many of our jog-trot Country-men would revolt at being made my instrument of sacrificing good corn land to the visions of Mr. Price's theory'.[15]

While Scott went along with Price's argument for a moral value to landscape that can override economic profit, his response to Pennant was more complex. An example of how his storytelling became a vehicle for a critique of the picturesque Highland tourism that Pennant inspired can be seen in the episode in Chapter 22 of *Waverley*, titled 'Highland Minstrelsy', where Flora Mac-Ivor literally takes Edward Waverley's breath away by waving to him from the 'perilous pass' of a pine-tree bridge, 150 feet over a rocky chasm. In a moment of sensibility, Waverley is 'unable, from the sense of dizziness which her situation conveyed, to return the salute'.[16] The scene demonstrates Burke's theory that the Sublime is a force capable of producing psychological terror and physical paralysis in a viewer who can enjoy both sensations only by remaining at a sufficient distance. At the same time, Scott's levity in using a comic tone interleaves a lightness that tempers any realistic threat to life into a perspective that readers would recognize as more consistent with the picturesque: the spectacle looks like a landscape painting or an illustration from a book. Scott's edition of Pennant's *Tour* contains a description and accompanying illustration of just such a bridge at the Fall of Fyers in the Highlands, made famous by Robert Burns's 1787 poem 'Written with a pencil, standing by the Falls of Fyers, near Loch Ness'. In the illustration, a woman and a man stand on a narrow pine bridge, while the narrative describes 'a true *Alpine* bridge of the bodies of trees covered with sods, from whose middle is an awful view of the water roaring beneath'.[17] Landscape painter Thomas Walmsley painted the falls in 1810 using a similar composition, with print copies sold through commercial printmakers.[18]

Edward Waverley's swoon at Flora's apparently dangerous behaviour is set in 1745, twelve years before Burke's *Enquiry* would have explained his condition.

---

[14] Thomas Pennant, *A Tour in Scotland, and Voyage to the Hebrides; MDCCLXIX* (London: printed for Benjamin White, 1790). Scott's Library at Abbotsford, now held by the Faculty of Advocates Abbotsford Collection Trust, also contains Pennant's *Journey to Snowdon* (London: printed for Henry Hughes, 1781); his *Tour in Wales* (London: printed for Benjamin White, 1784); and *The History of the Parishes of Whiteford, and Holywell* (London: printed for B. and J. White, 1794).

[15] *Letters*, III, 237.

[16] *Waverley*, ed. by P. D. Garside, EEWN (Edinburgh: Edinburgh University Press, 2007), p. 113.

[17] *A Tour in Scotland; MDCCLXIX*, 5th edn, 2 vols (London: Printed for Benjamin White, 1790), I, 219 and plate xxix.

[18] Thomas Walmsley, *Upper Falls of Fyers, Near Lough Ness, Northern Highlands, Scotland*, aquatint print (London: F. J. Sarjent, 1810). British Library.

He reverses eighteenth-century gendered behavioural and medical conventions in which women, rather than men, would be expected to display such heightened physical signs of fear at the sight of a dangerous situation. To that end, Scott anticipates, and satirically derogates, the 'man of feeling' that emerged from the culture of sensibility at the turn of the nineteenth century. At this midway point in the novel, Waverley's incapacity falls notably short of the masculine vigour that the rugged country of the Highlands might be expected to inspire. Unable to do anything to render Flora's situation safer than he believes it to be, and about to join the losing side of an armed conflict that ends with the 1746 massacre at Culloden, he is a failure as a 'natural' soldier and protector type.

There is more to explore in this episode, though, in terms of the function of the land in question beyond its aesthetic agency. Waverley is a tourist, not a Highlander. He views the land north of the Highland fault line from a cultural as well as a physical distance, perceiving it to be simultaneously magnificent and vulnerable. But the bridge on which Flora stands, barely three feet in width and made of two Scots pine trees, is familiar and entirely safe from her close-up perspective. She is firmly in touch with the trees, rocks, cataracts and expansive skies; so much so that rather than being suspended in air, as Waverley fancifully imagines, she is securely part of a connected ecology at the top of which she stands. While Waverley displays a less-than-masculine misunderstanding of a scene viewed like a painting or book illustration, Flora is part of the land itself. Even her name implies a natural system, rooted in sympathy with plants. Scott's 'Highland Minstrelsy' chapter grounds Flora Mac-Ivor's story in a complex system that comprises geology (rocks), botany (pine trees and flowers) and the elements (air and water). Moreover, her gestural wave draws attention to a natural harmony that establishes a point of contrast with the ending of *Waverley* where, as I have shown elsewhere, an act of violent intervention attempts to terminate the land's capacity for revealing stories.[19] That violence against the land centres on the removal of ancient trees, a subsequent levelling of land contours, and the planting of a monoculture of grass at Tully-Veolan. The re-landscaping, which extends deep below the surface of the soil and affects everything that lives in and grows from it, tells its own story of how the Highlands as the managed 'estate' of modern Scotland was transformed into sheep pasture from an older, mixed system of land use dominated by cattle husbandry and wild game hunting. That process is ultimately identified by Scott as an act of violence against the land as well as an act of cultural erasure. Moreover, the abrupt discontinuities of Davie Gellatley's consequential forgetting of his old songs and Flora Mac-Ivor's silence after entering a convent represents an enforced muteness that bleakly contrasts with the onwardly rolling music of the Yarrow

---

[19] 'Sir Walter Scott's Transatlantic Ecology', *The Wordsworth Circle*, 44.2/3 (2013), 115–20.

that concludes *The Lay of the Last Minstrel*, and the 'brawling' mountain rivulet 'heard among the stones or in the clefts of the rock that occasionally interrupted its course' that gives 'life and animation' to a different landscape of massacre and remembrance in *The Tale of Old Mortality*.[20] In order to enjoy the sight of Flora at the cataract, Waverley must come to his 'senses'. He must defer to a Romantic myth driven by picturesque aesthetics that underpins the politics of creating a desirable pastoral out of a wild and threatening wasteland.

Scott's combination of Romantic adventure and comedy in 'Highland Minstrelsy' accords with his dislike of Pennant's representation of Highlanders as barbarians whose behaviour was in keeping with the savagery of the land. Scott mentioned that matter in a late letter to Donald Gregory, dated 17 July 1831, writing that he had 'been shocked at the anathema [Pennant] has pronounced' on the Clan MacGregor, in particular, and had 'tried my best to laugh the world, the southern world at least, out of these absurd prejudices'.[21] As successor to a tradition of poetry rooted in the soil, he adds that 'the border Minstrels made a man of me'.[22]

Changes in land use had altered the appearance of much of Scotland during the second half of the eighteenth century, largely due to the agricultural revolution and economic pressures that affected the Highlands in particular. These had been recorded and investigated before Scott began writing *Waverley* in 1808, but sufficiently recently to influence that novel. The most comprehensive enquiry was John Sinclair's twenty-one-volume *Statistical Account of Scotland* (1791–99), which included descriptions of every parish. Sinclair's survey, with its reports commissioned from local contributors, tells its own story of the decline of cattle farming in the Borders and Highlands, and particularly in older native breeds of cattle, along with a rise in sheep numbers. Scott's fiction addresses those changes in ways that respond to Sinclair's manner as a storyteller. In *The Heart of Midlothian* (1818), part of the *Tales of My Landlord, Second Series*, the narrator, Jedediah Cleishbotham, repeatedly refers to the Duke of Argyll's contributions to animal husbandry in the agricultural revolution. His account is at least a twice-told tale, since the conceit of Scott's frame narrative is that it has been filtered through the papers of the fictional schoolmaster and clerk, Peter Pattieson, who in turn had heard the details from the landlord of a local inn. The layered narrative and distancing of a historical setting in the second and third decades of the eighteenth century works similarly to the aesthetics of the sublime

---

[20] For an analysis of the landscape of *Old Mortality*, see Susan Oliver, 'Walter Scott and the Matter of Landscape: Ecologies of Violence for Our Time', in *The Bottle Imp*, 16 (November 2014), n.pag. <http://asls.arts.gla.ac.uk/SWE/TBI/TBIIssue16/Oliver.html> [accessed 12 May 2016].

[21] *Letters*, XII, 24.

[22] Connections made in Scott's fiction between clan MacGregor and the land are discussed in my forthcoming book, *Green Scott: Historical Fiction and National Ecology*.

and picturesque already mentioned. But *The Heart of Midlothian*'s treatment of human tragedy and misfortune is packed with a different kind of detail that relates to land use. Again midway through the novel, a letter from Jeannie Deans to her father anxiously comments on Argyll's introduction of Devonshire dairy cattle in place of the older native Ayrshire breed. Jeannie expresses her affection for the native cattle and traditional Dunlop cheese. Her father later becomes the Duke's cowman. A parenthetical narrator's note inserted into the letter refers to a report intended to be sent to the Board of Agriculture: 'Here follow some observations respecting the breed of cattle, and the produce of the dairy, which it is our intention to forward to the Board of Agriculture.'[23] Many rural readers and landowners would have understood the implication of that foreshortened note of intent in Scott's own time. Jedediah Cleishbotham has already just said of the letter that 'it is too long altogether [...] so we only give a few extracts'.[24] Scott is likely here satirizing the length of agricultural reports such as Sinclair's — the kind that Mr. Knightley and Robert Martin discuss in Jane Austen's *Emma* (1815). Indeed, he remarked that Sinclair could be tiresome because of his obsession with detail.[25] The references to cattle and farming practices continue throughout *The Heart of Midlothian* in a dialogue about the agricultural revolution that forms an aside to the main story.

The Board of Agriculture and Improvement perhaps needs some explanation. Established in London by Royal Charter in 1793, with the intention of producing a full survey of the parishes of England in the style of the Scottish *Statistical Account*, its founder and President until 1798 was John Sinclair. While the English survey was never compiled, the reports that Sinclair sent from Scotland to the Board provide a detailed account of changing farming practices north of the border. Sinclair's edited two-volume *General Report of the Agricultural State, and Political Circumstances, of Scotland*, produced for the Board of Agriculture and published in Edinburgh and London in 1814, contains sections about climate, rivers, trees and livestock farming. The volumes include some direct storytelling, while their overall narrative builds into a saga of rural Scotland. The section on trees includes a brief history of the *HMS Glenmore*, an 800-ton frigate built in 1796 entirely of Scots pine, a species that Sinclair notes to be exceptionally valuable for its compact and durable wood.[26] The *Glenmore*

---

[23] *The Heart of Midlothian*, ed. by David Hewitt and Alison Lumsden, EEWN (Edinburgh: Edinburgh University Press, 2004), p. 350. Not the modern Ayrshire breed of cattle, which was first recorded in the 1870s and recognized as a herd in 1877. See Cattle Society of Great Britain and Ireland breed standard at <http://www.ayrshirescs.org/ayrshires-cattle-society/society/the-breed/> [accessed 12 May 2016].

[24] *Heart of Midlothian*, p. 350.

[25] *Letters*, VII, 231, 296.

[26] *General Report of the Agricultural State, and Political Circumstances, of Scotland*, ed. by Sir John Sinclair. Drawn up for the Consideration of the Board of Agriculture and Internal

survived service in the Far East, the Americas and the Napoleonic wars and was sold into merchant naval service in 1814. Sinclair includes a passionate account of the value of the Scots pine generally in shipbuilding and architecture, which entirely accords with Scott's love of that species. He includes details of by-products from the wood, including turpentine, lamp-black and even the potential food value of the bark (for which he references Carl Linnaeus). In Scott's *Tales of my Landlord, Third Series* novel *A Legend of the Wars of Montrose* (1818), Highlanders use blazing torches made of bog-pine, with Scott adding: 'this wood, found in the morasses, is so full of turpentine, that, when split and dried, it is frequently used in the Highlands instead of candles'.[27]

Trees

It is no secret that while writing poetry and novels alongside his work as a lawyer, journalist and public intellectual, Scott invested time, effort and money that he did not sufficiently have in his passion for planting trees at Abbotsford. The move of house from Ashiestiel in 1811 involved his relocating downstream along the Tweed, close to Galashiels and Melrose, where the river was wider than at his previous, rented home. The new estate included half a mile of river frontage with flood meadows that lived up to their reputation. There were few trees. Scott wrote of the new property to his brother-in-law Charles Carpenter, 'it is very bleak at present having little to recommend it but the vicinity of the river', but adding 'the ground is well adapted by nature to grow wood'.[28] The story of Scott's growing of that wood, and his passion for the Tweed, reads like a ballad of love and near loss. The cost of planting trees without doubt contributed to his insolvency crisis of 1826, after which he was able to continue living at Abbotsford on a life-rent but had to sell his Edinburgh house. Journals and letters comment on the unfolding arboricultural programme, but the most intimate and concentrated record of tree species and where they were planted, along with Scott's notes about their success or failure, is the unpublished manuscript journal in which he made entries between 1819 and 1825, *Sylva Abbotsfordiensis*. The *Sylva Abbotsfordiensis* pays attention to soil types, aspect, and local climate: sandy, wet, exposed or sheltered. Those accounts, combined with descriptions of water sources and notes on the competition between wildlife, domestic animals, wild plants and tree species, build a picture of the ecology of the estate as it was during six of the busiest years of Scott's planting activity.

Improvement, under the Directions of The Right Hon. Sir John Sinclair, 2 vols (Edinburgh: Archibald Constable and Co; London: Longan, Hurst, Rees, Orme Brown, 1814), II, 206–07.

[27] *A Legend of the Wars of Montrose*, ed. by J. H. Alexander, EEWN (Edinburgh: Edinburgh University Press, 1995), p. 33.

[28] Lockhart, p. 201.

As Alison Lumsden and Gerard Carruthers have argued, the 'Preface' to the *Sylva* indicates that it was probably intended to become a public document about land use and tree cultivation: Scott addresses an imagined reader using a conversational tone and concluding that he was writing 'at least to amuse myself and to interest those whose lot it may be to walk under the shade of the trees which I am now engaged in planting'.[29] The *Sylva* can indeed be read as a source of interesting stories that develop across the different parts of the estate, based in the experiments that Scott conducted, and linking arboriculture to the ecological and literary history of the region. His acquisition of the 'Glen at Huntley Burn', and description of 'The Rhymer's Glen' are cases in point. Both are connected by name and, even if only arbitrarily, by location with Thomas of Erceldoune, the Rhymer and archetypal Scottish poet of the old Borders ballad, which Scott had extended by adding a third part for the 'Imitation of the Ancient Ballads' section of *Minstrelsy of the Scottish Border* in 1803. Scott's entry in the *Sylva* on the Rhymer's Glen demonstrates the extent to which he combined a Romantic sensibility with a practical approach to livestock farming and cultivating trees:

> A romantick glen with a rivulet wandering down amongst rocks with remains of natural wood and a quantity of underwood of different kinds. The timber-trees of the upper part were estimated to me at £14, on account of the difficulty in clearing them out of the ravine.
>
> In 1817–18 many full-grown plants of from six to ten feet high were planted in this glen but without inclosing. They have sufferd by the sheep as was to be expected but still live & may thrive when cut over.
>
> The glen has been inclosed this season 1818–19 and it is proposed to plant it up but so as to preserve its wild & natural character.
>
> It was accordingly planted up in spring 1819 and must succeed well.[30]

The Rhymer's Glen, located not far from the stone that then as now commemorates a location where Thomas just might have composed his verses underneath the fabled Eildon tree, is an enigmatic presence in the *Sylva*. Describing it also in other sections, in terms of and with a perspective from the land that surrounds it, Scott seems to have wanted to preserve its sense of mystery. Near to the glen's entrance at Mar's Lea, Toftfield, oaks and larches are the main planted species growing in what Scott describes as an 'indifferent soil' that slopes to the east. He records that 'the hares have done much damage among the larches'.[31] The larches are not thriving. The soil is indifferent. Furthermore,

---

[29] *Sylva Abbotsfordiensis: Memoranda concerning the woods and plantations of Abbot's Ford. Commenced 1st January 1819*, p. 5. See Lumsden and Carruthers, 'Introductory Note' to transcript for the Faculty of Advocates Abbotsford Collection Trust <http://www.advocates.org.uk/media/1606/sylvafinalrevisedtranscript-web-version-010512.pdf> [accessed 10 March 2016].

[30] Ibid., p. 58.

[31] Ibid., p. 57.

at Ushers Stripe, 'a small stripe running south east from the south side of the Rhymer's Glen', ash and larches are 'choked by coarse grass' and the trees are 'bent', while 'a few sweet or Spanish Chestnuts' are just 'beginning to thrive'. North and west, and running to the bottom of the glen, more larches are affected by strangulation by coarse grass. In each of the instances just mentioned, tree species introduced to the area — planted ash, but also non-native larches and Spanish chestnuts[32] — have had their growth curtailed by the quiet violence and silent resistance of local ecologies manifest in the aggressive action of hares, and tangled and coarse grass. It is as if the land were protesting against invasion.

If the *Sylva* tells part of the story of Scott's planting programme, it also reflects on the connection between Scottish literature and the land made in Scott's *Minstrelsy of the Scottish Border* (1802–03). Partly an old, anonymous ballad, probably from the fifteenth century, and partly an improved fragment, 'Thomas the Rhymer' recalls a legend set in the late thirteenth century that, as Scott says in his notes to the *Minstrelsy*, is mentioned in early Scottish literature in the fourteenth-century long narrative poem *History of Wallace*, by Henry the minstrel (Blind Harry), in Andrew Wynton's *Chronicle*, and by John Barbour.[33] In these respects, 'Thomas the Rhymer' demonstrates the evolution of Scottish literature down through five centuries to Scott's own lifetime. Set in a particular, although legendary, location in the Borders — Huntlie Bank,[34] near the Eildon Hills, not far from the village of Erceldoune, and under the Eildon tree — the ballad argues for a literary rootedness in place. Included in all editions of the *Minstrelsy*, 'Thomas the Rhymer' grounds the origins of Scottish literature in the material substance of the soil of a local community, in the country of the Borders more generally, and in the land of Scotland as a nation. However, the earth in the poem begins as a strange place, alien, primal, prior to, and outside the socio-political structures of nationhood. It constitutes the deep history and material ecology on which Scotland is founded. Thomas must discover the nature of what lies beneath the tree and sustains its growth before he can transcend the limitation of mere verse to become a truly inspirational poet. The soil is the catalyst for that process, both symbolically and as a substance made of particles with their own history.

The first and older part of 'Thomas the Rhymer' is explained by Scott to be a composite of two source copies: one copy he gained from Anna Gordon, Mrs.

---

[32] Ibid., p. 59.

[33] Scott, *Minstrelsy of the Scottish Border*, 3 vols (Edinburgh: James Ballantyne, 1802), II, 247–48, 258. The poems Scott refers to are Harry's *The Actes and Deidis of the Illustre and Vallyeant Campioun Schir William Wallace*, Andrew of Wyntoun's *Orygynale Cronykil of Scotland*, and John Barbour's, *The Brus*.

[34] 'Huntlie' is the spelling used in the *Minstrelsy*, while 'Huntley' is used in the *Sylva Abbotsfordiensis*.

Brown, of Aberdeen, but the other is described only as being 'obtained from a lady, residing not far from Erceldoune'.[35] While Mrs. Brown's copy indicates the mobility of ballads through their transfer from one place to another, the second copy remains rooted where the poem was originally set. Its source is enigmatic: 'a lady, residing not far from Erceldoune' tantalizingly suggests a character from the ballad itself, the 'Ladye' or Elf Queen whom Thomas encounters, not far from Erceldoune. It is that first, composite part of the ballad that I am interested in here. The ballad begins with the story of how Thomas came intimately to know the soil of the land through an encounter linked to a tree. The process is one of immersion, like a Scottish vernacular version of the classical literary trope of the visit to the underworld. Before his encounter, we know only that Thomas composed verses. Then, while sitting on Huntlie bank beneath the Eildon tree, he 'spies wi' his ee' a 'ferlie', or strange lady, riding a horse. A supernatural creature whose 'skirt was o' the grass green silk', and, I argue, representing the land's compelling and magical strangeness, she carries him down under the surface of the soil, among the roots of the tree. Beguiling him, the Ladye sings 'Thomas, ye maun go wi' me', urging him to sing his rhymes:

> "Harp and Carp, Thomas," she said;
> "Harp and carp along wi' me:
> And if ye dare to kiss my lips,
> Sure of your bodie I will be."
> [...]
> All underneath the Eildon Tree.
> (5–6. 17–24)

The Rhymer lives with the elf queen underground for seven years before returning to the surface. When he returns to the world of late thirteenth-century Scotland, his poetry has been transformed by this environmental version of the visit to the underworld: he is changed, and his words now take the form of prophecy, involving wisdom as much as an ability to see the future.

'Thomas the Rhymer' is fundamental to the deep ecology of the *Minstrelsy*. The ballad tells a history of the land on which all of Scottish literature depends, putting that land first. Poetry comes afterwards. Dirt, like soil, as ecocritic Heather Sullivan has argued, is usually regarded as a 'less glamorous' substance.[36] The Rhymer's encounter with the 'ferlie', however, recognizes the earth precisely as entrancing matter: something that not only cannot be ignored, but that absolutely cannot be resisted and that will not be forgotten. The success of the ballad, which is evident in its endurance down through centuries, relies on the

---

[35] *Minstrelsy of the Scottish Border* (1802), II, 250.

[36] 'Dirt Theory and Material Ecocriticism', *Interdisciplinary Studies in Literature and Environment (ISLE)*, 19.3 (Summer 2012), 515–31 (p. 515).

agency of the earth both as matter and symbol. The Eildon tree, with its roots in the soil and its branches above the poet, connects the human world with the material earth. Beneath its canopy, and coming to know what normally remains unseen, the creative imagination is transformed into part of something more expansive in time and space than the temporally limited and changing world.

Rivers

By the time Scott published the *Minstrelsy*, he knew that not just the appearance but also the substance of the soil of the Borders had been changed. An older, more densely wooded landscape has been transformed into one dominated and defined by pasture. Sheep farming changes the soil. The animals' grazing habits and the matt-like roots of the grass affect the water content and composition of the earth, which in turn defines everything that lives below the surface of the ground. Scott's later poem, *The Lady of the Lake* (1810), the story of which concerns a sixteenth-century situation of human conflict on the geological fault-line that marks the border between the Highlands and Lowlands, notoriously includes an anachronistic reference to that very matter of land use change in the Borders (anachronistic because what is being described was actually the result of changes in times much closer to Scott's own):

> From Yarrow braes and banks of Tweed,
> Where the lone streams of Ettrick glide,
> And from the silver Teviot's side;
> The dales, where martial clans did ride,
> Are now one sheep-walk, waste and wide.
> (Canto 2: v. 28)

Those lines spoken by Roderick Dhu also identify four Borders rivers, each of which meant a great deal to Scott: the Yarrow, Ettrick, Teviot and Tweed. Indeed, the first three are tributaries of the Tweed. Despite significant changes in land use, including 'the sheep-walk, waste and wide', and a number of artificial alterations in their own courses, the rivers together constitute images of permanency over that of mutability. If we read Roderick Dhu's words as intertextual dialogue as well as a statement about environmental degradation, they reflect on Scott's first poem from five years earlier in 1805, *The Lay of the Last Minstrel*. They also hint at the opening of Wordsworth's 'Lines Written a few miles above Tintern Abbey', where the poet comments on hedgerows close to the river Wye that had changed from their appearance of only five years earlier to become 'hardly hedge-rows, little lines | Of sportive wood run wild (16–17)'.[37]

The 'last minstrel' as character in the frame narrative of *The Lay* wanders alone, a creative composite from medieval romance (Scott was deeply influenced

---

[37] William Wordsworth, *Lyrical Ballads and Other Poems* (London: J. and A. Arch, 1798), p. 202.

by the Italian Romance poets Pulci, Ariosto, Boiardo and Tasso), Scottish Borders folklore and a Romantic peripatetic Wordsworthian solitary. He is a figure strangely out of time and place, with no one to sing to and no one to hear him. Culturally reduced to the status of a sturdy beggar or vagabond, his harp is out of tune. But he walks until he comes to a castle by a river, where he is offered lodging, regains his ability to sing and play and — using all of the tropes of chivalric love and martial action — brings alive after a banquet a vigorous tale of knights and Ladyes, goblin pages, enchanted woods and magic books. Indeed, the minstrel is able to sing again only when he passes 'where Newark's stately tower | Looks out from Yarrow's birchen bower' (27–28). The river Yarrow not only features at eleven other points in the poem but becomes the place where the minstrel finally makes a new home that enables him to continue singing. He chooses a cottage close to its banks where he can hear its music, rather than reside in the castle. Again, Scott draws attention to the connection between storytelling and the land, in this instance not through subsoil but the sound of flowing water:

> When throstles sung in Hare-head shaw,
> And corn waved green on Carterhaugh,
> And flourished, broad, Blackandro's oak,
> The aged Harper's soul awoke!
> Then would he sing achievements high,
> And circumstance of chivalry,
> Till the rapt traveller would stay,
> Forgetful of the closing day;
> And noble youths, the strain to hear,
> Forsook the hunting of the deer;
> And Yarrow, as he rolled along,
> Bore burden to the Minstrel's song.
> (6.576–87)

Scott was writing here about rivers that had materially inspired his own imagination. As mentioned, his houses at Ashiestiel and Abbotsford were both close to the banks of the Tweed, at points downriver from the confluence with the Yarrow. A well-known anecdote is that when Scott was near to dying, he asked to be brought back to Abbotsford so that he could to hear the sound of the Tweed once more from his bedroom. The river is indeed audible from Abbotsford.

Scott continues to stress the importance of rivers in his novels, not least in his treatment of the Solway Firth in *Guy Mannering* (1815) and in *Redgauntlet* (1824). In both novels the liminal nature of the estuary contributes to the mystery of the plot. The epistolary chapters of book 1 of *Redgauntlet* not only establish how protagonist Darsie Latimer's part in the novel's plot is shaped by 'the great estuary' and its 'fatal sands', but also allow for a discourse on changes in fishing practice, in which game fishing and commercial stations had taken over from less efficient, common practices in which fish supplied food for every social class.[38] The subtitle of *Redgauntlet: A Tale of the Eighteenth Century* promises a story about time looked back upon. That time concerns Scotland's transition from older traditional ways of life towards modern innovations associated with improvement and *laissez faire* economics. Darsie Latimer recalls to Alan Fairford in letter III how he was scorned by a local village urchin for his lack of skill in using a rod, landing net and 'gorgeous jury of flies' — the game fishing gear of a sporting gentleman. The urchin, who is revealed to be a skilled fisherman and probably a poacher, borrows the equipment and within an hour has 'not only filled my basket [...] but taught me to kill two trouts with my own hand'. The social class implications of the encounter are compelling. Darsie reflects dismissively on Charles Cotton's additional 1676 treatise to Izaak Walton's *The Compleat Angler*, a copy of which Scott owned: 'old Cotton's instructions, by which I had hopes to qualify myself for one of that gentle society of anglers, are not worth a farthing for this meridian'.[39]

The next letter establishes the point of departure from which the plot develops as a mounted fish hunt that ends only moments before the ebb tide turns. However, even that episode serves as the prelude to an argument over new and old methods of fishing for salmon, with implications that extend much further than the 1765 setting of the story. Old Jacobite Mr. Herries and Joshua Geddes, a Quaker fisherman who owns a share in a salmon netting business, quarrel over the effect of netting on communities that had traditionally fished for and eaten salmon. Their dialogue concerns salmon stations:

> 'Friend Joshua [...] has thy spirit moved thee and thy righteous brethren to act with some honesty, and pull down yonder tide-nets that keep fish from coming up the river?'
>
> 'Surely, friend, not so [...]. Thou killest the fish with spear, line, and cobble-net; and we, with snares and nets, which work by the ebb and flow of tide.'
>
> 'I tell you in fair terms, Joshua Geddes, that you and your partners are using unlawful craft to destroy the fish in the Solway by stake-nets and wears [...]. You will destroy the salmon which make the livelihood of fifty poor families.'
>
> 'I tell you, we are under the protection of this country's laws; nor do we the less trust to obtain their protection.'[40]

---

[38] *Redgauntlet: A Tale of the Eighteenth Century*, ed. by G. A. M. Wood and David Hewitt, EEWN (Edinburgh: Edinburgh University Press, 1997), pp. 20–21.

[39] Scott's 1797 edition of *The Complete Angler; or, Contemplative Man's Recreation: being a discourse on rivers, fish-ponds, fish and fishing: in two parts. The first written by Mr. Isaac Walton, the second by Charles Cotton, Esq. With the lives of the authors, and notes, historical, critical and explanatory. By Sir John Hawkins, Knt.* is in the Library at Abbotsford.

[40] Ibid., pp. 43–44.

Redgauntlet is the last of Scott's Jacobite novels, set in 1765.[41] While Scott clearly uses the motif of fishing to comment on the hardships experienced by remaining Jacobites two decades after the '45 rebellion, he also shows interest in the efficiency and ethics of modern techniques of fishing in an environment where the river maintains an ancient and enduring power. The Solway Firth and its fish in *Redgauntlet* exert an overwhelming influence over the story, as does Egdon Heath and its furze in Thomas Hardy's *The Return of the Native* (1878), another novel in which violence erupts in a society transitioning into modernity.

Scott was interested in salmon and trout fishing as more than a marker of political or social development. His treatment of fishing in *Redgauntlet* and other novels responds to topical anxieties from the early nineteenth century. In 1824, the same year that *Redgauntlet* was published, a report was made public on Scotland's salmon fisheries with particular attention to the effects of 'the stake-net mode of fishing, the regulation of the close-time and the necessity of a legislative revisal of the antiquated Scots statutes'.[42] Observations in the report include a detailed description of tide-net fishing in the Solway Firth, tracing its development into the more recent stake-net method and arguing that the innovation transformed the yield of Scottish salmon fishing.[43] Scott owned a copy.[44] The Rivers Tweed and Tay are also covered in the report. A further, separate statement that was published on fisheries in the River Tay blames stake-net fishing for the reduction in fish numbers upstream.[45] As already mentioned Scott and a group of other interested parties established The Tweed Commissioners, in 1805, with the aim of responsibly managing the river so that the salmon population could be protected.

The best-selling status of Scott's fiction enabled him to address a wider audience than could be reached by official and scientific reports. His interventions on the decline in salmon stocks in Scotland's rivers, delivered through narrative digressions that often take the form of dialogue between commonplace characters, drew popular attention to an important ecological debate. The episode from *Redgauntlet* makes use of the technique of *entrelacement*, which he learned early in his life from the early sixteenth-century poetry of Ariosto.[46]

---

[41] G. A. M. Wood and David Hewitt, 'Historical Note', *Redgauntlet*, p. 440.

[42] *Observations regarding the salmon fishery of Scotland: especially with reference to the stake-net mode of fishing, the regulation of the close-time and the necessity of a legislative revisal of the antiquated Scots statutes* (Edinburgh and London: printed for Bell & Bradfute, and James Duncan, 1824).

[43] Ibid., pp. 7–10.

[44] A copy of the above report is in the Library at Abbotsford.

[45] *Statement relative to the fisheries in the River Tay* (Edinburgh: G. Ramsay, 1824).

[46] Scott's fuller involvement in this debate is explored in more depth in my forthcoming *Green Scott*. I address his adoption of *entrelacement* as used in Ariosto in my essay 'Walter Scott and *Orlando Furioso*', in *Proceedings of the British Academy* (forthcoming 2017).

Meals and letters are frequently the point of departure for telling these digressive stories. In *Old Mortality* (1816), salmon is the subject of a narrative aside describing a meal served by the Laird of Milnewood: 'A large boiled salmon would now-a-days have indicated more liberal housekeeping; but at that period it was caught in such plenty in all the considerable rivers in Scotland, that it was generally applied to feed the servants.'[47] Jonathan Oldbuck comments in *The Antiquary*, also published in 1816, on 'the space allotted for the passage of a salmon through a dam, dike, or weir, by statute [being] the length within which a full-grown pig can turn himself round'.[48] While the narrative here represents Oldbuck as being concerned with the finer points of language, the topic draws attention to an environmental concern of Scott's: the increasing number of impediments to the movement of salmon caused by the weirs, caulds and dams introduced to control the flow of rivers or divert their courses. Published seven years later, *Saint Ronan's Well* (1823) links the history of western political systems with natural law and the management of rivers:

> There must be government in all society — Bees have their Queen, and stag herds have their leader; Rome had her Consuls, Athens had her Archons — and we, Sir, have our Managing Committee.

The committee in question is the Tweed Commissioners. In the 1805 minutes of that NGO's nascent founding association, *The Western Association of Noblemen and Gentlemen for Procuring due Observance of the Laws respecting Fisheries in the River Tweed*, the purpose and aims of the association are established:

> 1st For the express purpose of enforcing a strict observance of the act regarding the Period when the river is to remain open and unmolested [...].

> 2nd For obtaining a free course for fish thro' such Caulds, Dams, or Damheads as are already erected or hereafter may be made in the River Tweed or other rivers connected with it.

> 3rd For the protection of the water in close time and the preservation of the young fry.[49]

Those minutes also report that 'a very inadequate proportion' of fish returning from the sea were able to reach the upper streams of river, a fact not surprising when 'no fewer than fifteen thousand Salmon, Gilses & co. were shipped from Berwick for London in the course of one week'.[50]

---

[47] *The Tale of Old Mortality*, ed. by Douglas Mack, EEWN (Edinburgh: Edinburgh University Press, 1993), p. 61.

[48] *The Antiquary*, ed. by David Hewitt, EEWN (Edinburgh: Edinburgh University Press, 1995), p. 66.

[49] From 'Section 1: Introduction: Fisheries Management on the Tweed — its Background and present day Structure', *The Tweed Foundation* <tweedfoundation.org.uk> [accessed 26 May 2016].

[50] Ibid.

By the early nineteenth century a booming industry in supplying Scottish salmon to London had developed, helped by faster shipping transport. David Montgomery has shown that by 1817, a year after publication of *The Antiquary* and *Old Mortality*, 750,000 pounds of chilled Scottish salmon per year was being exported to satisfy demand in the British capital.[51] Salmon stations using stake-netting technology in estuaries, as well as landowners further inland taking advantage of the trade, were depleting stocks. Sinclair's *Agricultural Report* comments on the extent to which commercial fishing was contributing to Scotland's economy, noting the problem of overfishing only insofar as it threatened the value in property of fishing rights:

> There is no species of property in Scotland, that has, in various instances, so much increased in value, as the salmon fisheries, owing to the more effectual means employed for catching the fish, the improved modes of conveying them to market, and the increased consumption and luxury of the metropolis, where this fish is in great request. In some cases, however, the value of that description of property has rather diminished, in consequence of the laws for the protection of the fish not having been properly attended to.[52]

Conclusion: where do we go from here?

This essay has explored a small segment of Scott's attention to the land and his interest in the developments of environmental management in Scotland. My aim has been to provide a brief investigation of how his storytelling drew public attention to real ecological problems, and how the agency of his writing mediates relationships between memory, mythmaking and the biosphere. That investigation shows why it is necessary to look comparatively across the range of Scott's writing, with attention to topical debates and concerns about environmental degradation and land use at the time that he was writing, if we are fully to understand the extent and importance of the history of Scotland's environment that he provides. Scott's dexterity in using different kinds of writing — poetry, fiction, letters, journals, and official documents including statements to parliament — in its turn responded to a variety of already existing texts including ancient ballads, treatises on aesthetics and land surveys. In so doing his responses to Scotland's evolving ecology closely match Scott Slovic's recent definition of the environmental humanities as a set of related and intersecting discourses embodying 'a loosely shared vision or set of concerns', in which agency is produced from solidarity in diversity.[53] Strength founded in unity in diversity has long been recognized as the foundation of Walter Scott's writing about

[51] David Montgomery, *King of Fish: The Thousand Year Run of Salmon* (Cambridge, MA: Westview Press, 2003), pp. 66–67.

[52] Sinclair, *Agricultural Report*, I, 119.

[53] Scott Slovic, 'Editor's Note', *ISLE*, 23.1 (Winter 2016), 1.

Scotland as a meeting point of diverse cultures and social practices, and as the underpinning motivation for his belief in the political union of the United Kingdom. A question that demands an answer, then, is whether Scott's writing about the environment is more than of a process of instrumentalization of the land, in which trees, rivers and the soil as the points of origin for stories are agents of a nationalism that function by representing Scots as intimately related to the land on which they live? It would be wrong to claim that Scott was not interested in the political and social identity of Scotland. But I find sufficient evidence to argue for a commitment to an early form of land ethic in his critique of environmental negligence and irresponsibility, made through a sustained series of remarks and digressions in best-selling poetry and fiction that continually engaged with topical ecological anxieties such as overfishing, the extension of sheep farming, and the planting of non-native trees in unsuitable locations.

Scott's novels and poetry recognize the value to Scotland's sense of identity of separate social and ecological cultures of the Borders, central Lowlands, Highlands, western Isles and Hebrides, east coast, and Orkney and Shetland Isles. In doing so, they look beyond the simple polarity of the Highlands and Lowlands with which he is usually associated, to establish ways of seeing a more complex set of interconnected communities that each had a deeply rooted relationship with its particular environment. This essay has not allowed for a more expansive investigation of his attention to each of those regions, so attention has been focused on particular locations that feature in some of Scott's best-known poems and novels. I began with a question as to whether Scott anticipated an ethical approach to the land that is in any way similar to the version proposed by Aldo Leopold. Leopold's land ethic demands that humankind change from 'conqueror of the land-community to plain member and citizen of it'. He argued that an 'ecological interpretation of history' shows man to be 'only a member of a biotic team' in which 'the characteristics of the land determined the men who lived on it'.[54] History is a keyword here, for Leopold tells the story of land ethics as an evolutionary social process 'impeded' by a society where 'the space between cities' means little to people who imagine they have 'outgrown the land'. Scott's voice can be heard in that account. Moreover, Devin Griffiths has persuasively argued that 'the literary mode that made it possible to narrate the evolutionary past convincingly [was] the historical novel, particularly as authored by Scott'.[55]

The problem of fetishization of that land for national interests remains, however. Taking a recent critical perspective, Jane Bennett warns that we should be cautious of the urge always to demystify the vitality with which the nonhuman

[54] Leopold, p. 205.
[55] Devin Griffiths, *The Age of Analogy: Science and Literature between the Darwins* (Baltimore, MD: Johns Hopkins University Press, 2016), p. 5.

is invested in literature.[56] On the one hand, the assumption that human agency has always been 'illicitly projected into things' is acknowledged by Bennett to be a valuable theory for exposing hidden systems of socio-political domination. The pastoral mode and aesthetics of the picturesque referred to earlier in this essay must surely be included in the exercise of such political and ideological power. But on the other hand, Bennett warns that habitual demystification can obscure the existence of a contrapuntal subversive vitality through which the nonhuman in the environment acts in its own ways, challenging the authority of anthropo-centric control. The echo of human agency *in sympathy* with nonhuman nature emerges as a necessary counter to many of the abuses of power that result in violence towards the land. Scott's emphasis on the marvellous power of the soil as an originary source for Scottish literature in 'Thomas the Rhymer', his recourse to the Tweed to recover the sound of the border minstrels, and his depiction of Flora Mac-Ivor's place in a Highland ecology all bear out that argument. The disrupted grounds of the modernized estate at Tully-Veolan become increasingly troubling. Ultimately, the contribution that Scott made to writing the environ-mental history of Scotland must be read in terms of what he displayed, and of what further might be expected, by way of a recognition of the value of the land in itself.

---

[56] Jane Bennett, *Vibrant Matter: A Political Ecology of Things* (Durham, NC: Duke University Press, 2010), pp. xiv–xv.

Lightning Source UK Ltd.
Milton Keynes UK
UKOW01f2339250917
309875UK00004B/185/P

9 781781 882931